Sorrow and Joy among Muslim Women

The Pukhtuns are numerically and politically one of the most significant ethnolinguistic groups in Pakistan and Afghanistan. This important study of Pukhtun society concentrates on the lives, thoughts and *gham-khādi* (funeral-wedding) ceremonies of the women, especially of the elite, wealthy and educated women (*Bibiane*) who have largely been overlooked in previous studies. Contesting their conventional representation as idle, it illustrates their commitment to various forms of work within familial and social contexts. It challenges the commonly assumed models of contemporary Pakistan society, which make a simplistic divide between rural and urban, Punjab and non-Punjab, and feudal and non-feudal spaces and peoples. It also contributes to broader debates about the nature and expression of elite cultures and issues of sociality, funerals and marriage, custom and religion, space and gender, morality and reason, and social role and personhood within the contexts of Islam in the Middle East and South Asia.

AMINEH AHMED HOTI received her PhD from the Faculty of Social Anthropology at the University of Cambridge and is a Visiting Scholar at Lucy Cavendish College. She runs the Society for Dialogue and Action, which promotes understanding between people of the Abrahamic faiths, namely Jews, Christians and Muslims.

University of Cambridge Oriental Publications 63
Sorrow and Joy among Muslim Women

A series list is shown at the back of the book

Sorrow and Joy among Muslim Women

The Pukhtuns of Northern Pakistan

AMINEH AHMED

CAMBRIDGE
UNIVERSITY PRESS

CAMBRIDGE UNIVERSITY PRESS
Cambridge, New York, Melbourne, Madrid, Cape Town, Singapore, São Paulo

Cambridge University Press
The Edinburgh Building, Cambridge CB2 8RU, UK

Published in the United States of America by Cambridge University Press, New York

www.cambridge.org
Information on this title: www.cambridge.org/9780521861694

© Faculty of Oriental Studies, University of Cambridge 2006

This publication is in copyright. Subject to statutory exception
and to the provisions of relevant collective licensing agreements,
no reproduction of any part may take place without the written
permission of Cambridge University Press.

First published 2006
This digitally printed version (with corrections) 2008

A catalogue record for this publication is available from the British Library

Library of Congress Cataloguing in Publication data
Ahmed, Aminch, 1972–
Sorrow and joy among Muslim women: the Pukhtuns of northern Pakistan / Aminch Ahmed.
  p. cm. – (University of Cambridge oriental publications; 63)
Includes bibliographical references and index.
ISBN-13: 978-0-521-86169-4 (hardback)
ISBN-10: 0-521-86169-1 (hardback)
1. Women, Pushtun – Rites and ceremonies. 2. Women, Pushtun – Psychology. 3. Women, Pushtun – Social conditions. 4. Pushtuns – Marriage customs and rites. 5. Pushtuns – Funeral customs and rites. 6. Pushtuns – Social life and customs. I. Title. II. Series.

DS432.P4A46 2006
305.48'891593 – dc22
2006011421

ISBN 978-0-521-86169-4 hardback
ISBN 978-0-521-05270-2 paperback

The colour images in the plate section have been reproduced in black and white for this digital reprinting.

Cambridge University Press has no responsibility for the persistence or accuracy of URLs for external or third-party Internet websites referred to in this publication, and does not guarantee that any content on such websites is, or will remain, accurate or appropriate.

CONTENTS

List of plates	*page* vi
List of figures	vii
List of maps	viii
List of tables	ix
Acknowledgements	x
Note on transliteration	xiii
Glossary	xiv

	Introduction	1
1	*Gham-khādi*: framework and fieldwork	15
2	From the inside-out: Bibiane's 'dual lives' in and beyond the house	47
3	The work of mourning: death and dismay among Bibiane	79
4	Celebrating *khādi*: communal Pukhtun weddings and clandestine internet marriages	107
5	The work of *gham-khādi*: 'Not to do *gham-khādi* is shameful (*sharam*); to do it a burden'	132

Conclusion		156
Appendix 1	Pukhtun putative genealogy	166
Appendix 2	Kinship terminology: affinal and consanguinal	167
Appendix 3	Time	169
Appendix 4	Maid performing *gham-khādi* on behalf of her Bibi	170
Appendix 5	Income and household expenditure	171
References		173
Index		192

PLATES

Plates appear between pages 106 and 107. *

1 Swat: view from Bareengal (Badshah Sahib's house)
2 Rooftop view of Hoti Mardan from the Nawab's *hujra*
3 The Faisal Mosque, Islamabad from the Margalla Hills
4 The Murree Convent
5 In (white and red) summer uniform with author's convent class-fellows (1988)
6 Entrances within the house to the *hujra* and *kor* in Hoti, Mardan
7 Sketch of the Wali of Swat's house (right); Dalbar (centre); and Bangla (left)
8 Saidu Baba's grave inside his mosque
9 The *mashra* (elder) Bibi (centre) directing maids while cooking for her guests
10 A maid called 'Babo' (mother) performing the *nazar-māt* for a little Badshah
11 A two-bedroom city flat
12 Bamboo-covered Khan's and Bibi's semi-detached rented house in Islamabad
13 Swati and Mardani children of Bibiane with friends and maids at a birthday ('minor *khādi*') in Islamabad
14 A maid in white with young Bibiane in 'Hot Shots'
15 Old *qabar* juxtaposed against new grave
16 Bibi distributing meat to the villagers from the *kor*
17 A Bibi at the wedding of her *dai*'s granddaughter (her 'niece')
18 Village children at a madrassa opened by a Khan in Mardan now supervised from Islamabad by Bibiane
19 Women in *sazare* seen for the first time outside their homes for this kind of Islamic activity in a Mardan madrassa (school) now supervised by a Bibi who lives in Islamabad
20 Displaying the bridal gold jewellery at the *Nakreeza* event
21 A young male performer (*dum*) collecting money thrown over the groom's father's younger brother's wife's head
22 The bride's unmarried sisters and cousin in 'modern' short-sleeved, non-traditional clothes dance 'Indian-style' in Mardan
23 Young Bibiane and children dance in a Swati wedding to an audience of Bibiane and male performers

The colour images in the plate section have been reproduced in black and white for this digital reprinting.

FIGURE

1 The regional reach of a Bibi's *gham-khādi* network across Pakistan   *page* 42

MAPS

1 Pakistan, its provinces and neighbouring countries *page* xx
2 Swat, Mardan and Islamabad xxi
3 Pukhto-speaking regions xxii

TABLES

1	*Gham-khādi*	*page* 8
2	'Pukhtun'	17
3	*Gham-khādi* as perceived by Al-Huda Bibiane	73
4	Food hierarchy	94
5	A bride's wedding expenditure	115
6	Money given by Bibi for *gham-khādi* during a four-month period (March–June 2001)	139

ACKNOWLEDGEMENTS

Bismillah ar Rahman ar Rahim. In the Muslim world, everything ideally begins like this, the beginning of a journey, a birth, a marriage, the bathing of the dead, and the various such *gham-khādi* events of life, including life itself.

This book is based on my PhD dissertation at the Department of Social Anthropology, University of Cambridge titled: '"The World is Established Through the Work of Existence": The Performance of *Gham-khādi* among Pukhtun Bibiane in Northern Pakistan'. It seems appropriate that this ethnographic research on Pukhtun women, for a PhD, was conducted at Cambridge University. It was at this very university where Professor Fredrick Barth, some fifty years ago, shaped the first ethnographic image of the Pukhtun people in social anthropology in his own PhD thesis on the Swat Pathans (1958). His ethnography published as *Political Leadership Among Swat Pathans* (1959) became a classic in anthropology – thus any subsequent study on the Pukhtuns refers to his work. But it is precisely because of this reason that his important ethnography has been challenged and revisited by many distinguished anthropologists such as Professor Akbar Ahmed and Dr Charles Lindholm, and it continues to be debated. I am grateful to my predecessors for their rich ethnographic contributions on their respective areas to the study of the North-West Frontier Province of Pakistan.

There are many people without whose support and various levels of contribution this work would not have been possible. For the awards they have granted me, I am grateful to: Trinity College, Cambridge University for a grant from the Wyse Fund (2002–3); Lucy Cavendish College, 2002–3, 2003, and Alistair Duncun (1999) at Altajir World of Islam Trust. At the University of Cambridge, I deeply thank Professors Marilyn Strathern, Caroline Humphrey, Alan Macfarlane, Dr Stephen Hugh-Jones, Dr James Laidlaw, Dr David Sneath and my supervisors Dr Helen Watson who showed remarkable support and friendship and Dr Susan Bayly whose academic rigour challenged me intensely to give my best. I warmly acknowledge Dr Alison Shaw, whose work on Pakistanis in Britain inspires me. Thanks are due to Margaret, Sally, Pat, Terri and Paul at the social anthropology department office. For their critical input, comments and valuable time, I am very grateful to: Mr James Griffiths, one of my best teachers, Lenora Fisher, Professor Sheikh Abdul Mabud from The Islamic Academy Cambridge, Jacqui and Dr Grae Worster, Sir

Acknowledgements xi

Nicolas Barrington, Dr Soumhya Venkatesan, Dr Magnus Marsden, Salma Akhtar, Rosellen Roche, Dr Maria Carranza and Tanya Richardson. I am grateful to Dr Gordon Johnson, Dr Michael Sharp, Elizabeth Davey and Monica Kendall for their supportive role in the publication stage of this work.

At Lucy Cavendish College, many people showed great warmth and support: Dr Anna Abulafia, Dr Sarah Brown, Dr Orsola Rath-Spivak, Susan Sang, Bill Nelson, Gaby Jones, Sumaira Noreen, Helen Hamilton, Jane Rowan and the working staff: Tim, Hugh, Tom and Vince Woodley. Thanks to Marcel, Chris and Adrian at the Cambridge University Computing Service's Help Desk. Outside the university, I wish to acknowledge Mrs Osla and Fawcett School for their computing facilities, Gila Margulim, Priya and Prue; and Dr Dipti Chitnavis, Naima Crossley, Dr Susan Fell, Katrina Perrin, Jill Tsoi, Lucy Bentall, Caroline Sebastian, Babar, Umar and Nafees Ahmed for helping me with childcare while I studied; and Muntaha, my children's Swati nanny, who before the last days of submitting the thesis willingly slept on the library floor of the computer room while I worked through parts of the night.

In Pakistan, I thank Dr Sarah Safdar, Director for the Centre of Women's Studies; and Shaheen Akhtar at Peshawar University for kindly allowing me access to the library and theses; Dr Huma Haq (Quaid-e-Azam University); from Al-Huda, Dr Farhat Hashmi, Amina Ilahi; among my elders, friends and informants: Nawabzada Amir Khan Hoti, Abbas Khan, Azam Khan and his wife Dr Parveen Azam Khan for showing me around her Dost Foundation, a drug rehabilitation centre she opened and runs in Peshawar, Sharafat Ali Khan, Fateh Muhammad Khan, Shujat Ali Khan and especially their families. I deeply thank Zebunnisa Jilani, Begum Chaman Aslam, Colonel and Mrs Hisam Khan, Begum and Colonel Iqbal Jan, Mr and Mrs Ahmed Shah Jan, Farida Khor, Naureen Wajiullah, Umbreen Faisal, Safina Habib, and in Paris Jahanzeb and Humaira. For their continual support, my deep gratitude also to: Shahin Khalid (Nazigul), Ambassador Akbar Zeb, Dr Anwarzeb, Shahzada Aman-e-Rum and Asmat Bibi, Falaknaz Asfandiar, Ejaz Ahmed, Mahmooda Bibi, Nilofar Khor and Shahryar Lala, Dr Nafisa and Dr Ahmed Khan, Saira Khorand Humayun Lala, Abida and Sarbiland Lala, Mrs Marium Faridullah Khan, Mrs Qadir Khan Hoti, Pinny Hoti, Afshan Toru, Nadia Toru and Dr Shahin Habibullah. I am grateful to all the other people whose names I am unable to mention here but who allowed me to lift the veils from their lives and share their very personal experiences.

I would also like to remember the people who either directly or indirectly contributed to this work, but passed away during or before its completion: the Wali of Swat, whom I saw as a child, but rediscovered as an adult through anthropological accounts and fieldwork, Shahzada Sultan-e-Rum, General Jilani, Ghani Khan (the Pukhtun poet-writer), Begum Nasim Aurangzeb (the First Lady of Pakistan as President Ayub Khan's daughter, who opened up a girls' orphanage school called *Maskan* in Swat); Adalat Bibi (the sister of the Wali of Swat), Major Miangul Aslamzeb, Begum Farhat Munir, Dir Bibi Mehreen from Wazirabad and also the remarkable *daigāne* need mention who left a marked impression on generations of members of Bibiane and Badshahyan: Sheereena Dai, Kharo Dai and Amrojan Babo.

Undertaking this work has meant many personal sacrifices for my family members and for myself. My greatest debt is to my husband, Arsallah Khan, who is a Pukhtun and has shown remarkable support to me at many difficult stages of this study and who sacrificed his *gham-khādi* networks in order for me to complete this work. During several difficult months of the writing-up period our children, Mina and Ibrahim, remained with my parents in Washington DC; I am hoping that they may some day read this work in an attempt to rediscover their own roots, for my present today will be their past, as in Bourdieu's terms, 'today is tomorrow, because yesterday tomorrow was today'. Finally, to my parents, I owe a debt more than I can acknowledge in words: my mother, the granddaughter of the Wali of Swat, symbolises to me a dynamic Pukhtun woman – a woman of substance. My interest in anthropology was first awakened by my father, Professor Akbar S. Ahmed, and his work on the Pukhtun people. Our conversations over the dining table and during his evening walks, his endless stamina and extraordinary academic output have been a continual source of inspiration for me.

Note

In accordance with anthropological convention I have used pseudonyms in the text. For any shortcomings that may remain I take sole responsibility.

NOTE ON TRANSLITERATION

In this book, I have translated Pukhto words and phrases according to Pukhtun Bibiane's own pronunciation and understanding and as I understood them. Pukhto (Pashto or Afghani) is one of the East Iranian group of languages; it has several dialects, and is spoken by seventeen million people across north-eastern Afghanistan and North-West Frontier Province, Pakistan (although the national language of Afghanistan, Pukhto has no official status in Pakistan). Written in a variant of the Persian script (itself a variant of the Arabic script) since the late sixteenth century, Pukhto has a number of alphabets modified for sounds specific to it. Pukhto distinguishes two grammatical genders as well as singular and plural with a strict word order being: subject–object–verb. Although primarily borrowing from Persian and Arabic, a number of words in contemporary Pakistani Pukhto are derived from Urdu, the national language of Pakistan, as well as a few from English (e.g. 'formality', 'raydoo' from radio and 'TW' from TV). The adjectives 'Swat' or 'Swati' and 'Mardan' or 'Mardani' follow the usage in local English. I have tried to capture this linguistic diversity in people's everyday conversations throughout this book.

GLOSSARY

abay/abaygane (sing./pl.) mother, wet-nurse (also *dai* and *aday*).
abaya Arab-style stitched garment covering a woman's entire body.
adab respect; comportment; bodily habitus; rules of conduct; civility.
adam Adam: human.
Akhtar Muslim festival (Urdu: *Eid*). There are three Eid festivals: *Eid-ul-Fitr*, celebrating the end of fasting during the month of Ramadan; *Eid-Milad-un-Nabi*, the birth anniversary of the Prophet (SAW); and *Eid-ul-Azha*, commemoration of Prophet Ibrahim's (Abraham's) willingness to sacrifice his son Ismail. Pukhtuns, in general, mainly celebrate the first *lakotay* (small) *Akhtar* and last *loi* (big) *Akhtar*; and rarely celebrate *Eid-Milad-un-Nabi*. Eid celebrations often last three days.
aql social reason, intelligence and knowledge manifested in actions.
bāng call for prayer performed by a mullah (Urdu: *azān*).
bad/badi/badda bad/hostility/unpleasant woman.
badal (1) revenge – a primary principle of *Pukhtunwali*; (2) exchange – marriage.
badmash/badmashee a villainous man/woman.
Badshah/Badshahyān (sing./pl.) king; title of male descendants of Badshah Sahib, the ruler of Swat.
bar Swat upper Swat (e.g. Sher Palam, Jura etc.) (*kooz* Swat is lower Swat or Saidu).
Bareeze Pakistani designed, machine-embroidered, unstitched three-piece suits sold in *Bareeze* shops across Pakistan; widely worn by wealthy Pakistani women.
bazār/bazāroona shop/s; non-segregated public space.
be-aql a person displaying a lack of knowledge, social reason or wisdom.
be-gherat a person without *gherat*, courage and honour.
Begum a title of rank and respect for a noblewoman: such as Madam.
Bibi/Bibiane (sing./pl.) a respect title for a woman from a wealthy family.
chalāk clever in a cunning way.
crore 100 lakhs: Rs.10,000,000.
daftar/daftari Pukhtun land which enables the Khan to participate in the council of elders and make major and significant socio-political decisions.
dai/daigāne (sing./pl.) wet-nurse/s.

dalbar from Persian, originally: *darbar* (court); the inner, often women's, quarters.
dars Islamic segregated lectures where the Quran and Hadith are translated.
darzi/darzian tailor/s.
Deoband An Islamic movement and academy founded in 1867 in the north Indian town of Deoband which played a reformist role at the time of the British colonial rule in the subcontinent by calling on Muslims to commit themselves to religious and moral perfection and to embody Islam.
dera a type of *hujra*; a men's house in Swat.
dimagh the mind; the intellect.
dodai (1) cooked food/meal/feast; (2) flat rounded bread baked in a *tanoor* (oven).
dolai palanquin carrying brides on the '*Rukhsatee*' (departure to her husband's house).
dozakh hell.
dum/dummān professional dancer/s, performers, musicians and actors; locally of very low status and reputation: prostitutes.
ezat reputation (public persona); honour and family pride.
faqir in Pukhto: '*pakir*'; landless, beggar or mendicant.
fikkar thought; pondering.
fikkroona (pl. of *fikkar*) problems; worries.
geenay young and often unmarried girl; *geenakai* – girls.
gham (1) specific meaning: death and mourning; (2) general meaning: sorrow, difficulties, sadness, loss, worry, anxiety.
gham-khādi (1) life-cycle gatherings: of which the most significant or major *gham-khādi* are, in order of priority: funerals and then weddings; minor *gham-khādi* events are births, illnesses, birthdays etc.; keeping up relations; (2) sadness–happiness.
ghara/ghare (sing./pl.) (1) dirge; (2) literally, throat.
gharib/gharibi poor/poverty.
gup (1) nonsense, gossip, idle talk; (2) friendly conversation.
Hadith (pl. Ahadith) the sayings and traditions of the Prophet (SAW).
haj pilgrimage to Makkah (Mecca): one of the five pillars of Islam.
haqiqa celebratory ceremonies of a newborn baby (e.g. shaving of hair).
hijab headscarf worn by Muslim women to cover the hair.
hujra/hujre (sing./pl.) men's house; guesthouse.
janaza funeral.
janimaz prayer mat.
jannati a person who is thought to deserve *jannat* (paradise).
jazbah the force of uncontrolled emotions.
jihad primarily spiritual struggle.
jirga council of Pukhtun elders.
kacha temporary, or makeshift; raw.
kafir unbeliever; infidel.
kāl celebrating ceremony of the completion of a year after death.

kamaql/kamaqla/kamaqle person/boy/girl who lacks social understanding or wisdom: 'foolish'.
kār work.
kasabgara maid who does *gham-khādi* work for a Bibi.
kashar/kasharān (sing./pl.) a person younger in age.
katke stool.
khār city.
kha-bade *kha* – good = *khādi*; *bade* – bad = *gham*.
khādi includes ceremonies of: *wada* (weddings), *sunnat* (circumcisions), *paidaish* (births), *koydan* (engagement); more general meaning: celebrations, happiness, joy.
kha-ikhlaqa a woman of good virtues and morals.
khairat charity or meal given to relatives, the needy and poor. In *gham-khādi* and other religious ceremonies it often takes the form of a meal or 'feast' which is consumed by wealthy guests and the community.
Khan/Khanān (sing./pl.) a title for a landlord. Pakistanis in general address Pukhto-speaking men (particularly merchants), regardless of class, as 'khan'. Here the term 'Khan' more specifically refers to landlords.
khapa to be sad; *khapgān* (pl.) sadness.
khattam (to finish) recitation of the entire Quran.
khaza woman/wife.
khidmatgar/ān, khidmatgare/Naukar/Naukara helper/s, male servant/female servant.
khor sister.
khpal a complex term indicating a relative or close friend. *Khpalwali* – keeping up relations as relatives are expected to do.
khwashhāli happiness.
kille village/town (often *kor-kille* 'home-village' implies to do *gham-khādi*).
kille-kor village house characterised by courtyards, large spaces and several rooms.
kor/koroona house/s.
lakh 100,000 Pakistani rupees: Rs.100,000.
lās niwa holding up the hands in prayer (Urdu: *dua*) for the deceased; condolence.
lewane/lewanai mad man/woman; socially inadequate people.
mairazane sharing the same father but born from different mothers.
mashar/mashari/mashartia senior/seniority, older person with authority; *masharān* elders.
mashara/masharāne older female/s.
mazhab/mazhabi religion/religious.
meeshtha the bond that develops as a result of living together.
melmastia hospitality – a major feature of Pukhtun identity or *Pukhtunwali*: (1) offering one's food, home and gifts; and (2) on a symbolic level, one's time and self.

Glossary xvii

mina   love, or affection.
moonz   prayers.
mullah/*mullahyan*   (sing./pl.) religious teacher, often based in a *madrassa* (religious school).
naghare   coal hearth.
Nakreeza/Nakreeze   (1) the first of the three days of a wedding (Urdu: *Mehendi*); (2) *nakreeza* is henna which is applied to the bride's palms on the *Nakreeza* event.
na-mahram   marriageable persons, i.e. not of the men forbidden by propinquity.
Nawab/Nawabān   (sing./pl.) a Khan of a very large area with considerable power, authority, prominence and above all land. Bestowed by the British, the prestige of the title, locally, is inheritable by the male descendants of a Nawab: e.g. nawab, nawabzada (son of Nawab), sahibzada (grandson of a nawab).
nazar   (1) insight; vision; (2) evil eye.
nazara   struck by the ill-effects of *nazar*. *Nazar-māt* – breaking the *nazar* by reciting Quranic verses or by burning the leaves *nazar-para*.
neeat   intentions.
okhyār/okhyara   (masculine/feminine) clever, perspicacious or having a ready insight into and understanding of things.
ombaraki   congratulations; congratulatory visit in *khādi* marking the beginning of a stage in the life-cycle, e.g. following births and marriages.
paband/i   restricted/restrictions.
parathe   local type of bread cooked in plentiful oil.
pareshani   anxiety.
partoog-kameez-loopata   (Urdu: *shalwar-kameez-dupatta*) Pakistani national dress consisting of tunic-like shirt typically with full-length sleeves, baggy trousers and matching veil.
peeshare   criticising a person to his face; compare *zghaibat*.
peghor   insulting public taunt when one falls short in acts of Pukhto. This is often an effective way of exercising social control and causes great anxiety among Pukhtuns.
pookha   before, previously, in the old days.
pradee   outsiders, strangers, opposite of *khpal*.
Pukhtana   the Pukhtun collective self-reference in the Pukhto language.
Pukhtanna   a Pukhtun woman.
Pukhto   (1) the language of Pukhtun people belonging to Pakistan's North-West Frontier Province; (2) Pukhto is also the synonym of *Pukhtunwali*, the customary practices of Pukhtun people such as spontaneous hospitality (*melmastia*).
Pukhtun   (1) a person originally from the North-West Frontier Province in Pakistan or from Afghanistan; (2) who speaks and does Pukhto; (3) a landlord (a Khan), as opposed to a barber (*nai*), etc.: by virtue of being a landlord a 'Pukhtun' is of the highest social status in the wider Pukhtun hierarchy.
Pukhtunwali   previously defined as a 'code'; or customary practices of Pukhtuns.

purdah (1) curtain; (2) veil of two distinctive types, not limited to gender assignments: (a) 'literal *purdah*', this often applies mainly (but not only) to women taking such forms as covering the body, head and face, and (b) 'metaphoric *purdah*', this is *purdah* of the heart, mind, eyes, ears and soul applying to both men and women.
qismat   fate as decreed by Allah.
quom   tribe/nation.
Ramadan   Muslim month of fasting from dawn to sunset.
rewāj   customary practices.
rishtinee   direct confrontation. This is seen as being equal to open conflict.
rogh-ranzoor   *rogh* – well (e.g. birth, new house); *ranzoor* – ill (e.g. accidents, miscarriages)
rogha   fixed, made up; healed. Opposite: *wrana* – fighting; broken, ruined.
roje   Muslim month of Ramadan: fasting.
rozgār   employment.
sakhta   hard, strong; *sakhte* – hardships, difficulties.
salām   salutations or greetings (peace).
Salwekhtamma   a specific event forty days after burial; part of burial rites.
saritob   display of masculinity and manhood.
sartor/sartora   (1) literally, blackhead; (2) bareheaded.
sath   (1) reverence, politeness; (2) invitation.
sattar   veiling/*purdah*; concealing, covering.
sawāb   religious merit.
sazar   (Urdu: *chador*) a large unstitched piece of cloth worn by Pukhtun women in various ways to cover the entire body, head and face and is often white in colour and embroidered. This contrasts with the Pakistani *loopata* (veil) – a length of cloth varying in size and typically, but not always, of lighter material.
shamiana/shamiane   (sing./pl.) brightly coloured tents which serve to enclose or segregate outdoor garden spaces in *gham-khādi*.
sharam   (1) shame, embarrassment; and (2) honour, self-respect.
speen   (1) white; (2) purity; (3) to peel.
sunna   traditions of the Prophet Muhammad (after every mention of the Prophet, it is conventional to put the following: Peace Be Upon Him: Pbuh, or in Arabic: SAW).
tajdid   revival of the authentic Islamic practices based on the Quran and Hadith.
tapos-pukhtana   to ask; enquiry visit: part of *gham-khādi* exchange.
tarburwali   agnatic rivalry – primary law of *Pukhtunwali*. Enmity with *tarbur* (father's brother's son). An alternative Pukhto word is '*thrabgani*' (derived from the term *thra* meaning father's brother).
thamma   expectation.
thor   (1) black; (2) a disgraced woman; (3) impure, or to be put off food or even a person.
tlal-ratlal   'going and coming', reciprocated visiting and a basis upon which *gham-khādi* is built.

tleen   the term *tleen* is derived from *talé* which means 'gone by', e.g. a death anniversary celebrated after a *kāl* (year).
uzar   to attend or express sorrow at the time of *gham* (death).
wāk   (1) will, choice, authority, command, sway, control, influence; (2) power, might, force, capacity.
wada   (1) the wedding day when the *Nikah* is typically performed (often the second day following the *Nakreeza*); (2) a promise.
Wali   ruler, chief, sovereign.
Walima   the third day of the wedding (celebrating the consummation of marriage).
warwal   bride price.
weenze maraee   a maid who is also a lifelong companion.
wesh   a past practice of decadal land redistribution within and between villages.
zamindar   (1) a landlord; (2) a man who works the land for a landlord or Khan.
zan/zanana   (1) woman/women; (2) women's section of the house; (3) female, feminine, effeminate, womanly.
zeest-rozgār   (1) *zeest* – life, living, existence; (2) employment. Or keeping up relations by going and coming (*tlal-ratlal, zee-razee*), reciprocating gifts (*warkra-rakra*: give and take). *Rozgār* – employment or work (*kār*).
zghaibat   criticising a person behind his or her back.

Map 1 Pakistan, its provinces and neighbouring countries.

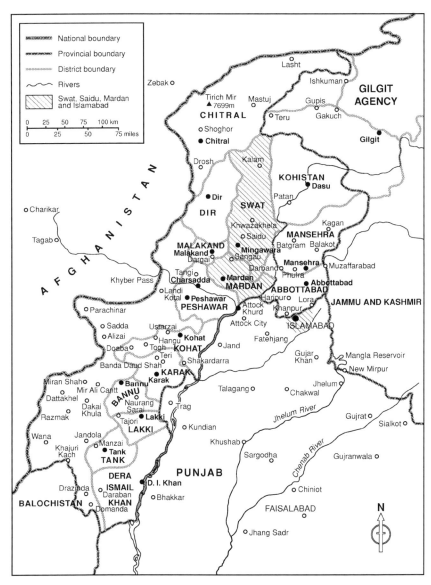

Map 2 The shaded areas correspond to Swat, Mardan and Islamabad.

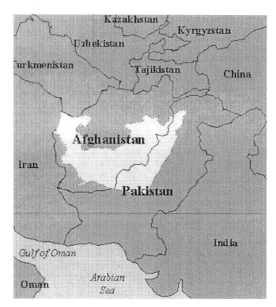

Map 3 Pukhto-speaking regions are roughly indicated by the light-grey shade.

INTRODUCTION

Death and destruction on 11 September 2001 in New York and Washington DC and on 7 July 2005 in London forced the world to ask fundamental questions about the nature and society of Islam. Unfortunately in the rush to provide answers inadequate and even distorted explanations were provided. Some sections of the media explicitly equated Islam to fanaticism and terrorism. Muslim groups like the Taliban in Afghanistan and Pakistan with their stringent and brutal ways came to symbolise Islam. In this din and confusion the normal and ordinary lives of Muslims threatened to be lost. More than ever we need to know and understand Muslim society.

This book is one such attempt. It is based in Pakistan which is important for a number of reasons: first, because its founder Mohammad Ali Jinnah believed in the vision of a modern Muslim nation; it is the only nuclear Muslim country; Pakistan has a population of about 160 million people; and there are millions of Pakistanis living abroad in the West, in the Middle East and the Far East (see footnote 19). Finally Pakistan is situated in one of the most sensitive and turbulent places in the world. All these factors make Pakistan an important geopolitical nation to study.

My anthropological work is based on an examination of the Pukhtun people of northern Pakistan (locally referred to as Pashtun or 'Pathan' from colonial English) who live not only in Pakistan but also along the eastern half of Afghanistan. Pukhtuns are one of Pakistan's and Afghanistan's numerically and politically most significant ethnolinguistic groups. Karachi, Pakistan's main commercial city, has one of the highest concentrations of Pukhtuns. Yet the Pukhtun people are too often conceptualised as occupying a timeless world distinct from other regions of Pakistan. Pukhtun families and clans have traditionally migrated from outside their homeland to other parts of the subcontinent.

With the focus of the United States shifting to Afghanistan after 11 September 2001 the significance of Pakistan on the international stage was confirmed. Pakistan became a key geopolitical ally to the United States: in 2004 President Bush called Pakistan its 'major non-NATO ally': billions of dollars of US aid were earmarked for the country. Yet, so little is known of its culture and traditions and even less about its women. The need to understand Pukhtun society specifically and Muslim society more generally through a diachronic and in-depth study is thus even more urgent. This book is therefore an attempt to portray ordinary Muslims leading their lives in an important part of the world. It is an attempt to explain how Muslims organise their lives through an examination of rituals conducted by women. Using anthropological perspectives and analyses this work lifts the veil from the lives of Pukhtun women – the ethnic group identified with the Taliban – known traditionally for their stringent observance of the veil and segregation; and because the author is a woman from that part of Pakistan it allows unprecedented access to the lives, stories and dreams of women in northern Pakistan. The reader hears how women cope with the burden of death and how they prepare to celebrate the joys of marriage. This particularistic account has far-reaching ramifications for the study of Muslim society.

One older Bibi (wealthy lady), sitting on a *kat* (straw bed) alongside various other visiting Bibiane (plural), village guests and maids – all sipping tea under a persimmon tree in the cool mountainous Swati breeze – told me, 'The world is established through the work of existence!', *'dunia pa zeest-rozgar wadana da!'* This profound saying emphasises the significance of events such as death and weddings for the women and men living in Pukhtun society. This book explores this aspect of the social lives of Pukhtun women through Bibiane in northern Pakistan. Its ethnographic focus is on the enactment of particular life-cycle or *gham-khādi* ceremonies (such as funerals and weddings). The widely used Pukhto term *gham-khādi* both refers to specific segregated gatherings commemorating death, marriage, birth, illnesses and other such events, and designates the emotions of sorrow (*gham*) and joy (*khādi*) which they elicit. While I focus on the *gham-khādi* of Bibiane and their maids in this work, it is important to make clear that *all* Pukhtuns generally, across the social hierarchy, practise and actively engage in *gham-khādi*. This study thus explores the emotional practices surrounding funerals (*gham*: sadness) and weddings (*khādi*: happiness) among Pukhtun women generally with a specific focus on elite women from Mardan and Swat, now living in Islamabad. *Gham-khādi* comprises a body of ideas and practices of life, in which happiness and sadness are understood as indissoluble, and are celebrated communally within networks of reciprocal social obligations. Different *gham-khādi* occasions are categorised in a hierarchy of importance with attendance at *gham* (the paramount emotional, thoughtful and bodily experience) taking priority over *khādi*. The scale descends through illness (*najorthia*), birth (*paidaish*) and relatively minor *tapos* (enquiries) on moving, *afsos* (condolence) following an election defeat, or felicitations (*ombaraki*) to winners. Thus, were a death and a wedding in two separate families to fall at the same time, an individual expected to attend both should go to the funeral (*gham*) (see also Lindholm 1982: 156). Although highly complex, in order to illustrate the concept of *gham-khādi* from a local perspective, I intentionally look at the concept to imply mainly funerals and weddings, the two most hierarchically important events of *gham-khādi*. *Gham-khādi* has been divided into two categories of priority: 'major': funerals and weddings, and 'minor': births, accidents, illnesses, returned-*haj* visits and birthdays, and so forth by Benedicte Grima, an American anthropologist, who conducted a groundbreaking study on the performance of *gham-khādi* emotions and narratives among Pukhtun women (1998). In this book, I focus on 'major' *gham-khādi* events of Bibiane, as these are considered most significant in the making and breaking of social relationships. Preparation for and attendance at *gham-khādi* events is locally understood as 'women's work', a set of complex activities integral to Pukhtun identity or *Pukhtunwali*.[1]

The term 'Pukhtun' is widely used, and has been previously defined, in three principally variable ways. First and more generally, all Pukhto-speaking people, the ethnolinguistic group predominantly living in Pakistan's North-West Frontier Province (NWFP, or Frontier), are known as Pukhtun (or Pashtun, 'Afghan' (Hoti 1942), or, more commonly, 'Pathan' by people living outside the Frontier areas). Pukhtuns are described as 'the largest tribal society in the world' (Spain 1995: 23), as sixty Pukhtun tribes comprise six million in Afghanistan and ten million of Pakistan's total 2002 population of 147,663,429 (S. M. Khan 1997; Shinwari 2000). Second, though the ability to speak the Pukhto language distinguishes the Pukhtun, speaking in itself is not sufficient. A Pukhtun must also 'do' Pukhto, i.e. seek to live up to a set of honour-based practices, also called *Pukhtunwali* (Barth 1981b: 105). Pukhtun identity is thus bestowed by adherence to notions of honour, especially in tribal areas where people are supposed to revert to 'ideal-type behaviour' (or *Pukhtunwali*) in order to be recognised as full members of society (A. S. Ahmed 1980). Third, lineage and genealogy distinguish the wide majority of the Pukhtun population, i.e. Pukhto-speakers, from landowning persons of the dominant Yusufzai tribe, also called Pukhtun, as opposed to a Pukhto-speaking *nai* (barber). 'Pukhtuns', descended from a common ancestor, have the right to 'full citizenship' on the basis of previous conquest (Barth 1986: 3). In its 258 interviews, at least, this work focuses on the Pukhto-speaking saintly and lordly landed families (particularly the Wali of Swat's family, the Khanān of *bar* (upper) Swat, the Nawabān of Hoti and the Toru of Mardan). These families are connected to a wider range of families in northern Pakistan.

Conventionally, anthropologists have characterised *Pukhtunwali* as an 'ideal-type code' based on such principles as *badal* (revenge), *melmastia* (hospitality), *nanawatee* (refuge), *tor* (female honour) and *tarburwali* (agnatic rivalry) (e.g. A. S. Ahmed 1980; Barth 1986; Grima 1998; Lindholm 1982; Singer 1982). This study suggests that *gham-khādi* has come to assume a priority among Pukhtuns as a contemporary principle of *Pukhtunwali*. Many of the concepts characterising *Pukhtunwali* (such as forms of hospitality, revenge, agnatic rivalry) are acted out in funerary and wedding events (*gham-khādi*). On the basis of ethnographic data, I will argue that *gham-khādi* constitutes a 'work of life' (*zeest-rozgār*), through which Bibiane maintain the fabric of social life by sustaining inter- and intra-family relationships.[2] This book identifies and explores a Pukhtun construction of work

---

[1] *Pukhtunwali* has been defined as the core of Pukhtun identity, and its social and cultural life (see A. S. Ahmed 1980: 3, 89; Q. I. Ahmed 1994; Banerjee 2000; Barth 1970: 119; 1986; 1995: 104; Grima 1998: xi; A. M. Khan 1994; G. Khan 1990; M. T. Khan 2000; Lindholm 1982: 210; Mohmand 1966: 44; Singer 1982: 51; Tahir 1980; Tair and Edwards 1982: 71).

[2] The Western concept of the 'family' fits uneasily with indigenous models (see Altorki 1986: 13; S. A. Khan 1996: 13; cf. Le Wita 1994: 118; Shore 2002: 2), which involve extra-familial networks

divergent from professionalism or physical labour measured and quantified by production output. What I seek to show is that the Pukhtun construction considers work as producing not things but social relations and transactions (cf. Strathern 1990: 177).

This book, therefore, seeks to contribute to anthropological debate on a number of issues. First, it attempts to establish the distinctive sociality of Pukhtun Bibiane in terms of their participation, within and beyond the household where they observe *purdah*, in *gham-khādi* festivities, joining them with hundreds of individuals from different families and social backgrounds.[3] Second, in tracing the extent of the *gham-khādi* networks of the wives of the landed wealthy ('Bibiane'), the study adds to the ethnography of 'the elite' of South Asian and Muslim societies (see Shore 2002: 1, 12 on 'studying up'). Moreover, it presents an alternative perspective to the characterisation of elite South Asian women as 'idle' (Alavi 1991: 127) by documenting their role in Pukhtun families in the household and in the wider society.[4] Third, it contests the conventional academic portrayal of Muslim societies as contexts in which men claim a greater measure of reason or social sense (*aql*) than women (Anderson 1985; Shalinski 1986; Torab 1996). In describing the segregated female contexts of *gham-khādi* as a space of agency, it reconstructs how, in one educated Bibi's words in English, Bibiane 'call the shots', exercising minutely differentiated senses of both social propriety and personal strategy in negotiating procedures. Focusing on this agency helps us to revise previous anthropological accounts of Pukhtun society, which project *Pukhtunwali* in predominantly masculine terms,[5] while depicting *gham-khādi* as an entirely feminine category (Grima 1998). Attention to Pukhtun society's *rites de passage*, as these represent key elements of social structure and behaviour, makes it possible to re-examine widely held views about Pukhtun society as a domain of male-dominated honour and shame values through considering the role, organisation and actions of its women. Fourth, the book is concerned to capture the contemporary dynamism of Pukhtun *gham-khādi*, which is subject to negotiation, in particular as relatively young married Bibiane take issue with its 'customs' (*rewāj*) as offending against Islamic precept.[6]

---

of alliance (Bourdieu 1991: 178). In the vernacular, the term 'family' is variably: a) the descendants of a single ancestor consisting of some twenty-five or more households but sharing one family name; b) a husband and wife unit; or c) a wife.

[3] The Arabic/Urdu word '*purdah*' denotes curtain (Papanek 1982); *purdah* is an entire system of segregation entailing veiling and avoidance behaviour.

[4] I use the term 'elite' not so much analytically as a local reference to members of landed families; it should not obscure some degree of social mobility only partly captured in my account. For comparative definitions of 'elite cultures' see Altorki 1986: 14–18; Altorki and El-Solh 1988: 52; Deutsch 1998; Hoodfar 1991: 122; Gilsenan 1996; Le Wita 1994; Shore 2002: 10; for calls for a redirection of anthropological attention to elites, see Comaroff and Comaroff 1992.

[5] Elsewhere I have analysed *Pukhtunwali* from a female perspective (A. Ahmed 1994; 2000).

[6] Henceforth, when I refer to 'Islam' I am referring to the principles prescribed or proscribed in the Quran and Hadith. From a Muslim perspective, Islam as a set of rules is distinct from the diverse and multiple practices and experiences of Muslim peoples. Contrast Gilmartin and Lawrence who use Hodgson's term 'Islamicate' to describe ways of life 'not restricted to the practice of Islam as a religion' (2000: 2).

Based in three localities of northern Pakistan, this study was conducted in Pakistan's capital city, Islamabad, and two villages (*killee*), Saidu in Swat and Hoti in Mardan, both in the North-West Frontier Province.[7] Mardan and Saidu Sharif are significant fieldsites in the study of Pukhtun society specifically and Pakistan more generally for a number of reasons. First, as the home regions of the elite Yusufzai Pukhtuns, they represent what are understood as 'essential' or the 'traditional' fieldsites. The Yusufzai are the most hierarchically important and widespread Pukhtun tribes. They have lived for centuries in their traditional location and define themselves through political action and literature. The Yusufzai are traditionally recognised as the embodiment of *Pukhtunwali*. By studying the Yusufzai Khanān and Bibiane, I am arguably looking at the core, the heart of Pukhtun identity. Second, both sites are the seats of historical crossroads: one of the most ancient civilisations in South Asia, Buddhist monasteries and archaeological finds have been located in both sites, Alexander's army crossed both cities, the British encountered the Pukhtun tribes in both areas. Third, the rich legacy of history in these sites together with the unsubmissive nature of the Yusufzai Pukhtuns prompted historians, colonialists and anthropologists to write on the Pukhtuns of Swat and Mardan. Fourth, the town is of considerable significance for the understanding of contemporary Pakistan society and the understanding of the Muslim world more generally, yet anthropological accounts tend to focus either on 'tribal' settings or on large cities, and there are only a few accounts of small town life in Pakistan. Swat and Mardan being the two major towns of the Frontier and close to the border of Afghanistan are significant entry points. The events of the past decade have caused a spill of Afghan refugees into Pakistan – many of whom live in Mardan and Swat. Although I am aware of these transformations I did not want to shift my focus from the Bibiane. I worked with Bibiane in Islamabad but this would not have been possible if they were from the Wazir or Mahsood tribes living in the remote tribal areas. Lastly, the valley of Swat with its ruling family allowed a striking contrast with the plains of Mardan and its lordly families. Yet in interesting ways these families are connected, as I document, through several intermarriages.

The districts of Swat and Mardan consist of several villages and may be characterised as segregated *purdah* contexts, in which patrilineal descent is common and marriage is typically both endogamous and virilocal. Swat is dominated by

---

[7] NWFP lies to the north-west of Pakistan with its western border or FATA, the Federally Administered Tribal Area, contiguous with Afghanistan along the Durand Line. The Frontier covers 41,000 sq. miles. It is one of the four provinces of Pakistan and borders Afghanistan to the west and Punjab Province to the east; anthropologists have variously placed studies of the Pukhtuns under the rubrics of Middle Eastern and South Asian Studies (Grima 1998: 2; Nelson 1974: 552). Donnan (1987: 21) attributes this definitional difficulty to the course of the Indus River across the south-eastern Frontier as it marks off the subcontinent (see also Banerjee 2000: 21). Historically, the Yusufzai Pukhtuns conquered the Frontier in successive waves from 1500 to 1600 (AD). During British rule in India the Frontier served as a neutral zone, interposed between the two Imperial frontiers of Russia and British India (Chakravarty 1976: 53; see also Richards 1990). The Frontier has retained its English colonial name despite many attempts to rename it *Pukhtunistān* (the land of the Pukhtuns) (Hanifi 1976: 442; Jansson 1988).

landowning Pukhtuns, referred to as Khanān. It was governed between 1926 and 1969 as an autonomous state under two rulers, Badshah Sahib, and his heir, the Wali, who were descended from the famous shepherd saint, the Akhund of Swat (1835–77). The Akhund's male descendants are referred to as Badshahyan (descendants of a ruler). Mardan is also dominated by landed lords or Nawabān, whose families, from the Patriarch Nawab Akbar Khan, were incorporated into British colonial rule as a landed elite. Women of both saintly and landed descent go by the honorific Bibiane.[8]

In both Swat and Mardan, the village (*kille*) is still, as Barth observed in the 1950s, 'the most important unit of territorial reference' for Pukhtuns (Barth 1986: 13). The Pukhto proverb: 'no matter how far you go, you'll eventually return to your village' (*che ze ze no Abazai la ba raze*) insists on an ideology of Pukhtun identity being vested in its rural heartlands, as well as in Pukhtun villagers, who are said by many Khanān and Bibiane to embody a purer form of Pukhto. While complex, village organisation is shaped by the dominant role of landlords on whose hospitality, patronage and landownership all other categories of villagers depend (cf. Barth 1986: 3, 10). Khan status derives from tenants' allegiances and patrilineal land inheritances. Land is mainly agricultural in both the valley of Swat and plains of Mardan. Among the categories of villagers (discussed in more detail later in this chapter), farmers, tenants, agricultural labourers, shopkeepers, barbers and dancers are all directly or indirectly dependent politically, economically and socially on landlords' families with whom they share reciprocal visiting relationships of *gham-khādi*. In addition to these, an entire category of male and female villagers belonging to these occupational groups as domestic helpers (wet-nurses, servants and maids) come to hold quasi-familial degrees of prominence and power in Bibiane's houses. Bibiane's performance of *gham-khādi* thus affects their relationships both with other families of equal status and with a variety of socially subordinate villagers.

The importance of focusing on the funerals and weddings of Khanān and Bibiane as a social group is not that their embodiment of *Pukhtunwali* is taken to be more authentic than that of the *gharibanān* (poor) – on the contrary it is the *gharibanān* who are seen by Bibiane and Khanān to embody *Pukhtunwali* in its most authentic form – but that the practices of Bibiane and Khanān have potential to disseminate more widely across village and metropolitan contexts. As many as two thousand people drawn from a broad social spectrum may attend big landlord families' funerals. As this study documents, landlords' migration to the capital Islamabad is precipitating transformations in these Bibiane–villager bonds. Transregional patterns of habitation mean that the observance of *gham-khādi* ceremonies in natal villages represents a vital ligature connecting often absent landlords to their traditional dependents and patrimony. Interactions between urban Bibiane and

---

[8] My use of the plural 'Bibiane' refers to Pukhtun women from landowning families, not the Urdu usage, 'bibi/an', a gender-specific respect title for women of various social strata. More widely, see Dalrymple 2002.

rural villagers demonstrate divergences in the understanding of convention, while the migration of Bibiane to a provincial region outside their own thus challenges some of the core features of Pukhtun identity. This creates many painful paradoxes for Bibiane as wedding and funerary procedures are revised, and the acceptable forms of ethnic and cultural continuity called into question.[9]

Bibiane from Frontier families who have left the village context for the city, for at least some part of every year, form the ethnographic focus of this study. Married Bibiane in Swat and especially in Mardan rarely leave the home for tasks not connected to *gham-khādi* (principally weddings and funerals, but also covering a range of other procedures of congratulation and condolence). These excursions, which take place as often as two or three times a day during the spring and autumn 'wedding season', and as infrequently as once a week in winter, tie them to a wide network of relations with hundreds of individuals from different families and social backgrounds.

According to an interpenetration of personal and social concepts of identity within Pukhtun conceptions of the family and kinship, Bibiane apprehend *gham-khādi* as both an enactment of social relations and a source of personal self-definition. A person's identity, as Daniel has argued, in a South Asian context, is not 'individual' but includes his or her spouse, offspring, kinsmen and so forth (1984: 103).[10] Every adult of a given family – both men and women – occupies a unique position within a thick web of relationships in local, regional and national contexts. Kinship among Pukhtuns is typically conceptualised as dense and multi-filiated. Individuals conceive themselves as having relations not only to immediate kin (parents, children and siblings) but also to a range of distant relatives and affines, usually connected through the marriages of female relatives (who may be cousins several times removed). Bibiane's sense of social identity derives from a married person's participation in circles of *gham-khādi* formed primarily through kinship and marriage, but also through friendship, clientage and political faction. Likewise, families are conceptualised as large corporate structures, belonging to different households but sharing a common ancestor (see footnote 2). *Gham-khādi* circle membership bestows on Khanān and Bibiane the obligation to attend fellow members' *gham-khādi* occasions, creating a complex pattern of overlapping bonds, loyalties, allegiances and debts between families (extended and nuclear). Each individual *qua* family member is bound to others by a pattern of reciprocal visiting.

At major *gham-khādi*, funerals and weddings, Bibiane engage in a number of practices of hosting (preparing the house, giving food) and attending (gifting, offering congratulations or condolence), observing 'proper' or ritualised forms of procedure and decorum. Bibiane (and not their husbands) in these contexts

---

[9] On the topic of inherent paradoxes within forms of religion (Islam) and practice (Pukhto), see A. S. Ahmed 1976; Tapper and Tapper 1986: 65; Titus 1998: 675.

[10] In contrast, quoting Foucault, Rabinow writes: 'What is distinctive about Western culture is that we have given so much importance to the problem of the subject ['objectified by a process of division either within himself or from others'] in our social, political, economic, legal, philosophical, and scientific traditions' (1986: 7).

Table 1 *Gham-khādi*

Pukhto:	*gham*	*rogh-ranzoor*	*khādi*	*paidaish*
Translation:	(sadness) ↓	(well-ill) ↓	(happiness) ↓	(birth) ↓
Event:	death ↓	illness/accident ↓	wedding ↓	birth ↓
Performance:	*lās-niwa* (condolence) ↓	*tapos* (enquiry) ↓	*ombaraki* (congratulations) ↓	*ombaraki* ↓
Offering:	money/food	money	money/(cloth)	money (baby clothes)
Offerer:	Wife or mother-in-law on daughter-in-laws' behalf (Iqbal 1997: 85)*			

* Naveed-i-Rahat, in the context of Meharabad in Punjab (Pakistan) notes: 'Transfer of roles from senior to junior generation takes place in Meharabad not from mother to daughter but from mother-in-law to daughter-in-law' (1990: 58). Further, Mernissi notes: 'The mother-in-law's role as imitator of *savoir-vivre* is as important as her role as instructress in matters of birth, sickness, and death' (1985: 126).

characteristically offer money, food or gifts in accordance with family status and accounts (*hisab-kitab*) of earlier debts and donations (Table 1). These activities represent the most pronounced forms of a general social system of *tlal-ratlal* ('going and coming'), conceived of by Pukhtun women generally, and Bibiane specifically, as an ongoing 'work of life'.

It should be stressed that, although the primary material of this study concerns funerary and wedding ceremonies, this analysis provides only an indirect contribution to the anthropology of death and marriage. *Gham-khādi* events among Bibiane are, rather, understood as complementary aspects of the concept of 'life' or 'existence' (*zeest*). This study draws on local understandings of marriage and death that do not rehearse established anthropological distinctions between the two, since Pukhto idioms consider such distinctions foreign. Moreover, as annotated in Raverty's dictionary, usages of '*gham*' (sadness) and '*khādi*' ('joy, happiness . . . gaiety') (1982: 670) suppose essentially public or ceremonial contexts for emotions. A speaker may denote a defining condition (say, childlessness or widowhood) as their *gham*, as well as gesturing towards personal feelings. The spoken verb, '*khādi kawal*', denotes the 'manifest(ation)' of 'gladness' specifically at weddings (*wada*), birth-visits (*ombaraki*), circumcisions (*sunnat*), naming and hair-shaving ceremonies (*haqiqa*), as well as less formal events such as returns from the *haj* pilgrimage, birthdays, election victories, professional promotions and housewarmings. Partly eliding the distinction between ceremonial and everyday visits, Bibiane specifically and Pukhtun people more generally place the term *gham-khādi* within the context of *tlal-ratlal* and a third expression, *zeest-rozgār* (literally the 'work of life'), thus confounding any anthropological attempt to establish a separate ontology of *gham-khādi* ceremonies (cf. Humphrey and Laidlaw 1994). Pukhtuns use variants of the word '*rozgār*' in contexts other than *gham-khādi*, referring to professional work ('*kār-rozgār*') as 'employment', which is distinguished from less specified purposive activity, '*kār*' ('*kor-kār*', housework). The word tends to relate more to people's roles or identities than to the effort invested in contingent tasks. The two available English–Pukhto dictionaries amplify these verbal transfers in defining *zeest* as 'life, existence, employment' (Bellew n.d.: 88; Raverty 1982: 537), and *rozgār* as 'employment', 'service, earning' and also 'time' (Bellew n.d.: 82; Raverty 1982: 516). Bibiane's own discourse suggests that visiting, gifting and attending ceremonial events are all parts of a conceptually single, though highly complex, process of 'making kinship' (cf. Carsten 1997) and building social relations – a process, moreover, experienced as a form of work.

Such a concept of 'work' – first, a practice of social relations not completely identified with any one task; and second, an array of conceptual (not only physical) activities – necessarily complicates and enriches debates within anthropology as to the definition of this term.[11] In the 1970s–80s, a number of women anthropologists took issue with the broadly Western conceptualisation of work as a salaried, professional task taking place in a 'public sphere', adducing the domestic context of socially meaningful labour (Mackintosh 1979: 175; Povinelli 1993; and Strathern 1984: 13, 18). Others criticised the then-dominant model of work as 'patriarchal' (Grint 1991: 33, 40; Kondos 1989: 29; Lewenhak 1980; 1992: 1, 16; Morris 1990: 3–5; Novarra 1980: 35; and Wallace 1987: 1). This book builds on such work by presenting an ethnically specific concept of Bibiane's 'work' as they enact 'proper' ceremonial observances. Attendance and participation count as Bibiane's work under a number of headings: first, these actions entail conformity to or negotiation with conventional practices. Second, they are physically and mentally arduous (a matter of strategy). Third, the participating women collectively perform a 'work' as a means of Pukhtun self-representation ('*Pukhtunwali*'). And last, they are understood by Bibiane as an ongoing social effort, characteristic of living itself. The analytical concept of 'work' I deploy in this book identifies the term with the small- and large-scale, highly organised, transactional activities that make up social relationships. Bibiane's entry into a *gham-khādi* circle, on marriage, commits them to a category of social relationship with other families in which *gham-khādi* obligations subsume all other ties, as *gham-khādi* and *tlal-ratlal* participants understand themselves to be performing an identity-making practice of 'Pukhto'.

---

[11] Western female anthropologist have been at pains to problematise assumptions about work, e.g. Andersen 2000: 144; Franks 1999: 4; Gray and Mearns 1989: 29; Hochschild 1997; Humphrey 1992: 179; Kelly 1986; Mackintosh 1979: 175, 179–90; Novarra 1980: 22–5; Oppong 1994: 1–13; Pahl 1989; Reagan and Blaxall 1976; Singh 1992: 3; and Wallman 1979: 12–13. On other activity in the hidden economy as 'work' (Daniels 1988), such as voluntary work, see Jahoda 1982: 8–9, and on charitable work, see Reynell 1985: 232–3.

10   *Sorrow and joy among Muslim women*

This study aims to build upon a rich body of anthropological literature about NWFP Pukhtuns, from a female context, for its representation of the actions of individual Bibiane in *gham-khādi*.[12] Most anthropological enquiries in the NWFP discuss 'tribal' village contexts (Donnan and Werbner 1991: 3).[13] Barth's account of political leadership among Swat Pukhtun Khans ('chiefs' or landowners) of the Yusufzai tribe (1986)[14] showed that although Pukhtun society, in theory, is egalitarian, in reality it is structured by caste-like divisions. The 'Pukhtun' (conventionally landowning and widely referred to as Khan) forms the apex of such structures, along with certain religious groups (for example the Wali's family). Barth argued that 'Khans' derive authority from the ownership of land, provision of hospitality and reputation for honour. In Swat, Khans, in the capacity of autonomous agents, build support and status by receiving visitors in their men's guesthouse (*hujra*). In a series of 'games', both the landed (*mōr sarī*: satisfied men) and their adherents (*wúge sarī*: hungry men) are granted an individualistic agency in exploiting their respective resources (land or support and labour). Barth argued that in a series of temporary choices, relationships are dyadic, contractual and voluntary (ibid.: 3). In contrast, I argue below that although Bibiane are able to exploit relationships within society to further their individual choices through *gham-khādi*, such relationships are, however, characterised by a complex, and sometimes negotiable, sense of duty and obligation.

Although Barth's focus on singular actors, agency and negotiation marked a new phase in anthropology (from that of Evans-Pritchard's and Radcliffe-Brown's models of social structure), and was the first substantial ethnography on 'elite' Pukhtuns, his theoretical presuppositions were challenged variously by Marxist, indigenous and feminist anthropologists. Asad (1972) argued that Barth obscured Khanāns' exercise of systematic domination through their control of scarcity. Second, Ahmed questioned Barth's Western presumption of individual interests, which downplay the emergence of the self-abnegating ruler (Badshah) or Wali and his Sufi ascetic ancestry in Swat (A. S. Ahmed 1976; cf. Comaroff and Comaroff 1992:

[12] A. S. Ahmed 1975, 1976, 1980, 1984, 1988; Asad 1972; Banerjee 2000; Barth 1958, 1986, 1960, 1961, 1970, 1981a, 1981b, 1995; Caroc 1992; Dupree 1978, 1984; Edwards 1996, 1998; Grima 1998; Lindholm 1981, 1982, 1988, 1995, 1996; Safdar 1997; Singer 1982; Shah 1993; Shah 1999; Spain 1962, 1963, 1995. On Afghan Pashtuns, see Lamb 2002; Tapper and Tapper 1986; Tapper 1981, 1991; Tapper 1984. Historical and colonial accounts include Bellew n.d., 1986, 1994; Beveridge 1987; Elphinstone 1815; Goodwin 1969; Howell 1979; King 1984; Kipling 1987; Merk 1984; Raverty 1982; Thackston 1999.
[13] A Pukhtun 'tribe', in this context, means the group of people who claim descent from a common ancestor, Qais bin Rashid in the seventh century, who had three sons: Sarban, Bitan and Ghurghust, from whom all Pukhtun tribes trace their descent (I shall elaborate on this in Chapter 1). All Pukhtun tribes also share a common 'culture' called *Pukhtunwali*; speak a common language, Pukhto; and usually occupy a specific geographical area, such as the North-West Frontier Province in Pakistan. For a definition of 'tribe' in the Middle Eastern context, see Khoury and Kostiner 1990: 4.
[14] Among the Pukhtun tribes the Yusufzai Pukhtuns who make 'the class of *khans* and Pukhtuns' (Charles Lindholm 1996: 78) aspire to 'positions of leadership' (Lindholm 1982: 213). They are one of the most powerful tribes in the Pukhtun hierarchy. Both Mardan and Swat regions are dominated by the Yusufzai Pukhtuns (see A. S. Ahmed 1976: 7, 1977a: 14; Barth 1986: 7–11, 25–8; Bellew 1994; Caroe 1992: 12–13; Wadud 1962: xxiv).

10, 16; Dupree 1977: 514). Third, anthropologists focusing on Pukhtun women and gender issues have also proposed a revision to Barth's 'political' conceptualisation of power, presenting power less as a quality vested in certain institutional offices or factional leaderships (like the Khans'), and more in terms of a 'particular kind of social relation' (Nelson 1974: 553).[15] In these terms, Bibiane's activities of 'brokering' 'information', 'control' and 'influence' through the 'negotiated order' of *gham-khādi* (Nelson's terms in her germinal 1974 article on women in the Middle East) achieve new theoretical visibility (cf. Roded 1999).

This account of Bibiane's *gham-khādi* as an important form of Pukhtun social activity explores dimensions and perspectives only partially investigated by earlier anthropologists.[16] In the context of Frontier ethnography, Barth viewed *gham-khādi* ceremonies as an adjunct to Khan factionalism, understanding the strengthening of affinal ties at weddings and funerals as essentially political acts (Barth 1986: 40, 41; cf. A. S. Ahmed 1980: 177). Charles Lindholm gives greater weight to Bibiane female agency in describing the activities of 'Khan women' in organising gatherings (1982: 134) in the village. Yet Lindholm describes women's position in terms of 'the centrality of the womb in a system that denies the existence of women as independent entities' (ibid.: 159; see also Charles Lindholm 1996). For Lindholm, the organisation of Pukhtun society 'on the basis of kinship' subordinates women to an essentially transitive role in the transfer of lineages and consolidation of patrimonies (Charles Lindholm 1996: 74). Grima's ethnography of the lives of Pukhtun women generally offers a first, more substantial, account of *gham-khādi* as emotions centrally 'performed' in women's self-conceptualisation and narration. However, in focusing on 'poor families' (1998: 28), Grima overlooks the Bibiane; and therefore attributes far more emphasis to *gham*, rather than noting its complementarity with *khādi*.

My account describes Bibiane's *gham-khādi* as segregated but not apolitical.[17] In suggesting places to look for Middle Eastern female agency, Tapper argues that any society prohibiting women's access to a professional sphere tends to develop alternative, quasi-autonomous female networks of circulation. Gossip and gifts between women demarcate a 'sub-society' serving as a 'psychological outlet . . . in a situation of male domination' (Tapper 1978: 395), as women exercise both tacit and overt forms of jurisdiction over the domestic environment. Yet, in the Frontier,

---

[15] I distinguish between a woman's gender perspective and that of a feminist. Indeed my interest in women does not necessarily entail feminism as a theoretical stance (Strathern 1990: 36).

[16] More widely, however, forms of South Asian and Middle Eastern women's visiting and feasting have been extensively documented (see Das 1986; Khedairi 2003; Sharma 1980: 234; Tapper 1991: all are gender-specific female activities around life-cycle events in India, Iraq and Afghanistan). For Bedouin and Turkish Muslim women's practices of bonding through visiting and exchange, see Abu-Lughod 1986; Aswad 1978; and Delaney 1991: 14 (contrast, also, Sexton 1984; and Strathern 1990). See Gilsenan (1990) on Arab women's visiting. Striking parallels are Shaw's account (1997) of the Punjabi reciprocity '*lena-dena*' (gift-giving) which corresponds to the Pukhtun *warkra-rakra* (give-take) gift-giving; and Nancy Tapper's *kheyr-u-sharr* (good-and-evil) among the Shahsevan Iranians (1978) is comparable to the Pukhto *kha-bade* (good-bad).

[17] 'Females . . . play a full part in the political and economic life of the Pukhtuns . . . an aspect of society . . . overlooked for lack of data and therefore . . . unanalysed' (A. S. Ahmed 1980: 15).

female visiting reflects and underpins Khanān and Badshahyan's explicitly political position-building. In a country in which its elite maintain dominance by controlling appointment to influential political positions (Ali Khan 2003: 31–2),[18] Bibiane's canvassing on behalf of male family-member MNAs and MPAs (Members of National and Provincial Assemblies) at Bibiane's ceremonies, brings them into contact with circles of a wide range of people (rich (*maldar*) and poor (*gharib*), from various familial, ethnic and multicultural backgrounds).[19] Bibiane command a significant degree of respect on the basis of family history but at the same time they must also put much time and effort into the work of reputation-building in the household, village and *gham-khādi* network analogously with their husbands' 'political' efforts.

Another dimension of the study is the exploration of the role played by wealthy middle-aged and young convent-educated Pukhtun women in the Islamisation of elite lifestyles in Pakistan. Through the unfolding of a number of case studies this work seeks to show Pukhtun women who have taken to the Islamic reform teachings of Al-Huda International who have sought to Islamise the very types of 'traditional' Pukhtun *gham-khādi* or funeral and marriage ceremonies that are central to their lives and also to their broader sense of Pukhtun identity. As case studies in this book suggest, the Al-Huda women's movement, particularly among Pukhtun women, aims to ingrain a sense of religiosity in Pakistani society generally within the existing structures and policies of the state, and is distinct from the state-oriented Islamic political groups that have been the focus of much academic studies of the Islamist movement. Yet the Al-Huda Islamic women's movement should not be seen as disconnected from socio-political engagement as the form of religious piety and practice it seeks to realise entails the transformation of many public, though segregated, aspects of social life in Pakistan.[20] I will thus examine Islamic revivalism through one particular study.

Recognising that Pukhtun Bibiane practices overlap with a political arena necessitates the reformulation of an idea of the public sphere from the 'inside-out' (Gray and Mearns 1989). Female anthropologists have challenged the equation of a governmentally administered work-space in the 'public' realm, with the home being considered a lesser, 'private' domain. The division deprived domestic women and children of status, self-determination and even complete personhood (see Colen and Sanjek 1990: 4; Strathern 1984: 31, 1990: 133; also Waterson 1990: 169).[21]

---

[18] On the continuing hold of elite tribal families in Pakistan's national politics, see Ali Khan 2003; Weiss 1991: 2. In 1999, 126 of the 207 National Assembly seats were held by members of the Frontier Khans, the Sindhi *waderas*, Punjabi *zamindars* and Baluchi *sardars*.

[19] Donnan and Werbner (1991) also note a large number of Pakistani migrants live in Euro-American and Middle Eastern cities; see Raj 1997; cf. Shaw 1997, 2001; and Werbner 1992.

[20] Compare the women's mosque movement in Cairo described brilliantly by Mahmood 2001. Brenner locates a comparable Islamic women's movement in Java (1996: 680); cf. also Abu-Lughod 1998a: 4, 15.

[21] On the Greek origins of the Western concept of 'work', see Grint 1991: 15. On work outside the house as a salaried male occupation differentiated from women's domestic tasks, see Weber 1968: 21–2; Hoch-Smith and Spring 1978.

Yet both Western and non-Western anthropologists working in South Asian, and particularly Muslim, contexts have tended to apply and continue to apply this framework to indigenous studies (see Deutsch 1998; Hirschkind 2001: 4; Kondos 1989: 165, 176; Papanek 1982: 28; Sharma 1980: 214, 226; Weiss 1998: 125), despite the lack of Islamic categories that correspond to Western notions of 'privacy' (Cook 2000: 80).[22] Henrietta Moore correctly suggests that 'even where such a distinction exists we must not assume that the Western terms . . . are adequate or reasonable translations of the categories other cultures perceive' (1997: 20). In this line of thought, York, within the context of Pakistan's Yasin valley, argues that the private and public domains are flexible and tend to overlap (1997: 209, 216). 'We call events and occasions "public" when they are open to all, in contrast to closed or exclusive affairs' (Habermas 2002: 1), as *gham-khādi* is understood to be. In the 'all-women context' of *gham-khādi*, Grima observes: 'every social interaction is public to a degree. There is not so much an opposition between public and private as . . . a continuum stretching from "less public" to "more public". The interaction between women, even if it takes place inside the house, has a very public aspect to it' (1998: 71, 118; see also A. S. Ahmed 1980: 243; and Barth 1981b: 28, 1986: 31).

The theoretical premise of the 'inside-out' approach allows social relationships to be delineated from the perspective of women observing *purdah*. In the context of her work in Papua New Guinea, Strathern (1984) calls for the 'dislodg[ing]' of one's thought from a binary Western matrix of 'work [inside and] outside the house' if the full complexity of affiliation between kin, affines and dependents is to be captured. This is a perspective that I seek to apply to the Pukhtun house as a place where both male and female (segregated) work, especially the work of *gham-khādi*, assumes a public aspect. At weddings and funerals the familial house is thrown open to all, with men visiting the *hujra* (men's guesthouse) and women the *kor* (house). Rather than dealing with these spaces according to any implicit hierarchy of importance (Grima 1998: 71, 118; Tiffany 1984: 6), I refer here to the *bazār* and other external spaces as 'the non-segregated public' and the house with its men's and women's areas during *gham-khādi* as the 'segregated public'.[23] These are very important theoretical distinctions that I urge social scientists to take account of when describing such complex societies.

In outlining the layout of the book, the following chapter introduces important contextual material relating to Pukhtun ideology (*Pukhtunwali*) and introduces the Bibiane, my fieldsites and methodology in the field. Chapter 2 documents the house, as the centre of Bibiane's social world, from the 'inside-out'. It orients Bibiane's 'dual lives' as they move between Islamabad and the Frontier,

---

[22] In an Arab context, Gilsenan dichotomises gendered space (1990: 17–173), as does Barth (1983: 74). Price furthermore alleges the tendentiousness of many academic appropriations of local (Indian) formulations of the 'public' (2000: 28). Cf. Reiter 1975. On a critique of the 'private–public' dichotomy, see Abu-Lughod 1986; Habermas 2002.

[23] In a Middle Eastern context cf. Abu-Lughod 1998b: 260; Altorki 1986; Altorki and El-Solh 1999: 44; Aswad 1978; and Tapper and Tapper who refer to the 'public context of hospitality, especially in life-cycle feasts' (1986: 74).

and between domestic (private) and public *gham-khādi* contexts. Chapters 3 and 4 present ethnographies of the procedures observed in Bibiane's funerals and weddings respectively. An examination of mourning or *gham* in Chapter 3 focuses on expressions of grief as socially expected forms of behaviour which reassert prior relationships against a background of 'natural' feeling. It also shows Bibiane's funerary practices simultaneously taking new and complex forms under the pressure of purist Islamic revision. Chapter 4 extends Bibiane's sense of self as performed during ceremonies across their lifelong efforts of planning and preparing for weddings, finding a suitable match for offspring and equipping the house. This pattern of weddings is contrasted with an internet love-marriage illustratively contracted outside of social sanction. Chapter 5 details the complexities of *gham-khādi* by focusing on its inherent contradictions and by describing Bibiane's anxieties in juggling different kinds of work (professional employment, childcare, housework) with the culturally imperative obligations of *gham-khādi*. My guiding questions throughout are: how are Bibiane's performances of specific *gham-khādi* duties more broadly constitutive of their self-image and personhood? What motivates, and what might justify, Bibiane's conceptualisation of attendance or preparation as 'work'? How are wedding and funeral ceremonies related to people's ideas of their (enactments of) Pukhtun ethnic identity? As with visiting, funerals and marriages are grasped as ceremonies for the transmission of social and ethnic identity through public and communal efforts of building social relations. I argue that an ethnographically detailed account of Bibiane's funerary and wedding ceremonies, besides its inherent interest, can renew our understanding of the modes of kinship and social organisation and cultural continuity among Pukhtuns.

1
Gham-khādi: framework and fieldwork

This chapter provides a taxonomic account of Pukhtun concepts of *Pukhtunwali* and *gham-khādi*. It also socially and geographically establishes the Bibiane whom I observed practising *gham-khādi* in northern Pakistan. In this way the chapter outlines the layout of the Pukhtun context and social setting.

Pukhtunwali: Pukhtun identity and *gham-khādi*

Gham-khādi does not only lie at the heart of making and sustaining social relationships, but also symbolically resumes Bibiane's representations of their identity (Castells 1999: 6). Many of the women I spoke to invoked an ideal of 'Pukhto' or *Pukhtunwali* for the establishment of norms and precedents of 'proper behaviour'. The Pukhtun as a distinct ethnolinguistic group organise their lives around what has been described as a defined 'code' called *Pukhtunwali* (A. S. Ahmed 1980; Barth 1995: 104; Caroe 1992: 24; Easwaran 1999: 55). One writer has observed that *Pukhtunwali* 'is an emic concept which includes everything which a Pashtun should or should not do. It is thus a means of ethnic identification and differentiation in relation to other ethnic groups' (Steul; in Grima 1998: 3). Furthermore, *Pukhtunwali* may acquire a normative force as a set of values internalised by individuals (men and women) as an ideal (or 'habitus', in Bourdieu's terms (1991: 18)), which they must embody to secure full symbolic legitimacy as ethnic Pukhtuns.

Explaining their behaviour, Bibiane refer to Pukhto (or *Pukhtunwali*) as their 'culture' so frequently, especially during *gham-khādi*, that one could be forgiven for seeing ceremonies merely as the instantiation of pre-existing codes or 'customs' (Lindholm 1981: 465). The problem for anthropology is to avoid essentialising Pukhto, while taking account of people's constant recourse to it in describing themselves (Thomas refers to 'reifications positively upheld' (1992: 213) in his discussion of Samoans' conceptualisation of their 'tradition'; but see Banerjee 2000 for a statement of Pukhto's dynamism). Werbner argues, 'cultures may be grasped as porous, constantly changing and borrowing, while nevertheless being able to retain at any particular historical moment the capacity to shock through deliberate conflations and subversions of sanctified orderings' (2001: 134). One highly respected Bibi, convent-educated and recently an Al-Huda graduate, told me: 'Being a Pukhtun, I know that the people of the Frontier Province have great respect for their religion and most of them are practising Muslims.' But while Pukhtuns insist on a Muslim identity, Pukhto is considered separate from adherence to Islam. Prohibitions of divorce and female inheritance in *Pukhtunwali* are increasingly seen as non-Islamic by new Al-Huda Islamic women's movements sweeping Pakistan. This ethnography focuses upon the perceived contradictions between the religious (Islamic) and customary (Pukhto) forms of mourning practice, such as a forty-day period of funerary commemoration. Despite Al-Huda graduates' and others' pointing-out of inconsistencies, in practice many Bibiane defer to the 'customary' forms.

With reference to Pakistan's Frontier Province, anthropologists (working in the 1950s and 80s) have defined *Pukhtunwali* on a basically schematic model, which revolves around the key concept of honour (*ezat*).[1] Accordingly, the central constitutive features of *Pukhtunwali* are: an intense sense of egalitarianism expressed through hospitality (*melmastia*), agnatic rivalry (*tarburwali*), revenge (*badal*), honour (*nang*), trust (*jabba*), respect for elders (*mashartia*), assembly of male elders (*jirga*), male honour (*gherat*), the men's house (*hujra*) and above all manliness (*saritob*).[2] On *Pukhtunwali* 'a tough code for tough men', see Dupree (1978: 328) and Keiser (1991) who notes that Conan the Barbarian, the American hero, is directly inspired by the Yusufzai Pukhtuns (9, 14).

Male anthropologists' access primarily to segregated male areas, in a stringent *purdah* society, has resulted in a largely androcentric picture of *Pukhtunwali* (cf. Nelson 1974: 553).[3] In contrast to the male view of *Pukhtunwali*, more recent work, such as Grima's (1998), recognises the necessity of overcoming 'women's analytical "invisibility"' (H. L. Moore 1997: 3) in conceptualisations of *Pukhtunwali*.[4] Yet Grima dichotomises *gham-khādi* into a classificatory scheme of 'Men's Paxto [Pukhto]' (the gun, the turban, honour (*gherat*), manliness (*saritob*), feuds or blood revenge (*badal*), hospitality; and granting exile) on the one hand, and 'Women's Paxto' (honour (*gherat*), shame, modesty, tears, upping the ante, *gham-xadi*

---

[1] 'Honour', argued Pitt-Rivers, 'is the value of a person in his[/her] own eyes, but also in the eyes of his society. It is his estimation of his own worth, his *claim* to pride, but it is also the acknowledgement of that claim, his excellence recognised by society, his[/her] *right* to pride' (1966: 1). The pursuit and theme of honour lies at the heart of Pukhtun literature and poetry. Khushal Khan Khattak (1613–89), a celebrated Pukhto poet, wrote in a famous couplet: 'I despise the man who does not guide his life by honour. The very word "honour" drives me mad' (A. S. Ahmed 1980: 91–2; cf. Bourdieu 1966).
[2] See A. S. Ahmed 1980: 90; Barth 1986: 83, 106; Lindholm 1982: 211, 1995: 69, 1996; Singer 1982. On the various accounts of the Pukhtun's 'manly warrior' image, see S. Bayly 2001: 141; Easwaran 1999: 64; Eliot 1963; Elliot 1968: 69; Titus 1998. On the image of the manly Pukhtun homosexual, see Banerjee 2000: 38, 40. Cf. Sinha 1995.
[3] Contrastively, for the prioritisation of a colonialist perspective on the colonised in conventional academic accounts, see Asad 1983: 15. Cf. A. S. Ahmed 1987: 58; Beattie 1985: 4; Boon 1982: 26; Mead 1950.
[4] Contrast Ardener 1975; Beck and Keddie 1978; Collier and Rosaldo 1981; Gray and Mearns 1989; Kabbani 1986; La Fontaine 1992; Leonardo 1991; Lewis 1996; H. L. Moore 1997, 1999; Okely 1996; Tiffany 1984. Slocum 1975 suggests anthropology's emphasis on the 'macro' tends to exclude women's accounts of ceremony. On alternative approaches to Pakistani anthropology, see S. A. Khan 1996; more widely, Broch-Due and Rudie 1993: 8.

Table 2 *'Pukhtun'*

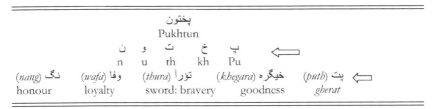

		پختون			
		Pukhtun			
ن	و	ت	خ	پ	⇐
n	u	th	kh	Pu	
نگ (*nang*)	وفا (*wafa*)	توړ‍ا (*thura*)	خېګړه (*khegara*)	پت (*puth*)	⇐
honour	loyalty	sword; bravery	goodness	*gherat*	

(*gham-khādi*), tapos and gifts) on the other (1998: 73). For Grima, men's Pukhto remains dominated by those features described by earlier male anthropologists, while she associates *gham-khādi* primarily with women.

In my analysis of Bibiane, by contrast, contemporary local understandings of *Pukhtunwali* apply broadly but unevenly to both sexes. *Gham-khādi* is incumbent on both men and women, as is hospitality and respect for elders (*mashartia*) within the men's (*hujra*) and women's spaces of the house (*kor*). Equally, *'gherat'* denotes modesty, bashfulness, courage and honour on the one hand, and jealousy and enmity on the other (Raverty 1982: 745). Both women and men talk about their lives and *gham-khādi* practices in reference to *gherat* and honour. In one Pukhtun home, a husband and wife showed me a formula, which analysed the concept 'Pukhtun' into its various sub-elements (Table 2). The gendering of these terms is complex. While some terms are martial, both Khanān and Bibiane recalled childhood images of the women of their households embodying qualities of Pukhto.[5] Mothers, aunts, maids and *daigāne* (wet-nurses) were idealised as honourable (*ezatmande*), loyal (*wafadare*), brave (*narre*), patient (*sabarnake*), prayerful (*moonzgoozare*), modest, strong (*zreware*) and *purdah*-observing (*sattarnake*).[6]

In a study on the Egyptian women's mosque movement in Cairo, Saba Mahmood suggests that female modesty, shyness and piety in being aspirational Islamic virtues are forms of potential female agency, if we see agency as 'a capacity for action that historically specific relations of subordination enable and create' (2001: 203). She argues that a particular openness to exploring 'nonliberal traditions' is intrinsic to a morally and politically responsible scholarly practice, considering the motivations, commitments and aspirations of the people studied, even if considered

---

[5] Elderly Bibiane and Khanān stated how mothers, not fathers, influenced childhood behaviour; e.g. Badshah Sahib's ninety-year-old daughter told me that she saw her father about four times in her lifetime; and a male elder living in Virginia (United States), General Jilani (1913–2004), said that a Pukhtun's habits and way of life (*Pukhtunwali*) were ingrained by mothers' teachings.

[6] Contrast Matthews 1996. On the importance of *purdah* as a practice of *Pukhtunwali* for women, see Singer 1982: 74; Rifaqat analyses the Pukhtun veil or *sazar* as a symbol of the honour (*ezat*) of Pukhtun women so that observance confers status and gender identity (*be sadara khaza kho khaza na ee*) (1998). On *purdah*-observing Pukhtun female rulers in nineteenth-century Bhopal, see S. M. Khan 2000.

'uncomfortable for feminist scholarship' and 'objectionable' (to 'liberals') (ibid.: 205, 225). Mahmood makes a valuable point here, despite her usage of some problematic terms. For Bibiane, the relation between different components of Pukhto was arguably less significant than the implication of Pukhto itself in a host of subtly differentiated cognates, respectively *kale-wlas* (village-gathering); *kha-bade* (good-bad); *kor-kille* (house-village); *tlal-ratlal* and *zeest-rozgār*.[7] For Pukhtun women and men, distinctively ethnic concepts are related to moral ideas, so that a critical measure of honour (*ezat*) for women is their diligence in discharging *gham-khādi* obligations. The interrelation of this evaluative framework for women with the performance of religiously contentious rites ensures the precarious nature of any innovations, which Bibiane may wish to introduce into *gham-khādi* practices.

With migration to Islamabad and elsewhere, widespread access to cable television, and motorised transport reducing the remoteness of 'tribal' areas, many Pukhtun men and women across various social backgrounds stated that Pukhto has 'changed' (*badalla shawe da*). The effort of driving three to six hours to a Frontier funeral from Islamabad means that *gham-khādi* has taken a greater prominence among markers of ethnic identity. '*Gham-khādi kawal*'[8] (literally, practising *gham-khādi*) implicitly means the embodiment of Pukhto for Bibiane and their families who admit feeling estranged from their roots. Spongmai, a Bibi in her mid-thirties with three young daughters, asserted in English:

I would always want my daughters to do *gham-khādi* because it 'is' *Pukhtunwali*, it's part of our family, it's part of our heritage and it's part of who we are, which we can't cut ourselves off from.

Here Spongmai makes it clear, as other Pukhtun informants have done, that *gham-khādi* is integral to a Pukhtun understanding of the self. In contrast, South Asian groups generally do engage in activities similar to *gham-khādi*: for example, *lena-dena* (give and take) or the *khatam* performed on the fortieth day of the death among Pakistani Punjabis (Shaw 2000), and *afsos karna* among Hindu Indians (Sharma 1980). For the Pukhtuns, however, *gham-khādi* is distinctly stressed as an *ethnic* marker. Tiffany writes, 'what women are is paradigmatically linked to what they do' (1984: 6), yet, what women 'do' also reflects who they 'are' and the conceptualisations of themselves they embody and seek to advance. This is the focus of the book – the enactment of the 'work' of *gham-khādi* as it becomes a self-conscious expression of the personhood of Bibiane in northern Pakistan.

---

[7] The collective aspect of *gham-khādi* is continuous with similar concepts in Muslim societies. Ibn Khaldun, the fourteenth-century Muslim 'sociologist of history', analysed society through the concept of '*asabiyah*' (group feeling). *Asabiyah*, like *gham-khādi*, binds groups who are not necessarily related by blood but connected by 'long and close contact as members of a group' and through a common language, culture, family, clan, tribe or kingdom affiliations. Muslims have reverted to the concept of *asabiyah*, and its social life-cycles, in expressing concerns over the breakdown of traditions in modernity. On Khaldun, see A. S. Ahmed 1993: 62; Ibn Khaldun 1986, 1989.

[8] The verb '*kawul*' is translated as 'to do, to act, to perform . . . to practice' (Raverty 1982: 821).

Village organisation

The immediate context of all Bibiane's *gham-khādi* is the natal or virilocal site. Pukhtuns more generally and Bibiane more specifically have conventionally lived in settlements, towns and villages, with village organisation being shaped by two main lines of common mythical beliefs.[9] In the first, religious ascendancy as embodied in virtues of religious learning, piety and devotion confers a variety of social statuses on persons. These statuses are inheritable, and it is typical for a diverse range of decent groups to claim high rank and authority as descendants of the Prophet (SAW) and saints. Both saints and their descendants are recognised by the occupants of the village as holding an important status in the Pukhtun social order. Holy men can come to hold large amounts of lands donated to them permanently either as acts of devotion or in return for political mediation. They may even eventually acquire the rank of independent political rulers. The second belief that affects village organisation relates to the status of landlords and land tenure: driven out of the Kabul valley from Afghanistan, the Yusufzai tribe conquered Peshawar (the present provincial capital of the NWFP), and eventually came to dominate Swat and Mardan between AD 1500 and 1600. Descendant Yusufzai claimed ownership of almost all lands, but could not organise an equal division of land among themselves. An 'important and pious' man, Shaikh Malli (in c.1530), was then called to implement an equitable system whatever the uneven quality of the land, dividing the region between a number of sub-tribes (or major segments of the tribes) according to a rotatory system known as *wesh*. This meant that no one lineage segment possessed a permanent right of ownership to land. Instead, they held shares in the landed assets of the sub-tribe. This egalitarian system worked alongside another hierarchical set-up. While the periodical reallotment over long distances (e.g. 30 miles) meant mass migration for the landlords, most of the non-Yusufzai population remained sedentary. The land tenure system consequently came to emphasise the division between the powerful Yusufzai and their tenants (who served a succession of different Khanān under the premise of an egalitarian relationship in *Pukhtunwali*).

The division within the system between landlords and tenants was also underlined by the prevention of intermarriage, so that distinct social groups emerged. Pukhtun parents will ideally give their daughters in marriage to men of equal or higher, but not lesser, status. As a group, then, landlords typically marry endogamously, while also marrying women of lower status. In contrast to the big Pukhtun Khan or landlord, who may delegate all agricultural activities to his tenant (*zamindar*), men with smaller landholdings work their own lands maintaining their independence. In addition to holy groups (Sayyid, Mian, Miangul) and landholding Pukhtun tribesmen, at the top of the hierarchy, a diverse range of occupational groups exist in villages, such as the priest (mullah), farmer (also *zamindar*), shopkeeper (*dukandar*), goldsmith (*zargar*), tailor (*darzi*), carpenter

---

[9] On the village in an Indian context, see Dumont 1980; and Madan 2002.

(*tarkan*), butcher (*qasai*), shepherd (*gujar*), musician and dancer (*dum*) and barber (*nai*). This order of social hierarchy in the village context follows the rubric of Barth's typology, who, most importantly for this study of Bibiane, emphasised that, '[a]ll alike are directly or indirectly dependent on the landowners' (1986: 10).

A village, comprised then of a complex composition of occupational groups, is often led by a recognised 'chief' or a big landlord. The landlord, and by extension his wife, maintain a range of relationships with the families of their various fellow villagers and dependents, including the families of other landowning Khanān (these are possible opponents as lineage equals), prominent members of holy families, tenants, dependents and servants. In the modern context, relations are maintained with local politicians and administrators and their wives. Partly formalised practices of house visiting, usually with the landlord's *kille-kor* being visited, substantially tie these families. Landlords, whose status and sustenance is derived from their title to land and not on physical labour, typically own large, solid (*pokh*) houses, divided in complex ways into the men's house (*hujra*) and family house (*kor*). Each house is built so as to accommodate large numbers of visitors (discussed in the following chapters). Extended patrilineal families emerge among landowning households, as married sons of landlords are discouraged from engaging in any occupation not befitting their status, and property inheritance is deferred until after fathers' death. Thus in the village context, married sons and their wives (Bibiane) live virilocally as dependents and helpers in the hosting of the houses' various guests. 'Allegiance to the chief is expressed by the mere act of visiting' the landlord's house, and further strengthened by the reciprocal hospitality offered by the landlord (Barth 1986: 11). Every Khan's *hujra* characteristically has an adjoining mosque (*jumāt*) and the religious priest or mullah of the mosque has the potential, through Friday sermons (*khutbas*), to increase the religious standing of the Khan in the perception of villagers while himself financially benefitting from the Khan's household generosity. During religious festivals (Eids, *Akhtar*), for instance, the Bibiane of the Khan's household traditionally keep one of the largest portions of distributed food and meat for the mosque and its mullah (as in Plate 16). The landlord's status in the village is thus enhanced by the domestic activities of the women (Bibiane and maids) of his house. Through the act of (his household's women) offering spontaneous hospitality, the landlord in the village consolidates his own and his family's reputation, while creating a complex pattern of debts and dependents, which may in turn be drawn upon in times of the landlord's own socio-political and religious needs (for instance, in national elections). While there is a mutual dependence between a Khan and his mosque mullah there is also a parallel sense of rivalry between the two: with the mullah seeing the Khan class as too westernised and less Islamic, and the Khan sometimes seeing the mullah as a hypocritical proselytiser (as in many of the verses about the mullah by the famous Pukhtun poet Ghani Khan).

Bibiane play an active role in hosting the houses' various guests and organising weddings and funerals, but their movement in the village to non-segregated public areas is typically restricted. Village *bazārs* (shops) are dominated by men. Women in drastically fewer numbers walk hurriedly behind their men, or in groups under large white veils (the *sazar*) or heavy black shuttlecock *burkhas*. The strict observance of *purdah* for women is a symbol of status in both Swat and Mardan (where *purdah* in the latter area is comparatively more stringent for Bibiane). In contrast to the women of the village, Bibiane of landowning families are distinguishable by their heavier veiling, avoidance of non-segregated public areas or the *bazār* and abstention from walking. Instead, they may be driven in cars to their destinations typically by old male 'family drivers'.

Fieldsites

The valley of Swat

Among the Islamabad Bibiane I worked with, half belong to Swat, which lies in a valley at the foot of the Hindukush Mountains, 270 km from Islamabad (Plate 1). Orderly meadows, green fields and fruit trees flank the meandering trunk road. To the north, the 'Swat' River (from 'Sweta' meaning white or clear, a name bestowed by historians attached to Alexander the Great in 326 BC) flows from the crevasses of mountains reaching 18,000 feet for about eighty-six miles. Swat's history is shaped by the region's distinctive legacy. It was progressively settled by the Buddhist Gandhara civilisation in c. AD 100, the Hindu Rajas, under whom Sanskrit was the language of the Swat people, and then by a series of conquerors: the first Muslim Mahmud of Ghazni entered in 1001; the first Mughal Emperor Babar in 1505 (Beveridge 1987); and, finally, the Yusufzai conquered Peshawar in c.1485, taking over Mardan and Swat.

Some of the Bibiane I worked with belong to the most prominent family in Swat as descendants of Badshah Sahib, whose family transformed itself 'from asceticism to kingdom' over two generations. In resisting British rule, the Sufi shepherd and ascetic Abdul Gaffur, known as 'the Akhund of Swat', acquired a large following of devotees who gifted him (*wakf*) lands (*serai*).[10] Sherani observes that donors and followers attribute to the saint (*pir*) an almost 'superhuman' status on account of 'his sacred genealogy and his relationship to God' (1991: 223; cf. Fazlur-Rehman 1999). In 1845, the Akhund selected Saidu as his centre, henceforth the capital and focal point of Swat politics (A. S. Ahmed 1976: xvi); it is now known as Saidu Sharif (holy) after Saidu Baba (father of Saidu). Saidu Baba's mosque in Saidu is a central place of pilgrimage in Swat transcending boundaries of gender and class; village-men and women, beggars, Bibiane and their families pray as equals in devotion.

[10] In Islamic law, the institution of '*wakf*', introduced and practised at the time of the Prophet (SAW), denotes the permanent dedication, by a Muslim, of his or her property for any purpose recognised by Islamic law as religious, pious or charitable. *Wakf* transfers the symbolic rights of ownership, of the thing dedicated, to God. However, as the nature of God transcends any use of the property, its benefits are reverted to the welfare of people. The recognised motive, in offering *wakf*, is to secure spiritual advancement, reward (*sawāb*), and social and political recognition (Asad 2003). On the political power of nineteenth-century saintly landowners in Sindh, cf. Ansari 1992: 63, 101; in Punjab, Gilmartin 1984: 223–4. Contrast Ewing 1988: 2.

The Akhund's grandson, Abdul Wadud, became the first ruler (Badshah Sahib, or 'Wali') of Swat in 1917 through fratricide. He was recognised by the British colonial authorities in 1926 (Barth 1995: 27, 42, 60; Toynbee 1961: 144). Male descendants of these families, individually called 'Badshah' in differentiation to the landowning Khan, retain a local aura of religious prestige. The term 'Badshah' or 'Khan' as an indicator of social class does not capture the full complexity of landed/saintly, ethnic and family distinctions among Pukhtuns. Mardan and upper (*bar*) Swat are dominated by the Yusufzai Khanān, while the Wali of Swat's descendants (Miangwalān; 'Mian' denotes religious affiliation) are further differentiated from the 'Miangān' (pl.) and are not lineally related to the saint Saidu Baba, whose descendants are indicated by the suffix '*gwal*'. Miangulan's less prestigious Safi Mohmand origin contrasts with the Sadozai descent of the Afghan ruling family. As the progeny of saintly and lordly ancestors, Bibiane distinguish themselves from persons of different tribes and family backgrounds while interacting with them during *gham-khādi*.

Swati villages (as do those in Mardan) physically comprise a collection of single-storey mud houses, arranged around a central, often white mosque, which serves as the centre of the non-segregated communal life. The Wali's descendants' houses are dispersed among the smaller mud and brick village homes in the mountains' foothills. Some Bibiane's houses are built overlooking the valley so that, with 'load shedding' (power cuts) at night, the gleam of other houses' *laatain* (lanterns) can be seen as clearly as the stars from their courtyards. Male and female villagers visit Bibiane's houses daily. While some *ghariban* may resent the rich's dominance over their lives through wealth and influence (Asad 1972), they may also venerate them as descendants of a saint. Circumstantial connections of charity, trade and retainership tie the community to the *kille-kor* of Badshahyan. Both marriage connections and the large gatherings at local *gham-khādi* bind Bibiane by reciprocal *tlal-ratlal* to several Khan households in upper Swat, Sher Palam and Jura. Swat proper (excluding Swat-Kohistan[11]) is divided into *bar* (upper) Swat – where the Khanān of Sher Palam originate – and *kooz* (lower) Swat, the natal lands of the Wali's family.

Swat borders Chitral to the north, Kohistan to the east, Malakand and then Mardan District to the south and Dir to the west, comprising a population, in 1998, of 1,257,600.[12] The Swat population depends on a complex subsistence economy, growing wheat, rice and maize, potatoes, tomatoes, walnuts and apples, persimmon and pears. Swat's hottest month is June, with the maximum temperature rising up to 33 °C, and its coldest, January, with the minimum temperature falling to −2 °C. There are two hospitals in Saidu: medical care in Swat is basic and sometimes inadequate, with emergency cases rushed by ambulance on often fatal

---

[11] The people of Kohistan – Kohistanis – are not Afghans and speak a dialect resembling Khodwari Hindko. In addition, *Gujjaran* (dairymen and agriculturalists) and *Parachkan* (businessmen) inhabit the region. The population however is predominantly that of the Yusufzai clan (Wadud 1962: 1; Wali Swat 1953).

[12] 1998 District Census Report of Swat: 21.

Gham-khādi: *framework and fieldwork* 23

four-hour journeys to Peshawar (as the capital, the largest city of the NWFP). Swat has a number of government and private schools including Sangota Convent and Jahanzeb College (named after its founder, the second Wali of Swat). Some Bibiane at primary level attended Sangota Convent day school, where a few have also taught.

While I was in the field, Swat's capital Saidu Sharif was accessible by a forty-five-minute flight from Islamabad or a six-hour (270 km) car journey. Bibiane rarely travel by transport other than planes (returns cost Rs.1,000, or £10) or their personal cars, while their maids frequently accompany them (otherwise, the bus or 'flying coach' costs them about Rs.150). More recently, the unprofitable airport has been closed down. Swat is, however, connected to Pakistan by the visits of politicians, state leaders, tourists and Swatis who work outside the region and in foreign countries (UAE, UK, USA). The importance of the ruling Wali's family of Swat in connecting it to Pakistan and the world more widely is its direct and personal connection with Pakistan's President Ayub Khan, whose two daughters married the Wali's two sons. The elder daughter, Naseem Bibi, who was the First Lady of Pakistan, married Aurangzeb Bacha, the Wali's heir. Through the First Lady of Pakistan the family remain connected to various high-profile people: photographs of President Kennedy with Naseem Bibi adorn various corners of her Swat and Islamabad houses, and Queen Elizabeth II visited Swat to meet the Wali's family. Moreover, many houses, not only the elite's, have telephones and televisions, and a few houses have internet access. Swat is thus not remote from the outside world.

The plains of Mardan

The Mardan District, with comparatively flat terrain, lies to the south of Swat, through the Malakand Pass. More than eleven different marriages, hence *gham-khādi* reciprocities, join the Swat families to the Mardan Khan Nawabs with whom I worked.

Occupied by the armies of Alexander the Great, ruled during the Gandhara kingdom by Buddhist emperors (321–297 BC) and Brahminical Hindu rajahs, the ancient Buddhist remains, old British colonial railway stations and Victorian buildings of contemporary Mardan attest to its dense historical past (Plate 2). In 1904, only two years after the NWFP was officially named, the British sanctioned railways and roads and set up the elite Guides Cavalry in Mardan from which to govern the rest of the Frontier. Established separately from the Peshawar District in 1937, Mardan has housed the divisional headquarters since 1988. The Pakistan army's Punjab Regiment is stationed in Mardan and some socialise with local Khanān. Mardan's population of over a million (1,050,992) comprises predominantly Muslim Yusufzai Pukhto-speaking client farmers and shopkeepers, who work for small landed Khanān or the big landed and politically influential Nawab Khanān. A small community of Hindu merchants and Christian sweepers work in Khan households and government schools. In terms of wealth, status and prestige the two Nawabs of Hoti and Toru are the most influential families, with members playing national political roles as Governors, Ministers and Ambassadors. The Hotis and Torus share kinship and affinal relations, yet often distinguish their family boundaries through rivalry: representatives of each family suspect the other of *kanjoosi* (parsimony), a quality opposite to the Pukhtun ideal, generosity and hospitality (*melmastia*).

In the strict Mardani style of *purdah* for Bibiane, male cousins and servants are avoided, shopping in the *bazār* prohibited, and visits to schools and hospitals take place outside the district.[13] The curtaining-off of the backs of the Toyota and Honda cars in which Mardan Bibiane travel to *gham-khādi* portrays a notable adaptation of *purdah* strictures to contemporary circumstances. Curtained cars are perhaps adaptations of the *palki* or *doli*, which was once a common way of travelling among (wealthier) women in the subcontinent (Ikramullah 1998: 18).[14] Bibiane's expected location in the *kor* sets up relays of maids for cloth and toiletries shopping, and summoning family doctors in case of emergency, besides longer filiations for schooling and *tlal-ratlal/gham-khādi*.

The temperature in Mardan in summer rises to a scorching 42 °C in June–July, while the winter months of December and January are very cold. Both the villagers' small mud houses and the Khanān and Bibiane's large *pokh* (brick and cement) houses are ill-suited to withstand either extreme, necessitating respectively fans or wood-fires. Electric power cuts are common, and the wealthy install home generators. Topographically, Mardan falls into two areas: the plains lying in the south-western areas, and the north-eastern hills. Mardan is reputed to be one of the most fertile agricultural areas in the Frontier, growing sugar cane, tobacco and fruits (oranges, peaches, apricots, pears, apples, plums, persimmons, lychees and lemons). *Ber*, acacia, jand and mesquite trees grow in the fields. The region's Khan proprietors have sold many of the first-stage food processing industry (sugar mills) they owned more than a decade ago. Others engage in politics, a few in service, and possibly in opium and commodity goods smuggling. Apart from agricultural and horticultural interests, the Khanān of Mardan generally own and keep livestock, poultry and guard dogs. Some Khanān are said to have previously kept horses and lions in their *hujre* (men's houses). Despite the reputed munificence of Khans' hospitality, there are no hotels in Mardan (which is 180 km away from Islamabad). One Khan told me, 'Mardan has the population of a city, but not the facilities of a city.'

[13] On veiling as a practice among upper-class Muslim women, see L. Ahmed 1992: 5; Brijbhushan 1980. Veiling is relatively loose among non-elite women in Frontier villages (Toormang, Dir) who leave their homes to bring wood from the jungle, water from the wells and fodder from the fields (Mannan 1994–6: 78); cf. Shabnam 1994–6; Yasmeen 1995–7. On *purdah* as predating Islam (being practised in the first century AD in the Byzantine Empire), see Beck and Keddie 1978: 25. Jacobson, however, points to textual evidence that Hindus practised veiling and restriction on movement of upper-class women in the Mauryan period (322–183 BC) (1982: 81, 86). On Hindu *purdah*, see Saiyid 1997: 8; Sharma 1980; Papanek 1982; Parry 1972: 217; and among Jains in Jaipur, see Reynell 1985: 72–3, 114–19.

[14] During my fieldwork, I came to think of the curtained back of cars in which I wrote my notes after conversations as a scholarly *purdah*-enclosure in the midst of an otherwise non-segregated public space.

Islamabad: '15 minutes away from [the real] Pakistan'

Swat and Mardan's lack of facilities makes Islamabad attractive to its Bibiane and their families on account of its range of 'English-medium' schools and colleges, relatively good healthcare, shopping amenities and a higher standard of living (Plate 3). Overlooked by the range of the Margalla Mountains (meaning 'string of pearls'), Islamabad has carefully planned roads, with relatively few traffic jams, slums and crowds compared to Pakistan's villages (Shah 1980–2). Its relative exemption from power cuts and extremes of climate puts it, popularly, '15 minutes away from [the *real*] Pakistan' (Nizami 2001). More importantly, Bibiane can access social and medical facilities without the same degree of *purdah* observance they face in the villages. Bibiane remarked that restraints applying in rural contexts hold less in the city. For instance, some Bibiane who leave their houses in curtained cars in Mardan do not wear the *sazar* (large Pukhtun veil-like cloth) in the *bazārs* of Islamabad.

Khanān and Bibiane's relocation to Islamabad is part of a wider process of urbanisation. A vast array of Pakistanis from all ethnic and tribal backgrounds have moved into the city from rural areas, particularly the NWFP (see Donnan and Werbner 1991: 11, 12). Islamabad's heterogeneous cosmopolitan population engages in such activities as commerce, national and state politics and diplomacy under the dispensation of a technically independent capital authority (Capital Development Authority, CDA). The city's population has grown from 204,000 in 1981 to 621,000 in 2000.[15] Ethnically, Islamabad's range of Muslim peoples – Baluchis, Kashmiris, Pukhtuns, Punjabis and Sindhis – sits alongside a small community of Christian Punjabis, whose women work in homes as hourly domestic cleaners or 'waxing women' (beauticians) for a large number of Bibiane. There are also communities of Afghan and Iranian refugees, and a community of multinational diplomats (M. S. Khan 1979–81). Almost all denizens of the 'city' have retained local family homes, so that during the two Eids, Islamabad empties like a 'ghost city'.

In contrast to Rawal Pindi (locally called 'Pindi'), about fifteen miles from Islamabad and one of the oldest cities in Pakistan, Islamabad was named and founded only recently in 1960 by President Ayub Khan, the father-in-law of the Wali Ahad (heir) of Swat. Islamabad attracted its first settlers in 1963; older Khanān and Bibiane in their seventies told me that they regarded Islamabad as a '*shaar*' (uninhabited valueless land) in the 1960s and 1970s. Houses there were a much less attractive investment than in Islamabad's more populous twin-city, Pindi (the site of the Islamabad International Airport and General Army HQ). In the past decade Islamabad property has become much more expensive than in Frontier villages, and after 11 September 2001, when many American Pakistanis returned

---

[15] Pakistan's population, according to the Economic Survey (2000–1), was 140.5 million and its growth rate 2.1% a year (Wasti and Osmani n.d.), while the rural population has declined from 71.7% in 1981 to 67.5% in 1998, which according to the survey 'means that every third person now lives in the city or town', *The News International* 2001.

to Pakistan for fear of increased counter-attacks and persecution, property jumped up seven times in price within a period of three years. Many Bibiane and their families cannot afford houses of the same size as in the *kille*.[16] With no concept of mortgages, some Bibiane live in rented houses. Others have sold substantial amounts of inherited land in their villages to buy small flats in the city. This, as illustrated in the next chapter, has serious implications for concepts of status, tenancy and dependence for Khanān and Bibiane. Some Swati Bibiane sold their gold wedding jewellery to purchase a place near their children's boarding schools in the hill station Murree, an hour's drive from Islamabad.

City houses are relatively modern, fitted with air conditioning and gas heating units to cope with the average 34.2 °C heat in May–August and the winter chill of 2 °C in February. In the intense summer heat, few people (among those I studied) leave the precincts of their home, families watch television indoors (of fifty-eight households I observed in Islamabad, all Pukhtun houses owned two television sets, while ten houses contained three, in private bedrooms for the children and maids). In addition, an increasing number of Bibiane own computers; some young and middle-aged Bibiane with sole unsupervised access reported how they acquired information from the internet or 'chatted' under the guise of a pseudonym on designated sites. Furthermore, Islamabad's leisure industry, particularly its international restaurants and Marriott Hotel, allow Bibiane's families to host weddings and offer hospitality (*melmastia*) in a context of globalised consumerism. Pukhtun Khanān, Badshahyan and Bibiane live as a social community in Islamabad and Pindi, and engage in increasing interactions with Punjabi, Sindhi and Baluchi friends and neighbours. Many of the characteristic *tlal-ratlal* practices in the city also intensify the social bonds between kin groupings whose natal lands are distant from each other. It is typical to do *gham-khādi* with all of one's *tlal-ratlal* connections. City life paradoxically releases Bibiane from some Pukhto constraints. At the same time, however, anxiety increases as other behavioural expectations increase.

The relative permissiveness regulating the wearing of the *sazar* serves as an example. Some Bibiane choose to forego the garment as they walk with female and male cousins and friends in the Margalla Hills, take picnics on the Rawal Dam or visit the *markaz* (markets), while others adhere strictly to veiling. An increasing number of Bibiane now participate in clubs, committees and women's organisations like the International Foreign Women's Association (IFWA) and the All Pakistan Women's Association (APWA). These associations possibly represent an embryonic form of female political organisation and activity in a Muslim country, raising funds through *meena-bazārs* for female education, development, income generation and rights (Alavi 1991; Mumtaz and Shaheed 1987: 52–4). Bibiane also take courses ranging from cooking to Islamic *dars*.

---

[16] In 2000 a Mardan Khan sold 2 *jrebs* of inherited land in Mardan for 4 lakh rupees to his shopkeeper's son (4 *jreb* is estimated as 1 English acre). In Islamabad, the same Khan bought a property equal to half that size – 1 *jreb* – for 100 lakhs (i.e. 1 Pakistani crore).

A particularly significant contribution to the contemporary lives of Bibiane in northern Pakistan, linking them to the wider global Islamic revival movement,[17] stems from the increasing enrolment of many in the Al-Huda International Institute of Islamic Education for Women of Islamabad. Dr Farhat Hashmi, the founder of Al-Huda, from Sargodha, Punjab, took her PhD in Islamic studies at Glasgow University before opening Islamabad's Al-Huda Institute in 1994. Al-Huda operates its main thriving centres in Pakistan in Islamabad and in Karachi (Ali 2003; Matri 2003). Supported by private funding, Al-Huda centres may be based at homes, schools or *madrassas* (recently a local *madrassa* (religious school) in Mardan has been converted into a centre for Al-Huda activities and teaching by a Khan and Bibi; both husband and wife are medical doctors trained in the UK and United States). When I asked which branch of Islam Al-Huda subscribed to, the answer was always simply: 'Islam', and its students said they enrolled in order to learn the meanings of the Quran and Hadith. When I asked one very respected Bibi, a graduate of Al-Huda, whether the Al-Huda women's movement was Wahabi or Deobandi. She answered:

Al-Huda teaches the Quran and Sunnah and they do not follow any particular sect. They call themselves 'Muslim' as was done during the lifetime of the Prophet (SAW). Dr Farhat Hashmi, the person running Al-Huda, follows a Hadith of the Prophet (SAW) which says, 'All my Sahaba are like the stars; follow any of them and you will be rightly guided.' She is in fact doing *jihad* [struggle] against Muslims calling themselves anything but 'Muslim'.

Pukhtuns who adhere stringently to their ethnic 'traditions' and 'culture' (Pukhto/*Pukhtunwali*) are perceived by fellow Pukhtuns from Al-Huda as being in some form of opposition to Islam. Dr Hashmi has stressed in one of her taped sermons that: 'Islam is a universal religion. It is not for a special culture or a particular place – it is for every time, every people and every place.'

The Al-Huda school offers a range of courses on the word-to-word translation of the Quran juxtaposed with the Hadith (sayings of the Prophet SAW) in Urdu and English. In the *Fahm-al-Quran* course, one *para* (chapter) of the Quran is expounded daily, juxtaposed with relevant Hadith. A website announces lectures and contains articles about the organisation, and on prayers (*dua*) and Islamic practice in weddings and deaths. Dr Hashmi appears on television and radio and her lectures are sold on audiocassettes. While the school awards diplomas to graduates of other universities after a year's study, its most popular classes are the open two-hour daily *dars* on the Quran during Ramadan, which have been attended by most Islamabad Bibiane. One Al-Huda graduate estimated that 5 per cent of the approximately 1,000 Al-Huda students in Islamabad at any one time are Pukhtuns. The reach of Al-Huda spans a broad range of ages, classes, ethnicities and nationalities – Dr Idrees Zubair, the husband of Dr Hashmi, offers separate courses for men (however, I know of only a few Khanān who have attended these courses compared to

---

[17] For some insightful discussions on the Islamic revival movements in Cairo, Egypt, see Charles Hirschkind 2001, and Saba Mahmood 2001, 2003.

Bibiane's attendance at female sections). Several Bibiane enrol their children in programmes for ages two to twelve, introducing prayers and tales of the Prophets. Al-Huda also offers correspondence courses to women and men; and former Al-Huda students outside Pakistan – in the United States, Canada, Australia and the United Arab Emirates – are also taking an active part in the proselytisation of a down-to-earth, textually responsible Islam.

Al-Huda advertises itself as a non-sectarian, non-governmental organisation 'actively involved in the promotion of Islamic education and the service of mankind' or *dawa*. The term *dawa* encompasses a wide range of meanings. In the Quran, it refers to God's invitation, through the Prophets, to mankind, to live in accord with God's commands. Over the course of Islamic history, the concept of *dawa* has come to be used interchangeably with another important Islamic term, *Sharia* (Islamic law: the juridical codification of God's commands), and with *din* (religion). Another significant line of thought in the contemporary discourse of Islam, from its early development, is that *dawa* is seen as a 'duty', binding every member of the Islamic *umma* (community) by actively engaging fellow Muslim 'brothers' and 'sisters' to pursue greater piety in every aspect of their lives. *Dawa*, in its contemporary form, has come to suggest the need for an individual and communal praxis to revive the Muslim *umma* in response to, for example, in one convent Pukhtun Bibi's words: 'an Americanised version – MTV, McDonalds, Disney, KFC and all that world'. Comparatively, Hirschkind talks about the urgency felt among the Egytian *du'at* (preachers of *dawa*) to practise *dawa* as a result of 'the erosion of the Islamic character of society under the impact of what is most often referred to as *al-ghawa al-fikri* (ideological conquest, i.e., Western cultural imperialism) and particularly its forms of consumerism and sensualism that are seen to be corrosive of the virtues enabling one to live a Muslim life' (Hirschkind 2001: 14).

Although the concept of *dawa* cannot be historically linked to a particular person or institution, its contemporary importance may be seen in its use in Islamic opposition movements, particularly the Muslim Brotherhood in the late 1920s. In the context of increased secularisation under the khedival rule and the perceived failure of established Islamic institutions to oppose it, the aim of the Brotherhood was Islamic reform and the restoration of the Islamic *umma*. In using modern political methods, such as print and recorded media, the Brotherhood transformed from a small local group to an international organisation which came to hold an enormous degree of religious and political power and authority. According to its believers, *dawa* 'defined the mode of action by which moral and political reform were to be brought about' (Hirschkind 2001: 7). Although its members were arrested and the Brotherhood banned by the Egyptian state, *dawa* itself has increasingly become a 'space for the articulation of a contestatory Islamic discourse on state and society' (ibid.). This discourse, as with the Al-Huda women's movement, is embodied in a diversified array of institutional forms such as teaching centres and (home-based) preaching groups, and an expanding network of media and publishing houses. Consequently, there is available in Islamabad a large body of Islamic literature (books, magazines, pamphlets) and media forms (videos and tapes) in English and

Urdu aimed at improving moral and social conduct. *Dawa* as an ethical form of increasing piety and encouraging an Islamic way of life may also include a variety of different spiritual, welfare and commercial activities, ranging from providing: education to women and children by sponsoring students in schools and universities; social services to the poor: monthly stipends to widows and orphans, medicines, food and clothes to the needy and wedding items to poor girls; and selling Islamic literature and cassettes. As a result, Islamic institutions like Al-Huda provide a context for the emergence of an arena of practice and critique that is largely independent and autonomous from the policies and interests of the state.

Although one might expect that Bibiane speak about their lives as unproblematic, the premise of a seamless connection between Bibiane's metropolitan domiciles and their village roots, by which Bibiane and their families periodically return to their natal lands to replenish their Pukhtun self-identification, is in fact challenged by the numerous contradictions between 'customary' ceremonial procedure and Islamic scriptural precept. These contradictions are being increasingly articulated by the female graduates of Al-Huda, which, part of a broader regional and arguably national movement of purist Islamisation, attempts to apply Quranic and Hadith prophetic teaching to everyday life (Ali 2003; cf. Metcalf 1990).[18] Contrary to certain academic assumptions (Mumtaz and Shaheed 1987), this reform involves educated elite and middle-class women. These women actively impart Islamic ways of living to family members across metropolitan–rural boundaries. The school's lectures (*dars*, classes) provide a basis for questioning 'customary' or Pukhtun lifecycle practices, authorising some Bibiane to amend visiting patterns in conformity with the Quran. The manipulation of life-cycle commemorations by elite and middle-class women as a vehicle of change, Islamisation and a particular mode of modernity becomes further significant in the light of recent socio-political Islamic movements in the post-Taliban Frontier Province (B. Khan 1999).

The people: Bibiane

My fieldwork brought me into contact with a total of 258 people, among whom I had close contact with 132 Bibiane of various ages: young (20–35), middle-aged (35–50) and older women (50+) from Swat, Mardan and Islamabad, and, by extension, a social spread of 126 others (Khanān and Badshahyan, children, village-men and women, wet-nurses and servants). Although an ethnography of Bibiane suggests that they form an exclusive elite group, the fact that they belong to larger Pukhtun society through genealogical, social and political connections bestows on them some measure of social representativeness. While most Bibiane are Pukhtun by patrilineal descent, a few acceded, in Barth's words, to 'membership' by marriage. The degrees of acceptance given to in-marrying Punjabis, Karachites and even

---

[18] 'The all-important, all-encompassing religious law of Islam is the codification of the practice of the Prophet, who realized in his life, more perfectly than other humans ever could, the revealed truths of the Qur'an' (Metcalf 1984a: 1). See also Gilsenan 1990: 17.

foreigners varies greatly, and largely depends on women's own initiatives and efforts to adopt Pukhtun *gham-khādi* practices. Bibiane may even welcome wives of non-Pukhtun ethnicities if the 'outsiders' (*pradee*) present no threat to the division of family properties or patrimonies, unlike 'insiders' or relatives (*khpal*) (see Lindholm 1982: 159). Yet others may not want their children to marry non-Pukhtuns, as one Bibi answered in response to my question: How do you see it as possible, despite the obvious attempt you make, to keep the Pukhtun self alive in either Islamabad or Britain and in what ways do you think about your relationship with non-Pukhtun Pakistanis, especially Punjabis?:

I believe that Pukhtuns are recognised because of their Pukhto language as well as the customs that they follow. In my view, it is essential that all Pukhtun parents should teach their children the Pukhto language, as this, I believe, identifies and distinguishes a Pukhtun from a non-Pukhtun. Despite living in Islamabad, we ensure that our children learn Pukhtun customs so that they are not treated as outsiders when they visit their home town in NWFP and that they can readily relate to the people there. I have non-Pukhtun friends but there are still many customs and habits that are very different from ours. I would not like my children to get married to non-Pukhtuns since our family customs, language and social values are very different from theirs.

The three defining characteristics of Pukhtun Bibiane are: family possession and patrilineal inheritance of village lands (Barth 1986); birth (through patrilineal descent) or marriage into a Pukhtun family: marriage is typically endogamous, with preference for first cousin marriage and virilocal residence; and participation in a web of *gham-khādi* networks. Wealthy Swat and Mardan families who, over the past thirty years, have bought or rented second homes in Islamabad, have retained their ancestral village houses (*kille-koroona*) as the primary sites for *gham-khādi* celebrations. Thus Bibiane's families' funerals and weddings link the village to the city, ideologically connecting city-dwellers to ancestral lands (*zmaka*).

Bibiane are thus socially identified by their membership in a particular family. Extended kin groupings in households may consist of between twelve to twenty-five households under one ancestrally derived name – the Hoti family, the Toru family, the Wali of Swat's family and so on. The size of each household varies between one and four generations. Households can have from one to ten children, servants and sometimes co-wives (*ban*) – though few Khanān under fifty have married twice. While no figures exist, a rough estimate allots some 3 per cent of the total Pakistani Pukhtun population to these aristocratic and well-known families. In the course of my fieldwork, I spoke to members of some hundred households in total which comprised four main extended families; leadership positions in Pakistan were, at one point, drawn from a limited array of elite families, famously the 'Twenty-two' (Weiss 1991: 2, 11).[19]

---

[19] At the time of President Ayub Khan (1958–69) 66 per cent of Pakistan's industrial capital was in the hands of the twenty-two families (Mumtaz and Shaheed 1987: 11).

Genealogy and historical background

Bibiane's complex and historically dense conceptions of local heritage represent a critical resource for their ethnic and familial identity. Claiming 'foreign ancestry', Bibiane and Khan families trace their collective descent from Adam to the Prophet Ibrahim (Abraham) through the grandson of King Saul, Afghana, whose sixth-century BC descendants fled Babylonian captivity to settle in present-day Afghanistan (Ahmad 1978; Cole 1984: 169; Spain 1995: 15).[20] Afghana (from whom the name Afghan is derived) had a son called Qais bin Rashid. Qais, the putative ancestor of Pukhtuns, legendarily left Ghor in Afghanistan for Arabia in the seventh century to be converted by the Prophet (SAW) himself, who was said to be so pleased with Qais and his group that he conferred on them the title 'Malik' (Arabic: king). The saying that 'every Pukhtun is a Malik' underlies societal attitudes to hierarchy and titles. Qais married the daughter of the renowned Muslim warrior Khalid bin Walid who bore him three sons: Sarban, Bitan and Ghurghust, and a fourth, Karlanri, was said to be adopted (see Appendix 1). Tracing their descent from Qais whatever their tribe, individuals in Pukhtun society necessarily orient themselves in relation to familial and tribal entities within the larger segmentary order.[21] Most Bibiane belong to the Yusufzai tribe, which claims descent from the eponymous ancestor Yusuf, another descendant of Qais.

In her book, *The Afghan Nobility and the Mughals (1526–1707)*, Joshi (1985) argues that as early as the eleventh and twelfth centuries, numerous Afghans settled in northern India in response to the invitation of Bahlol Lodhi, the ruler of Delhi, who gained the support of tribal leaders in exchange for land (*jagirs*) and renown. Dominant rulers of the Mughal and British empires repeated this pattern in order to secure loyalty from the Afghan people, depending on big landowning Khanān and religious leaders to gather revenue and keep order in the Indian subcontinent. In return, the rulers awarded the rural elite lordly titles, honorary military ranks, subsidiaries and substantial lands.[22] Rewards of land have benefited the Yusufzai who have a developed social structure based on irrigated land in Mardan and Swat. This structure further facilitated the formation of hierarchies dominated by powerful landlords.

This history of transmigration, clientage and feudalism established, in the words of Nawab Colonel Amir Khan, son of the Nawab of Hoti, Pukhtun '*quom* [ethnic origin] as *Afghan*. We won't say our *quom* is Pakistani, because we Pukhtuns

---

[20] According to one theory, the Pukhtuns claim descent from one of the lost tribes of Israel (for a historical account of this myth, see Parfitt 2002: 138).

[21] As Ernest Gellner noted: 'the notion of "segmentation" seems more useful than that of "democracy" for laying bare the actual mechanics of the society' (Gellner 1969: 28). 'However this is a structural rather than an ideological democracy. It is not based on a theory on a set of principles or norms' (ibid.).

[22] For accounts of the collaboration of elite families with the British in India during the colonial period, see Ansari 1992; Barth 1995; Bayly 2000; Cohn 1989: 318, 1996; Ali Khan 2003; Metcalf 1979. According to the *History of the Hoti Family*, Nawab Akbar Hoti was once noted to have owned forty Frontier villages partly as a result of his 'services' to the Mughals and British.

are from Afghanistan'. According to Banerjee, the British intervention (1868–80) became the decisive formative event in the Frontier class structure. The Khan's position was converted from one of patronage and symbolic pre-eminence, which superintended the communitarian system of land rotation (*wesh*), to an entrenched, 'feudalised' dominance exercised along property demarcations drawn up by colonial administrators (2000: 31). Both admiring and fearing the warrior Pukhtuns (see Elphinstone 1815; Charles Lindholm 1996), the British, in Banerjee's words, 'invented' a local ruling class to serve as their intermediaries. This ruling class received an English education befitting 'a class of persons, Indian in blood and colour, but English in taste, in opinion, in morals, and in intellect' (Macaulay 1935; see also Lees 1871: 5, 102). English-language literacy entered the Frontier through convents in Swat and Murree. The schools, namely: Sangota, St Dennies, Presentation, Lawrence College, Burn Hall and the Convent of Jesus and Mary (opened in 1876), have schooled hundreds of Bibiane, Badshayan and Khanān. A stroke of the administrator's pen made the English language the *sine qua non* of status and respectability. Elite Pukhtun Muslims sought to educate their children in 'elitist English schools' (Rahman 1997: 184) so as to retain social influence by staffing the emergent administrative positions of the state (Eickelman 1992: 644; Forbes 1999: 37; Kolenda 2000: 179; cf. Crystal 1997: 101; contrast Todorov 1984).

Education

The importance of these elite schools has not diminished in present-day Pakistani life, with both boys and girls being sent away for English-language instruction to boarding schools. 'These few public schools [remain] the pool from which the future leaders and intelligentsia are being, and will be, drawn' (A. S. Ahmed 1977b: 35, also 2003: 100–1). The Muslim elite sent their daughters to 'English-medium' schools because proficiency in bookkeeping and hence household management became desirable qualities in wives, and because officers' spouses needed to be minimally versed in social graces (Forbes 1999). Irish and Asian Roman Catholic nuns ('sisters') and priests ('fathers'), who often speak fluent Urdu, run the northern Pakistan girls' and boys' boarding schools. Murree Convent (Plate 4), for example, boards approximately 200 to 250 girls, often half of them Pukhtun. Other girls come from various ethnolinguistic groups; more than 90 per cent are Muslim. These *waray* (little) Bibiane follow in the footsteps of at least four generations of Pukhtuns, taking a pattern of education culminating in a final stage comparable to the former British 'O' level. Final examinations for fifteen- to seventeen-year-old students are termed 'Senior Cambridge' (being marked in the UK by the University of Cambridge Local Examinations Syndicate). The schools inculcate the moral virtue of obedience in the context of a scholarly (arts and sciences) and practical ('home management', 'moral education') curriculum.

Convent boarding establishes the patterned dualities (school/home; overt/concealed; individual/collective) that characterise Bibiane lives, as well as their continual movement between sites (as shall be discussed in the next chapter).

The Anglicisation process implicit in convent-schooling is neither simple nor straightforward. On one hand, convent pupils are widely said to become comparatively more 'westernised' than other Pakistani school students: they wear tunics and Western trousers in winter, and are expected to comply with the morals and manners set out by their instructors in English language and literature. The schools enforce English as the official tongue: 'convent-girls' now in their forties recall being fined a few *anas* (pennies) for speaking Pukhto. Yet, in other ways, the simultaneous supervision and care of convent-schooling approximates, for many Bibiane, to a 'protective' Pukhtun family. Girls moreover reject any suggestion of passive acculturation to school values, stressing actions of negotiation and even defiance. During Ramadan, the month of fasting, girls were allowed to fast only on weekends, but they secretly fasted on weekdays as well; and the day's missed prayers were performed after the sisters had turned off the dormitory lights. These acts, at the risk of the cane, sustained cultural identity through Islam in a Catholic context. A Bibi in her late forties remarked that possibly the convent's most enduring lesson was in cross-cultural adaptation: 'The convent was a Western institution; [at] home we had an Eastern culture, so we learnt to adapt between the two.'

Educational background creates differences between women. Convent-educated Bibiane speak English fluently, while older Bibiane, maids and many village-women speak only Pukhto and often remain illiterate, though a few are self-taught in Quranic Arabic. The speech of even younger Bibiane (ten to twenty-two) registers generational differences from their elders: while these girls may speak only in English, middle-aged convent Bibiane often dip in and out of English, Urdu, Farsi (Persian) and Pukhto, mixing colonial, vernacular and more modern idioms.[23] Many English-educated Bibiane and men thus defer to their *masharān* (elders) and even village-tenants in speaking better, and more 'proper' (*jukhtha*), Pukhto.

The non- or distant familial friendships formed at school endure into a Bibi's 'social' existence as a wife, as her schoolmates – some of whom may also be her cousins – become her in-laws and form part of her *gham-khādi* network. A few representatives of other religions and ethnicities – Christian, Shia, Punjabi, Sindhi and Baluchi – also attend Frontier weddings, as the bride's friends. Okely (1996: 151) describes school as a *rite de passage* mediating childhood and adulthood. The age to which families from different regions allow their post-menarche daughters to remain in school varies. Older Bibiane from the particularly *purdah*-observing Mardan Hoti and Toru families reported being sent to school in the 1950s and 1960s at the age of five and withdrawn at eleven and twelve (Class 6/7) (cf. Hussain 1979–81; Sehrai 1994–6; Sharma 1980: 226). Girls from Swat and Peshawar's Sadozai families typically completed Class 11 (aged about seventeen). A broad generational split exists among the Bibiane over what some regard as the pre-emptive curtailment of their primary education. While senior Bibiane uphold the prerogatives of 'custom', many middle-aged women in their forties and fifties

---

[23] In comparison to 48% Punjabi speakers, 8% of people in Pakistan speak Pukhto.

express regret over their unfulfilled ambitions for a professional career. As Maryam Bibi said: 'In recent times, Pukhtuns have started realising the importance of education and are now sending their children, both male and female, to school.' An increasing number of daughters of these Bibiane now pursue higher education, some studying Law (LLB) or Medicine. Others complete their BAs and MAs 'privately' at home without attending mixed-sex university classes, while most others get married.

Marriage

Marriage, a social obligation for both Pukhtun men (aged nineteen to thirty-one) and women (between sixteen and twenty-five), marks a particularly significant turning point in the lives of women (for the Islamic valence of marriage as an act of *Ibadat* or devotion to God, see Shaukat Ali 1997: 181). Marriage grants women social status, relatively greater spatial mobility, and social recognition within family networks. In the Frontier, being married is often thought of as preferable to girlhood. Their own *khādi* represents a threshold beyond which Bibiane may participate in the full Pukhtun complement of social events, of other *gham-khādi* (cf. Delaney 1991: 112; Tapper 1978: 393; Venkatesan 2001: 72). While unmarried *geenakai* (girls) may accompany their mothers to ceremonies, Bibiane perform *gham-khādi* in their own right as wives. Beginning to undertake visiting, mourning and celebratory practices thus signify Bibiane's first steps as independent social actors.

This agency is necessarily exercised within a context of existing social relationships. Pukhtun marriages are endogamous and based on kinship networks. Choice of marriage for girls is commonly determined by preference for parallel and cross-cousin marriage, as among other groups of Pakistanis such as Punjabis (Shaw 2001). These alliances aim to consolidate patrimonial lands and strengthen political and social ties. Political leadership is thus reinforced through marriage alliances. While referring to first cousins by sibling names ('sister' (*khor*), 'brother' (*ror*), rather than 'cousin' which lacks a Pukhto equivalent), Bibiane say that many of their relationships are 'six times' (*shpag wara*), that is, multiply connected by marriage. One elderly Bibi stated:

Only ten to fifteen years ago, men wanted to keep their lands in the family so daughters were married to the *Mama zwe* [mother's brother's sons] or to the *thre zwe* [father's brother's sons], not to *pradee* [outsiders]. It didn't matter if the cousin was short, illiterate, *jaiz* or *najaiz* [appropriate or inappropriate]. But now parents are clever [*okhyār*], they do not ruin the girl's life; and girls want educated husbands with good jobs.

This comment highlights a shift towards 'marrying out'. Locally, contact between the family of a potential 'girl' and 'boy' is highly fraught with tension and often mediated by a female intermediary. Families distantly related will also belong to the same extended *gham-khādi* circle. In this way, Pukhtun families may cement political alliances through exogamy (Barth 1986; Lindholm 1982; Safdar 1997).

The marriages of President Ayub Khan's two daughters, Begum Nasim and Begum Jamila, to the Wali of Swat's sons, Aurangzeb Bacha and Amirzeb Bacha, provide locally well-known examples.[24] Bibiane may marry Pukhtuns of equal or higher status (or hypergamy); hypogamy is rare, and Bibiane have never been known to marry servants or the sons of wet-nurses. The reasons here are both social and religious, with the Quran forbidding marriage to the offspring of a wet-nurse who is, in effect, a sibling (Q4: 22–4).

Marriage for Bibiane remains an inter-class transaction, through which women may express their social relations of dependence and indebtedness to immediate and wider families. Pukhtuns are acutely conscious of how marriage, more than any other social act, creates relationships between distant kin. A thoughtful married Bibi, Seema, with two daughters and one son, told me:

It is daughters that spread you, like *zele* [roots of a tree]. It is their marriages into other families that create [ties of] *tlal-ratlal*, going and coming.

These ties tightly interweave Pukhtun families, although marriages to non-Pukhtuns, once frowned upon, have become increasingly acceptable among certain families. A few now middle-aged Bibiane married men from 'outside' (*baharani khalak*), including Punjabis and Sindhis, and, in religious terms, adherents of Shia and Qadiani sects.

Although Pukhtun families consider the birth of sons prestigious, as they inherit family titles and land, the birth of daughters is not considered socially negligible, since they are seen to maintain the social fabric of society and sustain Pukhto (Sayyed analyses the 'psycho-social implications' of the lack of male offspring for Mardani women (1994–6)). Deliberations as to affiancing suppose people's *gham-khādi* network as the sphere from which marital candidates are drawn, and to which they will return as full social participants when a couple (cf. Abu-Lughod 1986: 11; Delaney 1991: 112). Bibiane are expected to fulfil family expectations in marrying, especially marriage to a person of their mother's choice. While in some families brides increasingly refuse marriage arrangements, family interests, rather than individual volition, determine marriage choices. The concept of a love match (discussed in Chapter 4) remains uncommon, despite the legends of old Pukhto romances (Heston and Nasir n.d.; Walter 1967).

Inter-household tension and deference

While marriages and their celebration may connect households, the female *kor* (house) serves the immediate context of Bibiane's sociality and of any *gham-khādi* preparation. The house therefore is the centre of social and familial life for its women (see Aswad 1978; York 1997). The main issues in Pukhtun society

---

[24] For an extensive exposition of political marriage alliances among the Swat elites, see Charles Lindholm (1982). Gilmartin traces cross-class or saintly-to-lordly transitions through marriage in the Punjabi case of Khwaja Allah Bakhsh, originally a Pukhtun, whose son 'emerged as a wealthy landed proprietor' in allying himself to Ghulam Qadir Khan Khakwani of Multan (1984: 237).

revolve around the rivalrous pursuit of power, status and honour among agnatic kin as represented on the tribal genealogical charter. While anthropologists have discussed the centrality of agnatic rivalry (*tarburwali*, or enmity with the father's brother's son over shared patrilineal inheritance) in the Pukhtun lineage system (A. S. Ahmed 1980: 3; Barth 1959: 11; Charles Lindholm 1996: 30, 74), social relationships among Muslim women tend to be described more peaceably, for example as 'an explicit women's ideal of "loving" everyone' (Barth 1983: 142). This book examines these concepts from a different perspective than the conventional perception of Pukhtun society, arguing that a parallel system of rivalry and competition exists among women, particularly in joint-family households. This '*indrorwali*' (enmity between the *indror*, or husband's sister, and the brother's wife (*wrandar*); or between a mother-in-law (*khwakhe*) and daughters-in-law (*ingorane*); or between brothers' wives (*yorāne*)) conditions Bibiane's lives to a pervasive degree.[25] Most of the married women with whom I worked (Bibiane, maids and villagers) described recurrent, often unsettling, levels of tension and conflict in families, which noticeably influenced *gham-khādi* gatherings. Yet familial tensions are concealed and unacknowledged beneath a level of Pukhtun hospitality (*melmastia*), kindness and etiquette, as demanded in the enactment of *Pukhtunwali*, even to 'enemies' (*nanawatee*).

Entering the marital household, a Bibi must establish positive relationships with an array of more senior women, including her husband's grandmother, great-aunts, mother, aunts, sisters and older sisters-in-law. Differences in degrees of household seniority manifest themselves most obviously through the system of respect names and honorifics given to Bibiane once they graduate to a position of family eminence (see Frazer 1993: 249). Apart from a woman's given name (Shaheen, for instance), she will take a generic respect name (e.g. Nazigul) identifying her to her affines and kin after marriage. Maids will not refer to an elder (*mashra*) Bibi by her first or second respect name unless they themselves achieve a status of respect and long-term familiarity with her. A younger person or maid who shares the same name as an elder Bibi may be given another, in order to avoid disrespect to the elder. Bibiane may take a third, yet more honourable name (e.g. Sahib Begum Bibi) which distinguishes her *mashartia* (seniority) after a further period of years. In removing the birthname of Bibiane from public knowledge, as its circulation would inappropriately breach *purdah*, the renaming process reflects a Bibi's increasing status and *ezat* (reputation or honour), and the reformation of her personhood in terms of her role in her adopted home. The effacement of origin in assimilating a Bibi may also progressively surmount the suggestion of taint in the family's alliance with a nubile woman. In addition, a complex set of fictive kinship terminology applies to all Pukhtun Bibiane, overlapping with designations for village women and maids – for example, *loor* (daughter) addresses someone younger; *khor/bibi*

---

[25] Cf. Bumiller 1991: 48. Bitter Pukhtun enmities also subsist between co-wives (*bun*) and *tarburān* (male paternal first cousins); in contrast to the potentially hostile relationship with the Fa's Bro, the Mo's Bro (*Mama*) is comparably affectionate.

(sister) a contemporary, and *thror/bibi* (aunt) and *wrandar/bibi* (brother's wife) someone slightly older (for Pukhtun kinship terminology, see Appendix 2). This terminology is also applied to servants and *khidmatgarān* (helpers).

Khidmatgarān *(helpers)*

Besides kin and affines, a number of *khidmatgarān* or *nawkarān* (servants: the term is used here to include maids, wet-nurses and male servants inclusively) will live in a given elite household. These helpers serve as the physical labourers in Bibiane's festivities, and as the hosts of their own. This is a topic which has as yet received little attention in ethnographic accounts.[26] Bibiane's households have between one and over twenty *khidmatgarān* including male servants, maids and sometimes one or more elderly wet-nurses (*dai/gane*). Bibiane address these persons as kin and consider their offspring 'like family'. Not all servants stay active around the house; Swati *daigāne* who weaned their charges fifty years ago stay in Bibiane's houses (*koroona*), coming eventually to make demands on their grown-up Bibiane. Domestic work among *khidmatgarān* is generally gendered in the house. Men work outside on *de saro kār* (men's work), such as shopping at the *bazār*, gardening, driving and even cooking (kitchens are sometimes viewed as ambiguous spaces lying both in and outside the house). Maids' *de khazo kār* (women's domestic work) involves childcare, cleaning, cooking and washing clothes. Importantly, trusted maids (addressed as 'aunt' (*thror*) or 'sister' (*khorai*), and less frequently as 'girl' (*geenay*)) may accompany Bibiane on *gham-khādi* trips.

Whether Bibiane do *gham-khādi* with their retainers and their wider relatives depends on their years of service and intimacy of the relationship. Bound by *purdah* restrictions, Bibiane may give clothes and money directly to maids before the maids leave for siblings' weddings, or may send cash for funerals through intermediaries (varying between about Rs.100 and Rs.10,000). Locally, maids may perform village-women's *gham-khādi* on behalf of their Bibi, repeating her words and presenting her donation (see Appendix 4). Although the maid performs the 'water-carrying' labour, the Bibi's work involves critical mental effort in directing the maid's actions, especially in terms of etiquette. The subtle differentiation between less and more intellectual forms of 'work' makes possible the conceptualisation of Bibiane's *gham-khādi* under that category, where a more simplistic understanding might see the work as being the maid's. On occasions of the misdelivery of goods or messages, for example, Bibiane, not maids, are thought to have failed. The social agency of the Bibi is thus embodied in her servants, and ideas of her personhood are corporate and extend to other subjects. I often heard Bibiane say: '[the maid, or wet-nurse] is my hands and feet' (*zama lasoona khpe da*). Relations between mistress and maid are even more complex than this formulation

---

[26] Charles Lindholm points out the lack of data on Pukhtun milk mothers (1996: 46). Yet the role of the wet-nurse is not unusual in Muslim contexts, see, for example, Delaney 1991: 72, 155; Mernissi 1988: 41; Thackston 1999: 65; see also the Quran: Q2: 233, Q6: 65.

suggests, in that maids both share interests and forms of social identity with their mistresses, and have distinctively individual desires, goals and own family (kin) affiliations.

Bibiane's relationships with *daigāne* (wet-nurses) are the most complex among her bonds with all household dependents. The practice, in which Badshahyan distinguish themselves socially by having one carer for each child, became less common around forty years ago; *daigāne* now in their sixties remain among the most imperiously powerful female members of households. Older Bibiane and established wet-nurses selected *daigāne* from thronging crowds of nursing mothers belonging to poor village families in Swat. In the case of the Wali's family, these women left their own families to suckle Badshahyan and Bibiane, who call their *daigāne* 'Abay' (mother). Many Swati Bibiane reported that their *abaygane* (pl.) were 'closer' than their biological mothers. Wet-nurses command loyalty and spur occasional inter-affinal antagonism, as ethnographic case studies in later chapters document. Despite the constraints on travel, many Bibiane in Swat and Mardan visit the houses of their *abaygane* for their *gham-khādi*. Likewise wet-nurses and maids seek financial and material benefits from their wealthy Bibiane.

Wealth and income

Anthropological accounts of Pukhtuns have paid little attention to women's property, ownership and land tenure, often suggesting women's dependent and subordinate status to men. Many present-day Swat and Mardan Bibiane, however, have substantial wealth in their own name. Bibiane own arable lands in parcels of 20 to 30 acres in Swat; in Mardan, the richest Bibiane may hold about 100 to 200 acres of relatively cheaper territory. Prime commercial property of between thirty-five to seventy shops and entire shopping 'markets' (arcades) also represent assets for Bibiane, while a few maintain flats in Islamabad or abroad, especially in London. Some Bibiane are sole owners of many village or Islamabad properties, others are jointly owned with husbands, siblings, paternal cousins and paternal uncles in a patrilineal set-up (in one family, the six offspring of two wives jointly inherited, after their father's death, one of the only two bus stations (*adday*) in Swat; the sons received twice the daughters' share). This property yields them substantial monthly incomes of Rs.30,000 (£315; $665) to Rs.70,000 (£736; $1,398), compared to the mean Pakistani annual per capita wage of $470 (Pakistan Country Statistics 1998). These figures are exclusive of their husbands' incomes, which vary greatly per year and may average 12 lakhs (£12,000); most Khan and Badshah landlords live off money they receive by selling inherited property. Other less wealthy or older Bibiane claim their brothers excluded them from shares of the family's inheritance. While older Bibiane consider it wrong to fight for property with their own family, various middle-aged and younger Bibiane have taken their closest kin to court in land disputes. There are as many as forty land cases among the various families I worked with (cf. Donner 1992; and Sung 1981). These ructions led to the breaking of *gham-khādi* reciprocities, attracting much comment.

Khanān and Bibiane nowadays express the fear that their power is waning to the detriment of a new professional or mercantile class, with the division of patrimonial lands in inheritance and illiquidity of property. Liaqat Khan, the older son of a big landlord from *bar* Swat, remarked to me: 'Our status is from land: the more the land, the bigger the Khan: *loi Khan*. But we are selling our lands simply to live; our capital keeps decreasing. My grandfather had 1,000 *jrebs* [500 acres] of land but now I only have 100 *jrebs* [50 acres].' Some people advanced an understanding of *Pukhtunwali*, especially *gham-khādi*, as making constant demands on capital, without clear expectations concerning return. This worries the Khan class, given female affinity for ceremonies bound with 'consumerist' patterns and impressive effects – especially clothes.

Social diacritica: dress

Dress and expected deportment, insofar as they express social relations of precedence, vary greatly between older and younger Bibiane. Older Bibiane often wear 'modest' clothing, typically consisting of *partoog-kameez* (baggy trousers and tunic) with sleeves below the wrists, baggy *kameezoona* (pl.) below the knees and high necklines. This accompanies the large Pukhtun veil-like covering (the *sazar*), often white in colour and worn over the head. Older Bibiane also wear opaque, and plain or unadorned, *partoogoona* (pl.). Local styles differ between Swat and Mardan Bibiane: Mardan descendants of Nawabān are said to be distinguished by their fondness for expensive clothes and jewellery in contrast to the relatively 'saintly' austerity of some Swati Bibiane. Moreover, older women are more 'conservative' than younger. Many summer *shalwar-kameez-dupatta* (trouser-tunic-veil) sold in unstitched three-piece suits are designed in Karachi, Lahore or Faisalabad. Often flimsier than the *sazar*, they do not suit the 'traditional' preferences of elderly Pukhtun Bibiane. In contrast, younger Bibiane often wear 'trouser-shalwars' with *lande-tange* (short shirts and fitted) half-sleeved or sleeveless *kameezoona*, which risk impropriety. More recently, styles of dress signify particular beliefs, as in the adoption of the headdress (*hijab*) and black cloak (*abaya*) over the *partoog-kameez* instead of the *sazar* by a few young and middle-aged Al-Huda Bibiane. Samina, a Bibi and popular Islamabad clothes designer (*zargul*), remarked that her clients, who formerly ordered sleeveless *kameezoona*, now prefer more 'Islamic' styles, and order long-sleeved outfits with matching *hijabs* due to the influence of Al-Huda.

Bibiane distinguish their everyday clothes from their special occasion *gham-khādi* clothes for going and coming (*de tlo-ratlo jame*). They invest a large amount of money and time in preparing clothes for *gham-khādi* occasions. Since women of the same network repeatedly meet each other at shared gatherings, changes of large wardrobes display status and *ezat* (public reputation; Mernissi 1985: 126). Carefully chosen veils and cloths match expensive foreign brand names of shoes and bags (e.g. Bally, Russell and Bromley, Gucci, etc.); some Bibiane may order fifteen to thirty pairs of *partoog-kameezoona* from tailors for each summer and winter seasons (costing between Rs.200 and Rs.3,000 (£2–£31) each). Women's clothes provoke competition, with a few Bibiane collecting seemingly inordinate numbers of garments.[27] Bibiane personalise garments to differentiate their taste from that of another purchaser of the same print. A number of young teenage Pukhtun girls told me that their *gham* was not having 'fashionable' clothes and that their *khādi* was shopping.

Generational differences

As has already been indicated, this study broadly identifies differences of attitude towards *gham-khādi* among three generations of women: older Bibiane, who insist on practices confirming their *ezat* (honour);[28] their middle-aged daughters who may view 'traditional' Pukhto as having deflected them from education or careers; and, more diversely, younger Bibiane, who may regard *gham-khādi* observance as a valuable expression of cultural identity or a form to be renewed by Islam (Mandelbaum distinguishes comparable attitudes towards 'tradition' among Pukhtuns in 1993; see also Eddy 1968 and, by contrast, Yin 1981). Some younger and a few middle-aged Bibiane did not exclusively identify themselves in their familial capacities and were striving to make a professional career (cf. Sherif 1999). Of the middle cohort, about a dozen Bibiane teach in English-medium schools in the Frontier and in Islamabad; a few are self-employed and offer private tutoring from home, and others have opened their own work centres. Yet the prevalent tone among the middle group is of regret for missed opportunities, and of a defiant commitment to the greater opportunities of their daughters. In one case, a Bibi in her forties told me she stood up to her 'conservative', authoritative father-in-law by insisting that he allow her twenty-one-year-old daughter to complete her law studies in Islamabad. Despite a family crisis and complaints from the Bibi's husband's brother (*lewar*) regarding the shamefulness of the male-dominated *kacharai* (magistrate's court, a non-segregated public space), the Bibi's father-in-law finally relented. Bibiane's motivation for professional employment does not necessarily reflect an ideological orientation towards 'Western' values. Yet the rewards of work, even if it engages the mind in an Islamic way, often prove incompatible with the demands of *gham-khādi*.

Gham-khādi networks

On marriage, a young Bibi acquires a greatly expanded circle of *gham-khādi* contacts, by joining her own kin to her husband's in new and strengthened bonds

---

[27] On the *Dubai chalo* (let us go to Dubai i.e. to shop) theme in Pakistan society, see A. S. Ahmed 1991: 257; on the symbolism of dress and cloth, see Sandborg 1993; Schneider and Weiner 1989; Veblen 1953.

[28] Some exceptional senior Bibiane – for example, Begum Nasim Aurangzeb (daughter of President Ayub Khan and wife of the heir apparent of the Wali of Swat), Begum Zari Sarfaraz and Dr Parveen Azam Khan – are accepted to have broken ground either through setting up social projects like orphanages and drug rehabilitation centres, or through political activism.

Gham-khādi: *framework and fieldwork* 41

of reciprocity and obligation. *Gham-khādi* networks connect different social segments to each other in multiple ways. Khanān will do *gham-khādi* in a seigneurial spirit to tenants and dependents, and, more obsequiously, to more powerful Badshahyan. Friends will do *gham-khādi* with each other according to gender. Persons peripheral to some family groupings become the linchpins of others, so that *gham-khādi* between extended families may represent dense webs of interconnection, or alternately looser lattices, held together only by the nodal observances of the festivities of a few powerful members.

One Bibi remarked, 'if women are best friends, then there is a bond between those two families'. In Strathern's words, '[t]ies through women are the essence of group definition' (1984: 19), especially if as married women they lie 'in-between' the two *gham-khādi* circles of kin and affines (comparatively, among the Hagen, Strathern shows how affinity is a state of being between groups of kin (1972: 130)). Both the number and nature of people with whom Bibiane observe *gham-khādi* is highly flexible. Kin may be resident in as many as twenty to thirty different regions of the Frontier and more widely in Pakistan, as may relatives of friends, family supporters, retainers and village-women. Figure 1 maps out across Pakistan's various regions one forty-eight-year-old Bibi's relational network with branches of comparable families to that of the Bibi's affinal genealogy. It shows a Bibi's affines who are also her own kin (father's sister's children). Each Bibi is at the centre of a *gham-khādi* network comparable to this Bibi's ramification of connections to various regions of Pakistan from Karachi to Quetta, and from Lahore to Saidu in Swat. The connections require visiting and being visited during *gham-khādi* by appropriate female family members. In this case, the Bibi's *gham-khādi* connections range from her DIG (Deputy Inspector General Police) husband's college, political and government friends to her own paternal kin in Saidu, her maternal kin in Peshawar, and to persons related by marriage to her four sisters and various cousins and aunts from other regions of Pakistan (e.g. Mardan, Quetta, Shamozo, etc.). The degree of a Bibi's participation in a particular *gham* (funeral) or *khādi* (wedding) depends on her closeness to the bride or deceased. Bibiane maintain continuity through various interactions ranging from brief visits to onerous, preparatory engagements. The 'close' relatives and household members forming the first circle of a Bibi's *gham-khādi* network are: her mother's kin (e.g. mother's mother; mother's father; mother's mother's sister; mother's mother's brother; mother's brother; mother's sister; mother's brother's son; mother's brother's daughter; mother's sister's daughter's daughter; etc.);[29] her father's kin (in a similar pattern), her cousins and their offspring; mother- and father-in-law, and their separate extended families. Bibiane also maintain a more extended network of ties with members of different unrelated families.

Gham-khādi, however, does not entail only symmetrical reciprocal visiting relations (where women of similar background visit each other); village-women from

---

[29] The term 'close' is an indigenous English idiom specifying those kin and affines upon whom one can rely for co-operation. Nancy Tapper describes the term 'closeness' as 'only indirectly related to genealogical distance' (1991: 18).

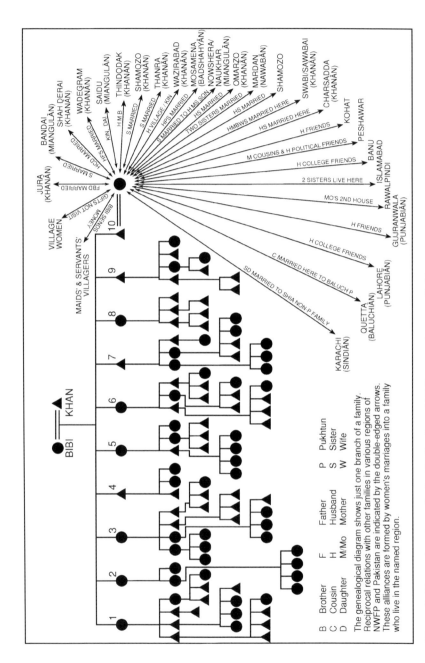

Figure 1 The regional reach of a Bibi's gham-khādi network across Pakistan

different social backgrounds (*gharib* or poor village-women, retainers, wet-nurses and their offspring) from both the Bibi's affinal and kin villages will also visit her on a daily basis and during her *gham-khādi*. Unlike Swat Bibiane, Mardan Bibiane do not typically visit the houses of local village-women (with the exception of their wet-nurses') but may send their maids with money, food and other gifts for their *gham-khādi*. *Gham-khādi* thus forms a network joining Bibiane to many different families all over Pakistan.

In *gham-khādi*, every married woman holds a unique position in the network of relationships. The focus of her own network of weddings and birth-visits, a woman becomes a satellite presence at other ceremonies. Participation in *gham-khādi* may be initiated by marriage or, more contingently, by invitation (as in the case of the non-Pukhtun school friends of former convent girls). Attendance at a wedding commits a guest not only to *gham-khādi* obligations but to the ongoing social form *tlal-ratlal*, which subsumes ideas of friendship, loyalty, personal duty and familial propriety. Where two people 'do *gham-khādi*' with each other, and one party fails to attend a ceremony, the other may choose to terminate relations with her. The importance that *gham-khādi* plays in inter-affinal and social relations cannot be overemphasised; to be excluded from circles in retribution for wrongdoing, real or perceived slights, or previous non-performance, is to suffer, in Bourdieu's words, a protracted and painful 'social death' (1966: 217). Social relations are severed and *ezat* lost in a society where reputation and honour determine Bibiane's social acceptability.

Gham-khādi works as the pivot on which matters of symbolic self-definition and identity, and matters of familial and political allegiance, turn. To quote Delaney, 'the ties that bind are not [only] *in* the blood but in culture . . . symbolically constructed within an entire system of meanings about the world' (1991: 14). Thus '[t]he Pukhtun say of a family with whom they have a close relationship: "We go to their weddings (*khādi*) and funerals (*ghem*)."' (Lindholm 1982: 131).

Fieldwork: participating and performing

This study is based on ethnographic fieldwork carried out in 1996–8, 1999–2001, 2005 and April 2006 in Islamabad, and in the Frontier in Saidu, Swat and Hoti, Mardan. Grima, doing fieldwork as 'an outsider in the village', admits she found Pukhtun female society impenetrable: 'it was difficult for me to break into the information networks and get women to think of me as someone to inform in the event of a crisis . . . I also had no obligation to go to any *gham-xadi* or *tapos* . . . So I usually found out about incidents after they had occurred' (1998: 88, 107). As an ethnographer working 'at home', my own experience was different but equally complex. While I came into close contact with a range of women (Bibiane, villagers and other Pukhto-speakers) whom I met for the first time during my fieldwork, I was also bound to a few Bibiane as maternal kin and had affinal ties to other women (cf. Altorki and El-Solh 1999: 52), some of whom were also my school-fellows at the Murree

Convent (Plate 5). While allowing me a great degree of access, these family relations and the *purdah* system necessarily determined some of my field practices (unlike conventional anthropologists, I could not live in unrelated men and women's houses).[30]

Having *gham-khādi* obligations as a participant deepened my understanding of the tensions Bibiane experience in discharging ceremonial roles, and complicated my self-understanding as an ethnographer (Mir-Hosseini 2000:10).

Furthermore, my level of access excited suspicions of impropriety as I 'lifted the veil' on women's lives. Ethnography involved reverting to Pukhtun styles of decorum (in conversation with many men I had to avoid eye contact and be circumspect in asking direct questions). It also involved breaching certain decorums in inter-class relationships, such as in visiting by foot the houses of the poor (*gharibanān*) in Mardan, and on one occasion bathing the corpse of a wet-nurse with several Swati village-women. While unable to divest myself of my familial identity, I had to establish a second self as an ethnographer if my notes were to capture *gham-khādi* as a practice involving interaction across, as well as within, household boundaries.

My initial aim when I first planned my research for a PhD was to investige the role of the global media, particularly television, in the lives of *purdah*-observing Pukhtun women. Yet the women I met expressed less interest in my painstakingly prepared questionnaires than in their constitutive effort of 'going and coming' from life-cycle events. These *tlal-ratlal* patterns obtrusively replicated themselves in my fieldwork practices: it was common to spend whole days visiting others or being visited.[31] Bibiane and their families constantly travelled: one day I would meet them in large-scale gatherings in Swat, a few days later in Peshawar, in Mardan, again in Islamabad, and then elsewhere in northern Pakistan at various *gham-khādi*. When my mother-in-law became seriously ill with cancer, her presence at my home in Islamabad brought in a daily flow of guests – Bibiane, Khanān, Badshahyān, villagers and retainers from a range of familial and social backgrounds from Swat and Mardan both related and unrelated to me. I utilised my local connections, and status as a wife and mother (cf. Abu-Lughod 1986: 17; Altorki 1986: 2; Altorki and El-Solh 1999: 12; Delaney 1991: 21, 28; La Fontaine 1992: 97; Watson 1992: 9; Youssef 1978: 86), to gain entry into women's networks, particularly during weddings and funerals. I thus observed and participated in Bibiane's houses, lives and complex behaviours in different regions of northern Pakistan at numerous major (funerals and weddings) and minor *gham-khādi* (births, illnesses, returned-*haj* visits and birthdays).

---

[30] See Abu-Lughod 1986: 11, 96; A. S. Ahmed 1980; Jeffery 1979: 5; Singer 1982: 74; Wikan 1982: 51. On the inevitably experiential nature of ethnography, see Ellen 1992: 27; James and Dawson 1997: 6; Morris 1995: 574; and Okely 1996: 27.

[31] My fieldnotes record at the most intense period of my research in the field, 'for me ethnography has become a passion – my way of life' (3.35 a.m. 16 February 2000), or in Scheper-Hughes's terms, a distinctively female 'work of recognition' (1992: 28; cf. Shostak 1982). One maid of about sixty in an elite village household said I was 'exhausting' myself 'to pieces' (*zare, zare shwe*) by writing down so many people's 'words and actions, both good and bad, like the *malaika* [recording angel]'.

In addition to my immersed participation, I interviewed a wide range of Bibiane and other people, 258 in all, whose accounts provided especially rich resources for my reconstruction of *gham-khādi*.[32] Interviewees were chosen to reflect gender, generational, regional and class distributions. While I have been careful not simply to defer to people's speech, interview responses proved helpful for building up more nuanced pictures of *gham-khādi*, for instance in highlighting divergences between 'accepted' and actual forms. Though some Bibiane expressed hesitation at my request for an interview and referred me to more authoritative elders, or to written codifications of Pukhto or villagers who still practised Pukhto, many ultimately expressed gladness for an opportunity to reflect aloud on their practices. Interviews, in English, Pukhto or both, were scheduled around prayer-times (see Appendix 3)[33] and conducted according to certain etiquettes, with personal names avoided. Many women perceived their own voices as part of themselves and subject to *purdah*. They often became shy (*washaramedoo*) about recording and listening to playbacks. Others felt that they had to speak well, as they were going 'in a book' (cf. Loizos 1981: 190). Recording itself lifted a metaphoric '*purdah* of the voice' from their experiences. Respectable Bibiane, self-assured during public *gham-khādi*, cried 'with an open heart' (*de zre kulawa*) when relating intimate life events (one Bibi broke down recalling her mother, in a land-dispute, disowning her in an open public court). I reciprocated this gesture of trust by expressing my own emotions through crying with them. The contacts forged during these processes are ongoing, as many Pukhtun families visit the UK (particularly London) each year. I also remain in touch with a range of Bibiane, through electronic mail (cf. Tapper 2001: 14).

This chapter has sought to introduce a number of themes through which Bibiane's enactment of the work of *gham-khādi* may be apprehended. I attempted to analyse *gham-khādi* within a wider structure of *Pukhtunwali*, placing *gham-khādi* for both Pukhtun men and women within a local framework of Pukhtuns' (self-)identity. It is within this frame of identity that Bibiane from Swat and Mardan organise their lives through marriage, domesticity, rivalry, wealth, clothes and, most importantly, *gham-khādi*. *Gham-khādi* ceremonies are ostentatious events in which families advertise and seek to consolidate their social status. In this way, they provide an occasion in which many of the organising, but more ordinarily submerged,

---

[32] The number of interviewees overlap: in total there were 258 of which 242 people were from the Frontier Province; 178 from elite Pukhtun backgrounds and 132 Bibiane. In addition, 16 interviewees were non-Pukhtuns for comparative material. Although I interviewed 64 men (elite and non-elite) in segregated areas, I also relied on the insights of my husband who is a Pukhtun from the Mardan area. The role of supportive spouses in Frontier's segregated society has already been noted in its ethnographic accounts (e.g. A. S. Ahmed 1980: 15; Barth 1983: 9; Lindholm 1982: xxiii; Singer 1982: 5, 72). On problematic access in segregated societies, see Keiser 1991: 2–3; J. D. Moore 1997: 245; Papanek 1982: 5.

[33] On prayer as punctuating other activities in Indonesia, see Bowen 1989. On a diverse range of complicated fieldwork experiences in different contexts, see Abu-Lughod 1986; Altorki 1986; Barley 1986; Ellen 1992; Epstein 1967: 15; and Madan 2002.

dynamics and tensions of Pukhtun life become visible. Rather than representing discrete and exceptional occurrences, during which people discard their habitual social identities, ceremonies knot the relations of kinship, wealth, domesticity and self-presentation otherwise negotiated in the course of Bibiane's everyday life. As an identity-defining practice, the terms of Bibiane's participation in *gham-khādi* are subject to both reiteration and revision; ceremonies may likewise be occasions of grief or joy, engagement or boredom, serenity or anxiety. The study's fuller description of *gham-khādi* ceremonies in the next chapter adduces an account of the necessary context of weddings and funerals in the experience of Bibiane, and the central site of their work, the *kor* (house).

2

From the inside-out: Bibiane's 'dual lives' in and beyond the house

Mother on the plains [in Mardan] and her luggage in Swat. *(Abay pa sama kadda a pa Swat)*[1]

When I call on you (at your place), what will you give me? And when you call on me, what will you bring me? (*Che staso kara darsham no sa ba rake? che zamoong kara rashe no sa ba rawre*)

(Pukhto proverbs)

When God wants to do it, it is done; when a *khaza* [woman/wife] wants to do it, it is also done. *(Che Khde a kai, agha keegee; che khaza a kai, agha keegee)*
(Stated by wet-nurse Sheereena *dai* (aged over seventy in 2001))

This chapter deploys an 'inside-out' approach to argue that the house as seen by Bibiane has 'a communal and political significance which goes beyond what anthropologists conventionally label "the domestic"' (Carsten 1997: 18; cf. Kondos 1989: 176). The houses of Bibiane host communal gatherings and feasting during *gham-khādi* ceremonies of wedding and funeral; women's activities play a central role in the symbolic reproduction of intra- and inter-familial relationships and inter-class social relationships, and in a representation of ethnic identity (Pukhto). As such a site, the *kor* (house), 'remains a crucial and an active source of reference' for Bibiane in all social contexts (Donnan and Werbner 1991: 140).

Bibiane and their families move from Islamabad to their village houses for holidays and religious festivals, including *Akhtar* (Eid), and 'life-crisis' events; some Bibiane superimpose these holidays and festivals upon seasonal translocations from the city to summer bolt holes in the hills of Murree and Abbottabad.[2] Bibiane's movement to and from the *kor* entails a multidimensional interchange

---

[1] The proverb originally refers to the Yusufzai annual migration from Mardan to Swat (Tair and Edwards 1982: 3) but is equally apt to the translocal nature of present-day Bibiane life. Contrastively, Humphrey describes how Buryat shamans in the Russian city of Ulan-Ude link citified individuals to half-forgotten rural practices by invoking clients' ancestors (1999: 8).

[2] The Pukhtun practice of relocation has been described as: '*nim-korah*': 'a person having two houses and residing in each occasionally' (Raverty 1982: 1,001); and '*dwa-kor*' (dual-houses; A. S. Ahmed 1980: 219). Only a decade ago entire Khan households moved servants and cattle to second homes in the hills away from the scorching heat of the plains.

47

of practices and behaviours between regions. On the one hand, modern houses in Islamabad are adapted to meet the stricter *purdah* segregations of the Frontier; on the other, new forms of knowledge, taught at Al-Huda, suggest alternative 'Pukhto' practices embodied at local sites in the exemplary actions of metropolitan Bibiane. Bibiane's identity, fluctuating between urban and rural sites, characterises their *gham-khādi* attendance, introducing modifications to *gham-khādi* procedures.

The house from inside-out

Certain anthropological accounts of domesticity in South Asian societies counter the more traditional emphasis on 'large-scale social phenomena', particularly in the political sphere.[3] Gray and Mearns (1989), for example, argue against simply perceiving the house through an 'outside-in approach' that 'devalues the endogamous processes of small-scale social domains, which are constitutive of actors' experiences' (18); Bourdieu, indeed, calls houses 'universe[s] of practice and discourse in their own right' (1991: 110). Insisting upon the theoretical validity of the female perspective, anthropologists seek to reconstruct external socio-political activities as seen from the 'inside'. Thus, 'the household remains absolutely central to bringing together the experiential and analytic interpretations of complex societies' (Gray and Mearns 1989: 31). The symbolic location of weddings and *gham* (literally and metaphorically) in the *kor* supports Kondos's assertion that the house is 'the site for people's existence [*zeest*] and continuity' (1989: 176).

Public gatherings of extended families and local community members affect this continuity during *gham-khādi*. As restated by Waterson (1990: 139), Lévi-Strauss identifies how 'house societies' return to symbolically localised origins by enacting ceremonies that legitimate the present in relation to the past.[4] The efficacy of these acts of transmission depends on the participation and approval of family and local community members. In other words, the house has public and private dimensions during *gham-khādi*.[5] Wedding and funeral ceremonies, however, represent less the interruption of an otherwise secluded space, than bespeak the duality of the *kor* as the site for transactions between outside and in. Even during everyday non-*gham-khādi* occasions, Bibiane understand the house as presumptively public in its general accessibility to guests and visitors and invest continuous efforts to prepare it for future events (storing up cloths, linen and bedding, extra-large cooking pots, cutlery and crockery in large quantities; getting together trousseaux). Furthermore, the acts of 'making kin' and of negotiating brides' marital assimilations portray the ongoing transactions between inside and out. Thus Pukhtun Bibiane's practices

---

[3] On the house as a critical area of ethnographic study, see Carsten and Hugh-Jones 1995; Gray and Mearns 1989; Morgan 1965; Rapoport 1976; Venkatesan 2001; and Waterson 1990 among others.

[4] For a critique that attempts to go beyond Lévi-Strauss's theory of 'house societies', see Carsten and Hugh-Jones 1995, who maintain that houses have animate qualities, and that 'an anthropology of the house ... considers houses and their inhabitants as part of one process of living' (37).

[5] The term private is 'far from self-evident' (Rapoport 1976: 4); here I imply a sense of certain rooms and spaces of the house as being closed to the general visiting public and guests.

demand the reassessment of certain contentious presuppositions within anthropology, primarily those that divide the home from the extra-domestic activities of the public sphere (see Abu-Lughod 1998b; Altorki 1986; Nelson 1974; York 1997 for critiques).

This homology (home is to private what non-home is to public) immediately breaks down in the light of Pukhtun practices. The Pukhto phrase '*kor kawul*' (literally, to do house) translates, 'to live . . . associate with' (Raverty 1982: 817). A close cognate of the term, '*kalaey kawul*' (to 'do village'), suggests the seamlessness of household interactions between Bibiane families and villagers (Delaney 1991: 202). For Donnan and Werbner, festivities show how the entire local and familial community '[imagine themselves] as an expanded house' (1991: 21), designating the village-crowd (*kile-u'las*) as synonymous with *gham-khādi*. The semantic connections between forms of female participation imply a network of reciprocal visiting extending outwards from the houses of women whose families enjoy *rogha* (fixed; friendly relations); more threateningly, relations truncated due to dispute are called *wrana* (broken, ruined). In returning to the *kille-kor* for *gham-khādi*, families renew a long-standing and typically moralised relationship of co-dependence with the village. Village houses, continuously occupied for five generations or a hundred years, reportedly tap reservoirs in people's hearts (*zre*) and thoughts (*soch*) that go deeper than more pragmatic ties to residences in Islamabad (on the significance of village land for Pukhtuns, see Lindholm 1982: 91; and Spain 1995: 24).[6] The following account describes different house forms (and different female domestic practices) in Islamabad and in the Frontier, deploying ideas of familial and gender relations (such as *purdah*) as analytical categories.

Houses and purdah

Most Bibiane with whom I worked lived in Islamabad but frequently returned to visit their relatives living in Swat and Mardan. While behaviour, dress and styles of thinking varied between locales, styles of *purdah* or *sattar* (concealing, veiling (Raverty 1982: 584)) portrayed the most obvious differences between city and village. This system of gender relations, instantiated most obviously through the veiling of Muslim women, cannot be separated from the house-structures that both cause and facilitate it (see Shalinski 1986: 329). In Frontier contexts, Bibiane's honour (*ezat*) is kept through close adherence to *purdah*. Pukhtuns commonly refer to women by the circumlocutory toponymic '*kor*' (house) or *kor-wala* (women of the house), a term of respect. *Purdah* represents a regulatory system which applies to both genders. Although often articulated in local idioms of shame (*sharam*), honour (*ezat*) and purity, *purdah* determines both gender and class distinctions.

---

[6] Ibn Khaldun (1986, vol. 1: 176) classically adduced an idea of the 'house' in the Middle Eastern context as connoting familial prestige, extrapolating from the term an idea of social interconnectedness (*asabiyah*) extending from kinship. Comparably, in the context of Elmdon, a village in north-west Essex, England, Strathern suggests the close relationship, even identity, between a house and a (social or familial) unit's conception of their defining origins (1981b: 6).

Anthropologists have observed that elite women in the Middle East and South Asia generally keep stringency in *purdah* as a sign of privilege and status among Muslim communities (L. Ahmed 1992: 5; Hoodfar 1991: 105, 106; Mernissi 1985: 142; Papanek 1982: 10; Rifaqat 1998: 181). In the Frontier, Bibiane's status is signified by exemption from social exposure. Large, well-buttressed village houses advertise families' social pre-eminence (Carsten and Hugh-Jones 1995: 2). Houses with 20-foot-high walls open with multiple entrances and are clothed in dense foliage, providing 'an architectural analogy of the veil' (Humphrey and Vitebsky 1997: 53). This structure excludes male strangers while allowing village-women and other Bibiane access to the house.

In terms of this scheme, the *kille-kor* may be conceived as the embodiment, extension and covering of the self, so that, for example, a 'daughter of the house' when marrying from the ancestral home, symbolically throws off its protective veil. In death, the body is again enshrouded back into the veil's folds.[7] Recognising the symbolic dimensions of women's ceremonial activities within the house, the *kor* plays as central a role in constituting *Pukhtunwali* as the male *hujra* (A. S. Ahmed 1976: 39, 42, 1980: 6; Q. I. Ahmed 1994; Barth 1986: 52; Lindholm 1982; Singer 1982: 46–8). The layout of the *kille-kor*, conterminous with the 'system' of Pukhto relations, observes a segregation between female and male areas, with a *hujra* adjoining the women's quarters (Plate 6). Male and female roles are generally viewed as complementary and equally but differentially important, rather than hierarchically organised (see Ardener 1981: 12). This premise of equivalence nevertheless assigns women to domesticity, exemplified by the Pukhto saying, 'for a woman either the house or the grave'. Gendered distinction of spaces gives women control over their own enclosure (cf. Sharma 1980: 218). Walls separate the *kor* from the men's areas to sustain the propriety of women in the family, and to establish lines of communication along which messages pass. In daily life, male and female family members share the same space in the *kor*. During *gham-khādi*, house-spaces become distinctively gendered between the female *kor* and the male *hujra*. Female and male spaces are both independent and interdependent, with messages relayed by servant and child intermediaries.

In the *kille* context, Bibiane interact with close men of the household, visiting village-women, children and maids. While Swat Bibiane observe *purdah* from unrelated men, married Mardan Bibiane observe *purdah* from all men from their first male cousins outwards (contrary to Papanek 1982: 19).[8] For excursions to the

---

[7] Carsten and Hugh-Jones have noted that '[b]ecause both body and house constitute the most intimate everyday environment and often serve as analogies for each other, it may sometimes seem unclear which is serving as metaphor for which – house for body or body for house' (1995: 43). Their 'alternative language of the house' assumes neither the 'priority of kinship [n]or economy' in developing an analytics of domesticity in its metaphorical dimension (ibid.: 2). See Csordas 1999.

[8] First cousins are often potential marriage partners; a large number of middle-aged married couples in my marriage diagrams were first cousins who observed *purdah* from (i.e. avoided) each other. Carsten and Hugh-Jones note that cousin marriages are fraught with ambiguity and tension due to implications of incest, which are countered by creating a 'formal category of affines' through prior avoidance (1995: 38).

bazār or hospital, they are driven (by old family male drivers) out of the vicinity of the village with other female relatives and maids to Peshawar's cloth market (*Kochi bazār*) or Hayatabad, where household goods smuggled into Pakistan from the tribal areas are sold. In Islamabad, Bibiane's range of interaction is wider, with their *purdah* allowing contact with merchants (contrary to Singer 1982: 74). Some leave the house without the *sazar*, others drive and a few swim in public segregated pools. For *gham-khādi*, Bibiane change back to severer styles of dress and observance, travelling in the curtained-off backs of cars.[9] These adaptations of behaviour rehearse a set of metaphorical relationships between the conscious mind, the properly regulated body and the arrangement of house-spaces.

Layout of the *kille-kor* (village house)

Kille-koroona, with different compounds and open courtyards, are much larger than the modern Western-style detached and semi-detached houses which Bibiane rent or buy in Islamabad. Their spacious architectural layout allows various households and nuclear families from the city to live together as one extended family during *gham-khādi* (cf. Singer 1982: 79). An elder mother, one or more married sons and servants (sometimes as many as twenty-two) occupy the *kor*. Other married sons may build separate adjoining city-style houses retaining the gendered compounds and large gardens (*chamman*) of village houses. All such households have a mistress or senior Bibi, designated by her second respect name; she will owe this position to marriage or (in the case of unmarried women) to her age and *ezat*. Joint-family structures typically assume a hierarchical form: *masharān* (the mother/father or eldest son/s and his wife) preside over *kasharān*, the younger sons and their wives. In turn, these younger brothers and their wives may be the heads of their own independent nuclear households in Islamabad. In the family house, however, they are expected to show great levels of deference to their seniors at *gham-khādi* (and sometimes to contribute financially towards the *kor*'s upkeep (A. S. Ahmed 1980: 294)). The house appears as a working 'bio-moral unit' (Daniel 1984) which co-ordinates the efforts (*koshish*) of its members by presenting a united front to kin, dependents and villagers in times of happiness (*khādi, khwashhāli*) and sorrow (*gham, khabgān*) (cf. Marsden 2002).

My specific example of a house in Swat, Dalbar (represented diagrammatically in Plate 7), exemplifies certain features of Bibiane's village houses. As the house formed part of the Wali of Swat's court, its name stems from the Persian word *darbar* (court). Dalbar embodies many characteristic features of joint-family houses of Khanān in *bar* Swat and Mardan. Situated in the midst of poorer (*gharib*) mud and brick village houses, Dalbar stands in Saidu, some five minutes' walk

---

[9] Comparatively, one Bibi, who had married outside her family to a Sudhum Mardan Khan, reported that only fifteen years ago the women of her affinal household did not travel by day as it was considered shameful. Women bearing lanterns travelled for *gham-khādi* at night, in order to conceal their height and body shapes from men. York, by contrast, denies the existence of any 'public arena' (1997: 229) at night inside houses.

away from Saidu Baba's mosque and the mausoleum of the family's saint ancestor (Plate 8). Villagers visit daily for the distribution of alms initiated by the Wali. The main road to Saidu Sharif passes Jahanzeb College, a hospital and a row of small shops selling wares, videos, cassettes and glossy posters of glamorous Bollywood film stars. In stark contrast, groups of Swati women pedestrians pass by fully covered in large head-to-toe veils or *sazare*.

The house is situated between the complex's three central entrances on to the road. The Wali's residence, its integral male guesthouse (or *dera*, a type of *hujra*) and a second further compound reserved for his second wife flank the road. Dalbar, first occupied by the Wali's first wife (now deceased) and the mother of all his children, is accessible via a public way and a 'secret door'.[10] Several rooms built in the entrance (*dewdai*) serve as a *dera* for male guests; from an inside-out view, this area forms the periphery of the *kor* and regulates the ingress of non-related men (Badshahyān, Khanān, servants or villagers). It also serves as the egress and the place of veiling for Bibiane. In this exceptional case, the Bibiane may undertake a form of pilgrimage via a *kacha* (muddy) pathway to Saidu Baba repeatedly on their return to Swat. After the death of the Wali's first wife, Dalbar has been successively inhabited by various offspring; the current occupants are his second daughter-in-law, Sahib Begum Bibi, now in her seventies.[11] The Wali's eldest son, 'Walayat Seb' (from Wali Ahad Sahib: heir apparent), lives in the adjoining Bangla (derived from the same root as the English 'bungalow'). Dalbar and Bangla share an interconnected internal side door locked from both sides but permitting Bibiane, on knocking, to visit each other without a *sazar*. Children pass freely through these doors, and maids also use this route to pass on messages and meal invitations (*dodaigāne*).

The central courtyard in Dalbar provides its largest shared household space and is often the scene of segregated public hospitality and *gham-khādi*. In contrast, private rooms are allocated to Bibiane, their children and maids according to changing family membership (cf. Delaney 1991: 116). Though maids may accompany Bibiane as personal servants, they have their own private quarters, adorned by gifts including televisions, radios, clothes-trunks and cupboards. Maids also frequent a courtyard space near the entrance of Dalbar where they oil and comb their hair after their weekly Friday bath or perform prayers on their *janimaz* (prayer mat) in the warmth of the winter sun. Many also use the kitchen space as a place to cook, talk and rest. Storerooms around the central courtyard in Dalbar and generally in *kille-koroona* (village houses) hold large quantities of cloth, bedding, quilts and

---

[10] On the marriage of Wali Sahib at the age of seventeen in 1925, see Barth 1995: 41. As with the Hageners (Strathern 1981a: 183), in the past it was rare for Khanān and Badshahyān to spend much time with women. It is said that when the Wali's first wife, Mashra Begum Sahib, heard about her husband's second marriage – to a woman rumoured to be a dancer – she locked the door which connected the Wali to her in protest. This physical act symbolically severed her connection to her husband.

[11] For a discussion of Sahib Begum Bibi's husband, the Wali's second son, see Barth 1995: 93, and on her father, Khan Bahadur Sahib, see Lindholm 1982.

clothing for *gham-khādi*; these items represent the household's symbolic capital. Food is served to the *kor* and the *dera* from the kitchen, the symbolic, not merely functional, hearth of domestic life (Otterbein 1977: 52). Women who live together – mother-in-law, daughters-in-law, wet-nurses, maids and even children – sit around the hearth in winter.

The *dera*, which physically adjoins the *kor* in Dalbar, consists of a row of simply appointed rooms fronted by a garden and 10-foot-high bushes. Comparatively, the Khan's men's houses or *hujras* I visited in upper (*bar*) Swat, Mardan and Abbottabad are much larger and more decorative, with hand-woven Persian carpets, European furniture, grand monogrammed crockery and crystal chandeliers. Barth described how saints and their families lacked large men's spaces due to their disconnection from local politics; in contrast, Khanān spent lavishly on their *hujras* and guests to build a network of political supporters; Barth makes a distinction between Khanān with *hujras* and saints without (1986: 52).[12] Yet, in the present context, where most of the male heads of the Swat family hold top positions in local politics, rooms have been added to houses which still differ from the old structures of the quasi-independent men's houses. Many Khanān's private rooms are connected to the main house through a labyrinth of secret passageways, leading from mirrored cupboard doors to the *kor*. These passageways allow a husband access to his wife and family while, in the eyes of guests and male servants, resting in the *hujra*. In comparison to general attitudes about conjugality some thirty to forty years ago, the shame of men being seen in women's quarters while visiting their wives is nowadays much diminished. This is, arguably, in part due to the move outside the village context: village houses and *hujras* of Khanān living in Islamabad have fallen into disrepair, their paint peeling, carpets mildewed, windows broken and gardens untended.[13] The house is renewed only with the 'life-giving rituals' (Carsten and Hugh-Jones 1995: 37) of *gham-khādi*, which see the arrival of hundreds of guests and children.

As nuclear families shift to the city, the typical demarcation of spaces in the *kor* becomes more flexible. Senior Khanān who have lost their political jobs with a change of government may return to spend their days in the *hujra*; landlords and their families may also go back to manage their lands or cultivate political stock. Rather than representing a schematic set of relationships between people and spaces, the house is characterised by a porousness of division between boundaries dividing different classes of agents, both literally in terms of passageways, and metaphorically in terms of shared experience. The relationship between the exterior and interior spaces of houses in Muslim societies has been described as one of homologous opposition (Bourdieu 1990: 277, in Carsten and Hugh-Jones 1995: 40 who critique this homology), yet in Pukhtun village houses, a complex and

---

[12] See also Ewing 1988: 10 on architecture as a sign of legitimacy and prestige; also Metcalf 1979: 375.
[13] Cf. Bayly on the twentieth-century decay of the large houses of Kara *zamindar* families, 'now crumbling', with their inhabitants working in the cities of Lucknow, Hyderabad and Allahabad (C. A. Bayly 1980: 37).

continuous movement of goods (particularly gifts and food) occurs between the interior and exterior (Nadelson 1981). The delivery of goods, especially bulk, proceeds through a network of passageways that link public areas to the *dewdai* and kitchen areas to both male and female quarters. In other words, legitimate gender relations are performed through the orchestration of forms of difference, equally, based on class.

Visiting etiquette: Bibiane forging bonds

The *kille-kor* is not a hermetic compound, but part of the community: a site for exchanges between Bibiane's families and various classes of visitors and villagers. On the part of the host household, offering maximum hospitality means 'doing Pukhto', *Pukhto kawal* (Edwards 1996); on the part of the visitor, the mere act of visiting means maintaining a *tlal-ratlal* or *gham-khādi* relationship with the household visited (Barth 1986: 11). Landlords' offers of food ('hospitality') take forms varying according to recipients' social class. Within their villages, Khanān and Badshahyān earn the reputation of *ezat*, being *kha* (good) and *droon* (literally, heavy; respectable) among dependents through charitable donations (cf. Bourdieu 1991: 8; Lupton 1996: 2; and Shaw 1997: 147). In contrast, villagers regard those who are *kanjoos* (stingy), *tang zre* (closed hearted) or fraudulent in calculating future returns (the *matlabi*, their version of the 'economist-maximisers') less favourably. *Gham-khādi* is the principal occasion at which hospitality is disbursed to villagers. Landlords thus demonstrate their largesse, humility and 'commitment to [their] culture' in engaging *Pukhtunwali* forms (Edwards 1996: 67; see also Barth 1986: 11). On a micro-level, however, as Iqbal's ethnography in Abbottabad demonstrated, 'women exercise control through [the] distribution of food' (1997: 71) by favouring personal connections over affinal ones. Aswad argues that visits are not merely a 'domestic' function but 'serve as institutionalized forms of the important "grapevine" component of power and decision-making' (1978: 480).

Hosting visits allows Bibiane to perform intimate procedures of social cohesion. It is considered more prestigious to be visited and to offer hospitality, than to play the role of visitor and guest (cf. Wikan 1982: 36). Consequently, older Bibiane spend most of the day in their own homes. Visiting implies a 'process of incorporation' (Carsten 1997: 16), by which the acceptance of another's hospitality initiates *gham-khādi* obligations between recipient and donor (Barth 1986: 11; Naveed-i-Rahat 1990: 60). Grima observes: 'Visiting among Pukhtuns is more than an obligation. For the host it represents a tremendous expense and hence a source of social power and prestige . . . The value of lavish entertainment, often exceeding one's means, lies in being able to claim that many people have eaten one's salt and consequently are indebted . . . no visit is made without entailing a relationship of reciprocity' (1998: 43). Conversely, representatives of families in dispute will refuse the other's food. Anthropologists have theorised this refusal of commensality in terms of an unwillingness to partake in the host's 'substance' (cf. Delaney 1991: 196–7; Gray and Mearns 1989: 23; Papanek 1982), and thus to avoid submitting oneself to others' authority or household affiliation (Carsten 1997: 52). Khanān and Bibiane receive a wide range of unrestricted visits from members of their wider families from cities, from local villagers and the families of various wet-nurses and maids. Dependents will come for financial gain, advice on naming a newborn, or for consultation about marriage proposals and *ghamkhādi* matters. Other visitors include female politicians and the wives of regional administrators (the Deputy Commissioner or Assistant Commissioner).

Visits are carefully organised so as not to disrupt existing premises of reciprocal equality between parties. To take everyday female–female visits first, on arriving in the *kor*'s courtyard, guests will be offered the best places on the straw beds (*katoona*) and cushioned sofas; they will be promptly offered velvet cushions (*bojoona*). During mealtime, foods like chicken curry (*charg engwalle*), rice cooked in onions and chicken (*wreeje* or *pulao*), spinach (*saba, sāg*) and homemade yogurt (*mastha*) will be prepared and laid on a hand-embroidered table cloth. In offering hospitality, the host will sit attentively, arms folded and body leaning forward, towards the guests, urging them to take more tea and food: 'Have some more! Don't do *formality* [in English] [or *sath*],' to which the guest will reply: 'It's my own house' (*zama khpal kor de*, meaning, I am taking what I like, I feel at home here). Despite these formulae, the guest should be thoughtful of the host's limited resources, although the primary onus falls on the host to be munificent – gifts and money will often be given to younger visitors and villagers on their departure.

In the case of a Khan being visited by an equal, possibly a politician or prominent member of another distinguished family, the visit will again entail certain protocols. Bibiane are often unaware of visitors to the *hujra* until the male family member sends a male servant to communicate with a maid. The Bibi then begins to oversee the preparation of food in the kitchen. Communication between the genders can be frustratingly or comically scrambled – sometimes Bibiane fail to realise guests have left, and at other times Khanān wait endlessly for food. The high stakes in terms of social reputation of hosting mean visits can be experienced as strained, although some older Bibiane possess an air of serenity in directing experienced servants (Plate 9).

A Bibi may either cook a number of dishes herself, or sit in the kitchen supervising her maids on a low stool (*katki*) beside the gas or coal hearth (*naghare*). In contrast, younger Bibiane, with small children in the way, fear the social consequences for common errors. If the tea is too black (*tor*), or the food inadequately salted (*pheeka, balmange*), the guests may not drink and eat, which reflects badly on the house. It is said that only an experienced hand can achieve the right texture and crispness of *paratte* (oily bread). To some extent, ordinary cooking presumes the imminent arrival of a guest: the tea is brewed with plentiful milk and sugar, sufficiently sweet (*khog*) for immediate service.

As household managers, senior Bibiane take personal responsibility for the quality of service shown to guests (cf. Lindholm 1982: 233). Whatever the particularities of individual household practices, the social and political prestige of the Khan depends on the competence of his wife in household management and hosting (cf. York 1997: 231). It is assumed locally that only guests who have been treated well and given respect will return; guests not offered appropriate hospitality will shun the house and talk badly of the *kor-wala* (women of the house), making light (*spak*) of the Bibiane's reputation (there is thus a 'moral dimension' (Strathern 1981a: 175) to women's performance of household duties). This responsibility brings women a large measure of social power inside the house as domestic supervisors and financial managers (ultimately charged with keeping records of *gham-khādi* debts and credits). It is women who determine recipients and amount in ceremonial gifting; men who interfere in these decisions gain a feminised reputation, 'they are like women (*khaze*) and less like men (*saree*)'. Liaqat Khan from *bar* Swat confirmed that Bibiane hold the purse strings: 'Before, men put their earnings in their own pockets, but today they come home and give the money to their wife and she uses it in *gham-khādi* and in the running of the house.' It is widely said that the wife in a nuclear household 'is in charge'. Evidence (even among Pukhtuns living abroad) suggests that the wives grant husbands discretionary allowances (\$300, in one instance) out of a larger sum of money overseen by the women. An elderly Bibi in northern Pakistan stated in a humorous way that she would bluntly ask her husband '*raka*' (give) whenever there was a household shortfall; when he responded, 'Where shall I produce money from?', she replied, 'I don't know, that is your *kār* [work].' The underlying assumption among women more generally is that earning is men's work and spending (on the house, on *gham-khādi*, etc.) is women's work.

Bibiane enjoy a degree of self-determination in hosting visits, principally in relating to other household women. Over cups of 'mixed tea' (*gad wad chay*), they discuss various issues like the births, marriages, illnesses, deaths (the *gham-khādi*) of other people, as well as difficulties with maids, and familial, national and global politics (Singer 1982: 81; Tapper 1978: 392; York 1997: 218). In her capacity as host, a Bibi may distinguish her own kin from her husband's in her treatment of them as guests: on several *gham-khādi* occasions in joint-family village houses, I have seen close family members (sisters, sisters' daughters, mother's sisters' daughters) of the hostess lie on her bed with their (bare) feet up. This degree of informality contrasted sharply with the upright, crossed-leg posture of close female affines on sofas or chairs one remove from the bed. One Bibi's wet-nurse in her seventies, having lived many decades in a lordly household, explained: 'If you are a relative of Khan, then sit outside; if you are a relative of Bibi, then come inside' (*Ka de Khan khpal ye no warchane kena; ke de Bibi khpal ye no danna rasha*).

Household relationships

'Life', as one Bibi said to me, 'is in layers' (*jwand pate pate de*). This layered or multidimensional understanding of life characterises women's activities in relation to other women within the *kille-kor*, and in their hospitality and guesting. Above,

I discussed patterns of hospitality and generosity entailed in relations between household members and visitors. Below, I describe inter-familial rivalry and tension underlying household relationships. A specific Pukhto lexicon for household relations indicates the good and bad atmospheres that may prevail in a joint-family *kor*. Bibiane describe houses as either '*jannat*' (heaven) or '*dozakh*' (hell), depending on the nature of relationships within. Houses may be characterised by cooperation (*khegara*), trust (*yaqeen*) and love (*mina*). Sororal relationships within the house are frequently ones of sacrifice, affection and close bonding: sisters may raise their nieces and nephews 'like mothers' – feeding them by hand, bathing them and caringly telling them off. In sickness and pregnancy I have seen reputedly 'clean' (*shaki*) Bibiane sleep on 'dirty' (*skha*) hospital floors in order to nurse their sisters-in-law. In spontaneous acts of generosity Bibiane might give their favourite shawl, *sazar* or piece of jewellery to a guest who notices it. Yet sometimes the surface-level appearance of household harmony belies a maelstrom of private antagonisms between Bibiane and Khanān, Bibiane and maids, and Bibiane themselves. Household relationships are often marked, to use the Pukhto expressions, by the simultaneous fear and threat of jealousy (*swazedal*), mistrust (*be-imani*) and enmity (*doshmani*). Charles Lindholm observes, '[t]he public face, which is kept up for the benefit of others, is often in marked contrast to the face revealed at home' (1988: 233; see also 1982). For anthropological accounts of the dual nature of emotions among the people of the NWFP, see Keiser (1991); and see Marsden (2002) on a discussion in Chitral among Muslims of the open (*al zahir*) and hidden (*al batin*): 'The danger of the underside of life emerging in public discussion has the potential to bring shame and disrespect, [to] individuals ... families, and importantly, the moral unit of the village itself' (ibid.: 44).

Inter-female discord in houses is a matter of both personal friendship and antipathy, and follows certain social patterns comparable to agnatic rivalry among Pukhtun men. In joint families, the characteristic sequence is for recent brides to be assimilated into marital homes (for kinship to be 'made') through a gradual process of mutual negotiation. Above all, it is vital for younger wives to avoid direct confrontation (*rishtinee*) with their elders, which is construed as utterly insulting. While a *nawe* (bride) inevitably comes to be viewed by the dominant household Bibiane 'as a potential threat to family solidarity' when she makes demands that are different to theirs (Mandelbaum 1993: 12), family honour insists that she eventually gravitate towards their status (her mother-in-law's) in the family.[14] Bibiane begin to free themselves of the perceived tyranny of senior women with the further in-marriage of new wives, who pose a greater threat than they (Iqbal 1997: 66; Mernissi 1985: 124; York 1997: 225). As their confidence and skill grow in negotiating protocols, established wives increasingly attend *gham-khādi* on their own terms. These negotiations require the adroit management of

---

[14] Comparatively, in 'Chinese tradition the person with the most power over a married woman was always her mother-in-law ... When she in turn became a mother-in-law she would bully her own daughter-in-laws in the same way' (Chang 1992: 93).

appearance, polite language and behaviour (*adab*), personal privileges, alliances and authority between Bibiane and *khidmatgarān*.

For women within the household, rage and resentment may fester over perceptions of favouritism, preferential treatment of children and maids, room allocation, heirlooms, degrees of seniority and respect, and even access to food. The most common form of antagonism, or *dushmani* (enmity, rivalry), between women of the same household subsists between in-married Bibiane and unmarried sisters of their husbands. The latter see the house as their 'father's house' (*de plar kor*), thus laying claim to a greater blood-right (of kinship) than those who marry in (affines). Yet the kin of one house must become affines in another. A bride's bad relationships with other women more commonly have the potential to sour her relationship with her spouse. The sister/sister-in-law relationship is widely seen as fractious among Swat and Mardan Bibiane and Pukhtun women generally.[15] Politics within families can take the form of slightly elder in-laws angling for the favour of senior figures by exercising a repressive or critical authority over younger Bibiane. Alternately, newly married women untutored in the skill of manoeuvring can find themselves bullied as interlopers. On many occasions, I heard various Bibiane call a daughter *nazbina* (cared for) and 'protected' in her natal house, while in her affinal house she was said to be 'overworked' (*wagrabeegee*); 'one day she has to please one person, the next day another' (*kala yao te khapa kala bal*; cf. Kondos 1989: 164). Bibiane can take drastic steps to maintain their autonomy in marital homes or to hold themselves aloof from others. In one case, a Bibi had a wall built running down the side of her affinal ancestral *kor*, to block off her sister-in-law's (also her first cousin's) living space.

One case especially illustrates the disparity between outward deportment and inner feeling forced on Bibiane by household propriety.[16] Khadija, a wife in her late twenties with three children, always appeared at *gham-khādi* events in the close company of her affluent mother-in-law – they arrived and greeted people together, and left in the same car. Yet my conversations with Khadija as a friend revealed profound hostility between them. Her mother- and sisters-in-law, and their maids, waged, in Khadija's words, a daily 'cold war' against her in her '*dozakh*' (abyss-like) affinal house. They refused to return her *salāms* (salutations), avoided direct conversation with her and communicated directly to her husband (by-passing wives in this way is considered highly insulting). When Khadija went to her mother's house and phoned her affinal house, they would hang up or pass the phone to a maid on hearing her voice. Even the house's food was locked up: in one instance, she was unable to get at a 'single potato' for her hungry child without her mother-in-law's (and the maids') consent. In Swat and Mardan, Bibiane may normally put locks on fridges and go-downs (*godām*) to keep servants away (cf. Macfarlane and Macfarlane 2003: 8). The responsibility of the keys to the go-downs and the

---

[15] Charles Lindholm explains, 'one's most salient opponent is likely to be one's next-door neighbour, who is as well one's patrilateral first cousin [and rival for shared patrilineal property]' (1982: 233).

[16] An idea of social interdependence as 'morally entangling' and 'double-edged' in South Asian social life has been advanced by Laidlaw (2000: 629, 630).

related distribution of food on the orders of the Bibi lie almost always with the most senior maid of the house. Mernissi borrows Goffman's analysis of totalitarianism in showing how dominant parties maintain control through regulating others' access to simple necessities; for instance, in the Moroccan household younger wives may beg for food (Mernissi 1985; Goffman 1968). It is usual for conflictual relationships among Bibiane to be inherited by their male and female offspring, who are inexorably drawn into any inter-affinal female dispute (unlike in Carsten's Malay, 1997: 220). Within the space of a household, children are treated as extensions of their mothers, becoming the target of any ill-will directed at her. When Khadija confronted her in-laws, it led only to more tension and mistrust; only occasional visits to her own mother's house in Islamabad allowed brief periods of respite from what she called her heartache (*de zre dard*).

Given the impermissibility of confrontation, Bibiane and maids rely on certain recognised practices in many Pukhtun contexts to articulate contentious feelings. Describing dreams permits women to state or explore otherwise unvoiced desires. Rather than requesting gifts directly from Bibiane, maids may say, as in one case, 'I had a dream that Khan gave me land to build a house' or that 'you sent me to *haj*', challenging her Bibi's sense of generosity by an oblique request. Other common objects of tacit requests are money, to perform *gham-khādi* for grown-up offspring, or consumer items which become the maid's private property. Many Bibiane were also known to resort to this strategy. Otherwise, Bibiane told me they coped with household friction through strength of character. One remarked that she learnt to be strong (*zrewara*) in childhood by competing with her brothers. Fatima, a Bibi from Peshawar in her late thirties, stated in English:

Men are born with the idea that they are men and that's it; they don't have to do anything – just being men makes them great. And the woman, even if it is for a piece of meat she has to fight for that right, and she has to make herself felt. She has to constantly be on her toes to make herself recognised.

Various Bibiane remarked that they become: 'hardened' (*klak*), 'cynical' and 'insensitive' to life over the years, which made them proficient at *gham-khādi* under difficult conditions of intense pressure and public scrutiny (*de khalako nazar*).[17] In many *gham-khādi* I attended, some Bibiane performed the public offices of affection – embracing and exchanging *salāms* – without any real warmth of regard. (Bibiane on more openly hostile terms simply avoid their affines in *gham-khādi* gatherings entirely – averting their gaze when they pass by.) Women's travails are understood as a private matter. One Bibi said, 'a *Pukhtanna* [Pukhtun woman] will bear and hide her *sakhte* [hardships] from other people, especially other women, because if they hear about her problems she will look weak [*kamzora*] and seem inferior than them'. Charles Lindholm stresses Pukhtuns' personal autonomy as a constituent of their moral egalitarianism. Showing forms of dependence is 'reviled

---

[17] Comparatively, Pastner observed that women in Panjgur (Baluchistan) get their own way by means of pleading illness, complaining, playing off male affines and consanguines against each other, and by non-cooperation (1978: 411).

as weakness' allowing 'one's opponents . . . an unwanted advantage' (1988: 234). I was told: 'those who cannot hide *sakhte*, like Punjabiane, have no *zāt* [purity of one's ethnic identity: dignity]'. Through this ideology of ethnic distancing, Bibiane accentuate differences between themselves and other groups through claiming a greater ability to endure and conceal the dynamics of domestic politics. *Gham-khādi* events are perceived as problematic because (among other reasons) they risk exposing private discord to public knowledge. Conflicts may then become the theme for gossip and *zghaibat* (criticism behind another's back). On the other hand, the proper performance of *gham-khādi* obligations may rectify lapsed domestic or family relations.

Household relationships can deteriorate so much as to suspend Bibiane's profession of Islam, with their using witchcraft and malediction (*jādu* and *kode*) to pursue their enmities (cf. Iqbal 1997: 109). I was told by a maid in one Bibi's household of a mother who wished to break up her son's marriage concealing pellets of hair under her daughter-in-law's room carpet.[18] Unfavoured younger Bibiane within a *kor* will often fear subjection to their rival's evil eye (*nazar*). Castings-out are performed through the burning of *nazar* leaves, usually by a maid, atop a pan lid used as a type of censer and held under the *kameez* (*laman*) (as seen in Plate 10).

The protective smoke (*looge*) from the leaves may also be blown on each newly arrived household member. The recitation of Quranic verses, followed by a puff of breath (either on oneself or the 'victim'), and the wearing of *taweezoona* (amulets), are also imputed to have the power to dispel curses. Children and brides are seen as particularly vulnerable to *nazar*. A fluent English-speaking convent-educated mother of a particularly plump nine-month-old baby told me that she feared women who praised her baby while looking askance at her, because they could cast the evil eye over her child. To ward off the potential curse, she followed her wet-nurse's remedy in hanging an apotropaic *partooghaakh* (trouser belt) from the eaves of the cot.

Bibiane employ many strategies and tactics to deal with the ongoing tension of cohabitation. The Bibi who was walled off by her sister-in-law (also her patrilateral parallel cousin), speaking in a metaphoric sense this time, said: 'I build walls in my mind to avoid the people I do not like, but we still share our *gham-khādi*.' Meaning that despite personal conflict, the women presented a united front to their guests in times of joint-household *gham-khādi*. Other Bibiane described their defence of rights and territory. In joint-family households, an in-married woman's allocated private room/s, in contrast to the largely segregated public and shared courtyard, are often perceived as her own, or as a 'space within [a] space' (Ardener 1981: 13). Here she may lock herself away from the crowd, rest between prolonged *gham-khādi* gatherings, pray (*moonz*), reiterate guests' discussions of family politics to her husband and put her baby to sleep during the day. Both large village house

---

[18] Practising witchcraft and casting spells on human hair, forbidden by the Prophet, is noted to have been common during the seventh century (Al-Akili 1993: 89). D. N. Gellner describes women using magic to harm each other to improve their status and opportunities. This is done either by casting spells on their hair or through looking at them or their food (1994: 29, 34).

structures and women's own room spaces allow them to experience some degree of control. In one large household, a mother-in-law and her daughter-in-law separately told me they held the 'spoon and keys' – or dominant symbolic control – of the house (cf. Mernissi 1985: 130). Yet boundaries may be used indiscriminately by guests or by rival affines in order to test their limits. During one wedding gathering, a middle-aged non-Pukhtun daughter-in-law said that her sisters-in-law and guests used her room, which had two entrances and a shorter passage to other compounds in the house, as a public passageway. Perceiving this as a violation of her privacy, she put a lock (*thala*) on her back door – an act interpreted as *ajeeba* (strange) by her Pukhtun affines, who left many of their own bedrooms open to guests.

The starkness of this division of spaces among social categories of person is to some extent blurred by children, who are assimilated into the gender system only at adolescence. For children, houses may possess the internal variety of a 'microcosmic world'. As such, many Bibiane consider the *kille-kor* the ideal site for the upbringing of children: 'not claustrophobic like houses in Islamabad. It is paradise (*jannat*) – big lawns, big houses, lots of playmates (cousins and village children), swings, and a variety of pets and cattle.' Children's happiness, however, depends on that of their mothers. Some Bibiane, like Khadija, sent their sons and daughters to boarding schools to protect them from joint-family politics, to keep them out of the laps of maids, or to spare them the travel in *gham-khādi*. In other families, the *kille-kor* schools children for adult Pukhtun life. Children's freedom to transgress gender boundaries paradoxically inducts them in the *purdah*, and possibly class, divisions that shape Pukhtun sociality. Children are disciplined through both fear and favouritism. Some mothers beat their children, or slap them on the face in accordance with a Pukhto proverb: 'Only with a beating can manners be taught' (*adab da zakhma akhastal keegee*). Family members may call them *kharra* (donkey) or *kamaqla* (stupid), though *daigāne* (wet-nurses) meting out similar treatment risk being scolded by the child's mother. Instead, nurses instil fear through frightening stories about '*baoo*' and '*ballagān*' (demons and beasts).[19] Yet both mothers and *khidmatgarān* (helpers), in joint families, favour their own children over others' by calling them '*shahzadgai*' (princess) and '*khāperai*' (fairy). Innately 'innocent' (*masoom*), children thus quickly learn to be '*chalāk*' (streetwise) and '*shaitan*' (devilish). These qualities make them valuable agents in playing an instrumental role in *gham-khādi*, acting as messengers between their parents and other kin; they thereby learn to negotiate different levels of status, permission and interdiction.[20] Through observing *gham-khādi* practices, children of both sexes are inducted into Pukhtun social practices from an early age through games in the house (Carsten and Hugh-Jones 1995: 2). In games such as 'wedding, wedding' (*wada, wada*) or 'house, house' *(kor, kor)*, children play out the roles of hosts and guests, sipping

---

[19] Some children's stories told by wet-nurses are grim and gruesome with a macabre theme: for example, in the '*Sheen Thootee*' (Green Parrot), a boy is cut up by his father and cooked by his mother, his remains are collected by his sister. He then turns into a green parrot and flies off.
[20] On children's roles as messengers in segregated societies, see Humphrey and Vitebsky 1997: 52–3. On *chalāki* and the control of emotion learnt at childhood, see Lindholm 1982; 1988.

make-believe tea from plastic toy cups made in China, and gigglingly make appropriate conversation.[21] Unlike adult *gham-khādi*, children's are 'fun games' (*de maze lobe*), while they provide 'expressive models' and 'simplified representations of what actually occurs in the world of adults' (Otterbein 1977: 180–1).

Just as children receive provisional exemption from gender segregation, children of different classes – of senior Bibiane, junior affinal brides, maids and villagewomen – also play freely together in the *kor*'s courtyards. Within this context, some older children may take responsibility for younger siblings dominated by older cousins. Yet one Bibi told me that she always instructed her maid to bring her baby into her compound when her older children and their cousins got together in the village house. She said in English, 'the bigger fish eat the little fish' – meaning that some children lord it over their younger cousins and social inferiors. For the children of maids and 'helpers', playing in the elite *kille-kor* may be beneficial. In many cases, these children's mothers have been taken in charitably, shielded from the social consequences of male abuse or a husband's absence, whether through death, a second marriage or absconding.

Social relationships in the house feature not only symmetrical same-class relationships but also asymmetrical Bibi–maid ties, which if nurtured develop into what Pitt-Rivers has classified as a 'lopsided friendship' ((1961) in Tellis-Nayak 1983: 67).[22] The Bibi–maid relationship, like the patron–client tie, is one in which one party is superior to the other in her capacity to grant goods and favours (ibid.). Servants do not have a formal legal contract of rights – a Bibi can fire her maid at any given time but by the same rule maids can leave the service of a particular Bibi by opportunity or choice. Both parties in the relationship have forms of power: the Bibi obviously so, the maid through the ability to gossip, which could wreak permanent damage on any Bibi's *ezat* in the wider society. Comparatively, Najmabadi describes a transformation in Iranian women's identity and status, in late nineteenth- and early twentieth-century Persian texts, from 'house' (*manzil*) to 'manager of the house' (*mudabbir-i-manzil*) (1998: 91). The shift represented 'at once a regulating and an empowering moment', necessitating a sundering of 'homosocial' relations of solidarity with house-servants as the condition of a new form of elite female power (ibid.: 102). Najmabadi's argument captures in another context many ambiguities in how Bibiane relate to female *khidmatgarān*.

Maids may be conceptualised as having a complex, ambivalent nature as both independent persons and adjuncts of their Bibiane, and as both family and as non-family. Bibiane may be jealously protective of maids who have accompanied them since birth or marriage, both as companions and as forms of human capital

---

[21] Macfarlane and Macfarlane wittily explain elaborate tea ceremonies as indulging a 'human desire' for play and formality (2003: 55).

[22] On the relationship of mistress–servant as 'domestic enemies' in eighteenth-century England, and the ' "simultaneous closeness and distance, intimacy and enmity" which epitomised relationships between mistress and servant', see Hill 1996: 6. Maza notes the 'perpetual process of negotiation, conflict, and compromise between master and servant' in eighteenth-century France (1983: 6). See also Callaway 1994; Greenleaf 1977; Grint 1994; Gul 1995–7; Hansen 1994; Ong 196; Robina 1994–6; and Tamanoi 1991.

or labour-power. I observed cases where maids' movements between households provoked bitter power-struggles. In one instance, a maid moving in search of a better job caused a dramatic row between the senior Bibiane of the two households involved. Some Bibiane said that their maids were 'like family' to them and, conversely, that maids were capable of greater devotion than relatives. In one case, an elderly, bedridden Bibi, with four married children, reported better care from her young maid than from her children. The young maid bathed, dressed and spoon-fed the Bibi, she even took the Bibi with the driver to hospital, and slept on a mattress beside her. As surrogates of their Bibiane, maids necessarily become embroiled in household politics. Within households, old house-servants usually side with sisters against incomers, yet some maids and brides (*nawe*) share comparable positions as outsiders. Their role in supporting their own Bibi is said to be double-edged: one Bibi in her forties living in a joint family in the village remarked, 'all our fights are because of *khidmatgarān* and their "*wre-rawre*" [bring and take, gossip]'. Yet Dunbar argues that female gossip is not idle but is a mechanism for controlling behaviour, giving advanced warning and shaming people into conformity with certain standards (1997: 172; cf. Spender 1980). Maids and especially wet-nurses can exert leverage because of their power in the household and because of their freedom to move between the house and the village.

Households' relationships with maids necessarily entail some degree of negotiation between independent persons with their own desires. In one instance, a maid was suspected of having stolen her Bibi's gold earrings. After repeated insistence on the harm that would befall the thief's reputation and restatements of the religious immorality of theft, the maid said she dreamt of her deceased husband for two nights in a row, who told her that she was not a thief (*ghla*), and that the earrings should be in the Bibi's drawer (from which they had been abstracted nine months previously). After the earrings were found, the maid, drawing a veil over her acts, told her Bibi, 'See, my dreams come true [*reeshthia*]; I did not take them.' In this way, the maid, turning the situation on its head, aligned herself with a class of seers to whom religious respect is due. Describing dreams as 'constitut[ing] a field of force . . . between the living, and between the living and the only apparently dead', Gilsenan explores how they 'valoriz[e] . . . the person, authoring and authorizing experience' (2000: 611).

Even more intensely than maids' service, the wet-nurses' or *daigāne*'s breast-feeding of the Bibi's children creates a family-like tie between *khidmatgar* (helper) and mistress: 'the *dai's* milk', it is said, 'becomes the child's *weena* [blood]' (see also Delaney 1991: 155). In Swat, *daigāne*'s offspring refer to themselves as '*dwem number Badshahyan*' (second-class kings), claiming a status higher than that of villagers but lower than landed-family children. I heard one wet-nurse's middle-aged daughter declare, 'I am the *khor* [sister] of the Badshah; I am nobody's servant' (*zo da cha sara nawkara na yamma*). While in Swat, wet-nurses became members of Badshah households, in Mardan the children of Khanān were sent away to be nursed. The daughter of the Nawab of Hoti told me she was raised in a poor and *kacha* (uncemented) *dai*'s home. *Daigāne* I spoke to described strong competition for the honour of entering into the elite household. Throngs of women presented themselves at the *dewdai* and courtyard. Becoming a wet-nurse meant a better standard of living and greater social status, but at the cost of a five-year absence from their own families and children. *Daigāne* hired other nurses for their own children; in one case, a *dai*'s husband left his wife for the wet-nurse of his children.

Bibiane and *daigāne* participate in each other's *gham-khādi* in such ways as to create complex cross-investments of money, duty and care. *Daigāne*'s daughters demand financial benefits from household Bibiane for their own (and close family's) *gham-khādi*, as well as for the ceremonies of Bibiane themselves. *Daigāne* become *sharika* (joint, partners) in *gham-khādi*; a *dai*'s daughter explained that when she needed money, she would go to her Bibi's married daughter and say, 'she is my niece, she is obliged to attend my *gham-khādi*', in other words she must pay up (*da kho zama khwarza da zama gham-khādi la ba khod razee*). Bibiane's financial commitment to *daigāne* in gifts of money, property and land can be lifelong. One *dai* who received frequent gifts of Rs.20,000 (£210) from her Bibi 'daughter' remarked: 'of all my [four] sons she is the best one for me' (*pa tolo zamanno ke agha zama da para kha da*). Thus, among the poorer Pukhtuns who give sons relatively greater significance, the *dai* compared her Bibi-daughter to a status better than a son's. As trusted members of a household, *daigāne* sometimes attend villagers' *gham-khādi* on behalf of their Bibiane. In one case, while an elderly Bibi received medical treatment in the UK, her retainer of more than forty years undertook a *gham* visit on her Bibi's behalf, and distributed a sum of her monthly income according to the Bibi's phone instructions (cf. Appendix 4). In-married Bibiane do not always share this affection for long-standing affinal house *daigāne*. They often remarked that the '*gareebe khaze*' (poor women), who nursed their husbands as children, passed on unsophisticated and bad (*kharab*) language and behaviour. Another Mardan Bibi attributes the differences between her feuding seven paternal uncles and aunts to their lacking the bond of having been raised by the same woman.

Reaching beyond the village

Bibiane are contradictorily enjoined to observe *purdah* by remaining within the house and to make far-flung *gham-khādi* visits to rural and urban sites. Bibiane refer to their shifts of mindset between the different expectations of social life, dress, deportment and regional variations between practices as their 'dual life'.[23] Discussing the house, many Bibiane spoke of their frustration with the social constraints of *purdah* and the lack of stimulation in the village house. A convent-educated Bibi from Swat, Spongmai, compared Khanān and other men, who 'have the freedom to leave the house', with Bibiane in a village context, for whom

---

[23] Lévi-Strauss (1963: 161) rejects the theoretical presupposition of duality, rather than the availability of dual organisations of concepts to people's sense of their experience. My own use of the term is based on a local usage and not as a theoretical tool.

'there is no mental challenge – we may arrange a picnic in some scenic area where there are no people. If I want to see a movie, I have to write a list and give it to the *Mama* [male servant, like a mother's brother]. If it wasn't for TV and the Decoder I'd go crazy.' Another Bibi described how she would 'kill time' by watching TV soap operas like 'Santa Barbara'. 'I used to watch so much TV my father used to call me "The Prophet of movies", because I knew the name of every actor, both English and Indian.' Both Bibiane and maids resort to television to relieve the boredom of village-life. One unmarried Mardan maid, aged twenty-one, bought a television with her hard-earned, saved-up wages; another older married village-woman sold her gold earrings (*deeday*) to buy a second-hand TV set. As a result of the widespread popularity of television-watching within homes and the perceived influence of Western and Indian cultures corroding Islamic family values the Taliban took to burning television sets in public displays in village *bazārs* and streets across the Frontier Province of Pakistan.[24]

With no other entertainment in a *purdah* context, a few Bibiane confided that their dislike of living in the village stemmed from their difficult (*grān*) and restricted (*paband*) life among affines. One, an older in-married Bibi in her fifties, confided that her 'heart' belonged in Pindi, where her father was in the army General Headquarters and where she had lived with her parents as a girl. After the death of her husband, the Bibi moved permanently from her Frontier village house to Pindi. Now a widow with married (*wada shawe*) offspring, she travels for *gham-khādi* without restrictions across the Frontier and Punjab with her village companion-maids. Another Bibi, in her late thirties, who is married to her patrilateral parallel cousin in a 'conservative' village, Sher Palam, felt quite free to 'open' her 'heart' (*kulao zre*) to me:

In [*bar*] Swat, what sort of life is this! If I want to visit my parents or brother's house, I have to take permission from my husband because men don't like their wives to be seen travelling too much – it is *sharam* [shameful]. In the village, the more a woman stays at home, the more *ezat* [honour] she has and the more *droon* [respectable] she is considered.

In Swat and particularly Mardan, prohibitions continue to regulate female visibility in non-segregated public spaces or *bazāroona* (plural for *bazār*), as 'women in male spaces are considered both provocative and offensive' (Mernissi 1985: 143). This is reflective of a wide South Asian attitude: Sharma in her study, in India, notes women's uneasiness and feelings of 'being out of place' (1980: 228) in spaces outside their houses unless on 'some specific business' (ibid.: 218; see also Papanek 1982: 31). When Bibiane need personal or household items from the village *bazār*, they rely on their older maids or male servants to buy these for them. In Mardan, where Bibiane practise *purdah* in the presence of their male servants,

---

[24] On local violent Taliban-type reactions to the television, see *The News International* 2000a and b (31 July and 31 October). Local works on television are: Ahmad 1998; Ali 1984–6; Farhat-ul-Ain 1980–2; Muhammad and Jan 1992–4; Yusufzai 2001. More widely, see Abu-Lughod 1993a; Ang 1997; Baudrillard 1997; Fiske 1997; Hall 1997; Hobson 1997; Holland 1997; Kuhn 1997; McLuhan 1997; Modleski 1997; Warrier 2000.

they pass on directions to maids who relay them to male servants. Shahbana, a Bibi in her mid-forties with kin and affines belonging to separate Mardan families, admitted to having 'lost control' beyond the walls of her village house, due to the unreliability of her servants (in getting household items and ingredients from the *bazār*). She even reports being cut off from her husband and son in the adjoining *hujra*, who may come away from guests to the *kor* in response to her message 'forty-five' minutes or an hour after she has called for them. In 2000, Shahbana 'convinced' her husband to escape the restrictions (*pabandi*) of the village and move to Islamabad. She wanted to school their growing three daughters (aged two, eight and nine) and son (fourteen) in English-medium schools. With her husband, she bought a four-bedroom house in Islamabad, close to her parents' second home in Pindi. During the small *khādi* for housewarming she told me:

Here [in Islamabad] I am very much in control of my life and everything – the house, the servants, the children – they come directly to me if anything goes wrong: I have to put it right. If I need anything, I drive myself to the *markaz* [shops], *kana* [you know], it's according to my choice and there's no *jagara* [struggle].

Bibiane spoke of finding a balance between the ease of the village house even with the restrictiveness, and the greater freedom of Islamabad, which imposed its own strenuous set of social and household demands. A few Bibiane prefer the village for personal and ideological reasons, and urge their husbands to spend more time tending their land. Other families compromise on space by staying in Islamabad apartments during their children's term-time. The following section shows that the premise of 'cultural uniformity' (Arensberg 1968: 7) of Pukhtun 'urban society' is misconceived, given the cultural diversity of Pukhtun Bibiane's lives in Islamabad.

Bibiane in Islamabad

Bibiane's domestic relationships are being redrawn with the move from the joint-family *kille* to nuclear-family units in Islamabad. Where the village house (*kille-kor*) characteristically houses more than one marital unit with offspring and dependents, Khanān and Bibiane settle down with reduced ancillary help (maids, *daigāne*) in Islamabad. Arguably, a Bibi's primary relationship, which was previously with other familial or affinal women, is to some extent reconfigured into a dyadic marital partnership with her husband. It is said that he often becomes more involved in childcare and spends more time travelling with his wife to *gham-khādi*. One Bibi said, 'before in the village men spent most of their time in the *hujra*. If a woman was ill she would go to a doctor with a (female) relative or the doctor would come to her house. But now I have seen husbands want to take part and be there with the wife when she is sick; he will take her to the hospital and be involved. Men are more concerned about their wives, they are curious. They want to take part in their wife's life.' Ajab, a Mardan Khan in his early forties with two daughters said in English:

The main reason to live in Islamabad is because of our women. Society forces the husband to move out – if a man's wife has a toothache, he will go to Peshawar or Islamabad rather than locally in Mardan, where there may be a good dentist but he may be too shy [due to the *purdah* system] to take his wife to him.

Among the fifty-eight Pukhtun households I studied in Islamabad, twenty (semi-detached) houses were rented, and twenty-eight houses and ten flats only recently purchased within the past seven years. Most Bibiane and Khanān sold Frontier village lands and jewellery to buy their costly houses and flats. While sitting in his newly purchased and renovated Islamabad house, Khalid Khan, from Mardan, told me in 2000:

The good [wealthy] families in the [Frontier] villages are all selling their property and buying in Islamabad. I can tell you that in ten years the village will be finished. Only the newly rich families will remain.

These new financial pressures among the previously 'independent' landowning Khanān blur the boundary between them and 'dependent' non-Pukhtun tenants. The 'newly rich' referred to by Khalid Khan earn their money by working abroad, or through the drug trade or smuggling; gradually, and with a sense of ambivalence, these groups are marrying into Bibiane's *gham-khādi* networks. Translocality – owning in the country and renting or purchasing in the city – places Khanān in a potentially threatened class position. As Barth (1959: 9–10, 1970: 125, 1986: 44), Lindholm (1982: 74, 91) and Titus (1998: 668) stressed, the Pukhtun landowning Khanān derive village-council authority, power of patronage and ethnic honour through landownership – which frees them of 'dependence' as tenants and buyers. Barth notes, 'judged by Pathan standards, clientship places a man among the despised failures, subordinates among independent commoners' (1970: 125). For Charles Lindholm, the action of a powerful Pukhtun is to create bonds of dependence (1982: 206). Yet as lodgers in Islamabad houses, some Khanān have rather contracted client relationships themselves. The situation of Khanān, whose ethos was previously determined by the *nang* (free honour) of the landowner, becomes bound by the more contractual criteria of *qalang* or regulated rent (A. S. Ahmed 1976, 1980). A Bibi reported, 'I remember a time when to rent was considered degrading. We were the landlords; now we are tenants.' But in an inverse process, the ability to rent or purchase a property in Islamabad now implies the wealth to be able to do so.

Data from Islamabad fieldwork revealed that Bibiane from Swati families owned more than ten flats, and six others have been bought more recently (in other words, owners came from areas where *purdah* was more permissive in relation to male relatives, servants and neighbours; and second that the flats were in the names of wives who took direct possession of it). Residents view flats as modern, practical and easy to rent to higher-paying foreigners (Plate 11). Most Islamabad flats have a non-segregated, central area, with bathrooms connecting to main living spaces, rather than to gendered quarters. Flats often have only single-room servant's digs with a separate entrance (these may be allotted to maids). Pukhtun families with male drivers usually rent extra basement rooms with entrances in the car-park. In this way, gender and status distinctions not leading to differential treatment in the country are accentuated in the more 'modern' context. Bibiane and various men (family, servants) contend at different times for the use of spaces in the flat: maids may watch television and uncles visit (at different times) in the same lounge. In contrast to Swati flat-owning Bibiane, a Mardan Bibi said that her husband was 'too Khan-minded' to allow such non-segregated sharing of domestic space and preferred to rent a semi-detached house than to buy a small apartment in a shared block of flats.

Greater stringency of *purdah* among Pukhtuns generally, compared to Punjabis and other Pakistanis, means the customisation of modern city houses into more 'Pukhtun' spaces. Unlike the spacious houses in Pindi and Islamabad which Khanān owned for many years, the compact, more recently bought city houses often lack gardens and provide only one entrance for both sexes. Despite the CDA (Capital Development Authority) rule that the outer walls of Islamabad houses should not exceed a certain low height, some Frontier Khanān seek to reinstate *purdah* restrictions by putting wall extensions, matting, bamboo and other coverings on their house gates and balconies (Plate 12). Bibiane told me that separate entrances, allowing for *purdah* maintenance, were a criterion determining which houses they rented. On one birth-visit to a Mardan Bibi, whom I had not visited before, I recognised her house by the conspicuous *chackoona* (bamboo coverings) behind the front gate, on the balcony and behind the outer walls. Many families adapt the interiors of houses to supposed Frontier norms. Space in modern city houses does not entirely maintain gender segregations, meaning that men and women indiscriminately use bathrooms and kitchens. In one household, the maids refused to share the single or men's servants' bathroom of their Bibi's new city house. As a result, the Khan and Bibi of the house were compelled, by obligation to their maids and in conformity with Pukhtun conventions, to build the maids another room and bathroom. Shahbana, who had persuaded her husband to move house to Islamabad, also supervised the construction of a male backroom serving as a space for her husband's *zamindar* (village-tenants) in their Islamabad house.[25] This room took a separate entrance from the rest of the residence. For the village-men visiting the Khan his traditional men's 'house' or *hujra* is replaced in the city by a one-room space not so different from their own *betak* in the village. Yet Khanān's reconfiguration of space attempts to avoid the reconfiguration of gender roles and relationships implicit in the modern house typology.

---

[25] Some veiled Bibiane assertively instruct male constructors, painters and contractors (*thekedars*) in Islamabad. A Bibi whose husband left their half-built house midway during construction said: 'I built half the house myself. The work was done faster because they [the workers] know Bibi means business.' She continued: 'Everything is in order when I manage things – the house runs to the clock. But when he is home he picks on everything. I want him to get a job and leave the house in the mornings.' She says, partially mockingly: 'We can't have two bosses in one house all the time!'

Visiting in the city

Bibiane's *gham-khādi* activities do not lapse with their (seasonal) arrival in the city. Islamabad represents not just the base from which women return at short notice to ceremonies in the *kille-kor*, but is itself a flourishing scene of *tlal-ratlal* and female–female relationship outside the house. Indeed, the concentration of Pukhtun Bibiane in the city creates an intensification of visiting practices among distant and close kin.[26] These visits illustrate the dependence of specific forms of quasi-'codifiable' behaviour at gatherings on *tlal-ratlal* sociality more generally. Moreover, practices have arisen over the past twenty years by which Bibiane may belatedly discharge *gham-khādi* obligations they may have missed (through indisposition, or being out of the country). In such cases, Bibiane visit the families in question in the city, stating their purpose ('I have come to do your daughter's *ombaraki*'). While, on the one hand, Pukhto may thus be reinforced or clarified in Islamabad, on the other, Bibiane voice the concern that it might also be diffused, with Islamabad's greater frequency of inter-ethnic interaction, and with the relaxation of *purdah* and other strictly ethnic forms.

When a Bibi visits another in Islamabad, the hostess obligingly keeps company with her guest, receives her condolences or congratulations, and then may talk or sit in silence. Bibiane serve tea in special crockery sets (either heirlooms embossed with the family crest or purchased from Peshawar's Hayatabad market), arranged in *soigné* fashion. They may display and discuss the latest and most modern purchased consumer goods from Hayatabad or even from abroad. The Bibi and her guests (female or even male) sit in the enclosed 'drawing-room', as opposed to village house verandas and open courtyard spaces, while the maids, in some cases male servants, prepare meals which the visitor may initially refuse, doing *sath*. As in the village, Islamabad Bibiane prepare for unexpected visits: they commonly keep pre-prepared delicacies in the freezer, such as meat kebabs, *samose* or home-made chicken rolls. Foods are defrosted in microwaves and served as guests arrive.

City visits also create broader articulations of enacted relationships across regional sites. For some, city *gham-khādi* only represent transposed forms of rural ceremonies. Bibiane without access to suitable village houses may host weddings in Islamabad hotels, though Bibiane consider weddings in ancestral homes more 'prestigious'. In this view, city-residence is rootless, and modern amenities (cars, aeroplanes) serve to expedite people's obligations in attendance, compared to the era of the *tanga* (horse and cart). Reference to a supposed origin or 'watershed' (Munn 1990) provides substantial meaning for a displaced life, provided for more practically by the conveyance of a Khan's income, means

---

[26] Anthropologists have theorised identities and description of practices as 'translocal'. In a case reversing the Pukhtun example (where Pukhto is conceptualised as invariant, while accounts of practices have altered), Schwartz describes Guatemalan oral historians' intervention in folk histories as positing a continuity between relocated city practices and the past (1977). For a broader account (broaching concepts of kula exchange and nationhood) of how distant groups may translocally be imagined as related, see Munn 1990: 1; cf. Hagen 1999: 372.

of sustenance and resources – chickens, fruit, *ghanam* (wheat) – in bulk from the *kille-kor* to the city house. The reverse movement is a flow of modern commodities (Dettol, Pampers, cornflakes, pastries) in large quantities to the village house.

City visits – as specific forms – recapitulate village and convent ties and develop new and socially (or familially) expanded *gham-khādi* relationships. In Islamabad, four Mardani couples 'broke their *purdah*', allowing wives to socially meet their husbands' male cousins. This new step has important implications for changing forms of *purdah* outside the Frontier context. The 'information service' of Pukhtun visits increasingly features female–male as well as female–female interfaces: in one instance of hosting in Islamabad, I saw a husband turn around in surprise when his own wife passed on information about his patrilateral cousins' and uncle's property business he himself did not know about. In a cosmopolitan milieu, Bibiane mix with certain men, with women of other ethnicities at religious school, or as the mothers of their children's schoolfriends; they also interact with Christian Punjabi cleaners and beauticians ('waxing women'). Plate 13 shows Bibiane's children's *khādi* (birthday) in the city; guests are from different ethnic and national backgrounds.

Bibiane's greater exposure manifests itself in wider freedoms of movement than in village contexts: they may go to cousins' houses and associate with others in the context of women's or religious bodies (APWA, IFWA, or Al-Huda). The city boasts several dedicated amenities, such as 'Hot Shots', a family entertainment centre with a swimming pool, bowling, arcade games and bouncy castles, in Islamabad's central Fatima Jinnah Park (Plate 14).

Al-Huda

What we see in effect in Islamabad is the co-presence of multiple modes of modernity, Islamised in various ways according to different schools of interpretation. The amusement arcade represents an instance of globalised commodity capitalism. Another modern mode, of the greatest significance for this study's treatment of *gham-khādi* ceremonies, is represented by the reformist interpretation of scriptural Islam taught at the Al-Huda school. During my initial fieldwork in Islamabad in 1994, I accompanied a group of Bibiane to the series of Ramadan Al-Huda classes, which attracted over 500 women attendees. In crowds of predominantly Punjabi women, Bibiane gathered with friends and relatives, settling down on a particular patch of the carpet, to listen to the Urdu lectures given by the organisation's founder, Dr Hashmi. Approaching the lectern entirely cloaked in a black bodily covering (*abaya*) and headdress (*hijab*), Dr Hashmi said that women should make an effort to look 'attractive' in segregated public spaces and for their husbands, but should cover those parts of the female body which may unnecessarily attract marriageable men. Just before her lecture, she removed this outer garment to reveal an elegantly dressed, soft-spoken and charismatic person in a brightly coloured *shalwar-kameez*. Dr Hashmi taught a form of Islam perceived as outward-looking and relevant to people's everyday lives. She made jokes as she referred to her own and other women's mundane experiences. As one of her Pukhtun students, Marium Bibi, told me:

My experience of Al-Huda was really wonderful. In a short span of one year, I learnt so much about Islam. It was an intellectually stimulating class and Dr Farhat was very focused while imparting Islamic education to her students. She never imposed her will on anyone, neither did she condemn or ridicule anyone. In fact, she had great respect for all her students. Outside the class, she was quite friendly and got along well with her students.

More critically, Dr Hashmi stressed that women could potentially transform society, saying in one *dars* in Urdu: 'the example of a woman [*aurat*]' on her surrounding family and community, 'is not like a matchstick but like a flaming petrol pump – as a daughter, sister, wife and mother, her message can spread like fire!' Agency-conferring movements, like the Al-Huda women's Islamic movement in Pakistan, have resonance with other comparable movements, such as the women's mosque movement in Cairo described by Mahmood (2001, 2003). Insofar as these movements have affected change in a wide range of social behaviour among contemporary citizens, including how to speak, dress, where and how to invest one's money, and what is deemed correct forms of practices in *rites de passage*, they acquire a very public nature with political implications. For the first time in the Islamic history of these areas, large numbers of women in Egypt and Pakistan have mobilised to hold public meetings in segregated public spaces (e.g. in Al-Huda centres or in Cairo mosques) and by doing so altered the historically male-centred character of Islamic pedagogy. Indeed, Donnan and Werbner have observed that religious gatherings and mosques in the cities become central in communal public activities and a focus for status achievement, as well as 'focal meeting places' (1991: 24).

In contrast to certain harsh prohibitions by some mullahs (male religious functionaries based in mosques) in Pakistan upon women's agency in general, Dr Hashmi's teaching grants contemporary women an Islamic right (*haq*) of rebuke in relation to husbands and other in-laws.[27] According to her lectures, Islam imposes a moral duty on every Muslim 'to command right and forbid wrong' (*al-amr bi'l-ma 'ruf wa'l-nahy 'an al-munkar*). Under this concept, the individual believer recognises her duty to issue orders, albeit in a 'kind manner', in conformity with divine precept (Cook 2000: 9).[28] Every member of a community, male

---

[27] The status of women in Muslim societies is shaped by two main factors: the (male-dominated) ulama and societal patriarchy (Haddad and Esposito 1998). The Jamaat-e-Islami and other such parties, for example, 'have advocated [the] inferior status and complete segregation of women who should preferably be confined to their homes, but otherwise heavily veiled from head to foot; and the total exclusion of women from any decision-making bodies or processes' (Mumtaz and Shaheed 1987: 16); on the 'bigoted' mullahs, see Alavi 1991: 141. Wikan discusses how the ulama (religious leaders) see 'females as morally weak and irresponsible' (1982: 56).

[28] Cook points to the parallels of such an expression, in England in 1801, when a 'Society for the Suppression of Vice and the Encouragement of Religion and Virtue' was established; and may also be seen among the Buddhists and Confucians (2000: 561–2). Distinctively, for Cook, 'Muslims perform the duty in its most stringent form (*bi-akad al-wujuh*): fighting (*qital*), which involves the risk of being killed' (ibid.: 582). Contrast Hasan 1996; M. W. Khan 1998; Malik 1991; cf. Nadvi, Nadvi and Nadvi 1999.

and female, is enjoined by Quranic obligation to this service (see, for example, the following Quranic verses: Q3: 104, 110, 114; Q7: 157; Q9: 71, 112; Q22: 41; Q31: 17, and several Ahadith (plural)). The Prophet is attributed with the saying: 'Whoever sees a wrong [*munkar*] and is able to put it right with his hand, let him do so; if he can't, then with his tongue; if he can't, then with [or in] his heart which is the bare minimum of faith' (see Cook 2000: 33). The Prophet thus ordered a hierarchy of modes of responses (the 'three mode' tradition) to wrong: deed, word and thought. (ibid.: 34, 45). One cannot compromise or make exemptions, by commanding or forbidding those Quranic precepts that suit particular interests (Tabari 310/923, in Cook 2000: 24). The most professing persons take on the role of God's *khalifa* (deputy) on earth by zealously 'commanding right and forbidding wrong' among his or her kinfolk. 'Conversely, "a dead [person] among the living" is explained as one who fails to perform the duty' (ibid.: 38). The phenomenon of commanding right belongs to the public space of Muslim society (ibid.: 469), whether in a domestic environment or not (Ghazzali in ibid.: 505, 1,111). The necessity of instruction in Islamic precept places a scholar (*faqih*) in every town, to engage in *dawa* (as discussed in the previous chapter) or to 'go out into the rural hinterlands' to teach (ibid.: 445). In this way, Islamic traditions bring scriptural teaching into contact with the circumstances of everyday village-life. Those who take up the Quranic injunction to teach are not necessarily received as strident; indeed, the action of commanding right may be more effective because its proponents are viewed primarily as relatives, not religionists. Al-Huda teachings rooted in these traditions raise fundamental questions as to the meaning of scripture in the world in which Bibiane live.

Al-Huda's exegesis and commentary upon the sacred Islamic texts (the Quran and Hadith) implicitly dispute that customary *gham-khādi* life-cycle events conform to Islam. While Pukhtun Bibiane mark funerals by collectively commemorating forty days after burial (the *Salwekhtamma*) and a year after burial (the *kāl*; sometimes even for two years), the Prophet (SAW) prohibits Muslims from mourning any deceased other than a husband for longer than three days (Bukhari 1994: 324 (ch. 14: 650); see also the Quran 2: 234). Again, Pukhtun families celebrate marriages for over three days, while Al-Huda Bibiane say that the Hadith refers only to two events: the *Nikah* and *Walima* (making no mention of the *Nakreeza* or 'Henna day', celebrated by dancing and singing). It is even claimed that the *Nakreeza* and *kāl* are not Islamic, but derive from Hindu practices.[29] The Pukhto forms of *gham-khādi* and what might be expected of an Islamic pattern of observance, while not antithetically organised, depart from each other at significant points, as illustrated in Table 3.

The contradictory modernity of the reformist Al-Huda school equally promotes extra-domestic contact between women. Insistence on a literal Islam paradoxically binds women to stricter personal ethics and more consistent *purdah*-observance, while allowing greater freedoms of association at religious and religiously

---

[29] The Hindu *sraddhas* is the first year after death followed by 'the annual *sraddhas*' (Kondos 1989: 172).

Table 3 *Gham-khādi* as perceived by Al-Huda Bibiane

Gham-khādi Event	Length of Days	Perceived as
Death (*Gham*)	THREE DAYS EACH	Islamic
Marriage (*Khādi*)		Non-Islamic
Death, *Salwekhtamma*	40 DAYS	Non-Islamic/Pukhto
Birth, *Salwekhtee*		Islamic

sponsored events outside the home. While women cannot attend prayers at outdoor village mosques, in the city large groups of Bibiane may attend the segregated and screened-off upper floor of Islamabad's Faisal Mosque at their discretion. On one occasion, a long train of Bibiane, aged between eighteen and seventy, co-ordinated to pick each other up on their drive to a *dars*.

Differences in expectation between the Frontier and elsewhere enable a skilfully managed range of dress, varied according to implicit religious or social expectation (something I have learned to negotiate myself). Although non-scholarly younger women, accompanied by a male chaperon, loosely practise *purdah* while shopping or with children, Al-Huda students typically veil themselves consistently in Arab-style *hijab*s. One forty-year-old Bibi, ten-years resident in Islamabad, told me how her twenty-year-old daughter chastised her for going about *sartora* (black or bareheaded, connoting nudity or *barband*) without a *sazar* in the village (cf. Mernissi 1985: 144). 'Conservative' dress – a term used in local English – comprises longer shirts and sleeves and higher necklines; in contrast, Al-Huda graduates wear the black *abaya* (cloak), a garment considered Arab rather than Pukhtun in origin, to mark the completion of the one-year course. Paradigmatically, one Bibi in her mid-twenties remarked:

When I am in Islamabad I just wear a coloured veil across my neck which matches my clothes; when I go to Peshawar I wear a *sazar* around my shoulders; when I go further to our *kille* [village], I cover my body, head and face entirely.

This sense of a progressive compromise on characteristic practices, and the ambiguous coincidence of revivalist, new and reiterated cultural forms in the city, leads many Khan-minded Pukhtuns to be wary of translocation altogether. They tend to agglomerate all of the city's features into one perceived threat to 'traditional' Pukhto. Bibiane's debates around translocality, however, are far more nuanced and many-stranded than that suggests.

Socio-political dimensions of gham-khādi

Male faction-building is underpinned by oblique forms of female *zeest-rozgār*. In recent electoral campaigns, Islamabad Bibiane canvassed other female voters in their villages through house visiting, suggesting that the extent of women's agency within the larger national Pukhtun political association has yet to be fully appreciated. Contrarily, the *ezat* of in-married women depends upon their husbands' skill and willingness in ingratiating them with his own relatives, in whose eyes he (as kin, *khpal*) carries more weight. In both micro and macro contexts, then, the house is a political, as well as a social, site. Outside the political context, the individual reputation of particular Bibiane (certain Khans' *kor-wala* or wife) may be known in and beyond the house.

In recent years, characteristically Pukhtun styles of visiting have been modified for specific political activities. With the move to Islamabad, the politicisation of *gham-khādi* and other visits has gathered momentum among men. The brother of a former NWFP Chief Minister, Aziz Khan, from Mardan and a Cambridge University graduate, told me, 'a lot of [*gham-khādi*] has become political'.[30] Liaqat Khan, from Swat, diagnosed a reversal in the relations of precedence between landlords and tenants with democracy, with the Khanān dependent upon the people for votes. He explained: 'In politics, today's votes are bought. Khanān are dependent on people's votes. So they try to keep the people happy by doing *gham-khādi* with them. A hundred years ago there was no need to ask for votes because the land was ours [Khanāns']; today we ask even the *pakeer* [the landless beggars] and the tenants for votes, so we are like the beggars.' Asfandiar Bacha, grandson of the Wali of Swat and the youngest Minister in Pakistan (1998–9), explained in English:

Gham-khādi is the 'backbone', or 'key', to politics in Pukhtun areas. People will vote for me because they are returning a favour when I go to their house to do their *gham-khādi*. As a Minister, I asked my boss [the Chief Minister] permission to take Saturday [a weekday in Pakistan] off to do *gham-khādi*. With Musharraf's dissolving the assembly I still spend two days a week doing people's *gham-khādi*. I limit myself to going for people's *gham*, not *khādi*, because for the people *gham* is more important.

Like Asfandiar Bacha and other influential Pukhtuns in senior government posts, DIG (Deputy Inspector General) Shaukat Khan, who is married to his own cousin, said he did everything in his influence not to be posted out of the Frontier (he has been living in Peshawar for the past decade, a one-hour drive from his village house in Wazirabad) so that his family could maintain *gham-khādi* relationships. Compared to the model of religious leadership exemplified by the Swati saint Saidu Baba, who acquired moral authority by moving away from temporal political concerns, his descendants derive influence by engaging in the everyday political milieu.[31] Another member of the Wali's family, his eldest grandson Adnan Bacha,

---

[30] Barth notes that *gham-khādi* 'form[s] the background for political activity' (1986: 31, 41; see also A. S. Ahmed 1980: 177; Grima 1998: 44). Assuming a historical perspective, Ayesha Jalal observes that in the period from Partition, 1946 to 1957, local issues, not all-India or religious, determined the way the Pukhtuns voted (1985: 171).

[31] On sainthood, moral authority and political leadership during nineteenth-century British rule in Sind, see Ansari 1992; and in the Punjab, Gilmartin 1984: 230. As in Sindh, 'saintly families with very great social and economic landed interests . . . came to wield political power' (Ansari 1992: 159).

a former MNA (Member of National Assembly), also stressed the significance of doing *gham-khādi* in voters' houses. On one occasion, when a villager's cow was sick, Adnan Bacha's political rival came to the villager's home for *tapos*. Adnan Bacha said that when 'vote-time comes, the man tells the local people to vote for him. If they question him, he says: "I did your *gham-khādi*, remember" and they say: "Yes, of course – you have my vote". So how can I compete with a man who extends *gham-khādi* to people's cattle?' Although seemingly trivial, Adnan Bacha is pointing to the deep-rooted significance of *gham-khādi* among villagers who are also political voters. The difference in perceptions of *gham-khādi* among Frontier villagers and largely Western-educated city-based Badshahyān and Khanān is also partly due to a sense of their double-rootedness.

'Double-rootedness'?

In a recondite gloss on Bibiane's theme of 'dual lives', Aziz Khan described his life as one of 'Dr Jekyll and Mr Hyde', because he practised Pukhto in the Frontier and more modern manners in the city. Khanān and Bibiane debate the pros and cons of city life in terms of morality, ethnic authenticity, cultural continuity and convenience. Donnan and Werbner, in their work on Pakistani migration, call translocal living a 'double-rootedness' (1991: 14); Pukhtuns, however, downplay the strength of their affective city roots, which they say are shallow, compared to attachments to their native *kor* (Lindholm1982: 57).

As Ajab Khan remarked earlier in this chapter, Khanān have moved to Islamabad because of their wife's medical needs. Availing oneself of modern social and medical amenities is frequently conceptualised as the loss of a more organic connection with lands and dependents. Older village-bred Bibiane and older *daigāne* protested about their residentially scattered children in the nuclear households of Islamabad ('*zan zani shwa*'). Others remembered the past nostalgically as a period of collectivity and grandeur.[32] The elderly daughter-in-law of one Nawab family from Mardan recalled the village house and *hujra* as a symbol of family *Badshahi* (royalty), saying:

The past was a grand time; there were tremendous *gham-khādi* in the *hujra* and *kor*, thousands of people from all the villages would gather. Those were the days of the Nawabān and Khanān. Now it has changed: all the Khanān have left the village and moved out; there is more independence and less love.

---

[32] The grandiose scale of *gham-khādi* celebrated by Nawab Akbar Khan Hoti in Mardan in a sociopolitical context during twentieth-century British rule is described in the *History of the Hoti Family*, detailing the Nawab's celebration of King George V's Silver Jubilee in an act of 'loyalty' (Hoti n.d.: 60). This *khādi* event was celebrated (at the Nawab's personal expense) on 6 May 1935. The shops in Khwaja Ganj *Bazār* were decorated and illuminated and a large procession of horsemen, decorated camels, boy scouts, schoolboys and dancing girls led the local public of 50,000 men with the gentry in cars. The Nawab supposedly fed some 25,000 people (Muslims, Hindus and Sikhs included). Evening followed with a display of fireworks and continued festive dancing into the night.

The idea that the communal 'love' of reciprocal *gham-khādi* networks has become attenuated was echoed in another Swati Bibi's words: 'my heart is in the *kille-kor*. Our roots, our identity, are there. We are like the royal family there. In Islamabad we are nobody.' Such thinking deploys a nativist rhetoric of identity that looks to preserve a presumed cultural heritage in city conditions: 'The village house', remarked one forty-year-old Swati Bibi, living in Islamabad, 'is like a magnet, my daughter [aged twenty] has that same yearning for Swat as I did when I was her age.'

Speakers in the village context likewise bemoan the exodus of kin to Islamabad. I often heard female members of joint-family households in Mardan utter the common phrase '*tol laroo, kille khwasha sho*' (they've all gone, the village is empty). In these circumstances, *gham-khādi*, as a mode of producing (hierarchical) social relations through ritual, gains an even greater salience as the form reuniting Khanān, Bibiane and villagers. Aziz Khan stated, 'going back for *gham-khādi* is a learning process for our son [aged about thirty-eight], because of whose education we have lived in Islamabad. It has been a wonderful life but it has deprived us of living in our culture [i.e. Pukhto].' He continued: 'Before, we as Khanān were much more available to the common people. But now we have run away to the cities, our *Khani* [authority] and *zmake* [lands] are left behind. So what we were Khanān of is finished.' Voicing resentment at the withdrawal of the Khanān's patronage, the seventy-one-year-old family driver of the Nawabān and Bibiane effectively agreed, 'we are left in *thawān* [loss] and to God's mercy [*ao munga khde tha pathe shoo*]'.

Bibiane further debate the degree to which Islamabad-living weakens their conformity to *Pukhtunwali*. Gulloono, a Mardan Bibi, told me how her family made a conscious effort to remain Pukhtun in an unfamiliar environment:

Living in Islamabad doesn't mean we live like Sindhis and Punjabis who come here. We continue our traditions: we live segregated lives; we don't go to mixed parties because we think we may come across someone we know; we avoid our children's friends' fathers, we just interact with the mothers. If a man visits our house to meet our husbands, we don't come down. So all this is part of our [Pukhto] culture.

Yet these practices are only sporadically being kept up; many Bibiane do 'mix' more widely. Nor are variations in *Pukhtunwali* localised in city and village respectively. A variety of 'modern' modes of consumption and televisual spectatorship, *purdah* observance, inter-gender socialising and *gham-khādi* performance (as shall be discussed in Chapters 3 and 4) are transmitted back from Islamabad to the Frontier. One Bibi acknowledged as much in saying, 'the difference [between village and city] was becoming less'.

Appadurai describes how *rites de passage* 'produce locality' in a world where the notion of neighbourhood is threatened (1986: 180). Khanān and Bibiane return to their ancestral foyer to perform *gham-khādi*. This return reconnects them to their symbolic origin, which grows increasingly complicated as 'locality cannot be taken for granted [since] regular work is needed to maintain it' (ibid.).

This chapter has sought to establish the central importance of everyday living conditions for *gham-khādi* events: that of the village house and sphere of conflictual female relations; of the village community, of partly erased tenant–landlord relationships; and of the multi-ethnic city with its innovative forms of religious and social practices. My account of a range of Bibiane's social activities is intended to demonstrate the inherence of specific *gham-khādi* forms within wider networks of visiting. This observation implicitly supports the local conceptualisation of *gham-khādi* as work. The work of 'making relationships' requires continual negotiation between kin, affines, other Bibiane and 'helpers', within an intrinsically dynamic, domestic space characterised by agnatic and affinal rivalry. The elite Pukhtun *kor* has multiple identities between the constantly shifting male/female, private/public, non-political/political and ceremonial/everyday character of the activities that it hosts. The very layout of the house expresses its status as the site of *gham-khādi*, with storerooms for material trappings, courtyards and a general pattern of gender-segregated spaces. Yet typologies of the house evolve with changing family shapes and translocation. Some *kille-koroona* fall into decay when their families move to Islamabad. The frequency of displacement between the city and village for *gham-khādi* means that Bibiane live 'like modern-day nomads: sometimes we are here, sometimes there'. Yet while this form of mobility ties directly to globalisation, it also suggests continuities with older Pukhtun practices, such as the periodical egalitarian land redistribution (*wesh*) among the Yusufzai (A. S. Ahmed 1976; Barth 1986; Lindholm 1982). In this way, *gham-khādi* as a practice given meaning by migration suggests both the estrangement of Khanān and Bibiane from their ancestral lands and their reconnection with dependents in ceremonies of gifting and cross-class redistribution.

The 'translocality' of elite Pukhtun practices around *gham* and *khādi* makes them a vehicle for the communication of new ideas and goods into remote regions, and the transfer of certain 'conventional' ideas to the city (Edwards 1998: 725). As Donnan and Werbner have written, 'in migration . . . people themselves must manage moral relations spanning great distances and disjunctions of both space and time' (1991: 16). Political and institutional practices, notably those of modern elections, insinuate themselves into 'ordinary' everyday *tlal-ratlal* house hospitality. These new influences make conventional practices simultaneously both new and old, generous and self-interested. The constant need for adjustment in styles of female propriety between sites affects *purdah* observance, dress, comportment and Bibiane's way of life generally (Gilsenan 1990: 12–13 offers a comparison with the Arab case). 'Pukhtun culture is geographical,' says Spongmai, who lives between the Frontier village and Islamabad, 'it is like [having] a double personality. You can take off your *chador*, you can go for drives and movies and then you go back to Swat – you wear your *chador*, you can't go out, you can't go anywhere, you can't go to the *bazār*.'

These contrasting elements construct the 'hybridised' substance of Bibiane's contemporary life. Moving beyond the house for Bibiane, however, should not be understood as their accession to a previously denied agency, but as an extension of their space of agency within the house (Abu-Lughod 1986, 1993a and b, 1998a and b; Nelson 1974; Najmabadi 1998; Tapper 1978). Strathern states powerfully that Hagen women's identity 'as persons does not have to rest on proof that they are powerful in some domain created by themselves, nor in an ability to break free from domestic confines constructed by men' (1984: 18; cf. Devji 1994). Recognising the full extent of Bibiane's *gham-khādi* responsibilities allows us to grant Bibiane a 'quasi-professional status' as household managers, responsible for formal and informal payments to 'helpers' and service providers, and for keeping accounts of inter-family indebtedness (Abu-Lughod 1998a: 12). Translocation to Islamabad potentially heralds a major shift in social organisation for Bibiane, with the emotional and financial complexity of female-household relationships giving way to companionable marriages. Meanwhile, the practical problems of *gham-khādi*, as the next chapter shows, persist. The exploration of burials exemplifies such problems as they reinforce and transform Bibiane's sense of Pukhtun identity.

3
The work of mourning: death and dismay among Bibiane

Mother cares not for the mourning of others; she merely fulfils her obligation to add to the mourners. *(Aday me Gham tasawe wer garmawe)*[1]

At the time of mourning everyone cries for their dead. *(Pa wer ke har sook khpal maree la jaree)*

Without tasting sorrow human experience is incomplete. *(Gham ai na yee, no agha banyadam na de)*

(Pukhto proverbs quoted by Bibiane and 'helpers' during funerals)

This chapter develops the idea of *gham-khādi* as a form of domestic and extra-domestic work in the context of *gham* funerary gatherings. It seeks to present social forms new to Pukhtun anthropology. While describing patterns of funerary practice, this chapter shows how modified religious movements pluralise the enactment of Pukhto. As case studies in this chapter illustrate, young and middle-aged Al-Huda Bibiane graduates, accepting a Muslim 'obligation' to 'command right and forbid wrong', assert independent decision-making in mourning, superseding certain Pukhto concepts of seniority derived from age (*mashartia*). Conventional practices are not rejected wholesale but adapted, sometimes against familial resistance, into greater conformity with 'correct' forms of religion. In exhibiting many of the purportedly essential qualities of *Pukhtunwali* – *purdah* (veiling), *melmastia* (hospitality) and styles of public decorum within a context of agnatic rivalry – *gham* becomes both potentially a site for the reproduction of 'custom' and a privileged female arena where female-sponsored transformations may take hold (see Charles Lindholm on the unique prestige of *gham* (1982: 156); cf. Mahmood 2001).

In this and the next chapter, I describe the participatory acts of guests as meaningful expressions of the work of *gham-khādi* for Bibiane, as these acts affirm social relationships. At death the Pukhtun body is laid to rest in the village soil, with burial drawing Islamabad-residing Bibiane and their families back to the village house (*kille-kor*) in a symbolic and real linkage with their origins

---

[1] Tair and Edwards 1982: 16.

(Plate 15).[2] A large body of anthropological literature suggests that funerals reaffirm social connections, but must also deal with death in its negative aspect of disruption and loss. I am interested in drawing on these texts, not for their treatment of the cosmological or eschatological ideas (see Hertz 1960; Malinowski 1982) of various societies, but rather for their representation of mourning as a social act, in which different categories of mourners behave in ways distinct from the wider community.[3] This emphasis, following local ideas in devolving concerns with an afterlife to Islam, yields another set of theoretical issues from the arguably dominant approaches to death within anthropology (see Bloch 1971; Bloch and Parry 1989) or (Hindu) South Asian ethnography (see Parry 1989). In the context of an argument about the relevance of concepts of 'pollution' to Muslims, Das suggests a comparable shift of attention away from the conceptualisation of death to 'the grief of the mourners and the "work" of mourning' (1986: 182; see also Tapper and Tapper 1986; Vogel comparably points to the etymology of 'liturgy' as 'the work of the people' (2000: 7)). My account of *gham* attempts in this way to characterise the occasion's complex sociality, as constituted in a differentiation of levels of participation between attenders. For Das, the possibility of different (or graduated) mourning activities mediates two axiomatic but inadequate understandings of death, which view it as entirely continuous with life or as entirely disjunctive from it. Yet these ideas pertain more to the political ideologies (say, of a timeless order: Bloch and Parry 1989), than to forms of sociality which ordinarily arise around the commemoration of death. A more fruitful line of enquiry in relation to *gham* thus 'conceptualize[s] . . . mourners as having the structure of a heterogeneous rather than a homogeneous totality' (ibid.: 197), allowing us to make 'connections between individual grief and societal patterns of mourning' (ibid.).

Attention to these patterns captures the agency of a range of class of social person over the initial three days. The bereaved family gains credit for hosting a large event (close kin households contribute to the payment for the large meals that feed the guests and poor); Bibiane discharge reciprocal obligations and consolidate bonds with bereaved and other attending women; and the village poor benefit from the disbursement of food and charity. Some anthropologists argue that death breaches the social fabric (or implicit ideology: see Bloch 1996; Tapper and Tapper 1986: 87), and needs the repair of particular ritual procedures. In contrast, Pukhtuns think death reaffirms certain fundamental constituents of Pukhto through orchestrating them socially. (An individual may have died, but his/her *gham-khādi* network springs up intact.) Bibiane (especially) perform their grief in socially productive ways through the collective performances of mortuary

---

[2] On Turkish burial in the native soil next to kin, see Delaney 1991: 'to be buried elsewhere is to be consigned to eternal *gurbet* (exile)' (311); cf. Fazila-Yacoobali 1999: 186. For the Lugbara, 'the good death' falls amidst ancestral shrines, while 'bad death' occurs away from home (Bloch and Parry 1989: 16).

[3] Van Gennep describes mourning as 'a transitional period for survivors, enter[ed] through rites of separation and emerge[d] from through rites of reintegration' (1977: 147).

ceremonies. In claiming the emotions for anthropology, Lutz challenges dominant ideas that construe emotions as irrational, child-like, inferior, devalued and predominantly feminine (1986). Like Lutz, I interpret the varying mourning behaviours (of affines, dependents, village-women, professional mourners) of *gham* participants as 'taught' and not always 'natural', thus having some of the character of work (cf. Grima 1998: 16; Lindholm 1988: 231). At funerals, Bibiane express their sorrow through understood decorums, which vary according to their degree of familial and social closeness to the deceased. Personal and family interests at *gham* influence spontaneous feeling, while emotional prostration may alternate with resentment or boredom. The composed appearance expected of Bibiane is difficult to sustain during extended funerary events, which last beyond three initial days of close contact to weekly, monthly and yearly anniversaries, and – in terms of relations with the bereaved family – indefinitely into the future.

The sequence of *gham*

I begin with an account of sequenced events that describe accepted behaviours for specific occurrences. Funerary ceremonies are always carried out over a period of three days in the deceased's Frontier village house, with anniversaries marking every Friday until the fortieth day after death (the *Salwekhtamma*). This anniversary is also commemorated during the first *Akhtar* (Eid, Islamic festival) and after one or, in some cases, two years (*kāl*). A large number of people (ranging between 200 to 2,000) attend these funerals. *Khairat* (the *gham-khādi* meal) is distributed to the entire community, particularly the poor and guests on the ceremonial days and also on Fridays (*Jumme*) until the fortieth day of mourning. All Pukhtun relatives and those with whom one does *gham-khādi* are expected to attend the first three days, and then to return to the village house each Friday until a forty-day period has elapsed, to attend the *Salwekhtamma*, and to gather in the village house (*kille-kor*) after a year (*kāl*). Among Bibiane, close family members and friends stay in the *kille-kor* for forty days (till the *Salwekhtamma*). Maids also participate; some live in the house for longer than forty days and are relied upon (*etabar*) as *khpal* (relatives) of the afflicted Bibiane. Funerals usually impose the stipulation that family members of the deceased refrain from attending *khādi* events such as weddings, engagements and birthdays (but not births) until a year (*kāl*) or two have passed (*thleen*).[4] A Pukhto proverb states, 'When there is death, there is no *khādi* [joy]' (*che marg shta khādi neeshta*; Tair and Edwards 1982: 148). Though the passage of a year is marked as a formal event that officially

---

[4] Cf. Ansari 1992: 72; Das 1986: 196; and Metcalf 1982: 19. Among Bibiane, mourning is expressed by abstinence from events and things seen as symbols of happiness. A Mardan Bibi said she mourned her father-in-law's death for a year avoiding other weddings, while his daughters observed *gham* for two years. When she attended her cousin's wedding the guests there asked her why she had come when her sisters-in-law were still mourning: 'I said, the bride is my first cousin and I am *majboora* [obliged].' Another Mardan Bibi said that after her father's brother's death her family marked the mourning by not watching television for six months.

closes the period of death, in some families in both Swat and Mardan the day of the death is marked annually by a charity meal. Charles Lindholm notes that some families in Swat may even hold *thleen* (or '*tlin*') every year for a decade (1982: 158). This extended, obligatory and highly formalised pattern of Pukhtun funerals (*gham*) constitutes an established and pervasive convention for Bibiane's families and more generally for Pukhtuns; this commemoration is widely perceived as 'doing Pukhto'.[5] Participation and travel to and from the various events place great strains on Bibiane and their households, particularly on pregnant and nursing mothers, elderly Bibiane and children left in 'the house of *gham*' *(de gham kor)* from morning (10 am) till night (*maghreb*: after sunset). Bibiane returning from Islamabad come under particular pressure to behave appropriately in accordance with a more village concept of Pukhto. Respect to elder sisters-in-law and other affines, and propriety in *purdah* (wearing full-sleeved *kameezoona* and the *sazar*), is demanded. Yet some middle-aged and young educated Bibiane increasingly criticise the extended conventional pattern of *gham*, by calling for more rational, voluntary and Islamic practices.

My characterisation of *gham* events is elaborated in the form of a time-line.[6] An ongoing *gham-khādi* relationship is expressed by an enquiry visit (*tapos*) to someone who is ill (*najora*), and whose death in old age is anticipated. Friends and family fulfil *tapos* obligations in the ill person's house or hospital room (if the person, particularly an elderly Bibi, is in Islamabad). This is a preliminary step to observing *gham*. *Tapos* visits meet an obligatory *tlal-ratlal* pattern of reciprocity in hosting. These visits are incumbent on both men and women (cf. Abu-Lughod 1986: 67), but the primary burden of enquiry falls on women, who see sick female relatives in person. There is a wide array of reasons for undertaking *tapos* visits such as for accidents, miscarriages, even robbery. A variant of *tapos* is to enquire about a girl for marriage. In illness, however, the immediate female relatives (wives, sisters, daughters, mother, aunts and sisters-in-law) of the sick person take turns to care for him/her who must also receive constant and unannounced guests. When the sick person is a man, visitors usually consult his female family members, who stay by his side, even in the city hospital (Grima 1998: 92); in villages Bibiane are barred from visiting hospitals due to segregation, and instead visit female relatives of the patient at his or her house. Grima argues that *tapos* visits for men are less onerous a social procedure: 'simply a casual inquiry after someone, performed in a public space like the *bazār* or tea shop, with no ritual' (1998: 86). In fact, present-day Bibiane and their husbands (with Bibiane specially veiled in a *sazar* for the occasion) typically visit as couples. On arrival they may go to the door of the patient's room, knock and wait outside, then on directions from the sick person's kin, proceed to separate, gendered waiting rooms. In Pakistan, visiting

---

[5] Funerary ceremonies up to the fortieth day are also central to Punjabi Muslim ceremonies, even though they are not stressed as ethnic markers (see Shaw 2000).

[6] In this respect, the ordering of ceremonies in terms of 'stipulated' procedures of 'archetypal' elements, constitutively observed as the social form of *gham* events, fulfils at least two axiological perquisites of 'ritual' as defined by Humphrey and Laidlaw (1994: 88–9).

hours accommodate conventional visiting practices so that family members may tend a patient all day. Bibiane doing *tapos* will enter the female patient's room. The sick remain in bed, but may offer Bibiane who come and go throughout the day drinks and fruit. Bibiane's husbands accumulate in the lobby (if, however, the patient is in intensive care, both sexes may gather in separate spaces of the waiting room). In families whose *purdah* practices are relatively relaxed, the sick person's female and male relatives meet in the patient's room sitting on the chairs and floor mattresses. Absence (without adequate reason such as illness) from a *tapos* visit is taken as intentional, or an example of 'avoidance', and risks the severing of future relations. Bibiane describe *tapos* as both compelled by social expectation and religiously enjoined (*sawāb*) by Hadith.[7] Servants, especially long-standing maids, proved to be particularly observant informants about family participation as indexed by *tapos* attendance: one fifty-year-old maid classified after-comers attending the *gham* after missing the *tapos* as '*baharanai khaz[e]*' (outside or insignificant women) at the funeral, 'even if they were as close as aunts or cousins'.

Relatives of the dying person (*zankadan*) undertake different levels of work to prepare for the death. This may include a preparation of emotions and mind, in which family members reconcile themselves to the event. More practically, they prepare the *kille-kor* for the public ceremony. In the case of unexpected death, as in cases of suicide (of which there were three among Khanān and Badshahyān during my fieldwork (see Yusufzai 2000)), or accidents involving a young person or a child, mourners may typically say: '*Ai-hai*! [Alas!] s/he did not have a "full life"; s/he wasn't even ill so that we could have prepared ourselves for the death!' In a contrasting instance, the family members of a twenty-one-year-old Bibi who had suffered from a prolonged bout with cancer, told those doing condolence (*afsos*) with them that her illness had allowed them to be 'mentally prepared' (said in English). In laying out the house of death (*de gham kor*), it is widely held among Bibiane that daughters are 'too close' (*neezde*) to the deceased to offer practicable hospitality – their place is to mourn, not work. Thus daughters-in-law, whose *khoog* (hurt) supposedly does not penetrate so deep, do most of the necessary work. In the case of one expected death in Islamabad (of a seventy-year-old Bibi who had slipped into a coma on a life-support machine), the daughters-in-law packed their own suitcases, left their children in the care of maids and husbands, and drove to their affinal village house to prepare the house for death. Arriving in late evening, they opened the locked rooms and windows of the village house for airing and instructed the male servants, from behind the walls, to summon the morning caterers and arrange the rental of chairs, *shamiane* (courtyard tents), tables and crockery in anticipation of hundreds of mourners. Under these circumstances, the Bibiane also authorised payment from the joint family income.

---

[7] Bukhari 1994: 935 (ch. 5: 1,956). Quoting the Hadith, Bibiane widely say during *tapos* visits that illness purifies from sins (ibid.: 934 (ch. 1: 1,949)). Yet *gham*, due to its sorrowful nature, is carefully concealed from persons who are not obliged to attend, for example the young, the sick and outsiders (see Grima 1998: 88).

In conceptualising the 'work' of *gham-khādi*, at one level, it is important to note the genuine materiality and effortfulness of female labour – house preparation (keeping in mind the large spaces of village houses and their rooms) includes Bibiane's work of opening storerooms and trunks to air a substantial quantity of white sheets, bedding, quilts (*brasthanne*), prayer mats and towels. Work also includes supervising the maids' jobs of washing bathrooms and of sweeping and dusting all spaces used in the *gham*, many of which will be required for nursing, childminding, resting and prayers. Bibiane, who may remain in their 'old clothes' (their previous day's clothes) as a sign of full involvement, perform a great deal of preparatory organisation (which may include cleaning and dusting). They pay special attention to the space to which the body will return, which may be either the centre courtyard (common in Swat) or else the living-room (as in Mardan). The women must be able to gather around the coffin or *kat* (straw bed). If the body is laid indoors, furniture may be moved and white sheets spread over the entire carpeted floor. A few personal rooms and belongings are often locked away, as the house becomes a segregated public space and may be used indifferently by the guests.

Following death, the *gham-kor* is opened to rich and poor members of the village and other Pukhtuns with whom the family has *gham-khādi* reciprocal ties. At this point the segregated spaces of the house – the *kor* for women and the *hujra* for men – are designated as public but strictly gendered spaces. Male family members, previously allowed in the *kor*, are barred from it. As the community is reimagined as an enlarged, and equally suffering, family, family members are absorbed into this wider corporate body for the initial period of the mourning.[8] From the first announcement of death and burial-time over the village mosque loudspeaker, Bibiane begin phoning relatives locally, nationally and internationally, and connected family groupings begin to arrive at the *kille-kor*. On the way to one Bibi's funeral (that of the daughter of President Ayub Khan and wife of the heir apparent of the Wali of Swat), in the back of a car driven by her husband, a relative Bibi of the deceased remarked to me in English:

All the people of the village will come because, like when a royalty dies in England, everyone would want to offer condolences. In England there are restrictions and the public cannot enter Buckingham Palace, but in Swat it is the opposite, the house is open to the people, so everyone will come.

Indeed, Pukhtuns of all social backgrounds and non-Pukhtun friends are expected to immediately drop everything and see the face of the deceased (*makh kathal*), thereby registering the reality of their demise. Many Bibiane told me that if 'you do *kille* [literally, 'village', here implying the upkeep of social relations] with someone, you have to go immediately for their *gham-khādi* [event] because it is

---

[8] On communal aspects of Punjabi funerals, see Shaw 2000. For a comparison of the communal and public aspect of death in Borneo, see Metcalf 1982: 105. Cf. Huntington and Metcalf 1980: 102.

in death that you can judge who your *khpal* [closest] people are'.[9] The first day of death is the most important. When close relatives or children of a deceased woman do not make the first day, for valid reasons (for instance, being abroad at the time of a death), guests often say with great pity: 'Alas! she did not see her mother's face' (*ai-hai! de mor makh a wanakatho*).[10]

With the relocation of so many Bibiane and their families to Islamabad, procedures have been devised for the immediate return of the body to the familial village house via ambulance.[11] A cortège of cars drives from the city to the female section of the village house in an order determined by seniority, with *masharān* leading 'youngers', even when these are adult sons of the deceased and their wives. A large cohort of ululating women greet the corpse, regardless of its gender, which is then laid on a *kat* (straw bed) surrounded by as many as a thousand women straining for a glance of the deceased's face (cf. Darish 1989: 130, 133; and Metcalf 1982: 37). As Bibiane arrive throughout the day, they leave their children and maids in a designated room (children often cling to the mother's side, while mothers are themselves under pressure and anxious to fulfil their obligations). Mourners then proceed to offer their condolences to the closest female members of the deceased. The deceased's wife, daughters, mother and sisters sit on the floor by the body and touch its head, hands or feet (the body of a person who has died by accident, suicide or illness is not displayed).[12] Daughters of the deceased remain seated, while daughters-in-law may stand to receive guests and see to their comfort and needs. With each arrival of a close relative, women renew their wailing; some village-women strike their chests and temples, while other women restrain their hands; the mourners reply with cries of '*pre me da!*' (leave me!). The closer the mourner is to the deceased, the louder the crying on her arrival (Grima 1998: 58–63). Through this period, the *kor* is for the women participants transformed into a scene of turmoil (cf. Bloch 1996: 215).

Men's mourning space is confined to the *hujra* where guests sit on chairs or stand and may discuss various socio-political and economic issues; in contrast, the women, in the *kor*, mourn through emotional and bodily involvement, sitting on floor-mattresses and white sheets in positions of unaccustomed discomfort. Bibiane remove their shoes before entering the room and some hold up their hands in prayer (*lās niwa*) before gathering around the body. The lying-in room is conceived as a place of purity; it later hosts prayer and the women's collective consumption of the

---

[9] Local concepts of '*khpal*' may include wide and extended networks of people including non-related people (fictive kin) who may be called '*khpal*' due to mutually good relations and ongoing *gham-khādi* reciprocity. This relationship is locally termed *khpalwali*.

[10] On the importance of funeral ceremonies in maintaining translocal links among other ethnolinguistic groups, such as the Punjabis, see Shaw 2000.

[11] Women of poor *zamindar* (farmer) families working in Islamabad told me that they hired the 'flying coach' (van) for the return of their dead to their village home.

[12] Accidental or youthful death is seen as amounting to martyrdom (*shahid*) and deserving of paradise (*jannat*). Women always remember the good and talk well of a deceased person (even if the relationship between them was a hostile one). When the news of a person's death is first released it is said that s/he has reached the truth (God) (*agha haq waraseda/o*).

evening meal.[13] Bibiane see themselves as central by virtue of their proximity to the body, and its visibility. Men's position in the *hujra* is apparently comparatively marginal.

The body in the *kor* is dressed for burial according to decorum. The head is carefully covered in a continuation of *purdah* observance, with a *topai* (cap) for the male corpse and a veil for the female (see also Naveed-i-Rahat 1990: 110; Papanek 1982: 11). The clothed body is further covered in layers of white bed sheets, blankets and quilts. If the deceased is male, his body is washed by the village mullah and several of his own personal male servants. In contrast, companion-maids or *weenze maraee* (who may have bathed her during illness) see to a woman's corpse; more recently, relatives (daughters-in-law, sisters-in-law) have taken on a decisive role in directing this aspect of the work of mourning. Bathing is performed in a manner comparable to ablution for purity and prayers (*awdas-charadam, wadu*). Between three to seven ablutions lave the entire body, requiring several new bars of soap (*sabun*), scent and oil; black *ranja* (kohl), in the case of women, is applied to the eyes and sometimes eyebrows. The washed hair is braided in three plaits and wrapped in several layers of white cotton cloth.[14] Cotton wool is placed in the nostrils and orifices, before the prepared body is laid in a *kaffan* (coffin). The surrounding women may bend over the body of an elder and say, '*ombarak sha*' (congratulations), on having lived a 'complete life' (*poora jwand*). Strikingly, *khādi* ceremonies (centrally births and weddings) are the only other occasions on which the phrase is uttered, suggesting that death is subsumed into a more integral understanding of the life-cycle (*gham-khādi*).

The order of *gham* ceremonies both conforms to and diverges from *Pukhtunwali* gender norms. Grima asserts that women mourn by violating *purdah* (by casting off their veil (1998: 39)). Bibiane, however, carefully observe *purdah* on the first day of the funeral. The agitation displayed in the *kor* contrasts with the more sober and controlled actions of the men in the *hujra*. These gendered spaces are, however, trespassed during the Pukhtun burial procedure. Around four o'clock in the evening of the first day before *makham moonz* (fourth prayer), about ten to fifteen of the deceased's close male family members enter the *kor* even though many women there, particularly in Mardan, would normally be sequestered from them. The men and women do not speak to each other. The men instead cover the *kaffan* with another cloth (often green and embossed with Quranic verses), and stand in place to lift it away. The women begin to wail loudly, as they realise that the body is about to be borne out of their arena. Close female relatives tear at the *kaffan* cloth from all sides. Some women throw themselves upon the corpse, while

---

[13] Contrastingly, on female pollution through proximity to corpses, see Bloch 1996; Huntington and Metcalf 1980: 64; on the corpse as both pure and polluting, see Parry 1989: 79.

[14] *Da oobo na oobasee* is the Pukhto phrase meaning, 'to take out of water' or to bathe the body. On water as purifier and indicator of 'change of state', see Metcalf 1982: 145, 147, 151. Among Pukhtuns, water (bath: *lāmbal*; or '*pāk*-bath' in convent English) indicates ablution at significant *gham-khādi* or life phases: before five daily prayers; at marriage, after the fortieth day of birth; on becoming a *dai* (wet-nurse); after menstruation, sexual contact and at death.

men hurriedly push the *kaffan* free. Women who otherwise express the greatest care over their deportment now struggle bodily against the pall-bearers. In this short dramatic sequence, boundaries between male and female, *kor* and *hujra*, norm and exception, and this life and the next momentarily dissolve. For the Bibiane, who are prohibited from attending the interment, the bearing of the body from the *kor* indicates the deceased's social death.[15]

The rituals of the first day of a funeral end with a meal, cooked, prepared and served on behalf of close kin to guests and the village poor. Styles of consumption vary according to family relationship to the deceased and understood social position. Though wealthier guests (as *mara* (satisfied) people) take food, there is an underlying sense that eating in the house of the dead is shameful for Bibiane, befitting only the poor (*wúge* (hungry) people).[16] Bibiane are served meals first, and accept them under duress. Such 'formality' or '*sath*' leaves food on the table, which is then descended upon by village-women and children, who conceal plastic bags of leftovers under *sazare* to take back to their homes. The bereaved (widow, daughters, mother and sisters of the deceased) refuse food entirely, rejecting the persistent offers of relatives with the words '*zra me mor de*' (my heart is full) with '*khabgaan*' (sadness) (Lupton 1996: 36).[17] This rejection of food accords the emotions a measure of rationality or social sense in Pukhtun contexts. After the evening meal and prayer, messages will be sent for Bibiane through maids by husbands and sons, and most women disperse. Bibiane are picked up at the entrances of the *dewdai* along with children and maids with ideally as little *purdah* violation as possible. A small number of 'close' Bibiane (according to socio-familial relations, including women from the mother's side, father's side, husband's mother's side, husband's father's side, offspring, their spouses and families, and offspring's offspring and their spouses) stay with the bereaved relatives in the *kor*. The presence of twenty to fifty such women, who will reminisce about the deceased, is considered healing. One Bibi, whose father died, remarked, 'women's talk during *gham* distracts from the loss and diverts the thoughts'.

The customary second day of *gham* begins with the ten o'clock arrival of the guests who were present on the first day. This day is often marked by a *qul*, or Quranic *khattam*, reading of the Quran (Dube 1969: 52). In the living-room or veranda, large clean white sheets are laid over the floors, and trays of date stones and beads are placed in the centre for the telling of short verses (see Gellner 1993: 143). A group of elderly Bibiane and a few younger women sit in a circle, systematically reciting. Other Bibiane simultaneously read the entire thirty *siparas*

---

[15] On male Pukhtun death and burial, see Lindholm 1982: 156–8; Singer 1982: 135–6. Cf. Delaney 1991: 313; Jeffery 1979: 21.

[16] I was told that the people of Buner (south of Swat) do not eat in the house of the deceased and take their own tea to the *hujra* because: 'the food cooked in the house of the deceased is forbidden, "*harām*"'.

[17] This phrase is also used in a context of extreme anger and interpersonal dissatisfaction '*zre me te mor sho*', signifying a desire to break off relations. In some parts of Swat the deceased's immediate family and sometimes the entire village is obliged to fast for three days (Lindholm 1982: 157).

of the Quran. Some women look on and talk; others excuse themselves as '*napāk*' (unclean, or in a state of menstruation). The effort of recital is understood as redounding to the *sawāb* (religious merit) of the departing soul of the deceased. Meals mark the end of rituals and the (second) day.

The third day of mourning, the '*thdrayemma*' (from *thdray*, third), is less intense for the bereaved and other mourners. One woman who had lost her mother told me that the first day of a *gham* is like fire (*wor*), the second like burning coal (*skara*) and the third ash (*heera*) (cf. Huntington and Metcalf 1980: 105). With the exception of the widow and daughters, the Bibiane sometimes dispense with the *sazar* on the third day and wear colourful clothing and light jewellery, such as diamond earrings and gold bangles. While older women and a few younger women (including those both with and without Al-Huda training) adhere to covering the head, others intentionally remove the veil as a mark of informality. On one of my *lās niwa* visits that occurred on the third day of a death, I wore the *sazar* over my head in accordance with the decorum of a reputedly 'conservative' Pukhtun family; a young married Bibi from another family immediately asked, 'Where is your *loopata* [chiffon veil]?' When I answered, 'In the car,' she said, 'On the third day you should not wear a *sazar* over your head, just a veil [across the neck]; can you see anyone with a *sazar* except older women and maids?' Though (self-)authorised to impose moral decisions and determine meanings, this young woman saw herself as imparting advice to a 'friend', rather than treating a guest uncivilly. On the third day following death, friends and relatives, especially those who live abroad and meet only during collective *gham* or *khādi* gatherings, express their feelings with less restraint. Groups of women and girls may joke, gossip and even laugh aloud.[18] After the evening meal and prayer, guests return to their home cities and villages (as far as six hours away). The immediate family of the deceased remain in the *kille-kor* for forty days. On departure, other guests are reminded to return for the consecutive *Jumme* (Fridays) and particularly for the Fortieth day, or *Salwekhtamma*.

The *Salwekhtamma* is customarily marked by the gathering of people and a *khairat* feast for the poor, signalling the end of relatives' confinement to the *kor* (Metcalf 1982: 261). One Khan told me that he registered his father's death only after the forty days and the formal departures of the mourners. Unlike the first unrestricted three days of death, families increasingly invite people to the *Salwekhtamma* by phone. The bereaved speak fondly of those who make the effort to attend. Conversely, they criticise non-attenders openly and retaliate by not reciprocating their *gham-khādi*. Though the *Salwekhtamma* is thought of as a Pukhto rather than Islamic practice, people put themselves out to attend, knowing the offence that omission would cause.

Pukhtun Bibiane also commemorate the year anniversary (*kāl, thleen*), which ends familial *khādi* prohibitions and closes the socially demarcated mourning

---

[18] Charles Lindholm goes so far as to describe funerals as 'a vacation for [women]' (1982: 156); cf. Huntington and Metcalf 1980: 2.

period (Metcalf 1982: 262). Guests are invited by word of mouth or telephone, and the village house is prepared for hospitality. *Shamiane* are put in the courtyards, and caterers set chairs and tables for the *khairat* meal. Men dress in clean white clothes; women wear sombre colours but expensive materials. A Quranic *khattam* is carried out with date seeds on white sheets in the *kor*. Women collectively lift their palms and bless the deceased on completion of each prayer. Bibiane and their families also return to village houses for the festival of *Akhtar* (the two Eids celebrating the Abrahamic sacrifice, and the end of fasting in the month of Ramadan), with the family reunion after death explicitly styled as an act of remembrance.

Decorum and expression in *gham*

Pukhtun funerals demand certain behaviours from men, women, family and villagers, who enact the work of *gham-khādi*. 'Work' in the local usage refers to both enacted emotion and physical effort. Das's theory of the heterogeneous structure, or collectivity, of mourners allows us to determine 'the structure behind ... spontaneous and often unbearable expressions of personal sorrow' (1986: 188), as people behave in ways acceptable on the basis of their social relationship with the dead. Within such a structure, or at least formalised articulation of relationships, kin may injure themselves mildly; sisters-in-law look after guests, and visitors sustain a level of decorum at all times. Those who fail to adopt an appropriate demeanour or social understanding of the collaborative labour of 'making' the ceremony risk being dismissed behind their backs as *lewanai* or *kamaql* (mad, senseless). Within the normal allocation of roles, though, there is scope for individual variation in social manoeuvring.

On entering the *gham-kor*, Bibiane usually announce themselves with '*salām-a-laikum*' (peace be with you), to which the reply is '*walaikum-salām*' (and peace be on you). Yet in certain conditions of personal and familial conflict or in the extremity of grief, salutations are avoided. Closely related Bibiane may express the depth of their sorrow through the negation of greeting, making their way to the closest female relative of the deceased, embracing them and crying aloud with them. Women bow their heads to each other's shoulders, muffling their sobs. This restrained expression of grief is considered dignified, and forges bonds to the family afflicted by *gham*. Abu-Lughod notes in relation to crying:

Not only may such shared emotional experiences enhance the sense of identification that underpins social bonds, but participation in rituals that express sentiments might also generate feelings like those the person directly affected is experiencing, thus creating an identification between people where it did not spontaneously exist. (1986: 69)

Through *gham*, individuals of both sexes create ties of obligation, responsibility and care. Both strategy (in the Barthian sense) and disinterest may come into play. Among the whole gathering of mourning women in the *kor*, there are also 'sub-groups' and sub-networks of *gham-khādi* to which individual Bibiane are affiliated in multiple, sometimes entangled ways. Bibiane of all ages will be thoughtful not only of the closest mourner (widow, daughter, mother of the deceased) to whom she will incline herself in *dua* or *lās niwa* (prayer), but also of various women with whom, on the basis of family connection, she will normally sit throughout the day. Women swathed in white *sazare* and bowed under the pressures of distress, exhaustion, hunger and the anxieties of social conformity throng the *kor* during women's *gham*. 'Extreme' or 'symbol[ically] excess[ive]' female mourning behaviour – loud weeping, the beating of breasts and fainting – both participates in a religious or cosmological understanding – conjoining the states of life and death (Das 1986: 197) – and 'produces' grief socially. *Gham* is an occasion which is like typologically similar *gham-khādi*, and reasserts ethnic continuity through and against the deceased's death. In this sense, the hosting role played by widows remains paramount. '[T]hose most affected by the death are drawn into the centre of the community when they might otherwise feel most impelled to renounce it' (Durkheim, in Giddens 1978: 96). She may stand in the centre of hundreds of women, receive female relatives' *gham-khādi* money and answer the enquiries about the manner of her husband's death.

The sense of social discrimination as it exists around the display of grief and fortitude is very precise (see Das 1986: 196 on 'the differential symbolic functions of . . . family mourners and professional mourners'). In bereavement, Pukhtun women often engage in a ritualised funeral lament known as *ghare* (dirge) (cf. Huntington and Metcalf 1980: 74). In one *dai*'s funeral, the daughters of the deceased intoned in Pukhto, '*ya zama khdaya*' (Oh my God) (this is repeated in extended phrasal units), '*Alai zama khwaga mor mra shwa, ya moro pasa sta melmana chak chapera raghale dee* [Alas, my sweet mother is dead. Oh mother, arise, your guests have come, standing all around you].' Even in death, the necessities of hospitality in hosting are not forgotten. This chanted lament was intermitted with weeping and comparatively shorter chants, repeated in intense and sustained cycles:

We all depended on *Moro* [mother]; father was not so strong [*kamzora*]. We all gathered around mother. But now what will happen to us? And what will become of father? And what of Akhtar Ali, our youngest brother? *Ya Khdaya, ya Khdaya* [Oh God, oh God]. He said he would never live without our mother. But look! He lives. And so do we. *Ya Khdaya, ya Khdaya*. You should have taken me instead of our mother. You could have waited till all her children were married. She has unmarried children! And what of them? *Ya Khdaya, ya Khdaya*. Now who can I call '*Moro*'? *Ya zama Khdaya* [Oh my God], she was my mother as well as my father.

Such formulae are often personalised for the deceased through the insertion of short anecdotes adverting to those left behind. Women who might otherwise keep *purdah* of the voice now express grief, sadness, vulnerability and dependency in a segregated public context (cf. Abu-Lughod 1986: 198). Propriety, however, still governs the expression of grief as it relates to class position. I have seen poor women perform relatively more intense *ghare* than Bibiane, who rather than wailing and beating themselves are more likely to cry, faint or talk about their grief and loss. In the funerals of Bibiane, professional female mourners perform the most demonstrative dirge. Bibiane who cry excessively during the funeral are reminded to endure with patience (*sabar*) and to accept God's will (*qismat*), as relatives and guests, referring to the death, say, 'it is God's work' (*de Khde Pāk kār de*) (see A. S. Ahmed 1991: 261).

Men's expression of grief is characteristically more muted but those who cry in public at the time of taking away their mother's body from the women's space, for example, are discussed by the female spectators as having a *kamzora zre* (weak heart) (cf. Das 1986: 198; Grima 1998: 61; Lindholm 1982: 156). For men, regardless of their personal grief, 'immobility and silence are the only languages available' (Das 1986: 198). For women – as in *ghare* or spoken words in death – speeches become ritualised as they invoke repeatable verse-forms and set phrases. Both sexes, however, are expected to avoid laughter in mourning, which is emphasised in the following verse by Rehman Baba (n.d.), a renowned Pukhtun poet (cf. Bowen 1982: 13):

> What happened to those handsome people . . .
> I cannot laugh with those around me
> I'm mourning those departed people
> (from *Waste*. Enevoldsen 1993: 83)

Those who laugh inappropriately at funerals may be remembered critically for a long time. In one case, an elderly woman called 'Aunty' by Bibiane, the daughter of a powerful *dai* (wet-nurse), whispered to me about how an elder, Jahan Bibi, had acted with little social sense (*kamaql*) and breached the mourning code. 'Aunty' remembered the forty-year-old incident, where a child had died from the family into which Jahan Bibi was married, and Jahan Bibi had been seen talking and laughing (*khandal*) during the first day of the funeral:

Thousands of people had collected in the village house [*khalak raghwand shoo*], there was tremendous crying! But Jahan Bibi lacked understanding, she was laughing! A *kamaql* [senseless] person laughs, she did not consider the propriety of the event [*kamaqla wa dase a khandal. Napoyeda, kamaqla banda khandee – mauke ta a na katal*]. In *gham*, you are supposed to show *khabgan* [sadness]! It made me so angry that I told *mashra* Bibi [the elder Bibi of the deceased's house]: What sort of a *khaza* [woman] is this! She is laughing' [*da sanga khaza da, da kho khandee*]!

Even the slightest deviation from decorum – a smile, for instance – may be misconstrued as an expression of happiness during the mourning period. This exposes in-married younger Bibiane to the '*peeshare*' (mocking) of affines and observers. The place of new in-married women like Jahan Bibi is particularly uncertain, as they are not yet emotionally attached to their in-laws' 'hurt' (*khoog*), and they have not yet established *gham-khādi* relations as a means of building their own social standing.

Bibiane require much self-control to profess the appropriate and expected emotions over the initial three days of a funeral. The Pukhto proverb, 'people weep, but the damsel laughs' (*khalak jaree, kho peghla khandi*: Tair and Edwards 1982: 191), reflects a distinction between the uncultivated behaviour of youth and the developed social sense (*aql*) inculcated with age. In this context, feigned emotions enjoin the precepts of religious and cultural *aql*; they 'serve a legitimate end, for the Prophet [SAW] himself taught that one should pretend to weep if one did not do so naturally, in order to cultivate the appropriate emotion' (Metcalf 1984a: 10). Bibiane described this mindful simulation as onerous (*grana da*). Funerals are occasions on which members of an extended family may see their relatives and friends after long periods, sometimes years, of intermission. While the first day is grave, succeeding days are characterised by the sadness of the occasion and the underlying excitement of the reunion. Bibiane's skill in carrying themselves at the formal *gham* thus relates to their ability to evade the proscriptive attention of 'society' to engage meaningfully with distant friends and cousins.

Different voices respond to the pressures of *gham* by counselling some form of reversion to scripture. Asma, a convent-educated Bibi, now in her mid-forties, with a diploma from Al-Huda, told me at a funeral in Mardan: 'A man's *lāsh* [Urdu: corpse] should be brought to the men's space, not the women's; the burial should be quick, and the time-span cut short so that people don't have time to laugh and "do fashion". When *gham* goes on beyond three days, it turns into one big party: people laugh, joke and feast' (cf. Drucker-Brown 1982: 714). Asma's words reflect debates about the length of Pukhtun mourning and its violation of the three days prescribed by Islam. Bibiane hold varied opinions about these issues. On the fortieth day of a funeral in which I participated, many of the female guests sat in sub-groups, while certain village-women proficiently performed the Quranic *khattam*. Small verses were read over date seeds in order to keep count of the recitation. In contrast to the hundreds of Bibiane sitting in the courtyard, only twelve married Bibiane of various ages from twenty-three to sixty-five took part in the read-through. The elderly Bibiane were from the local village, while the Bibiane aged between twenty-three and forty-five had returned from Islamabad. One of the village-women, a professional mourner, raised her voice and sang in Pukhto during a moment of silence:

Where are the beautiful people of this house? This world is a temporary residence, the final world is eternal – how far have you people wandered – you are only involved in the *show sha* [superficial acts] of this world.

On hearing the village-woman sing religious themes, one *hijab*-wearing Bibi in her late thirties, a regular student at Al-Huda, walked away from this gathering, saying that she found the idea of a *khattam* mixed with singing both offensive and un-Islamic. However, a much older Pukhtun Bibi (in her mid-sixties) in this group, unaware of the reason for the younger Bibi's departure, told the singer: 'Such a beautiful voice you have; sing more about religion [*din*].' I often had experiences of this kind of multiplicity and variability in Bibiane's reactions to situations, which tested their notions of what was acceptably 'Islamic' in *gham-khādi* settings.

For some types of death, notably suicide, which is considered an unforgivable sin, Islam prohibits funeral attendance, yet many Bibiane and their husbands consider these funerary ceremonies obligatory to the practice of Pukhto. Following the funeral of an individual known to have shot himself, I witnessed one group of Bibiane and Khanān debate the morality of holding the burial in the conventional Pukhtun way. The eldest Khan, Lala (aged sixty-two), said that attending a *marg* (funeral) was 'compulsory; it *has* to be done.' His wife, Zainab (in her fifties), disagreed: 'But in Islam suicide is *gunah* [sinful], and the burial prayer [*da janaze moonz*] is not accepted; a *janaza* [formal communal burial performed by men] is not permitted; and the body should be bathed and then buried without any usual ceremonies. It is a great sin even to attend the ceremony of a person who commits suicide.' This Bibi, who lives in Peshawar and had not attended Al-Huda, felt empowered by conversations with her relatives (who were Al-Huda scholars), and challenged her husband on the basis of Islamic knowledge. In a double-edged manner, Al-Huda, an institution seen by some so-called 'liberal' women as bringing about 'conservativism' in society, empowered its followers. He replied defensively: 'Yes, I know, but I *had* to attend; I was doing Pukhto' (said in English). Ejaz, Lala's thirty-eight-year-old male cousin, asked: 'If you had known [attending was sinful] would you still have attended this funeral?' Lala replied ambiguously and deferred to Pukhto, 'I would have attended only to console the deceased's family.' The exchange illustrates the force Pukhto imperatives place on *gham-khādi* members. The stimulus for reconsidering Pukhto practices comes from Bibiane by appealing to an alternative religious standard.

Women's work in *gham* partakes both of spontaneous impulses and of a learnt order of emotion, which may be deployed with reference to personal interest (see Grima 1998: 6; and Goody 1962: 22). Parveen Bibi told me:

Crying in death is sharing the grief [of the bereaved]. The poor may cry more because they will get more in *warkra* [gifts/rewards]. If they cry a lot and you don't give them anything they will tell people, 'Oh, I performed so much *khabgān* [sadness, crying], and they did not [reciprocate] materially.'

Emotional intensity at weddings, births or funerals does not negate the awareness of social relationships among Bibiane but rather sharpens it. These events allow people to assess their place in social networks. Both the inter-affinal competition and the wider social regulation of funerals generate discourse among Bibiane and introduce the terms required for transforming 'custom'.

Obligations upon kin: food and hospitality

In *gham*, certain fundamental features of *Pukhtunwali*, such as *melmastia* (hospitality), surround the actual deposition of the body. The obligatory communal meal (*de khairat dodai*) is foremost among these features. The word '*khairat*' derives from '*khair*' (peace; wholesomeness; goodness), and denotes a form of Islamic charity. The giver and the recipients garner religious merit when food, money and

Table 4 *Food hierarchy*

High status (meat)	= *charg*, chicken: 'good food' (*droon khwarak*)
Intermediary	= *kacha ghwakha*, small meat (i.e. lamb meat)
	= *ghatta ghwakha*, big meat i.e. cow (*ghwa*), buffalo (*mekha*)
Low status	= *daal* lentils: 'poor person's food' (*de gharib khwarak*)

clothes are provided for the poor, the needy and relatives. Mortuary rituals significantly impact the hosting family financially, given the cost of food preparation, which includes the payment of labour and hired cooks (*degmarān*, named after their large metallic vessels, *degs*).[19] Relatives, who are forced by social pressures into significant expenditure, seemingly volunteer in order of seniority to pay for the *khairat* meal which is served to the entire assemblage of guests. It is said that the fire in the *gham-kor* should not burn for the three days after a death, so the relatives of the deceased serve and donate *khairat* meals on these days, on Fridays, on the Fortieth day and even on the *kāl*.[20] The house-context described in Chapter 2 is thus turned inside-out, as relatives and members of the village host the immediate bereaved. In contrast to Bibiane's *ghamoona*, poorer villagers practise a system of *tal-tole*, or a sharing of expenses incurred in *gham-khādi* among poor village households (Barth 1986: 31–5). Each wealthy household (including its Bibiane and maids) takes the opportunity to arrange, finance, prepare, serve and host the communal meal. As one *kasabgara* maid remarked: 'When there was a *gham* among the *naikān* [elite] I'd wash the dishes, and collect all the bedding, sometimes wash the dead, and *sambāl* [collect] everything for the death.' Different aspects of the 'work' of mourning – publicly attested grieving and the practical work of inter-class solidarity – are in this way divided among women according to their relationship to the dead person.

Meals served at funerals often consist of chicken (*charg*), rice (*wreeje*), meat curry (*engwale*; beef or mutton), spinach (*saba/saag*) and later tea. Pukhtuns consider food without chicken or *ghwakha* (cow or goat meat) *tasha* (empty; unfulfilling) or *spaka* (light, unprestigious), as indicated in Table 4.[21] Bibiane say that 'when there is a crowd in *gham-khādi* [the donor should] offer the guests chicken and meat' (*che garna yee khalak charg-ghwakha warkai*). Cooked rice without meat is said to be '*wache wreeje*' (dry rice). Pukhtuns generally consider *gham-khādi* meals without meat inadequate, particularly when the meal is being offered by a household as a form of gift (cf. Shaw 1997). Hosts present meat dishes in large

---

[19] Cf. Baily 1957: 64; and Metcalf 1982: 22.
[20] The *khairat* meal is also sent from a poorer household to that of Bibianes. One Bibi explained: 'when my sister's *abay* (wet-nurse) died her sons cooked *degoona* [large pots] of rice and sent it to our house', illustrating the variety of pathways of dependence and reciprocity between Bibiane and wet-nurses.
[21] On the significance and meanings of meat among Durrani Afghan Pashtuns during religious festivals, see Tapper and Tapper 1986: 64–7; cf. Ikramullah 1992: 27.

tray-like receptacles that run across a series of tables along one side of the courtyard. Younger girls and Bibiane themselves carry the trays to serve *masharāne* (elders). Guests appear impolite and non-participatory when they refuse to eat. People evaluate a family's discharge of *gham* according to the quality and quantity of food at a funeral meal and to the copiousness of attendance. Hundreds of guests carefully observe, critique and praise the women who provide the meal.

Operating within what Gilsenan describes as the 'fields of force' made up by the overlapping of different moral rubrics and societal expectations, Bibiane display their own family honour as they make, sustain and police relationships (1990: 173) at *gham* occasions. They also exhibit their capacity as 'important demonstrators of the status of their protectors' to challenge (or accept a challenge from) others (Papanek 1982: 8). Bibiane may raise, for example, the alleged non-reciprocation in their own festivities by other attenders. Cousins and sisters-in-law may use errors and misconduct to 'put' a Bibi 'down in order to put herself higher'. With such perceptions and matters of deportment, a Bibi's closest kin and affines (who may be rivals) constantly evaluate her reputation. Bibiane also care about the views of village-women, as their gossip shapes Bibiane's reputation in the *kille*. A Bibi's 'sacred self is most at risk in public, [and] has to be . . . jealously maintained by constant awareness of others' behaviour [and observation]. Everything is on show in such a setting' (Gilsenan 1990: 173). In this 'symbolic game of "seeing"' for Gilsenan (ibid.: 190), *gham* participation presents many risks. Women, under the knowledge that they may at any time be 'under observation' (ibid.), constantly reiterate behavioural rules and tacit norms at these ceremonies.

Daughters'-in-law service of the meal elicits much attention as they reflect the Bibiane's affinal household investment in the funeral. These Bibiane rush about laying plates, dishes and serving spoons (for up to a thousand people) ensuring the plates and glasses are clean, inspecting water jugs and co-ordinating the timing that dishes are brought to the table. Each household competes to present meals 'better than others' (*de bal na kha*). In this way, households 'up the ante', to adapt a phrase of Grima for inter-female rivalry, on their kin and affines (1998: 75–6, 78). Like *kor* hosting, successful *gham-khādi* hosting appears effortless and provides relaxed service, regardless of the laborious preparation. Some Al-Huda Bibiane express dismay about 'feasting' on such 'sober and sad occasions', one stating: 'I personally feel that instead of giving such lavish lunches and dinners for the rich at the time of death, one should collect that money and give it to the poor.'

After the Bibiane lay out the meal, they call individual attenders (anxiously and knowing they will be judged) to come for the meal. Every guest must be served before the hosts eat. Elders are not expected to rise, so Bibiane and maids ferry tables, trays, dishes and drinks to the different rooms, verandas and corners of the courtyard where groups of older women gather. Guests, particularly elders, will repeatedly be offered more food and drink (cf. Singer 1982: 27 on male hospitality). After the meal, many guests will want to wash their hands and say their prayers, so prayer mats (*janimazoona*) and rooms must be prepared beforehand. Many

Bibiane (both guests and hosts) say that the emotional and physical intensity of *gham* provoke heightened levels of 'tension' (in English), provoking severe headaches and bodily pains. In many funerals, I saw various Bibiane take aspirins and strong 'mixed' tea with milk (*tez gad wad che*) as cures when the day turned to evening (see Macfarlane and Macfarlane 2003: 46, 255 on the curative qualities of tea).

Although the wider circle of immediate relatives (siblings, first cousins, sons-in-law, other relatives) and even some village members take on feast obligations, many responsibilities revert to the bereaved after their designated period of grief. When a senior Bibi dies, the daughters, even ones younger than the deceased Bibi's sisters/sisters-in-law, distribute her clothes, jewellery, personal effects and books. Sororal and affinal Bibiane have a keen awareness of the material work required in the *kor* for *gham* preparations. One Pukhtun Bibi in her forties returning from Islamabad, told a group of Bibiane after the *Asr* (noon) prayer: 'We should all leave now; it will be less of a burden on the people of the house. You know, it is a difficult time and *gran kār* [difficult work] to entertain guests when the *korwala* [house-women] are burdened with their own grief.' She took a group of ten Bibiane with her to her brother's house in the same village.

After the three days, mourning lapses into a secondary and more extended period during which the death is absorbed into the texture of family and village-life. During this period, mourners gradually assume their former visiting activities. Within the village, as noted by Charles Lindholm, a sense of pollution accompanies the death, particularly regarding the ablution of corpses (1996: 36).[22] Bibiane, in contrast, are not so scrupulous that they shun the deceased's clothes – cashmere shawls or embroidered veils – which have personal value. After the three days, relatives who missed the initial ceremonies, through illness or absence from the country, are welcomed, indeed expected, to personally express their condolences (*dua*, prayer) to the deceased's daughters (Chapter 2 showed how these procedures may be performed in Islamabad). The patterns of timely, deferred or omitted performance of *gham-khādi*, besides the pace of mourners' reintegration into full *tlal-ratlal*, suggest the articulation of a Pukhtun experience of time in relation to commemoration of 'life-events'. When paying a deferred condolence visit, women keep their head covered, perform the *lās niwa*, then enquire about the death and burial, no matter how well these events are known. The visit expressing consolation or congratulation following a *gham* or *khādi* has affinities to the *tapos* or illness enquiry, as Grima showed in her typology of the 'formulaic apology' (1998: 88). A visitor states:

1. How she found out about the death (i.e. who brought the news);
2. How she responded;
3. Why she was delayed, and came as soon as she could for the *tapos* (ibid.: 103).

---

[22] Comparatively, death, in Japanese folk belief, pollutes (*kegare*) while ritual purifies (*hare*) (Namihira 1987). Cf. Bloch 1971; Bloch and Parry 1989: 14; Seaman 1981: 382.

A non-participant must account for her family's absence to a satisfactory level of detail, not merely stating but acting out her grief when she heard of the loss. Visitors share in mourning by virtue of their place in linkages of family relationship, obligation and communication, so that the performance of *gham-khādi* obligations crystallises a certain order of sociality. On the side of the host, *melmastia* obliges Bibiane to offer a whole meal spontaneously to all visitors at any time of the day, following the proverb, 'whether it is raining or hailing, give the guest the best hospitality' (*Ka barān we ka galai melma ghware kha nwarai*; Tair and Edwards 1982: 251). After this reciprocal enactment of *tlal-ratlal*, social relations between individuals and families resume to a formal level.

Failure to attend a person's *gham* entails serious consequences for continued social interactions with a slighted family. As Abu-Lughod observes among the Bedouins in the context of the Middle East, '[t]he worst form of trouble, of course, is death. Not to go to a camp in which a person has died, if you have any link . . . to that person . . . is to sever the tie' (1986: 67). Such consequences characterise the general sociality of Bibiane and their families, even in circumstances where late attendance is bound up in other conditions of modernity, cosmopolitanism and change (ibid.; and Strathern 1972: 176, 182). Even close relatives who miss the initial three days are not invited for the Fortieth. In Maryam's words, 'that's their clear way of telling you that they are sad or they are snubbing you'. In one case, a Khan's mother died while her son, Jahangir, accompanied her sister (his mother-in-law and aunt) to the UK for a medical check-up. He could fly back only four days later, after the three days. Jahangir took offence when his wife (who is his materilateral parallel cousin) reported that a younger nephew-in-law failed to come on the first two funeral days, and declared the end of relations between his immediate family and the renegade. The nephew, who is related to both Jahangir and his wife (as her nephew), had been embroiled in a land dispute with his aunt, which had strained the men's relationship. Jahangir said, 'I considered him "like a son". Fighting is in its own place; but *gham* is in its own place. As he did not do it with us, my relationship with him has finished for life! Finished! Finished!'

The incident illustrates the agency and privileged role Bibiane have in *gham-khādi* directing male political, or factioneering, behaviour in other contexts. Bibiane serve as family custodians, 'keeping the score' of goodness (*khawale*) and neglect in *gham-khādi*, and so determining the form of male and inter-family reciprocity for generations.

'Clothing matters'

For Bibiane, mourning symbolises a range of requisite actions and self-presentation (dark clothes without decorative patterns, make-up or jewellery). Tarlo (1996) uses the title 'Clothing Matters' to suggest the rich semantic implication of dress in statements of political belief and social role in a South Asian context. Many Bibiane in their sixties recall wearing the plainest clothes throughout the three days of mourning in Swat and Mardan, just two decades ago. A woman's self-neglect expressed her grief. However, as I was repeatedly told, this 'simplicity' has 'changed' and now even bereaved Bibiane change their clothes daily. On the third day and Fridays, many distant family members and mourners wear rich cotton *partoog-kameez* from *Bareeze* shops, costly foreign cashmere sweaters, foreign shoes and bags, 'light jewellery' (small earrings and rings) and make-up. In one Bibi's words, 'everyone dresses well for a wedding. But in *gham* most women want to show that they are high status and that they dress well at home. So the impression they give is that they were wearing the same clothes at home and as they heard the news of death they came "as they were".' This interpretation would see 'dressy' women making a statement about the importance of returning to the *kille* in an ostentatious style reinforcing their status. In a context where several hundred women sit collectively for extended periods, the attire of each mourner attracts much comment, placing great pressure on women to 'compete'. Bibiane's dress must neither be too fine nor too simple; at the same time her outfit must match or outshine the others' present. For instance, Arifa, a middle-aged Karachi-born Bibi who has been married into a Mardan Khan family for eighteen years, said in English:

My husband berates me: 'Why are you dressing so well for *gham*?' I tell him, 'If you go into those four walls there are these women – wearing make-up, they are fully dressed in their best clothes. Though now I am wiser – I dress up wearing darker colours and rich fabric – but earlier, for years I would go in my regular plain clothes because I'd think it's a funeral; nobody will be looking at me. But then you'd be sitting in a courtyard from morning till evening, everybody looking at you from top to toe, how many diamonds you've got, what's the latest designer, if you are wearing the latest print. That's one thing I found so typical to this society and this set-up.

Bibiane's emphasis on material effects such as clothes even at *gham* events makes their set-up distinct for Arifa who observes their world from a partial outsider perspective. Yet the line between dressing well to express status and dressing appropriately for *gham* is often ambiguous. Shaheen, in her early twenties and married into the Wali of Swat's family, dramatised her sense of contrary expectations in her account of wearing simple clothes to a funeral in Swat. At the event she was struck by the other mourners' garments: 'dressy clothes such as velvets and cotton *Bareezes*; I was surprised! It was all a *show shah* [a show]! They were looking at me carefully as if, she's from a *Badshah* [royal] family and look what she is wearing. When I came home I told my husband "was this a *gham* or a wedding [*wada*]" – I couldn't even see the difference!'

In the minds of many Bibiane, jewellery is more unambiguous in suggesting 'that you are happy in a sad time'. At the funeral of an older Bibi in Swat, the deceased's sister's daughter-in-law Uzma wore an expensive pashmina shawl, perfume, jewellery and bright clothing during the second day of *gham*. This outfit earned the opprobrium of the deceased's daughter, Inam, and the censorious conveyance of her activities to her mother's sister, Uzma's mother-in-law. *Gham* ceremonies become sites of remembrance and utmost propriety for the immediate family, as well as scenes for socialising and information gathering. Once her anger had died down, Inam found it sufficient that people should show their respect by attending. Yet a few find slippages between 'custom', negotiated social relationship and Islam unsustainable, and think dress codes should be regulated during times of observance. One *hijab*-wearing Bibi, Nazia, a student at Islamabad Al-Huda in her late thirties, commented at a funeral in Mardan: '*Gham* has become a place where everyone collects and gossips; it is like a fashion-show. Women should do useful things like reading the Quran.' For Bibiane like Nazia, written authority (Hadith) and 'custom' intertwine in multiple ways in authorising or prohibiting funerary practices. It is this contradiction that makes Bibiane's work in performing, authorising and debating proper procedures both especially fraught and especially significant in determining the character of Pukhto. Alongside the trauma of a relative's death, funerals offer the traumatic experience for Bibiane of exposing them to a scrutiny of their *ezat*, defined by the correctness of their ethnic self-presentation. At the same time, young Bibiane question the religious precedent of ethnic practices. The work of Pukhtun mourning thus builds ethnic identity and identification across regional and national boundaries, enacts inter-class solidarity under the auspices of *Pukhtunwali*, and contests non-Islamic forms. These various processes are all acted out in particular ways in the course of various individual funerary ceremonies in the Frontier.

Transcending seniority: a case in Swat

Begum Bibi, whom I had talked to several times in the course of my research, died in her sixties of a heart attack while I was in the field. She was an important personage since both her husband and father were senior Pakistani political figures, one a member of a Frontier royal family. Royal deaths are 'special because they are part of a political drama in which many people have a stake' (Huntington and Metcalf 1980: 122). After being informed by phone that she had passed away (*haq waraseda*), I cancelled my planned schedule and donned my *sazar* for the occasion; I arrived at her house in Islamabad early in the morning. There were already dozens of cars outside the house. The body lay covered by an English rose-patterned duvet, surrounded by several standing maids who intoned the following dirge, 'Oh, my Bibi! Oh, my sweet Bibi'. The room filled with veiled Bibiane and Punjabi women, some of whom were recognisable by their uncovered heads. After a six-hour journey to Swat, on arrival at the village house, women began to wail again. Women of different ages and backgrounds thronged the *kor*: older Bibiane on chairs and beds, younger women on the floor, maids on the verandas, and village-women freely jostling to see the face of the deceased.

The funerary procedure took a defining but innovative course in the washing of the body before burial. There was no doubt among the daughters-in-law, who, in the grief of the deceased's daughters, had assumed full responsibility about who would direct the bathing. The deceased's youngest sister-in-law, Kawsar, had followed an extensive course at Al-Huda and was the only immediate family member who wore a *hijab*. Middle Eastern anthropologists have emphasised that the wearer of the *hijab* conveys 'publicly the message that the wearer is a Muslim woman who adheres to the Islamic rules regulating the relationships, rights, and obligations inherent in the gender roles' (Hoodfar 1991: 106; cf. Cook 2000: 9–10). As a *hijab*-wearer and person of supposed high morality, the deceased Bibi's daughters-in-law authorised Kawsar to supersede the customary prerogatives of three elder (*mashar*) sisters-in-law (the wives of the deceased's husband's brothers, elder by up to thirty years). Her Islamic knowledge granted her priority over those who conspicuously outranked her in familial and social hierarchy. Kawsar was told to lead the bathing with maids and other women in the bathroom 'as you think right' – in other words, avoiding divergence from precept (see Brenner 1996: 685). Kawsar saw no insubordination in taking control, but rather she acted in a sense of responsibility and imposed her duty 'to forbid wrong and command right' (Cook 2000: 481). After the bath during the funeral Kawsar told me that she had ordered the sheets taken off and

> laid some towels over the body, so that she [the deceased] does not show, and then did her *audas-charadām* [ablution] in odd numbers such as three. Then we washed her from right to left, we washed her hair and braided it in three plaits. We wrapped five layers of white cloth around different parts of her entire body and head except the face: of which one piece was around the chest, another around [she whispered] her lower parts.

Kawsar stressed:

> I kept it very Islamic because I had done the Al-Huda course. But according to the *rewāj* [custom] of Pukhto, people do all sorts of things: like they write *kalimas* [Quranic verses] on the sheets, which they wrap around the body; they put the Quran on the corpse's chest; they put pieces of cloth from Kabah in the eyes. But, I think, Islam says only the person's *amāl* [good deeds] will accompany the person. None of these other *riwajoona* [customs].

The bath under the supervision of Kawsar differed from a *dai*'s death that I participated in myself, where Quranic verses were inscribed on the headdress and coffin cloth of the deceased. Kawsar saw herself stripping away all superogatory funerary conventions not demanded by Islamic texts. The rediscovery of scriptural authority thus poses a challenge not only to 'secularism' or 'modernity' but also to the widespread religious idioms and symbols of the village. Village Pukhto or 'customary' practices often strive for doctrinal supremacy which often contrasts with the Islam of the mosques and schools (Marsden 2002). Crucially, complex cases like these parallel themes from eighteenth- and nineteenth-century Islamic renewal movements. These movements from the subcontinent and elsewhere, notably in Egypt, demand a return to *Sharia* (Islamic law) based on the Quran and Hadith (Shakry 1998: 152). The call for 'a revival of Hadith studies (*ilm al-hadith*); a rejection of *taqlid* (blind imitation of customs and tradition . . .); a critique of certain forms of popular religion . . . and a reassertion of *ijtihad*, or independent legal interpretation' (ibid.) licenses individuals to act boldly in entrenched relationships of seniority, while it simultaneously subjects them to a criteria of propriety and self-conscience. Al-Huda Bibiane see themselves as carrying out an Islamic 'duty' by giving instruction at public events of *gham-khādi*. They assertively declare knowledge, without dogmatically insisting on principle (scriptural Islam leaving open many possibilities of tolerance and concession without forsaking the profession of religion).

In this case, the year of the funerary procedure was rounded off with a customary *kāl* observance. In the next case, and elsewhere, certain days that fall outside the prescribed Islamic days of mourning are beginning to be omitted, in a way which Bibiane say occasions confusion and upset to more conventional adherents of *gham-khādi* customs.

Bibiane's agency in the heart of Mardan

My second case study focuses on the funeral of an older Bibi, who was originally from Mardan but lived in Islamabad and whose three daughters-in-law had attended courses at Al-Huda. These women followed Islamic prescriptions and decided to waive the conventional Pukhtun *Salwekhtamma* (the Fortieth day) and the *kāl* for both male and female guests. In this instance, however, the women did not transform all 'un-Islamic' practices (as discussed in Chapter 2; Table 3) but varied the order of ceremony to combine elements of Bibiane's own understanding of Pukhto and Islam.

First, because a Hadith restricts mourning times for Muslim women to three days (widows exceptionally mourn longer, for the pragmatic reason that a pregnancy subsequent to her husband's death may affect her decision to remarry), the daughters-in-law substituted the customary Fortieth-day observances with a Quranic *khattam*. This was scheduled for the fourth day of the first *Akhtar* (the three-day religious festival) after death. Normally, on the first *Akhtar*, men and women separately participate in a *roombe Akhtar* (the first *Akhtar*), by sitting with the bereaved and consoling them through prompted reminiscences. The daughters-in-law also took in hand the obligatory distribution of *khairat*, food for the poor. This practice is typically carried out by the sons and mother of the house, prior to the gathering of female guests. An *alale* (sacrifice) of two goats and a cow was performed near the kitchen spaces of the *kor*. The daughters-in-law, who took immediate charge after their mother-in-law's death, distributed the butchered cubes of meat in handfuls and bags to local villagers, servants, mosques and *madrassas*.[23] They carefully measured prescribed quantities, distributing amounts befitting of status (Plate 16).

The deceased's second daughter-in-law, Nadia (aged thirty-one), in her black *hijab*, sat her blonde three-year-old daughter on her chair in the back-kitchen of the joint-family *kor*, ticking off her list of recipients as the cohort of Nadia's affinal maids went back and forth with bags to give to the male servants in the *hujra*. Nadia's challenge to precedence perturbed the youngest son of the deceased Bibi, Muhammed Khan (older than Nadia by ten years but younger than her husband),

---

[23] On the role of Maktab schemes in Mardan District, see P. S. Ahmed Abdul-Mueed and Khan 1980–2.

who had sometimes helped his (now late) mother during such *Akhtar* meat distribution over the past few years. During the earlier part of the distribution process, the eldest sister-in-law, Zubaida (aged forty; also Muhammed's mother's sister's daughter), had not yet arrived from Islamabad. Zubaida is also Nadia's father's step-sister, and several land-dispute cases exist between her and Nadia's father. Muhammed attempted to delay the distribution of *khairat* meat until Zubaida's arrival. He came repeatedly into the *kor*, urging Nadia to take account of particular servants whom he knew because he grew up in the house (Nadia, by implication, was possibly unaware of the various and multiple bonds of certain individuals to his mother's household). The maids, as they collected the *khairat*, gave some of the meat to village families who had already been given food, but had requested more.

When Zubaida entered, panic crossed the faces of the Bibiane and maids familiar with the domestic hierarchy of the house, and its breach in this instance. Muhammed Khan's wife whispered under her *sazar*: 'GHQ has arrived', likening the elder sister-in-law to a senior military army officer in Pakistan's General Headquarters. Zubaida dispatched her maid for the list so that she could take over. Warned by a glance from Muhammed, Nadia explicitly challenged her older sister-in-law's authority, saying boldly, but quietly, in English, 'Sorry, I have started the job, and she can't take the list from my hand, can she?' As Zubaida approached from behind a latticed partition (a *purdah* division separating the kitchen from the bedrooms), Nadia called the names on her list even louder, and instructed the maids in Pukhto, 'give this bag to the driver'; 'put more meat in that bag for the *jumat* [mosque]'. Still standing aside and observed by guests, her fellow sisters-in-law and the *kor*'s maids, Zubaida initiated an exchange in the most polite and guarded terms. Asked to reserve a double share for Zubaida's *dai*'s daughter (her 'milk-sister', whose marriage Zubaida herself had arranged with her husband's driver), Nadia replied '*Jee* [assuredly, a polite form of agreement or acceptance], I have already kept a share for her father-in-law [a household driver].' Zubaida pressed further, 'Keep one for her as well.' Nadia replied, '*Jee*.' When Zubaida left for her own compound, Nadia confided: 'Bibi [Zubaida] always takes credit for everything. She always says: "I did this and I did that".' Referring to this incident, she noted, 'Bibi was so shocked that her place was taken, I could see it on her face, that when she passed by [the kitchen] she didn't even come near me.' Zubaida's request that her *dai*'s daughter, or symbolic sister, specifically be favoured represented an attempt to wrest back control of the household from her younger affine. Nadia's polite refusal to relinquish a procedure which she had initiated was played out in a semi-public arena, watched by the various household women and visitors who stood to one side in nervous excitement.

The exchange illustrates a number of points about how intra-familial dynamics influence the work of *gham*. The overseer of the *khairat* donations holds considerable power in the eyes of household members. As Harrison points out, 'a community staging one of its important ceremonies may, at one level, be expressing its sense of identity and unity. But often this is only outwardly so, and the performance may in fact be preceded by intense power-struggles among its organisers' (1992: 225). Usually the eldest female in the family structure, the mother-in-law of the house, assumes this role. Zubaida was senior to Nadia as her eldest brother-in-law's wife and as Nadia's father's step-sister, yet the system of *mashartia* (seniority) was negotiable, reflecting Nadia's prestige as an active Al-Huda participant (Zubaida wears the *sazar*, whereas Nadia the *hijab*). They both adroitly managed the confrontation within the bounds of decorum. When Zubaida avoided a direct rebuff by sending her maid for the list, she underlined the important role maids hold as key agents in aiding Bibiane's work of *gham-khādi*. Her intercession on behalf of her *dai*'s relative, especially as it finessed procedures in asking for meat twice for the same household, subtly interposed her authority in such a way that it had to be carried out respectfully.

The different stages of *gham* provide contexts for these power negotiations among affines, where, as in this case, the faultlines ran between females. Alliances, like that of Muhammed and Nadia (despite the younger son's reservations over Nadia's actions), usually form across gender boundaries. All players and levels of society further their own interests from an allotted place. Maids, for instance, seek favour and status among the villagers in requesting bigger portions, while Bibiane may intercede on behalf of maids and younger relatives. It is important to note that there is no transcendental or non-transactional position which senior Bibiane can occupy in refusing requests: they have to either fulfil *tlal-ratlal* obligations or face the consequences of not doing so. In such a context, maids and junior Bibiane alike attempt to 'keep in' with village households by being responsible for having their share of food delivered, thus maintaining a social relationship. This act on the part of the interceding Bibi (possibly through her maids) represents the 'work' of interpersonal village relations. Looking at the whole procedure for distributing *gham-khādi* food, the pattern of affiliation of Bibiane through servants to village households ensures the nearly equitable sharing of scarce resources as they pass from the elite *kor* to the village.

Furthermore, the decision of Bibiane to hold a religious event (the Quran *khattam*) for their mother-in-law the day after this *Akhtar* (which lasts three days) represents the largest negotiated intervention of all. Many attending Bibiane (some 200 in this case) considered this alternative day 'untraditional', as it did not keep with the customary Fortieth-day procedures. Even the deceased would not have envisioned such a change to *gham* through her own death, but it is said: 'the living have the control over the dead' (*Da maro waak da jwando yee*). I heard one guest ask one of the daughters-in-law: 'Will there be a Fortieth? Because this is only the twenty-eighth day.' The women thought that the daughters-in-law temporised with the *khattam*, as it also fell outside the Islamic three-day mourning limit. Death and burial, nonetheless, underwent a partial 'de-secularisation' through a more textual interpretation of Islam. I found that women in Nadia's situation often viewed a successful *gham* less in terms of wealth shown and *khairat* (food) distributed, and more in terms of appropriately marking the passage of the deceased's soul into its next stage of life. Possibly because of their critical place in *Pukhtunwali*, *gham* rituals importantly unite divergent claims of custom – they do not, in other words, register pre-existing beliefs, but signify 'a realm of conflict... where new statuses can be asserted or destroyed' (C. A. Bayly 1998: 135).

The above case is not unique. Middle-aged Al-Huda Bibiane from various households and families today make great efforts to bring individuals into more Islamic ways of living. Styles of attendance, rather than hospitality, change, as women fit their visiting practices with the Hadith circumscription of mourning. One Al-Huda graduate, Bano Bibi, described how she once sought to curtail the attendance of a number of women at a *khairat* feast on the first Friday of a funeral:

At one death, I got up and left before the *dodai* [meal]. People close [to the bereaved] said to me: 'don't do this; they [the bereaved] will think you are treating our death lightly' [*che zamoonga marg spakawae*]. I thought we have to *break* this tradition because, you know, one meal costs about Rs.25,000 [£263]. So I thought that this is too much money and it is being given because it is a social pressure. So I got up and left.

Bano attempted to persuade others to join her, convincing 'five cousins, although' her 'own mother declined'. Her mother understood that she would jeopardise her own honour (*ezat*) if she left before the end of the ceremony. 'She was too scared of the people, you see', Bano shrugged, 'and then there was a lot of opposition. People were saying: 'They have devalued our death: they only attend funerals for one hour [*zamoonga marg a spak ko: dee ghenta ghenta oozar kai*].'' Although this Bibi and her mother agreed on the differences between customary *gham* and religious prescription, they were unable to act in concert at the actual event.

Bano left the event because she considered the system of obligatory condolences 'hypocritical' in that those closely afflicted only spend time and effort hosting for reasons of duty. The pressures of Pukhto force mothers to bear the work of *ghamkhādi* with conventional manners and restrain them from following their daughters' calls to new Islamic practices.

This chapter described attending, gifting, public grieving and personal self-presentation at Pukhtun *gham*. Funerals bring Khan and villagers together in ceremonial procedures to affirm the former's solidarity with the latter. The satisfactoriness of a *gham* as a social act depends on its successful enactment of sequence and propriety, and is performed each time a person dies. Families and participants produce the social meaning of death according to a 'structuration' (Das 1986) of tasks as they are allotted to people on the basis of family relationship to the deceased. These tasks also define women's personhoods in both an intimate and a public dimension. While stipulations of 'customary' form are sometimes oppressively present in Bibiane's minds during *gham*, and have great coercive force in shaping their behaviour, such norms are not immune from challenge. In this chapter, I demonstrated the modes by which Bibiane of different kinds (Al-Huda graduates, their relatives and non-Pukhtuns) modify, displace or resignify expected procedures, according to informed readings of scripture.

Pukhtun *gham* may be distinguished from the funerals of other ethnolinguistic groups in a number of ways. First, and arguably, the intricacy of the procedures of gifting and hospitality, and of performed social relationships to the deceased, is central to *Pukhtunwali*. Second, the transregionalism of contemporary Bibiane's lives exposes traditionally held theories about 'cultural identity' to multiple and contradictory modes of Islamic modernity.

Case studies and other incidents examined in this chapter suggest that the innovations into *gham* introduced by Al-Huda Bibiane are beginning to serve as a conduit through which distinctively novel forms of practice may penetrate elite village houses in the Frontier. Some anthropologists interpret female 'performative' or 'ritual' acts (in ceremonial contexts) as a Muslim woman's principal sphere of agency in the absence of 'direct, confrontational verbal' engagement (Hegland 1998: 255; 'rituals [in a Shia context] enable . . . participants to wield agency, share in creating meaning, and make more of their worlds' (ibid.)). Yet while it is rare for men and women to break out in open confrontation (*reshtheene*) over funerary arrangements, recent religiously inspired interventions in mourning do represent a form of engagement between the sexes, in which women gain leverage on account of the centrality of *gham* in Pukhto. Attention to religious Bibiane's reforms in *gham-khādi* thus takes a stage further two trends in anthropology: the representation of the 'ambiguity' or plurality of Muslim ideas of gender for women (Ewing 1988), and the documentation of a number of global Islamic movements, that put religion on a rational footing in connecting Islam to practitioners' everyday lives (Brenner 1996; Tapper and Tapper 1986: 70).

In one sense, it is possible to understand *gham* as part of a 'supervisorial' network, in which village-based identities and 'patriarchal' authority are enforced at participants' natal site (Hegland 1998: 247). Within the idiom of convent-educated Bibiane, however, the word corresponding to 'identity' is the Urdu term '*pehchan*', or, literally, recognition, suggesting that people's sense of themselves resides to some extent in social relations. Much more interesting and specific social transactions than any simple reiteration of 'village' identities go on under a surface of conformity to *gham*'s stringent prescriptions of female modesty. These dealings may take the form of intra-family disputes and tensions (or agnatic rivalry), but also involve the ongoing redefinition of the relationship between given extended families and the poorer communities they traditionally sustain. *Ghamoona* (pl.) are communal observances, in which a quasi-egalitarian distribution is undertaken under an aegis of Pukhtun ideas of responsibility. The charity meted out in *gham* suggests how strongly stratified and strongly egalitarian forms of social organisation may coexist in contemporary transregional 'tribal Islam' (Gellner 1993). I have suggested that Pukhtun women's role, particularly that of Al-Huda participants, in *gham* – classified as 'segregated public occasions' – begins to have socio-political implications in that change is brought about in many public aspects of the lives of Pukhtuns specifically and Pakistanis more generally.

Above all, this chapter has sought to unite a number of detailed descriptions of various hosting and attending decorums under the single local designation, 'work'.

I would align my account with a materialist ethnography in claiming that the symbolic work of making relationships is not entirely feasible without the physical labour of servants. There are other critical senses in which Bibiane's overseeing and visiting activities constitute the basis for such an analytical concept. Bibiane's activities represent mental efforts directed in a co-ordinated way towards a goal; they have the character of a duty, not a fully voluntary act; they are prosecuted according to recognisable rules and forms of legitimacy, and grasped as recurring or everyday tasks characterising life in a general way ('the work of life'); furthermore, they maintain the symbolic continuity ('work' in the sense of mechanics) of Pukhtun society. While these features may seem completely onerous, some Bibiane presented the duties of *gham* in a more affirmative way. The elaboration of mourning ceremonies is valued by many Bibiane as supporting and giving a social identity to their personal grief. It is in the critical junctures of *gham* and *khādi* (the central collective expression of joy in Pukhtun life and focus of the next chapter), that Bibiane depend on the complex mesh of social relationships that shape their social world.

1 Swat: view from Bareengal (Badshah Sahib's house)

2 Rooftop view of Hoti Mardan from the Nawab's hujra

3 *The Faisal Mosque, Islamabad from the Margalla Hills*

4 *The Murree Convent (notice the visiting Pukhtun mother in a white* sazar*)*

5 *In (white and red) summer uniform with author's convent class-fellows (1988)*

6 *Entrances within the house to the* hujra *and* kor *in Hoti, Mardan*

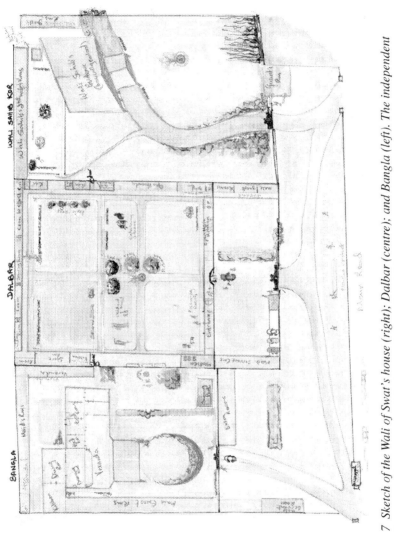

7 Sketch of the Wali of Swat's house (right); Dalbar (centre); and Bangla (left). The independent houses are interconnected by internal doors for visiting

8 Saidu Baba's grave inside his mosque

9 The mashra *(elder) Bibi (centre) directing maids while cooking for her guests*

10 A maid called 'Babo' (mother) performing the nazar-māt *for a little Badshah*

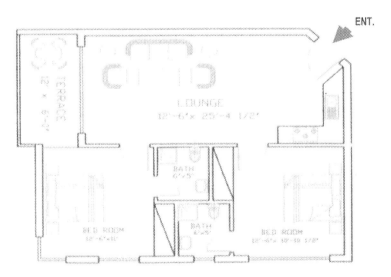

11 A two-bedroom city flat

12 Bamboo-covered Khan's and Bibi's semi-detached rented house in Islamabad

13 Swati and Mardani children of Bibiane with friends and maids at a birthday ('minor khādi'*) in Islamabad. The two women on the left (in sleeveless shirts) are Moroccan neighbours*

14 A maid in white with young Bibiane in 'Hot Shots'

15 Old qabar *(built structure at rear) juxtaposed against new grave. The new grave is freshly decorated by mourning women who just visited the grave and consequently come to terms with their loss in the house* (kor)

16 Bibi distributing meat to the villagers from the kor: *a maid bags portions of meat, while the Bibi's three-year-old holds the list with the villagers' names; the silver cooking pot under the* kat *(straw bed) is destined for the local mosque and* madrassa

17 A Bibi (to the left) at the wedding of her dai*'s granddaughter (her 'niece')*

18 Village children at a madrassa opened by a Khan in Mardan now supervised from Islamabad by Bibiane

19 Women in sazare seen for the first time outside their homes for this kind of Islamic activity in a Mardan madrassa (school) now supervised by a Bibi who lives in Islamabad

20 Displaying the bridal gold jewellery at the Nakreeza *event*

21 A young male performer (dum) *collecting money thrown over the groom's father's younger brother's wife's head (swat)*

22 The bride's unmarried sisters and cousin in 'modern' short-sleeved, non-traditional clothes dance 'Indian-style' in Mardan

23 Young Bibiane and children dance in a Swati wedding to an audience of Bibiane and male performers

4
Celebrating *khādi*: communal Pukhtun weddings and clandestine internet marriages

Marriage is easy, but its work is difficult. (*Wada asān de kho 'tak took' a grān de*)
(Pukhto proverb)[1]

The lover and beloved finally achieved unison, Adam and Dur Khanai became one. (*Mayan pa mayan pathe shoo, Adam ao Dur Khanai yao shoo*)[2]

The ethnographic focus of the previous chapter was on the procedures enacted by Bibiane in the context of *gham* funerary ceremonies. After establishing a discursive and physical context for elite Pukhtun life-cycle events in the first and second chapters, I sought to introduce to Frontier anthropology a more close-grained account of Bibiane's practices at funerals. This chapter presents the *gham-khādi* wedding festival in the same sequence. Like *gham*, *khādi* involves transregional and city-dwelling Bibiane in ceremonies which ideally bring them to the village-site or *kille-kor*, reaffirming attenuated class connections with villagers. Weddings are central or pivotal gatherings in which *purdah*-observing women may meet other women, the treatment of *khādi* therefore lies at the heart of Bibiane's sociality and close or extended kinship structures. As in funerals, meeting other women and satisfying attendance obligations involves gifting, deportment and self-presentation. Bibiane sustain an ongoing work of making relationships, which they conceptualise in conversation as 'the work of life'. This 'women's work' – insofar as *gham-khādi* is devolved by Pukhtun men on to female jurisdiction – grants Bibiane considerable autonomy in authorising the marriages of individual couples and thus, both literally and metaphorically, securing the continuity of elite Pukhtun life and experience.

A Bibi's 'work' during weddings reinforces kinship, responsibility of relationships and class and region allegiances. My account of Bibiane's 'work' at weddings (*khādi*) is comparable to my account of their activities during *gham*. Striving to reconstruct the conceptual interdependence of *gham* and *khādi* in Pukhtun thought,

---

[1] Tair and Edwards 1982: 269.
[2] Stated by a Mardan *kasabgar* woman called Almas, whose daughter was engaged to her cousin (father's sister's son) but who fell in love with and had liaisons with her parallel cousin. Almas broke the first engagement, marrying her daughter to her lover, as 'it was my Pukhto to prevent *sharam* [shame, honour], to *khlas* [release] my daughter from this boy and give her to the other whose name she had already been linked with'.

my presentation of the stylised (or 'ritualised') procedures for wedding ceremonies identifies similarities between *gham* and *khādi*'s allocation of space and gendered tasks. The Pukhto proverb, '*gham* and *khādi* are sister and brother', captures the close relationship of the procedures in local thought, an indissoluble philosophical relation which anthropology has yet to capture fully (see Grima 1998: 73, however, on the ceremonies' comparable solicitation of 'learnt' forms of emotion). Nevertheless, this chapter also distinguishes in important ways between *gham* and *khādi* as performances of female and familial bonding and social continuity. It explains how the necessarily different articulation of private and communal happiness ('*khādi*') at weddings involves different forms of gifting between women, and a different degree of openness of the elite *kille-kor* to the surrounding village. Moreover, the 'work' of Bibiane in confirming the identity and conformity to precedent, or *Pukhtunwali*, of individual *wada* is conceptualised in a slightly different way. While for *gham*, this 'work' took the form primarily of attendance in the face of a grief, for *khādi*, women serve as definitive visual witnesses, whose 'social presence' endorses the marital rite. Bibiane's celebration of weddings, through gesturing with money and dancing, validates weddings as consonant with a supposed earlier order of procedure, assimilating them to notions of a life-cycle governed by *gham* and *khādi*. These actions sufficiently constitute unity for many Pukhtuns, so that, in one Bibi's words, '*gham* and *khādi* are [inseparable] till the end, while there is life [*jwand*]'.

This chapter offers an account of *khādi* both as marriage (that is, as a specific sequence of acts leading up to and beyond a ceremony of betrothal) and as marrying (the forging of family alliances through social connection, and the associated consolidation of a kin network). While determining expected forms, it also examines a case study in which the legitimisation of weddings, and the enlargement of family identity, did not proceed as unproblematically as suggested in the above account of the exemplary nature of *khādi*. In other words, while Bibiane orchestrating weddings understand their satisfactoriness in terms of ceremonies' conformity to the ethnic specificity of *Pukhtunwali*, the analytical characterisation of weddings is necessarily misconceived if forced to coincide with the experience of participants. This is because, as case studies demonstrate, it has become impossible for *Pukhtunwali* to be reproduced through weddings, in terms of affirming Pukhtuns' religious faith and class responsibilities, without arousing painful contradictions in the minds of Bibiane.

Of all *khādi* (joyous) events, Pukhtun weddings may be accounted the most important, because they hold the greatest significance for the families, communities and the individuals involved (A. S. Ahmed 1980: 242; Lindholm 1982: 130). 'Elite' weddings bring families pursuing political alliances together with large numbers of their followers or dependents who stand to benefit or suffer the consequences of renewed affiliations. Bibiane's weddings also introduce the Frontier to practices debated in Islamabad, especially ones that relate to the scriptural warrant for 'Pukhtun' celebratory procedures. Bibiane's greater munificence in gifting and hosting, moreover, makes the material objects and signs of *khādi* more legible or available to ethnography. This chapter demonstrates how interpersonal transactions, effected through particular patterns of exchange, produce the social significance of weddings for different people (the couple, the parents, close relatives, more distant kin). Like funerals, weddings involve different social classes of person in differing degrees of centrality, according to their social relationship to the spouses. The bride and groom themselves marry; the natal household loses a daughter and the marital home gains a bride; the families' *gham-khādi* network contributes financially; all present testify to the propriety of the union, and are confirmed in their socio-familial bonds to each other and their hosts.[3] At a 'correctly' observed ceremony, marriage unions are sustained, or receive public approval, through the attendance of a *gham-khādi* circle. In this sense, weddings are understood as merely the culmination of difficult and ethnically specific procedures of betrothal, preparation and communal participation, all of which have their own requirements. Participants experience weddings through the same capillary network of obligations and reciprocal responsibilities described in Chapter 3. Moreover, Bibiane attend *gham-khādi* as the 'children' of their *daigāne* (wet-nurses), not merely as family representatives or the wives of their husbands.

Bibiane understand the 'work' of *khādi* as one undertaken by female relatives and attenders. While brides choose their cloths, *sazare* and jewellery, married Bibiane repeatedly described themselves as being swept into the process of their own nuptials. Marriage initiates the 'full' assumption of one's obligations as a social agent, henceforth the maintenance of *gham-khādi* relationships. The work of *khādi*, particularly weddings, is widely seen by Bibiane as having both physical and mindful dimensions. On the level of intentional action, *khādi* involves inviting all of one's social network, and involves observing food, dress and procedural standards.

The general characteristics of *khādi* in Pakistani weddings (such as large gatherings, a stress on clothing and lavish hospitality) are central to Pukhtun self-representation as they adhere to 'convention' and guarantee the social success of marriage procedures. Failure to observe certain prerequisites makes the wedding less efficacious as a form of bonding or position-building. The Pukhto proverb, 'Marriage is easy, but its work is difficult' (Tair and Edwards 1982: 269), begins to suggest how more is involved in a wedding than the reproduction of an invariant form.[4] One of the eldest Bibiane (in her seventies, and the mother of six married offspring) with whom I spoke told me that wedding preparations required '*der ghat kār*' ('a great deal of work'). While for those Bibiane hosting a wedding its work and pressures may be preparatory to the ceremony proper, for guests, questions of etiquette may play on their minds throughout the celebrations. Bibiane, as at funerals, are again judged on how well they perform certain ritualised or

---

[3] Nancy Tapper notes, 'Middle Eastern marriages establish a framework in which the intimate connections between the issues of marriage and group identity . . . can be investigated' (1991: 16).

[4] On marriages in northern Pakistan and Afghanistan, see A. S. Ahmed 1980: 242–58; Donnan 1988; Lindholm 1982; Safdar 1997; Tapper 1981, 1991.

formalised actions. Before *khādi*, relatives enquire about the bride or groom, pass on invitations and help prepare the bride, house and dowry. At weddings themselves, Bibiane distribute money, dance and serve food. Alongside this work of hosting, a range of village-women help lay the tables, clean, wash the dishes and relay messages locally. Female guests dress in finery, dance and eat, while verifying the observance of bridal *rites de passage*. The ceremonial forms of *khādi* and *gham* both suggest their complementarity, and show the possibility of celebrants at one feast being the mourners at the next.

Preference and choice: finding a bride

'Marrying' one's child comprises obligatory work that is construed as the mother's social duty (cf. Shaw 2001: 324). Yet this obligation, stated as such, obscures the many concerns that Bibiane must balance in choosing whom their daughters should marry. These concerns include *ezat*, the consolidation of land, access to wealth and status, preference for kinship and ethnic endogamy and the healing of family disputes.[5] Due to the segregation of public occasions, *gham-khādi* contexts provide the only means of viewing and encountering a girl's or a boy's family, in which married women typically play matchmaking roles.[6] In a comparative Moroccan context, in the 1980s, Mernissi observed the importance of women's matchmaking role, specifically mothers, whose: 'role is pivotal, because she has access to information relevant to the marriage that only women can have in a sexually segregated society. The mother is the one who can see the bride, engage in discussions with her, and eventually acquire a very intimate knowledge of her' (1985: 123).

It is often said, among Pukhtuns generally, that 'weddings make other weddings': in Bourdieu's terms, marriages take their place in a pattern of social reproduction, in terms of both identity-defining practices and the dominance of a social segment. Previously endogamy, especially patrilateral cross- or parallel cousin marriage, was favoured for preventing the dissipation of wealth; now, however, the criteria for a 'good family' includes money-wealth gains, political connections and also historical roots. Until recently, mothers did not take the religious observance or professed Islamic views of young women into marriage considerations (even beauty and fair skin were said to be more important). This situation is changing with the popularity of Al-Huda courses; two middle-aged Bibiane told me that their sons only wanted to marry girls who wore a *hijab*.

---

[5] In this I agree with Shaw (2001) who seeks to go beyond the 'culturalist' explanation for the high rates of inter-ethnic and inter-*biradari* marriage among second-generation British Pakistanis, to consider motivations of: maintaining class or *zat* status; marrying within *biradari*; discharging obligations to kin; upwards social mobility; and facilitating immigration.
[6] See Abu-Lughod 1990: 43; Altorki 1986; Naveed-i-Rahat 1990: 54; Tapper 1978: 397; Watson 1992: 8; cf. Humphrey 1992: 191.

Celebrating khādi   111

At *gham-khādi*, close female relatives of a marriageable boy or girl typically 'look' for potential spouses in the crowd, sometimes literally: the girl's physical appearance, her family and a simple exchange of *salāms* (greetings) may be enough for the boy's mother to consider proposal to the girl (see Barth 1986: 38; Tapper 1978: 392). In one of my fieldsites, a few marriageable boys' mothers kept asking me to find their sons a *speena* (light-skinned) and tall girl. In another case, of exogamy, a Bibi in her forties gave her twenty-one-year-old daughter to a very wealthy, non-related Shia Punjabi boy, whom she met through her sister's school connections. This inter-ethnic marriage featured both Pukhto and Punjabi ceremonies. A Sunni *khādi* in the girl's parental village house in the Frontier preceded a Shia function to which only the girl's immediate families were invited. The Shia boy's family was wealthy, and he had studied at Eton, but his denominational and Shia-Punjabi background caused great debate among Sunni-Pukhtun Bibiane. Some Al-Huda Bibiane among themselves declared the alliance impermissible. In another related case (in Islamabad), when a twenty-three-year-old female cousin of the above bride received a proposal from a less wealthy Punjabi Shia, she bluntly refused to 'marry a Shia', ending the matter there (as Sheriff notes, it is a Muslim woman's right to have a say in her own marriage (1996: 7)).

In determining a response to a proposal, mothers rely on information and research from other Bibiane and maids about the boy and his profession (*kār-rozgār*). Bibiane or maids may involve themselves in other women's weddings anticipating either *ezat* or economic benefits. Gossip among women on the subject of possible alliances circulates between affinal and friends' houses in a discursive network itself constituting an important dimension of Bibiane's life. Once a Bibi is married, she will think about and facilitate the marriage of her younger female family members. Married women sometimes act as links between metropolitan *gham-khādi* circles and more isolated family or tribal networks, who have more restricted *gham-khādi* relationships with other Frontier families. Women in the NWFP may communicate with their relatives in the city, or even abroad, on the subject of potential alliances over the phone. The whole texture of the lives of Bibiane is revealed in the spirit of wit, good humour and occasional malice in which marriages are projected. Much turns on the intimate relations of friendship between Bibiane in the run-up to a betrothal; senior Bibiane facilitate important alliances between families and withhold or disclose vital information to serve particular interests. Helen Watson, in the context of Cairo, notes: 'Information is a powerful tool in such circumstances; marriage plans either advance or collapse when women withhold or manipulate certain facts about the families concerned' (1992: 8). Men, on the other hand, are largely excluded from this field of activity, while their wives, mothers, sisters and daughters mediate the process.

Bibiane carefully consider intermediation to the degree that stock roles and attitudes exist around it. In one context of particularly restrictive *purdah*, a Mardan

Bibi sent a trusted maid to work for a year as a *khidmatgara* (helper) in her prospective daughter-in-law's natal household to assess, by proxy, her behaviour and character. More usually, in the absence of previous contact, families make connections based upon the shared Pukhtun assumptions of both sides. One Bibi, in the role of a go-between, helped to effect an alliance between distant relatives (through her husband's uncle's wife on one side and maternal first cousin on the other) who at the time 'had no *gham-khādi* relations'. She brought the unmarried girl, her mother and the young man's mother together in her Islamabad house, served tea and observed pleasantries. The marriage took place, and the Bibi who acted as the go-between stated that, because some of the work of the wedding fell upon her, she was *pareshān* (anxious) that she would feel responsible if the marriage was unsuccessful. At the same time, the Bibi was seen to derive *sawāb* (religious merit), similar to the reward for the *haj* (compulsory pilgrimage to Makkah), by successfully facilitating a marriage.

Bibiane arrange the place, invitations and procedures for their offsprings' weddings with concern for propriety and a strategic cultivation of family *ezat*. First of all, the choice of location projects the legitimacy of the nuptials in the eyes of one's *gham-khādi* network. The three-day wedding ceremonies of Bibiane's families are held most frequently in the village house (*kille-kor*). They may use sites belonging to either side of the match, with the first two days typically being hosted on 'the girl's side' and the third on the boy's (funerals, by contrast, are always held in one site at the deceased's *kille-kor*). Marriages potentially involve movement between cities, towns and countries, imposing logistical burdens on all participants. Bibiane without access to a village house, or who are living abroad, may hire a big hotel hall in Islamabad to organise a wedding reception according to the requirements of Bibiane (such as for segregated social spaces). Nazia, an Islamabad Bibi, said that, 'a lot of responsibility and work [*kār*] is reduced' with hotel weddings. Despite this, Bibiane say it is more prestigious and honourable (*ezatmand*) to hold a wedding in the village house. According to one Bibi in her mid-forties:

People who are typical Pukhtun – they don't want their daughters to get married out of a hotel. They want to go back to their own *kille* [village] because, you see, there is more respect in giving away the girl from the ancestral home.

The spacious courtyards and extra guest-rooms of Bibiane's *kille-koroona* accommodate hundreds of guests at any one time, including local villagers. Holding the wedding in the village house makes the event accessible to a large number of local villagers. Once the location is decided, the mother of the bride or groom, depending on the daily division of responsibilities, chooses the menu and decor, confirms the order of events, books cameramen and arranges for her daughter's *nawe* (bridal) make-up. In addition, she organises the distribution of about one thousand invitation cards, individually addressed to all the women in her *gham-khādi* network. It is an obligatory part of the labour of *zeest-rozgār* both to invite one's circle and to take up invitations by attending.

Sath and *tayyari*: invitations and preparations

Invitations express emotions 'from the heart'; customarily, hosts notify invitees through a formal visit. A village Bibi, Mehreen, whose brother was getting married, told me: 'all those people who we invited in person came for the wedding, but all those who were invited by telephone did not attend, because they said, "we have not been invited from the heart [*na-zre*] [meaning that the effort of invitation was not made in person and therefore only partially]"' (cf. Das 1986: 195). Among Bibiane, relatives and those held in respect (elders, influential persons and certain in-laws) are invited in person, while others are notified through hand-delivered invitation cards (rarely by post). The list of people personally invited to weddings may include two to four hundred people with whom the mothers of the groom and bride sustain regular social relationships. Bibiane are expected mentally to keep track of invitations and refusals, rather than through bookkeeping and through other means. These methods risk not inviting important kin or affines, whose non-attendance must be attributed to failure to send an invitation, inadvertence on the part of the non-reciprocating family or to conscious avoidance. Forgetting to invite someone for a *khādi* causes great anger and offence, comparable to that of missing a *gham-khādi* visit. While I was in Islamabad, several family disputes occurred over this cause. Thus Bibiane experience the receiving and issuing of invitations as fraught with anxiety. The procedures require the Bibi to balance reciprocal procedures with more specific judgements and obligations towards particular families.

The greater honour of being visited, for Bibiane, than of leaving the house to visit others means that village-women may be invited prior to the date by the Bibi's most trusted maids. In Toru, a village in Mardan that I visited during fieldwork, a Bibi reported that *purdah*-restricted Bibiane depend on their maids to pass invitations to other women in the Frontier. She elaborated: 'The trend for *gham-khādi* is not to invite people by telephone, but the maid will go around in Toru village or to Peshawar, circulating a slip of paper among other Bibiane, who have to sign their names to indicate that they are going to attend or not.' In other areas outside Toru, telephones and email are used to contact distant guests. Cards are distributed to each female head of a household and her married children, and invite both husbands and wives, with the exception of the first day of the wedding – the *Nakreeza* – reserved for women only.

Wedding cards are placed in an unsealed envelope on which the name/s of the invitee/s are written. Mothers of the bride or groom divide the cards among their close female relatives (sisters, married daughters, aunts, cousins and sisters-in-law) who share the work of distribution by relay along their wider social networks. For example, the mother of a bride may give about thirty cards to her eldest married sister to pass to each of the sister's affines. She will repeat this procedure with all her immediate kin. With some families who practise stringent *purdah*, male members distribute the cards to more distant relatives. Those people who take an active part in this work are considered 'close' to the immediate family, according to the distributional definition of social identities suggested by Bourdieu's formulation that '[I]t is practical kin who make marriages; it is official kin who celebrate them' (1991: 34).

The delivery of invitations is itself quasi-ceremonial. Bibiane put on appropriate attire for going and coming (*de tlo-ratlo jame*): expensive embroidered clothes, foreign bags, high-heeled shoes and either 'heavy' gold jewellery or more 'sophisticated' diamond rings. They may be accompanied by other Bibiane or maids as they visit the invitee's house. Even heavily pregnant sisters, as was sometimes the case, are obliged to participate in this round of work. Visiting prior to a wedding represents a major commitment of time and energy, as well as the deployment of *aql* (social sense). As food cannot easily be refused without some '*sath*' (reverence, polite decline to insistence), on the recipient's side, the Bibiane cannot refuse an invitation to a wedding (or to a relative's house) also called '*sath*' (invitation) without a serious reason such as mourning in her family, absence from the country or a dispute (*wrana*) with the family concerned. Even so, close relatives – aunts and cousins – come from foreign countries for *gham-khādi*.

After the delivery of invitations, preparation for the wedding among the mother and close female relatives begins in earnest. Future brides may choose their own materials, patterns and designs from separate shops with their mothers, sisters, aunts and female cousins. Suitable wedding and dowry items are gathered regionally, nationally and internationally: jewellery – a Bibi's personal property – for example, may be procured from Pindi, Lahore, Karachi, Delhi or London. Female relatives compile a trousseau of clothes, cloths and other adornments for the bride. Thirty to forty finely embroidered suits are stitched (*partoog-kameez-loopatte*) and another trunkful of unstitched pairs are expressly commissioned from various shops, tailors *(darzian)* and boutiques. The Bibiane either select or design their own embroidery (cf. Tarlo 1996: 155).[7] One newly married woman told me, 'My bridal dress was rust. Before, brides always wore red, but nowadays people are into designer bridal wear from magazines and designers. They want to make unique, rather than common, things, so they experiment with colour and designs.' The amount of work required for such embroidered clothes earn their Pukhto name, '*de kār jame*' (literally, 'the clothes of work').

A bride's mother, and sometimes her sister, prepare the trousseau of fine clothes over the course of a lifetime. They include household goods, particularly linens and crockery, to equip the house for *gham-khādi*. In Strathern's terms, these material effects signify their owner, according to a non-Western conception of work in which objects appear as people ('personification'), rather than as things ('reification': 1990: 177). For a wedding, a wardrobe of fine embroidered silks and *jamawars* will be ordered six months to one year before the wedding. Table 5 represents one example of a mother's approximate expenditure for her daughter's 2002 wedding, which cost about Rs.2,378,000 (equivalent to £25,031.58).

The sums of money spent on weddings or *khādiane* is high by Pakistani standards. Among Bibiane's families, weddings usually cost less than funerals, though

---

[7] On the tailor's tasks as involving 'women's work' and therefore degrading, see C.A. Bayly 2001: 296.

Table 5 *A bride's wedding expenditure*

ITEM	DESCRIPTION	AMOUNT (Rs.) (approx.)
Clothes	30 pairs stitched and embroidered by a local designer	100,000
Jewellery	New jewellery made in addition to older inherited pieces	1,900,000
Furniture	Double-bed; sofa-set; tables set; carpet pieces	100,000
Electrical goods	Fridge, TV, vacuum cleaner	100,000
Kitchen items	Cutlery, crockery, etc.	20,000
Toiletry	Shampoos, soaps, powders, etc.	2,000
Make-up	Make-up sets and expensive designs e.g. Chanel lipsticks	2,500 plus
Linen	Bed sheets, bedcovers, etc.	3,500
Asbab (Trunk of bedding)	12 *brasthane* (quilts); 8 pillows; 4 *bojoona* (cushions); 12 matresses, etc.	50,000
Preparation expenditure	*Shamiane*, chairs, food for guests	100,000
Total		**Rs.2,378,000**

the mothers' financial burden is sometimes higher as they individually bear the costs of their daughters' weddings (Ikramullah 1992: 79). In some cases, mothers may replace the purchase of household amenities with cash: in one instance of virilocal marriage, a mother-in-law forbade her daughter-in-law and mother from buying furniture or electronic items for her already fully furnished house. More frequently, the women laboriously prepare the girl's suitcases and room furniture, and they send electrical appliances and other necessities to the boy's house in instalments before the wedding. Mothers organise this work and often perceive it as tediously difficult and time-consuming.

While reactivating the formal ties connecting the Bibiane of a household, wedding preparations also provide an occasion for the clarification of Bibiane's relations with their *khidmatgarān* (helpers). The form of gatherings at Pukhtun weddings, like that of funerals, depends upon the more general idea of female sociality in *tlal-ratlal*, which reaffirms such cross-class female relationships. Plate 17 shows a Bibi at the wedding of her *dai*'s granddaughter. As intermarriage between the children of different wet-nurses is common, the bride is marrying the grandson of the *dai* of this Bibi's sister. The Bibi herself (on the left, with her grandnephew on her knee) lives in America where her husband is employed, and periodically visits her mother's house in Swat.

Maids' position is liminal in that they serve in different contexts as bound servants, to whom the Bibiane have responsibilities; as personal companions, in whom Bibiane vest much of their affective energy; and also as independent financial actors, who profit from their work for *gham-khādi* occasions. This relationship between mistress and maid is uncertainly divided among modes of 'trust' and of 'contract' (Freeman 1970; Tonkiss and Passey 2000), as *khidmatgarān* (helpers) seek rewards for services not specified in the context of any prior negotiated agreement. Women from the village are paid to undertake cleaning, serving and other labour, working beside Bibiane as they perform ceremonial procedures, especially hosting *khādi* meals. While the relationships between the Khanān and their *khidmatgarān* become strained with translocation, other maids have moved to Islamabad with their Bibiane. In one instance, an elderly maid joined her Bibi (in her sixties) in Islamabad by taxi (for which she paid Rs.12 from the *adda* (bus station)), then visited the Bibi's six married children and recouped ten times the cost of her fare; she also personally received Rs.1,000 from each for the engagement of the Bibi's youngest daughter.

In many cases, maids' economic interests would seem to be bound up with the weddings (and more tacitly, the deaths) of the close relatives of her mistress. One maid described collecting the money thrown at dancers at the *Nakreeza* function, which Bibiane shun as the money is meant for the performers. This maid would calculate the other gifts (clothes, for example) which she could expect from Bibiane during their *khādi* occasions, asking for 10,000 rupees when she expected to receive 6,000. This sense of haggling is present only in the relations between certain classes of maids and their employers, with reciprocity and augmentation in cash gifts between Bibiane themselves being calculated but not the theme of overt expostulation or debate.

Marriages also reunite families whose members live in different regions and countries, emphasising individuals' rootedness to the *kor*. The girl's close family (including aunts and cousins) arrive at least a month before the wedding (cf. Delaney 1991: 124). In the house, celebrations and group dancing practices begin days, even weeks, before the actual wedding. Unmarried friends and cousins stay close to the bride-to-be, offering 'moral support' in preparation for the life-changing event. Altorki, referring to the Jiddah elite, comments on female friendships: 'In a world of women, friendship ties play a more important role as they come to constitute a network of support second only to kinship ties and at times equal to them' (1986: 100). For people from Pukhtun families living abroad, absence from the country implies not so much the attenuation as the redefinition and renegotiation of the practical ties of kinship. In a personal instance, an older female in-law visiting Britain from Pakistan, within minutes of meeting me offered to make a list of people to whom I owed a *gham-khādi* visit. While attendance and involvement in the case of distant kin, supporters or equals may be exempted, different terms apply for those who are closely related.

The three wedding days proper are second only to Pukhtun funerals in the scheme of *gham-khādi* events.[8] While Pukhtun funerals are open to the public in a segregated context, weddings are largely 'by-invitation' events; thus, I define them as

[8] Comparatively, weddings in the Punjab are far more elaborate and extended. One Punjabi wedding that I attended of a neighbour in Islamabad spread over a period of ten days of formal celebrations, including: the bride's *Mayun*; the groom's *Mayun*; bride's *Mehendi*; the groom's *Mehendi*; *Barāt*; *Walima*; and two further days of mutual visiting to the bride's and groom's houses.

restricted segregated public events. A basic typology of Pukhtun weddings would include a three-day event; dancing, food and generous hospitality. Variations occur within this pattern, according to location, the minutiae of rituals during the first festive day (*Nakreeza*), the degree of *purdah* observance and emphasis on dancing.

Bibiane's weddings

In the marriage season, just before and after the summer heat, various weddings occur in different places at the same time. If weddings overlap, attendees will be expected to attend both occasions. Bibiane and their families will then visit the *Nakreeza* and *Wada* of one marriage and the *Walima* of another. Women's journeys from Islamabad to *kille-koroona* are particularly arduous due to prolonged travel in *sazare*, heavily embroidered wedding clothes and gold jewellery, and holding children on their laps on the rough and often dangerous roads to villages. The first day, or *Nakreeza*, of the wedding takes place for Bibiane on the night of their arrival. Women enter the courtyard of the *kor*, greet the female relatives by embracing and kissing them, and then approach the mother of the bride. They give her money in an envelope saying, '*ombarak shai*' (congratulations). While during funerals cash gifts may be restricted to substantial donations of about Rs.10,000 (even 30,000) from immediate family members, at weddings, all invited women are expected to contribute (as detailed in Chapter 5). After presenting herself to the bride's mother, a Bibi may then greet a large number of kin, affines, acquaintances and other guests with an embrace and kisses. In addition to relatives, and Bibiane from other 'respectable families' (*khandani koranai*), there will be a large presence of local village-women and poorer dependents.

The women of the boy's side, particularly his mother, prepare and pack the various suitcases, making sure that every last lipstick and bar of soap is packed. Mothers worry about leaving some important or minor thing out, fearing the impression of ineptitude might damage her reputation (*ezat*). Other female relatives place henna (*nakreeza*) on plates, which are encircled with shimmering tinsel and lit candles.[9] After adorning themselves with gold jewellery, the Bibiane from the boy's side veil themselves with their *sazare* and are driven in a cortège of several cars by close male relatives to the bride's house. This journey may last a few minutes or several hours, depending on the distance between the groom and bride's houses. Upon their arrival at the '*Nakreeza*' function (henna-night), the first of the three formal wedding days, women remove their *sazare*, which may be skilfully folded and put away by maids. The cohort of Bibiane variously walk or dance into the courtyard space of the house, which is enclosed by *shamiane* (colourful tents). The courtyard is ablaze with women in vibrant colours.

---

[9] I use lower case for *nakreeza* (henna) to distinguish it from the wedding event also called *Nakreeza*. Nancy and Richard Tapper describe henna as 'symbolic blood' (1986: 70) and the henna event among the Maduzai Pashtun of Afghanistan as symbolising 'good luck' (in the bride's marital defloration) (Tapper 1991: 163).

The boy's side women then place the henna on the centre table on the carpeted courtyard, while the male musicians, or *dummān*, dressed in jeans and shirts, sing popular Pukhto wedding songs:

> This is the night of henna,
> The girls beat their kettledrums;
> The people [*khalak*] have assembled for the wedding.
> (*Shpa da de nakreezo,*
> *Jeenakai tanbal waheena;*
> *Khalak pa wada raghale dee na*)

The song reflects the high spirits and dancing evoked at weddings. More importantly, it refers to weddings as integrally characterised by guests' attendance and participation. The aunts of the groom (his father's brothers' wives) brandish five or ten rupee notes above each Bibi's head during the dancing. The songs and dance halt for the public displays of the bridal gifts brought by the groom's relatives. A close female relative, such as the groom's paternal uncle's wife, may stand on a chair and present each item brought for the bride's wedding day: the bridal suit (*jora*), shoes (*paizar*), jewellery (*kalee*) and other accessories (*zaroorathoona*) (cf. Tapper 1991: 165). This display of reciprocal munificence asserts the new family relationship in a mode of abundance and economic largesse (Plate 20).

A few female guests may visit the bride in her room who typically dresses in yellow, without make-up or 'real' jewellery apart from glass bangles. This image of pure simplicity contrasts with the elaborate bridal make-up worn the following day. The bride's relatives and friends escort her under a silk veil on to the veranda. Several relatives place *nakreeza* on the palm of her hand. At this point, the groom's kin throw money over the bride's and other relatives' heads, which is collected rapidly by the musicians (see Plate 21). Groups of maids dance in circular patterns before an evening meal is eaten, which concludes the event. The guests finally disperse back to their village houses.

On the second day (*de wada wraz*), the bride's family host an event in their village house. Each female guest, on arrival, presents her cash contribution to the bride's mother (varying between Rs.300 (£3) to Rs.1,000 (£10) or more). Poor villagewomen do not necessarily offer monetary gifts, but present their attendance as a gift. If not already performed, the *nikah* (legal marriage contract) may be carried out in the girl's room (the *nikah* may have been formally drawn up months, even years, earlier).[10] The bride's male kin and close female relatives perform the *nikah* with a close relative, employing the girl's brother or maternal uncle to represent the bride. At this point, the mother of the bride often appears especially tense, as the responsibility of the entire wedding falls upon her shoulders; furthermore, at the point of *nikah*, her daughter will be married and shall leave the mother's house for another *kor*. Yet at the same time, parallel to a widow in grief, the mother

---

[10] Nancy Tapper notes that the Afghan Durrani Pashtuns visit their wives after the *nikah* in her parent's house until the marriage is celebrated publicly (1991).

must maintain her sense of hospitality – greeting and offering each guest her time, good humour and food. At this point, the bride's mother and female kin call each guest for '*dodai*' (food); Bibiane and maids of the house serve elders each dish of the meal where they sit. Other attendees claim their appointed share. The hosts renew their hospitality to guests already served, eating only when everyone else professes themselves sated. Village guests and maids often describe a 'good wedding' through reference to food: a '*garam*' (hot) and '*mazedar*' (tasty) wedding is one that is successful, meaning that both the quantity and quality of the wedding sufficiently fed a large number of rich and poor people.[11]

The bride is then presented to the guests on a veranda or a raised platform in the courtyard. A group of relatives and friends 'hold' the bride by her arms, while her face may remain fully covered with the red bridal dress presented the preceding day. The bridal colour red is symbolic of fertility and suggests the loss of virginity, while symbolising the vital and emotional participation of the guests in the life-cycle event (see Abu-Lughod 1986: 136; Delaney 1991: 142). 'Holding' the bride symbolises the significance placed on interdependence and solidarity between close kin and friends. The female guests approach the bride in turn, giving her money (if this has not earlier been offered to her mother), congratulating her on her appearance and blessing the match. The bride and the groom sit together on the sofa for an hour of photography with different affines, kin and friends. While photography, a symbol of happiness (*khwashhāli*), in *khādi* is seen as normal, in *gham* it is offensive (cf. Kurti 1999). In some weddings, the bride's sisters and cousins remove the groom's shoe (*juta chupai*), and return it for a sum of money. In one wedding, the young Bibiane began bargaining at Rs.50,000 (£526) and settled at Rs.20,000 (£210). There are a variety of wedding games that are performed on stage, some introduced by Punjabi friends and relatives. For example, the male and female cousins of the groom and bride attempt to push her/him down as they stand on stage; the last person standing, it is said, will be the stronger partner in the marriage. One bride told me that she got nervous at this point: 'Normally I am the boss, and I boss my cousins around, but as a bride, I couldn't.'

The next stage of *khādi* proceedings entails a male intrusion into the female *purdah*-space, comparable to the entry of the male family pall-bearers in the *gham-kor*. The men on the bride's side – her father, brothers, uncles and sometimes cousins – enter the courtyard to bear the bride away.[12] At the *Rukhsatee* (departure), the bride is walked by her father or brothers to the bedecked car after tearful farewells from the women of her family and household. Grima has interpreted this momentary sadness as '*gham*' (1998: 52);[13] Delaney, in another Muslim context,

---

[11] Comparatively, the Maduzai Pashtuns say that 'a big feast', which for the local Khans may involve feeding upwards of 2,000 people, 'tastes good'; it is also a clear sign of both economic and political success and is likely to bring yet further success in the future (Tapper 1991: 174, see also 173).

[12] Iqbal compares the '*Doli*' (bride's palanquin) to a '*zindajinaza*' (coffin) (1997: 108).

[13] Bibiane say weddings may include moments of '*khabgaan*' (sadness), rather than *gham* (in the sense of the event itself), just as death events may include laughter as the days of mourning wane.

120   *Sorrow and joy among Muslim women*

more aptly, notes, 'The crying symbolizes love; if a [Turkish] mother didn't cry, one would suspect she didn't care for the girl' (1991: 131).

The *jhanj* (convoy of in-laws) drive with the bride to the groom's village in a flotilla of cars.[14] At the threshold of her new house, the bride is brought from the car by her female affines. One bride described her arrival at her new house: 'When I arrived, it was from one set-up to another, I had a sinking feeling and I started to cry. Probably, it was the change; and none of my own family were there.' The Quran is then held above the bride's head. Later in the evening, the mother-in-law offers the bride a special drink made with sweetened milk and almonds, called '*goot*' (literally, sip). It is said that whichever girl drinks the *goot* after the bride will be next to marry.

The *Walima* or the third day of the wedding is carried out on the boy's side and publicly celebrates the consummation of the marriage in accordance to a Hadith (Tirmidhi) that states, 'make this marriage publicly known, solemnise it in the mosques and play tambourines in honour of it'. The *Walima* is seen to be a necessary symbolic public marker of marriage.[15] The successful prosecution of a *khādi* wedding and the production of the married couple as an accepted social sub-unit within a family are at stake on this day. The transfer of the bride between households must pass without any suspicion of premarital sexual expression or, as understood in *Pukhtunwali*, her being violated (cf. Werbner 1986). The repeated public demonstrations of the marriage bond explicitly link two families and their *gham-khādi* networks, and clarify the new social status of the bride as a junior Bibi in her affinal household. The fear of this change of status being inadequately conveyed is a great source of tension among the groom's female relatives, who usually host the *Walima* in the household into which the bride will be adopted.

While some guests attend all three wedding days, more distant relatives may attend only the *Walima*, driving down from Islamabad for the day and returning after the event is over. Lunch is served with the hosts from the marital household's side repeatedly urging food on their guests. The bride's mother may bring a number of large, silver trunks, displaying the dowry contents to the groom's family relatives and guests. This procedure manifests the bride's mother's fulfilled dowry obligation. Excluding immediate family and cousins, guests return home after tea. One particular *khādi* may end but the process of attending and participating in other *gham-khādi* continues for most men and women. One twenty-one-year-old Pukhtun bride from Swat, who married a Lahori Punjabi living in Pindi, described to me how only two weeks after her wedding, she was obliged to perform other *khādi* among her kin in Swat, thus illustrating the ever-renewed urgency of *zeest-rozgār* demands:

---

[14] Charles Lindholm notes that 'the *junj* . . . is a display of solidarity with the groom and his family' (1982: 137).
[15] In Shia Islam, one of the four conditions under which marriage may be void is if the marriage is not consummated, with the bride remaining a virgin (Ferdows 1985: 27).

After two weeks of my own marriage, a cousin of mine was getting married, so I went back to Swat. As this was my first time after my wedding, my mother gave me a gold jewellery set – this is a Pukhtun custom. I also called on all my relatives, and even though it was only two weeks after my wedding, everyone was asking me '*Sa dee?*' [Are you expecting?] [she laughs].

The honouring of reciprocal ties needs to be overt (and arduous) because marriage in effect enlarges kinship relations between families. My fieldwork uncovered a number of Bibiane marrying outwards, and thereby coming into intimate relationship with families who, two or three generations before, were merely acquaintances. Strathern notes, 'In societies where ... marriage rituals take centre stage ... often demanding lengthy periods of time, people make "transformed kinship" their chief problem' (1990: 264). Ceremonies 'work at making visible what works by being kept hidden; [as people] work at "reproducing" themselves, at making more kinship' (ibid.). This activity of 'making more kinship' proceeds the work of *khādi*: through the marriage itself, through the consecration of relations of obligation and reciprocity between guests and hosts, and through the affirmation of a body of common 'Pukhtun' perceptions and practices among invitees.

Wedding dances: the work of entertainment

The complexity of the work of *khādi* is suggestively embodied in wedding dances (Plates 22 and 23). For many Bibiane, dancing is an expression of the bonds of relationship – a sister may dance at her brother's wedding to express her kinship and affection. Though dancing occupies a central place in contemporary Pukhtun weddings, dancing excites much debate and verbal opposition, as I discuss below. During the *Nakreeza*, which is set aside for women, Bibiane of the boy's side and the girl's side, together with hired musicians and household maids, dance in festive celebration. Yet dancing is not confined to the *Nakreeza*. One Pukhtun Bibi, who is married to a Punjabi, reported that in her experience of non-Pukhtun weddings, people generally dance only on the first day, the *Mehendi (Nakreeza)*, While 'in the Frontier, women dance on all three days: the *Nakreeza, Wada* and *Walima*'. This statement supports my own observations that elite Pukhtuns' specifically and villagers' families more generally dance to songs from Indian movies, and other Pukhto and Urdu popular songs, on all three wedding days.

Dancing occurs immediately in front of the raised platform on which the bride is presented. As they arrive, the wedding participants arrange themselves on rows of chairs around the central stage and critically comment on the dancers. Some ask about the dancers' relationship to the bride or groom, and others even search for brides. Though usually segregated, male musicians remain present during the *khādi*. Cameramen and photographers – all of whom are *pradee saree* (male strangers) from whom *purdah* should be observed – are considered an inherent part of a contemporary wedding, even though their presence is contentious.[16] In one wedding I attended, Bibiane performed dances in the courtyard of the bride's village house, while local village-boys and girls watched with great interest from the flat mud rooftops of their houses. Some Bibiane may say they are 'shy' of dancing in public as they are being watched, and others avoid persistent requests by saying that they do not dance at all. (The word used here is *sharam*, suggesting that weddings are one occasion where Bibiane are expected to overcome their fear of shame or public display by bodily signifying their affiliation to the bride and groom's families.) The social éclat of weddings is evaluated by the performance and quality of hired singers and dancers (Tapper 1991: 175); Delaney, in a Turkish context, observes, '[t]he women's celebration is comparable to the community of men gathered at the mosque' (1991: 135).[17]

Bibiane dance in two distinguishable styles: the conventional Pukhto dance (*gadedal*) involves little bodily movement; only the turning of wrists or the bending of ankles diverts attention from the woman's body. Dances are typically performed in groups, although some dances arouse other women's critical comments.[18] In contrast to Pukhtun dance, a more contemporary and 'modern' style of dancing is imitated from Indian Bollywood movies.[19] Here movement is concentrated in the more provocative parts of a woman's body, her shoulders and hips, which are thrust back and forth vigorously. In various weddings, younger sisters of brides and grooms chose to dance 'Indian-style' (Plate 22); on occasions, male cousins were brought into the female space to dance among the women like Indian actors and actresses in movies. This often caused a stir among the female audience, prior to the boy's identification as a brother or cousin. Female relatives of the groom and bride dance separately, almost in a competition. Both sides are subject to scrutiny as they consolidate their kinship group through dance.

The crowd of dancers consists both of an indeterminate celebratory body, whose physical participation lends substance to the marriage contract, and of a group of individuals with determinate relationships to the bride, the groom and their families. Singers will typically select a particular member of the crowd and direct their songs towards her. Bibiane may dance towards others as a form of affectionate

---

[16] On scholarly debates on Muslim women's wedding dances, see Delaney 1991: 127, 135; Grima 1998: 43; Tapper 1991: 175.

[17] On the *adab* (respect and behaviour) of musicians, see Silver 1984: 327, 329, and on the Hindu origin of music and its problematic status in a Muslim or Pakistani context, see 324; on music as an act of devotion, see Marsden 2002.

[18] Bourdieu suggests that besides being an expressive or representational art form, collective dancing itself enacts a form of social order: 'The reason why submission to the collective rhythms is so rigorously demanded is that the temporal forms or the spatial structures structure not only the group's representation of the world but the group itself, which orders itself in accordance with this representation' (1991: 163).

[19] Comparatively, Imtiaz Ahmad notes: 'the customs and rituals observed by Muslim communities [in India] at the time of marriage are adaptations of the customs and rituals observed generally within the region' (1978: xxv). He observes further, 'the customs of presentation (*joran*), of singing of songs by women (*bainam*) and of the ritual purification baths given to the bride and the groom (*naoni*) are easily comparable to similar customs observed by the Hindus of that area' (ibid.).

notice. In one instance, after I had returned from Cambridge to my fieldsites, a senior Bibi distinguished me in this way. In village weddings, women will dance up to relatives and friends and move their hands, saying: 'Why? You have come all the way from Islamabad for the wedding; shouldn't I dance specially for you?'[20]

Audiences debate the different styles and meanings of the dancing. Nahida, a young Bibi in her twenties who lives in Swat, told me in Pukhto at her brother's wedding:

> Before people danced *sada* [simply]. Now they have learnt from TV *India-walla* dances. The *masharān* [elders] don't like it because the *badan* [body] shakes, and they think it is *behaya ao sharam de* [immodest and shameful].

Dancing in Swat and Mardan offers younger Bibiane a historically novel avenue for self-expression in the supposedly all-female space of the *Nakreeza*. The bodily expressiveness which it grants women has perhaps been tolerated insofar as it has articulated itself in the interstices of an important life-course (*gham-khādi*) occurrence, whose nature is determined by women. It would appear that dancing has passed from being a mere form of entertainment to being a physical sign of participation in the wedding and its happiness (female relatives of the couple are now pressured to join in, suggesting dancing has become a 'work' of entertainment). The following exchange between a Khan from *bar* Swat, reputedly one of the most 'conservative' and Pukhto-observing families, and an elder, Begum-Bibi, illustrates the complexity and historical mutability of dance:

> NASIR KHAN: Except for the mullah, almost every family watches TV, satellite and Indian channels. The other day in my nephew's wedding in Swat, my nieces were dancing and singing just like in Indian *filmoona* [films]!
>
> BEGUM-BIBI: There is a male *dum* [dancer] in Swat who said, 'Before [during the Swat state] you Bibiane and Badshahyan used to make us dance, now the Bibiane dance and I play the *sāz* [music].'[21]

This change is striking in the general context of Pakistan's wider Islamic society, where dancing and drumming in festive contexts are seen as 'un-Islamic practices' (see, for example, Ansari 1992: 151–2; Cook 2000: 68, 90, 444; Freitag 1988: 145; Marsden 2002: 128). Dancing has particularly been regarded as questionable in Swat, and more widely in the Frontier. Barth (1959; 1981b) and Charles Lindholm (1996: 37; 1982: 118–21) point out the lowly status of the *dum* (dancer) or *nai* (barber, whose wives may be dancers, *dummāne* (derogatory: prostitutes)) in Pukhtun social hierarchies. A number of Bibiane who attended Al-Huda did

---

[20] Bibiane may dance themselves since a troupe of male *dumman* or musicians charge as much as 3,000 rupees each; another source of expenditure is the hundreds of five and ten rupee notes thrown over the heads of the dancers and the bride. Three sisters arranging a wedding told me: 'We wanted to call [female] *dummāne* from Lahore but they are too expensive – some demand two and a half lakhs!'

[21] Indeed many older Bibiane and *daigāne* who were fully involved in the daily lives of Bibiane note that in contrast to the present, '*dumman*' used to be invited frequently for every *khādi*: weddings, births and circumcisions.

not participate in the *Nakreeza*, nor did they dance – although some may dance wholeheartedly on other days in the privacy of their bedrooms. It is even more striking for Bibiane, who observe strict *purdah* in the village, to dance. One older village Bibi condemned younger Bibiane's exposure of themselves as 'all *show sha* [showing off]'. In her mind, their thoughtless imitation of Indian films violated *purdah*: 'this is not Pukhto, but it has become the way of Pukhtun women'.

Abu-Lughod suggests that women's dancing at weddings represents a form of resistance to men (1990: 51). From this viewpoint, women control their own sphere by staging symbolic acts of protest and insurrection through bodily movements denied them outside the house or in the ordinary domestic environment. Nasrin, whose brother forbade her to undertake professional employment or to drive a car, told me: 'People will not say anything bad when the sisters or the mother of a boy dance, because they are expected to be happy and dance.' As a female expression of loyalty to male kin, dancing also allows women to present themselves subversively in terms of some men's expectations. Women may pressure others to dance and be refused, while onlooking Bibiane may approve or be critical of the communal, cross-class or inter-gender nature of the celebration.

In one wedding, Ranigul, a groom's father's sister (in her forties), danced close to her sisters and said:

I have a hurt hip, yet because of happiness I am dancing the most. But my sister-in-law [the groom's mother] will probably not appreciate it. She will say, 'So what? After all it's her brother's son! She is supposed to dance!'

Different relatives express kinship relationships in diverse and sometimes conflicting ways. Here, Ranigul risked her own respectability by dancing for her nephew, at one point even referring to herself by the derogatory term '*dumma*' (dancer). The wives of paternal uncles and cousins, with whom the groom's immediate family may have been in dispute, symbolically heal the breach in relationship by participating wholeheartedly in wedding festivities (dancing and throwing money). Bibiane conceal their feelings of stress from the guests of the wedding. To the public, Ranigul expressed her bond with her nephew, her brother and with his wife (Ranigul's sister-in-law) by extension.

So far I have presented the conventional sequence of events at weddings; other examples of *khādi* exhibit individuality by departing from this order of procedure. Weddings are characterised by a tension between what individuals wish to do (dance or not dance, socialise in families or more widely), and what they feel compelled to do at the essentially collective event. The sense of co-operative and collective work is maintained throughout the different phases of the *khādi*: in travel, through each married woman's donation of wedding money (which shall be discussed in Chapter 5), in sitting and participation, in receiving the hosts' hospitality, in the escorting of the bride, in the dancing during the *Nakreeza* and in a range of other complicated social interactions. Correct female participation in each of these actions bestows public respectability on individual *khādi* ceremonies, which are thus legitimised as relationships continuous with the other interpersonal and inter-familial kinship bonds of society. Peoples' marriages that fail to follow the precepts of *Pukhtunwali* by excluding members of their *gham-khādi* circle deprive themselves of such a constitutive social endorsement; such marriages are, rather, met with social disapproval. This 'non *zeest-rozgār*' is illustrated in the following case of a Pukhtun love marriage that developed over the internet.

An internet love marriage

The famous contemporary Pukhtun poet Ghani Khan wrote that a Pukhtun 'cannot think of love without marriage. If he does, he pays for it with his life' (1990: 13). In the account below, I show that individuals' choices in marriage were disconnected from the expectations of their community, defying the 'ideology that underpins a South Asian "arranged" marriage . . . that obligations to one's immediate and more extended family have priority over personal self-interest' (Shaw 2001: 323). Such a perception has informed a number of ethnographies within a South Asian context. Ask affirms that unmarried girls in northern Pakistan are conceptualised as 'creatures' of uncontrollable emotion, and are thus bound to forms of familial duty (1993: 208). The conflict between family ideals and self-will has provoked a broadly documented range of demands for love-marriage (see Abu-Lughod 1990: 47; Altorki 1986: 137; Alvi 2001: 60; Ask 1993; Beck and Keddie 1978: 4; Berland 1982: 89; Fischer 1991: 102; Mernissi 1985: 135; Mody Spencer 2000; Papanek 1982: 39; Shaw 2001: 324; Tapper 1991: 94). These accounts describe violent outcomes meted out to those transgressing parental sanctions. In the Mohmand Pukhtun context, A. S. Ahmed (1980) and Singer (1982: 74) describe husbands' killings of wives and their lovers in *tor* (*thor*) cases seen to have violated the family honour (A. S. Ahmed 1980: 202–12). Elsewhere, lovers may be killed by the woman's kin, partners separated and individuals disinherited, ostracised or otherwise sundered from interaction with kin.

As seen at the beginning of this chapter, Pukhtun mothers of brides and grooms typically play active roles in their children's marriages, often determining the type of family and bride, and are consequently involved in working towards achieving a successful wedding. The case here is of a rift between the groom and his Pukhtun mother, resolved peacefully, but through painful social compromise. Firoza and Zain's love-marriage developed over the internet. Many Pukhtun and Pakistani girls and boys have increasing access to the web in their bedrooms. In this instance, Firoza (a twenty-six-year-old with a Masters in Social Science from Karachi) began to correspond with Zain, a Pukhtun man (aged twenty-five, and a student in Canada), through email after meeting only once at a Karachi party. Zain's parents live in Islamabad; his mother is a Bibi from a less wealthy Pukhtun family, and is related to the Mardan and Swat families through marriage. Firoza's mother is Pukhtun and her father of Indian origin. The lovers married secretly, defying Pukhtun notions of collectivity and *gham-khādi* group involvement. The bond was found unacceptable by Zain's mother, as compromising her honour or *ezat*, impairing her full personhood and social identity in Pukhtun society. In the words of one anthropologist, the loss of honour means 'he or she is no longer able to face others. Honour is the public part of the self which, in order to remain communicable to others, must conform to social expectations' (Alvi 2001: 52).[22] Two years after the actual wedding, Zain's mother accepted the match, arranging a special collective *khādi* commemoration to reconcile the nuptials with *Pukhtunwali*.[23] The case is perhaps best told through separate conversations I had with Firoza and with Zain's mother. In the first, a taped interview from her apartment in Islamabad, Firoza explained the complexities of her marriage:

> The computer brings the whole world right up to your eyes [sic] . . . on the internet chat room, Zain's name was above mine, and he wanted instructions on how to use the internet, so we began to talk. After Zain's classes in Canada, we began to chat for ten hours straight, and then it went up to eighteen hours a day. Then my net used to be connected all the time. He wanted my photo to see me. After a year, he said he wanted to come to Pakistan to marry me. I told my mother – but being a Pukhtun she knew the society – she knew what the people would say, so we argued. From Canada, Zain phoned his mother, and spoke to her about me, but she told him that she wanted him to marry a cousin and would get him engaged, so he ended up disputing with her. Zain said, 'my mother is a Pukhtun, and once she puts her foot down she will not change. I know her. She will say, "this is not my choice, it's my son's choice!" ' But Zain came to Pakistan secretly, and we got married, *nikaofaied* [an anglicised term for the Arabic *nika*, legally wedded]. My husband went to Islamabad and showed his mother the *nikah-nama* (marriage certificate) to show her the proof. Zain's mother got very angry. They both fought fiercely, and Zain left the house. He had nowhere to go, so he came back to me to Karachi.

The incident illustrates how boys, as well as girls, are scrutinised and chaperoned, and how Pukhtun Bibiane's attitudes towards children's obligations are perceived as different from, but in constant contact with, the possibly more permissive stances of other Pakistani ethnicities. In a separate interview, Zain's mother presented her side, attesting a concern less for procedure than for the suitability of the marriage itself. According to her, 'Firoza's parents told us over the phone to send a proposal, and they'll marry them. I told her parents: "My husband was mad at the situation because of the way it happened. It wasn't the right way! Everything has a correct way [*Da har sa tareka yee*]. Now I'm very angry with him [Zain]." '

At this point in Firoza's account, her parents were also upset:

> My father really loves me, but this time my parents were angry when they found out – Zain's parents called my father. I was sorry . . . so my father accepted Zain on condition that we get wedded again 'properly' [i.e. publicly]. Zain came to my home, so my parents wanted to do a 'function' [Pakistani English implying 'gathering' or 'wedding reception'] for us to make it official. So they spoke to Zain's parents, but they were unco-operative. My parents still held the wedding function, so that if I had a child tomorrow people would

---

[22] Cf. Shah 1980–2: 9.
[23] Bourdieu theorises how '[r]ite[s] must be resolved by means of an operation socially approved and collectively assumed' (1991: 136). For a comparable case of elopement and marriage of a British Pakistani girl, who feared to renew contact with her angered father ten years after the incident, see Shaw 2001: 330.

not say it is *harām* [illegitimate].[24] For two years, his parents did not accept me; his mother kept telling him to divorce me. Zain almost had a nervous breakdown. I felt guilty and sad for him, because he had no one else and nowhere else to go to. But then a few months back, the mother called, and she said they wanted to patch up. So we did.

Zain's mother, just before her act of public accreditation of the marriage before all her female relatives, told me: 'I'm going along with it. He's my son, and he'll come back to me whether after five or ten years.' Clearly, the responsibility given Bibiane in marrying sons can foster feelings of maternal possessiveness and aggression towards sons' wives. Above all, the mother–son relationship is conceived as indissoluble. Firoza confirms:

Zain is very dominated by his mother. I have seen that in this community. Pathans usually get very dominated by their mothers. He had studied abroad; but the thoughts remained: if you are a Pathan, you remain a 'Pathan' [this colonial-era term is still used among non-Pukhtuns and some Bibiane]. When my husband is alone, he makes one decision, but changes his mind after he comes back from his mother's. Since we have moved to Islamabad, we have to go to see his mother every day, and they meet as if they have seen each other after a long time while I hang around. Looks like I have another wife to my husband, something like that!

Two years after his clandestine marriage, Zain's deferred wedding reception followed the conventional *khādi*-style, featuring an invitation event with a feast, singing and dancing, and the reunion of hundreds of kin, affines, friends and acquaintances (including myself). In reinscribing the potential transgression of the son back into the symbolic order of *Pukhtunwali*, the mother's own honour in the public eye – her *ezat* – was effectively restored, given that '[t]he code of honour weighs on each agent with the weight of all the other agents' (Bourdieu 1991: 196). To some extent, the wide attendance at such an unorthodox *khādi* gathering mitigated its exceptional quality, since 'a gathering of many people is also one's honour [*gara hum ezat sho kana*]'. A Bibi explained:

It shows that people are coming to see the host, because she does *gham-khādi* with them, people will come to see her. That is her *ezat*. But if she did not keep up with them, and her house was *tash-tor* [literally, empty and black: receiving no visitors], then people will say, 'What honour does she have? None.' So this is also her *ezat* that people say: '*gara raghla* [the crowd has gathered].'

The work of *khādi*, both in hosting and in attending, healed the breach in social relationships caused by Zain's liaison. However, because *gham-khādi* builds over generations, Zain's mother could not invite her circle to the 'second wedding' on the same terms as she had attended their festivities. Thus the reparative work of the festivity, exercising the 'right of a mother' (*de mor haq*), was only partially accepted by many participants. This case highlights how Bibiane understand the

---

[24] In relation to food the term *harām* implies 'strictly forbidden'. In a different context, Nancy Tapper points out that among the Durrani Pashtun 'the children of mixed marriages may be described as hybrids (*du-raga*, literally, "two-veined")' (1991: 57).

public wedding reception to be a marriage contract not only between a bride and groom, but also between families, kinship networks and widespread *gham-khādi* circles (see Tapper 1991: 14).

To enhance our understanding of the complexity of *khādi* I will briefly look at birth as another aspect of *khādi*. The local concept of the 'work' of attendance and giving money in birth is also categorised under *zeest-rozgār* and *gham-khādi*.

Birth: *ombaraki*

Bibiane specifically, and Pukhtun women more generally, often say that the birth of children (particularly sons) completes the personhood of a woman, both socially and in terms of a desirable life-trajectory. As a new member of her husband's household, a bride is not expected to work in the home for a year until she has her first child. One newly married Bibi remarked, 'I don't think a woman is complete without children.' This widely shared expectation means that Bibiane see birth as the next 'natural' phase of marriage. Birth-visits tend to be soberly happy, but less vibrant than weddings. During the period of my fieldwork, I participated in more than twenty birth *ombarakiāne* (pl.), or congratulatory birth-visits, accompanied by other Bibiane and maids or with my husband. A Bibi's location, context and family relationship determine who accompanies her for home visits. In the village context, a Bibi may go with a group of Bibiane (her mother – or sister/s-in-law) and a male family driver; in the city, she may undertake visiting with her husband or alternatively with a sister.

The general pattern of an *ombaraki* for many Bibiane is as follows: often a couple or a small group of Bibiane visit the mother and baby in the hospital or at home without prior notification. As on a *tapos* enquiry, visiting men do not enter the mother's room unless very closely related (brothers, uncles), and even then leave when a female guest from another family enters. While men discuss national and local politics with the father to one side, Bibiane sit beside the mother as she lies in bed, asking detailed and other intimate questions about the *khādi*. Much is said about whether the baby's looks 'have gone' to her father's or mother's side. Visitors may further enquire about the type of birth and the weight of the baby. In reply, the mother gives detailed descriptions of the first moments of birth and the father's reaction to the baby. After about an hour, the women wish the mother *salāms*, place an envelope with money (between Rs.300 (£3) to Rs.2,000 (£21, depending on the relationship and earlier reciprocal exchange) under the baby's pillow or give it to the mother herself, and depart. All the envelopes bear the name of the woman who gives the money, allowing the mother to tally the identities of donor families and the amounts given. At many events, I was struck by how well Bibiane remembered exactly how much money they had received from the different members of their *gham-khādi* networks, as much as ten years after the event. The assumption is that the receiver will repay the amount in *gham-khādi* events over the course of her lifetime.

Celebrating khādi 129

On departure, a Bibi may send her child or maid to her husband with the message '*Bibi wai, zoo*?' (Bibi says, shall we go?). Bibiane cover themselves appropriately with their *sazare*, and leave separately from non-related men (who will leave the room). In the car, I often heard Bibiane provide their husbands with detailed accounts of the baby's name, looks and birth, in addition to other important information about family relationships and disputes. The husband then enquires about issues he could not, in propriety, discuss with other men.

It is now possible to compare some structural features of *gham* and *khādi*. Both necessitate the gathering of people; as one Bibi told me on the way to a funeral, using the words of an Indian song: '*Kia barāt hoti hay, kia janaza hota hay, log jama hote hay. Aik hee bāth hoti hay*' ('Sometimes a wedding, sometimes a death, people come together in both events. It is the same thing'). Preparation for both requires similar effort – ordering and organising chairs, *shamiane* and *degoona* (large pots) – with the meals symbolising a form of gift. Furthermore, both *gham* and *khādi* obey the tripartite organisation of commemorative events proposed by Van Gennep (1977) – there are three days of observance in death and weddings; and forty days mark the initial phase of mourning (*Salwekhtamma*) and celebration after birth (*Salwekhtee*). These time-schemes regulate the reassimilation of mourning or celebrating families into the community.

This chapter has shown that a number of critical or constitutive female procedures in weddings take place in particular house-spaces (or spaces outside the house). Women's presence, or active forms of ceremonial participation (like dancing or scattering material or money), is determined by their familial relation to the bride or groom. Since forms like dancing make or perform kinship, bride's and groom's side relatives often dance or socialise separately in an assertion of kin identity, even as this is subsumed in a wider festive body of revellers. The allocation of duties and activities among women, as in the case of funerals, portrays the structure of reciprocal relations always implicit in female sociality. Aunts may hold up money in the *Nakreeza*, while *daigāne* dance on stage with their Bibi's daughters or granddaughters; less close but still dependent maids and village-women will watch the dancers from low roofs. This concerted, but minutely differentiated, effort among women represents the 'work' of participating at and 'making' a wedding.

My account of *khādi* also relates the physical and celebratory coming together at weddings with Pukhtun forms of elite-family and cross-class social solidarity ordinarily secured by *tlal-ratlal*. Chapter 3 described funerals as acts of social cohesion, predicated on ideas of *Pukhtunwali*, that bring poor tenants, village people and Khanān together. Bibiane's weddings are distinctive in bringing together people of both sexes from different social backgrounds, though attendance on the part of the poor is by invitation. Weddings secure social continuity in a comparable way to funerals: they produce unions as proper extensions to pre-existent patterns of kin (and thus social and *gham-khādi*) relationship. Women's 'work' in this connection centrally involves the certification of individual marriages as 'correct' enactments of Pukhto procedure, seen and approved by women's own eyes. The female activities and conventional procedures of *khādi* celebration – from energetic forms like dancing to more sedentary forms like accepting food – connote a mode of social presence and collective witness of wedding rites.

Pukhtun and Islamic notions of shame around bodily processes give women special authority to authenticate deaths, births and weddings. At weddings, the bride and groom are presented to a female audience; in *ombaraki* and *haqiqa* (head-shaving) ceremonies, women observe the baby at birth. Male kin depend on close female relatives to confirm weddings and births (Shaukat Ali 1997: 215). The public nature of festivities eases transitions across a liminal zone joining states of life – life/death and maidenhood/marriage. The explicit disavowal of *sharam* in the case of virginal brides safeguards the honour of both families. Thus Bibiane's confirmation of the giving away of the bride, of her marital relationship with her husband and her defloration, represents a form of engagement with men and male concepts of family honour, however temporary the ceremonial interactions between the genders within the *kor*.

My description of ceremonies within the house extends from my articulation of the *kor*-space in Chapter 2 where I posited analogies between the house and a range of Bibiane's *purdah* practices, such as veiling. The *purdah* system which insists on a segregated *kor* for women now generates analogous forms of *purdah*-enclosure (notably the cordoned-off backs of cars), which are being assimilated into ceremonial patterns. In striking contrast, *gham* and *khādi* stage the exceptional incursion of men into the segregated women's zone. The appearance of male kin in the *kor* (to bear away the coffin or *dolai* (bride's palanquin)) allows women to put faces to names, paradoxically making present the whole body of a (section of) society at the time of the loss or departure of one of its members. This particular scene, in which Bibiane expressly look at their male kin, may serve as an emblem for the role of visual witness which they play throughout *gham-khādi* events, consecrating the social legitimacy of proceedings.

The concept of 'work' developed throughout, particularly in my treatment of the anthropology of the house in Chapters 2 and 3, incorporates physical efforts (travel, food preparation) into broader notions of socially responsive, thoughtfully directed action (*aql*). The deployment of this word in a Pukhtun Bibiane's context, in a sense different from the religious meaning, enjoins the proper observance of ritualised actions or appropriate moods at life-event ceremonies. Bibiane are thus said to be deficient in sense, or in an appreciation of Pukhto, if they fail to perform expected emotions at particular ceremonial junctures. At stake in weddings for individual Bibiane is others' (and her own) assessment of her public reputation or *ezat*, as someone who complies with a requirement to attend. At stake for a family is their freedom from taint, as socially attested and (as discussed in chapter 3) their social status, implied by the size of attendance (the *khalak* or 'people'; see Barth 1986: 32; Bourdieu 1991: 171).

Yet if the outcome of Bibiane's participation in ceremonies is typically social approval (Delaney 1991: 135), the possibility exists of procedures going awry.

Relations can founder and be unmade. In one scandalous instance, an unmarried cousin broke up a marriage when she told a prospective bride about the groom's affair with another relative. The subsequent stigma, while not resulting in any honour killing, nevertheless stained all participants. In this way, actions intended to reproduce an immemorial order of *Pukhtunwali*, in practice preserve, adapt and problematise 'convention' in multivalent ways. If one way to describe *gham-khādi* ceremonies is through itemising their conventional forms, another is through exploring the ways in which these forms are internally contradictory, characterised by impossible demands and subject to revision in new circumstances. The next chapter examines how *gham-khādi* as a system of ideas is itself problematic in Pukhtun thought and practice in conjoining certain presuppositions – of Islam and 'custom', or 'tradition' and 'modernity' – in conflicting ways. *Gham-khādi* continues to project Pukhto into the future, but as the vehicle of new or distinct forms of female agency or Islamic knowledge. Such slippages, as well as such transmissions, of social meaning go on so long as marriage joins '*alak*' (boy, unmarried man) and '*geenay*' (girl, unmarried woman), and transforms their public status into '*sare*' (man) and '*khaza*' (woman) – that is, into people who become accountable, 'on whom the responsibility to do *gham-khādi* in turn falls' (*de wada na makhke de jeenai hisaab kitab na yee; wada na pas hisab shoro shee*).

5
The work of *gham-khādi*: 'Not to do *gham-khādi* is shameful (*sharam*); to do it a burden'

In my laughter there is grief; with sad eyes do I smile. (*Pa khanda ke me jara da; pa khapa stargo khandegam*)
Ghani Khan

Before there was little *Gham*, now these *Ghamoona* [pl.] have taken me off my *rozgār* [employment]. (*Pookha ba kala kala Gham wo was de Ghamoona da rozgār a ooweesthama*)
(From the popular contemporary Pukhto song '*Gham*', sung by Rahim Shah)

At times I enjoy it, at times I don't; *gham-khādi* is like a *duty* that has to be done.
(Middle-aged convent-educated Bibi)

This chapter examines the problematic and stressful aspect of *gham-khādi* as experienced by Bibiane not just physically in different milieux but in their reflection upon diverse areas of their lives. The performance of *gham-khādi* prompts women to think about its relation to Pukhtun categories of religion and 'custom', right and wrong, the individual and the collective, and the obligatory and the voluntary. Unlike other customs less identified with a philosophy of life or with particular celebrations, *gham-khādi* falls neither on one side of these dichotomies nor the other, but rather cuts across them in such a way as to arouse painful dilemmas for Bibiane. My analyses here begin to expose how *gham-khādi* is problematic for Bibiane in bringing to the surface deep-lying social contradictions, which demand some practical resolution given the priority granted to *gham-khādi* (or *zeest-rozgār*) over forms of professional employment (*kār-rozgār*), childcare and housework (*kor-kār*).

The term *gham-khādi*, as used by Bibiane, refers not merely to wedding and funeral ceremonies and procedures, but to a sense of social obligation underlying the performances. *Gham-khādi* as a principle of Pukhtun life and thought may be characterised not only in terms of the organising schemes above, but also as a negotiation between the poles of each; it is not simply the implementation of any single principle. Having focused ethnographically on ceremonies' features in Chapters 3 and 4, I now ask: should *gham-khādi* be collectively understood as having prior terms of enactment, or as subject to individual manipulation and strategy? Is *gham-khādi* for Bibiane governed by patterns of reciprocity that exclude personal choice, or does it represent a kind of morality, accessible to the subjective judgements of groups and individuals? If *gham-khādi* is an ingrained feature of

Pukhto, then is it in conformity with present-day understandings of Islam? Can the obligation to perform *gham-khādi* be made congruent with the Western idea of a professional career for women outside the home? The chapter draws on my observations and discussions with Bibiane, representing *gham-khādi* as the place where a number of normative and definitional concepts of gender, personhood, propriety and tradition are knotted – and are beginning to unravel.

Bibiane see the activities associated with *gham-khādi* – preparation, travel, financial and household management – and the consolidation of kin relationships through acts of attention and politeness as a form of 'work'. However, the injunctive force of work does not make *gham-khādi* an unproblematic performance of (a number of) narrowly defined acts. As we saw in Chapter 2, Bibiane describe their 'layered' lives in terms of ambiguities and contradictions – between city and village, home and school, *hujra* and *kor*. The fundamental paradox of *gham-khādi* (sadness-happiness) as a verbal formulation is yet more intractable in practice, in the sense that a funeral may take place in one village the day after a wedding in another. Bibiane also experience the paradox enshrined in the phrase in a series of daily quandaries as *gham-khādi* obligations may clash with other projects they wish to pursue, such as education, full-time employment and childcare.

References to *gham-khādi* are pervasive in people's accounts of their social experience. Bibiane and Khanān feel an overwhelming sense of responsibility in complying with expectations concerning their attendance, gifting, deportment and dress; this generates an agitated moral discourse of judgement and self-scrutiny. As husbands depend on wives to undertake *gham-khādi* on behalf of their households, the practices represent an instance of female power within a supposedly 'patriarchal' framework (Papanek 1982: 37; Shaw 1997: 149). Meanwhile, the specificity of *gham-khādi* as a distinct set of conventions between religion and Pukhto, moral choice and compulsion, grants it a language of its own, as documented in this chapter.

Collective and individual in *gham-khādi*

Gham-khādi in Pukhtun experience comprises a constant feature of life as lived and understood, yet is complex, contradictory and subject to transformation (Comaroff and Comaroff 1992: 38). One of the dimensions in which Bibiane see *gham-khādi* changing is in the different types of responsibilities required of individual subjects over the course of their lives. Another dimension concerns the always mutable question of social status (of both individuals and families) as negotiated through *gham-khādi* observances. Much of the complexity of *gham-khādi* inheres in its bridging of two levels: that of collective performance and of individual responsibility.

At one level, collective co-operation, through attendance, gifting and consumption of the feast-meal, is deemed essential to the correct performance of *gham-khādi*. As discussed in the earlier chapters, the success of an event and the prestige of a particular family are judged by the number of people (*khalak*) attending their wedding or funeral (see A. S. Ahmed 1980: 243, 288; Barth 1986: 32). A large attendance maintains honour, while scant attendance may lead to the ostracism of 'the person whose *gham/khādi* it is. It is as if she is not "recognised": she is "no one" in society.' Sumaira, in her late thirties, originally from Swat, married to her matrilateral parallel cousin from Mardan and now living in Islamabad, explained the significance of *gham-khādi* to me in English:

Gham-khādi has this importance, from *roz-e-awal* [Persian: from the beginning] both for men and for women, like when people get together collectively for prayers in a mosque. Why? The importance of this is that people come together collectively and understand and share each other's *dokh dard* [Urdu: sorrow and pain]. It's a community feeling. Tomorrow, God forbid, if it is your sorrow or illness the same people will ask and come to you when you need them'

In *gham-khādi*, the collectivity of kin and affines assembles from the same and other villages, cities and even foreign countries to gather at the site of origin. The *gham-khādi* event in this manner places emphasis on *Pukhtunwali* both in regulating social relations and on an individual level, and is an important constituent in the self-understanding of urban or emigrant Pukhtuns. In the case of one wedding, a Bibi who lived in the United States with her Pukhtun husband, praised *gham-khādi* for joining dispersed relatives. With increased global transport and communication, *gham-khādi* becomes crucial in the affirmation of people's Pukhtun identity. Close relatives living abroad are expected to return for the ceremony (cf. Shaw 2000; Werbner 1986); and more distant relatives phone. The work in *gham-khādi* makes itself felt in the literal and physical cost of travel and attendance.

Against an emphasis on collectivity (and cases where parents may act for married children, or wives for husbands), every adult individual is ultimately responsible for performing reciprocal cycles of 'going and coming' with his/her wider social network. Participation is said to engage different dimensions of personhood – the body (*jismi zor*: physical effort), mind (*dimagh*: intellect) and emotions (*zre*: heart). Bibiane are expected in a generalised moral register to keep up relationships with kin and affines (through visiting, solicitude, *gham-khādi* attendance), and also to carry off social performances in the ceremonial context (presenting oneself to the senior women of the afflicted or celebrating household, addressing people correctly by seniority and family closeness, gifting correctly and in accordance with an accepted procedure). Despite the usual practice of husband and wife attending *gham-khādi* together, in segregated spaces, individual women are understood as agents exercising control over these forms of behaviour. Actions in such a context inform a public view of one's female morality, in which 'psychological' and 'social' components are indissoluble. A common proverb is repeated among Bibiane, '*khpal ezat pa khpal las ke de*' (one's own *ezat* is in one's own hands; cf. Altorki 1986: 135; Lindholm 1995: 64). If distinct styles of behaviour are expected of Bibiane in *gham-khādi* contexts, then it is also understood that women may fall short of them. Thus two orders of moral thinking interlock in the context of *gham-khādi*: first, women's adept or inept performance of repeatable procedures; and second, individuals' knowing deviation from them (for example, through notably ostentatious or self-effacing styles of self-presentation).

The actual deployment of tactics in socialising and presenting one's gift as a household-head in ceremonies is far more subtle than schematic moral ideas of good/bad and conformity/deviance would suggest. Each woman (responsible for more than herself) in the act of giving money on behalf of her own family (and husband) will take great care to register her action with both the recipient and the attending assembly of women. She will announce her contribution, writing 'from Mr and Mrs Khan', for example, on the envelope. Bibiane are concerned to make an impression through the way in which they arrive and present their offerings, taking care to acknowledge the senior women of the household (see Chapter 3 for an analysis of Bibiane's discourse of skill in *gham-khādi*). Persons seek to maintain a respectable public face, even, in some cases, at the cost of excluding or asserting precedence over others. These manoeuvrings of position and status within extended families, with competing sisters-in-law, other affines and step-relations (co-wives and their children), make *gham-khādi* the site of peculiar conflicts (as was seen in Chapter 3).[1] These forms of female rivalry are often treated light-heartedly, with an undertone of deeper feeling. An approaching sister-in-law may be derided *sotto voce* as a '*balla*' (fiend) or '*badda*' (bad), before being greeted cordially. Thus, as we have seen, under the co-operative and collective sense of *gham-khādi* lies another level of relationships fraught with competition and tension.

Unmarried girls and women not obliged to attend *gham-khādi* are schooled in the skill and politics involved in *gham-khādi* from a young age. On one occasion in Islamabad, I accompanied a Bibi, her daughter and niece to the *bazār* for an evening drive. The Bibi bought a bouquet of red roses (*gwalāb*) through her half-opened car window from a persistent young beggar-girl. After the Bibi had given them to her five-year-old daughter in the car to present to her bed-bound grandmother, the child's seven-year-old cousin said, 'You hold the flowers now [in the car], but I will "give" them.' The Bibi turned to me and whispered, turning her eyes towards the seven-year-old, that the little girl displayed '*chalāki*' (sharpness). At the age of seven, she understood the social value of being the person to offer gifts, skilfully renegotiating the terms of exchange so that she could be the giver.[2]

Tension coexists with forms of tutelage into Pukhto procedures, as affinal relations (mothers-in-law and sisters-in-law) teach brides how to perform correct *gham-khādi* in the context of their own extended families. Anthropological accounts from the wider Muslim world, specifically South Asia, recurrently note the role extended families play in shaping individual behaviour. In her account of joint-family households in rural Rajasthan, Kolenda notes that early marriage necessitates 'the joint family function[ing] as [the] protector and guide of young couples' (1989: 103); for newly married Bibiane, this protection extends to their

---

[1] On competitive rivalry and 'upping the ante' among Pukhtuns, see also Grima 1998: 75; and Lindholm 1982: 74, 191.
[2] Barth noted that when faced with a choice, Swati Pukhtuns consider private rather than group interest, switching sides from one group to another when it suits their interests (1986: 2).

training as workers in *gham-khādi*. Nazia (aged forty-five at the time of this conversation) recalled:

> I was only fifteen when I got married. But my *yor* [husband's eldest brother's wife] taught me everything, like dressing up and how to meet people in *gham-khādi*. She has trained me the way you train your own daughter.

The mutual obligations of *gham-khādi* define for Bibiane the particular social and familial networks in which they will engage during the course of their lives. Older informants told me that every family has their specific *riwajoona* (ways/customs) of *gham-khādi* (i.e. who with and how they do *gham-khādi*), in terms of both whom they favour with attendance and their procedures of visiting, gifting and recognising reciprocity. Arrangements between families vary according to the amounts exchanged (e.g. between Rs.500 and Rs.2,000), the degree of non-kin attendance for political families and expectations of exact financial reciprocity for poorer scions. Beginning the performance of *gham-khādi* can be a daunting and bewildering experience for young women, who are treated as full independent moral agents for the first time. A non-Pukhtun wife, Aliya, captured in English the difficulty of establishing new affinal relationships:

> If you do not attend *gham-khādi* they say: 'she doesn't want to be part of the family'. It's very clannish. It took me a long time to understand that all these women are all cousins; and cousins of their husbands. If I don't go they say she is an 'outsider', and I am pushed out more. So I *work* hard to meet these people.

In-marriage, as proved time and again in family *gham-khādi* gatherings, is proposed as the making of kinship in two ways: not only does the non-consanguineous bride affiliate herself with the relatives of her husband, but she also works at building relationships with a network of household spouses who are also cousins, overcoming a further boundary of kinship. When such a woman integrates herself successfully, her choices in terms of small acts of compliance with group norms will have bound her to the collectivity of her affines.

Reciprocity and morality

In committing herself morally to a *gham-khādi* relationship, a Bibi reciprocates another's attention firstly with respect to time and presence, and secondly with respect to money. The quality of visiting is evaluated by the amount of money given, immediacy of attendance and time stayed (from morning to evening for three days, or forty days). All these represent criteria for how 'well' a bond has been discharged. The identity of *gham-khādi* as a form of reciprocal *tlai-ratlal* in theory guarantees a return on visits paid. Financially, this reciprocity takes the normative form of receivers giving back more than they were offered. One Bibi observed: 'You come to my house [for *ombaraki*] and give me a gift [customarily money]; in return I must go to your house for the same duration of time and pay back the equivalent or more, but never knowingly less [although in practice some people give according to their means].' Attendance at others' festivities is more important than money itself, and determines whether a relationship is sustained or ruptured. The gift of one's presence at ceremonies is normally, however, accompanied by a financial subvention, and vice versa; both together signify the continuance of family bonds (Abu-Lughod 1986: 69). To borrow Mauss's terms (1990), *gham-khādi* gifts do not exist as isolated and unsignifed objects, but rather carry a symbolic part of the donor: in a display of hospitality, women offer their guests their unconditional attention, time and presence. The gift of money also represents and embodies the donor and receiver's social relationship.[3]

Chapters 3 and 4 focused ethnographically on the particularities of hospitality, courtesies, entertainment, ritualised or repeated performance, dances and feasts (see Mauss 1990: 3). Procedures for the presentation and reception of gifts of money are calibrated to the family relationships of both donor and recipient and, more markedly, the recipient and the 'subject' of the gathering (the dead person, the newborn baby, the bride's mother or female guardian). Bibiane may accept money from *gham-khādi* guests in different capacities: as brides, mothers of newborn babies, wives of ill husbands or widows. At weddings, a bride's mother, who stands at the entrance of the wedding reception, will be greeted by each arriving guest, then handed an envelope containing money (this may vary from Rs.200 to Rs.2,000, the amount depending on reciprocity and, to some extent, means). This money is meant for the bride, and her mother hands over all the envelopes to her daughter after the ceremony. The mother may at this point write down the names and amounts of money given by each guest, often assessing her relationship with each woman according to the amount of money given. This list will be an important reference for the bride in her future reciprocations as, until individual sums of money are repaid, the receiver is in a state of debt.

Expectations of reciprocity in *gham-khādi* practically affect Pukhtuns in their day-to-day existence. Even many of the *gharibanān* (poor) maintain a public image by gifting large sums and hosting *gham-khādi* events.[4] Maids may depend on their Bibiane as patrons from whom to borrow large sums in loans (during my fieldwork I knew three maids who borrowed more than Rs.10,000 (£105) in one transaction from Bibiane for their families' *gham-khādi*). If someone is *na-chāra* (very poor), they procure loans (*qarz*) from village shopkeepers, wealthier relatives

---

[3] On hospitality as a special variety of gift-giving, see Barth 1986: 77. On unreciprocated or free gifts in 'Jain society', see Laidlaw 2000, who theorises that 'The self-negating free gift is . . . present, even if only for a moment, in the transactions which make up systems of reciprocal gift exchange' (628).

[4] One older maid told me: 'Here [in Mardan] there is a wedding of a widow's son – the *jore* [suits], clothes, the rice, everything are *qarz* [loaned]. I told the woman: "What is the sense in taking so many loans?" The mother of the groom replied: "People will laugh at me if I don't have these things to show at my son's wedding."' The speaker herself did not 'give a single meal' at the marriage of any of her four sons due to her unwillingness to take out a *qarza* (loan).

and neighbours. Many of these loans lead to life-long debt.[5] Financial gifts pass not merely between members of different households, but also, in a generally more symmetrical arrangement, between affines. The morning after her wedding, a bride also receives money from the closest of her husband's relatives: her married sisters-in-law (both her husband's sisters and his brother's wives) and mother-in-law, who typically determine amounts beforehand, so that all sisters-in-law give equally. The inscribed envelope is then presented to the bride with large sums of *ombaraki* money. In Mardan at the time of my fieldwork, close relatives such as first cousins or sisters-in-law gave Rs.10,000 to brides; in Swat some Bibiane even reported giving Rs.20,000. Funeral payments range from Rs.500 to Rs.20,000 for a very close relative. Births 'cost' from Rs.200 to Rs.2,000, and illness upwards of Rs.500. Distant relatives are not required to underwrite funeral expenses, though a wealthy elder who did so would be thanked after the gift had been politely refused in *sath*. (There are no forms for young people giving to the old in such circumstances.) The differences between funeral and wedding gifting points to the greater closeness of relatives in sharing grief; *khādi* are happier occasions, in which all may participate. Very tentatively, though, the movement among elite Pukhtuns from closely reciprocated patrilateral cousin marriages to exogamy suggests that *khādi* contributions keep alive a family's possibility of later marrying into the circle (benefitting from the 'good' of a bride or giving a bride).

Without ceasing to be obligatory, Bibiane's responsibilities in *gham-khādi* are graded according to their household seniority.[6] One of my older informants, Bibiji (aged sixty), stated: '*Masharān* [elders] give more in weddings and births of people not so close [distant relatives], about Rs.500 [£5] to Rs.1,000 [£10], while *kasharān* [younger women] give less, about Rs.300 [£3].' According to my observations and the statements of younger Bibiane, however, this was rarely the case. Bibiane in their twenties and thirties reported giving between Rs.500 (£5) to Rs.20,000 (£210) for weddings. The younger women considered the amounts suggested by Bibiji as far too little and 'embarrassing'; many women remarked that the larger sums they gave symbolised the value which they placed upon their relationship with recipients. Larger sums may also reflect younger Bibiane's anxiety to grow roots in their marital families. A twenty-five-year-old Bibi told me that she wanted to give Rs.2,000 for the birth money of a close friend, who was also her affine, but just before visiting their house her mother-in-law interceded, causing her to reduce the amount to Rs.500 (£5) in proportion to the elder woman's gift of Rs.1,000 (£10). The amount of money younger women give in *gham-khādi* clearly exceeds the amounts given by *masharān* (elders), suggesting younger Bibiane's gifts express degrees of voluntarity.

---

[5] '[H]ospitality and the large-scale entertainment required at *gham-khādi* events were the greatest burdens on the family economy, leading to the heaviest debts' (Grima 1998: 43).

[6] 'Social status, measured through conspicuous consumption and as part of Pukhto tradition, is maintained by senior lineages although their incomes may be considerably lower than junior or non-Pukhtun groups' (A. S. Ahmed 1980: 287; see also 288).

Table 6 *Money given by Bibi for* gham-khādi *during a four-month period (March–June 2001)*

Deaths	**Cash**
1) Brother's wife (*wrandar*)	= Rs.5,000
2) Older sister (*khor*)	= Rs.5,000
3) Sister's husband (*ookhe*)	= Rs.1,000
Food offerings	
4) Husband's brother's son (*lewarzay*)	(5 *darai* of) rice, *sarwe* (1 cow) and *sanda* (1 buffalo) = Rs.10,900
Weddings	
Relatives (*khpalwān*)	Due to the many deaths of close relatives there were no weddings in Bibi's family during this year. Amount given = None
Non-relatives (*pradee*)	= Rs.1,000 (varies from Rs.100 to Rs.2,000)
Births	
Amount given for two *ombarakiāne*	= Rs.2,000
Total	**= Rs.24,900**

Table 6 shows an estimate of a *mashara* (elder) Bibi's spending on *gham-khādi* within a period of four months. The total amounts to a large sum of expenditure by local standards.[7] Another Bibi estimated spending approximately 1 lakh rupee a year on *gham-khādi*: 'I give Rs.20–30,000 for relatives' death' (see Appendix 5 for a younger Bibi's *gham-khādi* expenditure). Anthropologists confirm the major economic impact of funerals and weddings on Pukhtun families, not merely among Khanān but across social classes (A. S. Ahmed 1980: 285–8; Barth 1986: 32; and Grima 1998: 43; cf. Metcalf 1982: 21).

Maids and *daigāne* participate in the reciprocal gift economy of *gham-khādi* in a number of ways. Though maids and *daigāne* may accompany their Bibiane on all their *gham-khādi*, they do not normally give money to Bibiane (wet-nurses may give, however; in one case I observed a *dai* give Rs.100 as a birth *ombaraki* to a particular Bibi). Among villagers the expectation of gifting is not waived, even for poor married maids who give the same amount as other villagers: between Rs.100 to Rs.200 for a close relative's death, and either Rs.30, Rs.50 or Rs.100 for weddings (if the wedding is of the offspring of a sibling or husband's sibling, the gifts for a bride may cost Rs.1,000, including a pair of clothes for her trunk (*de sundak jora*), a *sazar* and shoes). A maid may also give the same amounts for the birth of a relative's child, and at illness she may take a litre of milk, eggs or a chicken. The amount a maid has received from her own relative will be reciprocated with an increase of Rs.5 (surcharges on gifts are levied to save the face of the original recipient, or *zan kooz na khkara kai*). In contrast, those unable to offer anything

---

[7] In comparison a wealthy Khan's annual income may range from 10 to 12 lakh rupees (£10,000–£12,000) and a maid's pay may average from Rs.2,400 (£25) to Rs.20,000 (£210) a year.

but their person participate marginally in society, and are visited only by a small circle of close kin.[8] While in practice Bibiane send money and food to villagers and maids' houses during their *gham-khādi* without visiting them, *gham-khādi* is understood to impose mutual, though asymmetrical, obligations. For instance, when one twenty-four-year-old maid's father died in Swat, her thirty-year-old Bibi sent the maid's mother Rs.5,000 from Islamabad; several months later when the maid's mother came to visit her daughter's Bibi, she brought two chickens (costing Rs.50 each), and on another occasion a dozen eggs (Rs.3 each). Maids widely report that their state of poverty makes them *na-chāra* (unable) to undertake expenditure beyond their means. Reciprocity that involves *gham-khādi* money in figures of Rs.1,000 and Rs.2,000 is '*droon kār*' (heavy work), meaning it is beyond their means (*chār*) and befitting only Bibiane.

Widely stated comments thus indicate that people make *gham-khādi* contributions according to their means. While the *gham-khādi* of Bibiane and maids is lopsided, that between Bibiane should ideally be characterised by reciprocity. Given that each family maintains *gham-khādi* relationships with a large number of women in other families, Bibiane who receive *gham-khādi* money collect considerable sums. The cash may be earmarked for feast money for weddings and deaths, or used for personal purposes. Bibiane say that the money given to women belongs to them; what they do with it is, in one Bibi's words, 'women's business'. She revealed that in total she received $2\frac{1}{2}$ lakh rupees (approx. £2,631) for her two sons' births which she invested in the stock market. Several other mothers bought expensive jewellery with the money, purchasing new 'sets' (necklace and earrings) for future *khādi* events. Mothers with baby daughters said that the jewellery represented a long-term investment in their daughters' dowry (cf. Ward 1997).[9]

While some Bibiane benefit financially in the short term from *gham-khādi*, the deferred nature of reciprocity means that ceremonies' cash requirements place large, unpredictable demands on the household incomes managed by Bibiane. Many revealed that they spent a large sum of the house pay *(de kor kharcha)* on *gham-khādi*; and some Bibiane stated their reliance on their own sources of income. One Bibi reported that, as a young bride, she was too shy to ask her husband for the necessary cash and 'senselessly' (*kam-aqltob*) sold her gold jewellery to pay her close kin's *gham-khādi* money. Yet as Bibiane get older and more powerful within their marital households, their duty to be munificent in *gham-khādi* proportionately increases. Many Bibiane (young and middle-aged) argued that both Islam and Pukhto conventions give women a right to her husband's wealth, whereas her own income is her own. In one Bibi's words, 'I can save it; I can spend it; I can do anything with it.' Moreover, comments were made by Bibiane suggesting

---

[8] Similarly, a maid, Sherafzoon (aged about sixty) explained the reciprocal nature of *gham-khādi* among poorer Pukhtuns: 'No one does my *tapos* [enquiry] because I am poor [*ghariba*]. I cannot afford to do *gham-khādi* [i.e. give money].'

[9] On the symbolic significance of gold as a reflection of God's divine light (*nur*), see C. A. Bayly 2001: 291–2.

that Pukhtun husbands who 'regard themselves as the head of the household and responsible for the well being of the family take pride in earning for their families and prefer that their women look after the home rather than go out for [professional] employment'. Men would consider themselves ashamed to be supported by their wife's income, as Arifa, a professionally employed Bibi, remarked:

A Pukhtun man would not have his wife spending her money on the household to throw in his face and say: 'Oh, I'm supporting the family.' No way, he would go that extra mile to make sure *his* money is spent.

The reciprocity implicit in the practice of *gham-khādi* gives it affinities with characteristically Pukhtun forms of exchange, *badal*; analogous to *badal* in another sense – that of revenge (Baal 1975: 11; and see Grima 1998: 5, 70–2 on the reciprocal structuring of revenge). Just as men seek payment from those who have insulted their honour, so women exact vengeance for social slights and neglect (particularly in cases of land dispute) by selectively observing the obligations of *gham-khādi*. I have described reciprocity as a non-negotiable obligation, but it may in fact also be refused by Bibiane's deliberate choice. In one instance, an Islamabad Bibi referring to her second cousin told me: 'Zurina's son is born [in Islamabad], but she didn't come for my twenty-one-year-old niece's *tapos* [enquiry visit] when my niece was diagnosed with cancer. So I didn't go for her son's birth *ombaraki*, even though my daughter is named after her.' In this way, much of the otherwise suppressed and deflected hostility between female affinal and kin relations is expressed through reciprocation and non-reciprocation in *gham-khādi*. In terms of how reciprocal obligations are discharged, wide scope exists for individual moral choices, as perceived offences and antagonisms work themselves to the surface in voluntary actions.

In this sense of female choice, Bibiane's control over a family's *gham-khādi* relationships may be more typical of elite than non-elite families. Among the poorer Pukhtuns who tilled farmlands in Chak Shehzad near Islamabad as tenants of Pukhtun Bibiane, men typically exercised greater direction over their wives' *gham-khādi* relations. The wife of one *zamindar* (farmer) stated: 'We have this *rewāj* [custom] that if my husband doesn't get along with anyone, including my family, then I and my children avoid those people. But if the dispute is between me and another person then my husband will not break relationships with them. Men have more *ikhtiar* [authority]; women don't, because we live in such *gharibi* [poverty].' Unlike the range of many poorer women's positions in the family, Bibiane and even some of their husbands admitted that in upper social echelons men eventually follow their wives' lead in avoiding kin. With her affines, the case is more complicated and varied; husbands may here behave with a degree of independence in maintaining personal relationships with their own mother or sister. Yet during the time of my fieldwork, there were more than two cases where relations with men's mothers and sisters were entirely severed for extended periods through their wives' disputes with them. The machinations of family politics seem more involved among Khan families, where the connections between people are

Obligation and preference: the 'burden' of performing *gham-khādi*

Bibiane's actual *gham-khādi* practices show receptivity to some degree of choice. Bibiane actively discriminate in how much *gham-khādi* to do, how immediate one's family *gham-khādi* circle should be, how to prioritise double engagements and even whether to abandon social relations with families altogether. Yet the choice of whether to do or not to do *gham-khādi* is limited. The obligatory nature of *gham-khādi* is widely perceived as binding and burdensome as it constrains as well as shapes social visiting among women. '*Gham-khādi* is a *boj* [burden] because women want to visit each other, but there are all these rules of "give and take" which restrain them,' expressed Nasreen, a twenty-two-year-old *dai*'s granddaughter, employed as a 'Lady Social Worker' (visiting women's houses as a government employee in Swati villages with medicine and contraceptives). The *gham-khādi* visitor, regardless of social status, must give on arrival to avoid the appearance of dishonour (*sharam*). Likewise, full hospitality (as seen in Chapter 2) must be displayed to avoid damaging the host's social reputation. As one convent Bibi, in her late forties, originally from Mardan and now living in Islamabad, remarked:

If you do *gham-khādi* you can't go empty handed. That's not our way. To help in that *khairat* [charity meal] you have to take something – money [*paisay*], gift [*thofa*], rice [*wreeje*], oil [*ghwaree*] and sugar [*cheenee*]. With inflation, it is a financial burden and then we can't keep it up because nobody has the time. The performance of *gham-khādi* should not be prolonged [over a period of days]. But if you don't do *gham-khādi*, people get very offended.

Rabia Bibi, in her thirties, originally from Swat but also living in Islamabad, amplified this point in English:

Gham-khādi kills everybody, rich and poor. If you don't do it, people say, 'she's an outcast'. They will boycott her socially; because, they say, she hasn't done it with us . . . but once you start doing it, there is no end.

The impasse expressed by these Bibiane is one felt across class, gender and region. For instance, a middle-aged village-woman associated with a Khan household (rumoured to be the Khan's mistress) said following a week of several kin *gham-khādi* events that she had been obliged to gift large amounts of rice, oil and flour in the village:

The *boj* [burden] of *gham-khādi* is on our *kakarai* [skulls]. So in this age we're fed up [*der thang*] with *gham-khādi*! *Gham-khādi* has burdened us greatly. Because if we do not do it – it is *sharam* [a great shame]. It takes the clothes from off our backs [literally: I have been skinned for this: *sarman me wakhatha*]. It's a burden, because *gham-khādi* never ends and the [network of] people is vast, while our incomes are comparatively small. If we don't do it, people say they don't understand *rewāj* [custom]; if we do it, we pay out more than we get in. Oh, God! My heart is fed up with this *gham-khādi*.

As reflected in the words of this outspoken woman, Bibiane also entertain a range of spirited views about *gham-khādi* and the burdens it places on them.

Such views are possible because *gham-khādi* is felt to be obligatory by Bibiane, yet it is not always welcomed or liked. Many Bibiane insisted on the invariant nature of the forms and orders of procedure acceptable in *gham-khādi*. Visiting excludes, or forecloses upon, spontaneity, since visits follow conventional patterns. The greater the intricacy of Bibiane's kinship ties, the more *gham-khādi* there is, and the more arduous it becomes. The difficulty, intensity and frequency of *gham-khādi* visits leads to Bibiane and other Pukhtun descriptions of *gham-khādi* as a '*boj*' (burden) or a '*musibath*' (problem).[10] The *boj* is one that is seen to extend from the social to the core of familial life.

In relation to childcare, Bibiane experience great levels of distress over how their children's requirements, particularly schooling, might accommodate constant interruption by mothers' *gham-khādi*. Arifa told me, 'Every time there is a death in my in-laws', I have to leave everything in Islamabad and go to the village. But I cannot take my children with me, as they will then miss three days of school.' In one case of an aunt-in-law's death, Arifa resolved her dilemma by requesting an Islamabad friend to nanny her children. The demands made by ceremonies on mothers' time also detract from their childcare. Farah, in her late thirties, who studied at the Murree Convent and works as an English-medium schoolteacher in Peshawar, told me (in the presence of her father and male cousins) that Pukhtun mothers of wealthy backgrounds spent more time buying and ordering clothes for *gham-khādi*, and attending ceremonies, than they did reading with their children. Imitating the mothers, Farah gestured: 'No *jee*! there is a death here; a wedding there [*Na jee! zama khwata mare sho; alta wada sho*]. Mothers are busy with *gham-khādi*; the father is tired, he comes home from office – the children are neglected and ignored.' Farah further gives an example of a student in her class:

Like, this little boy, who was beaten by his father. I called his mother to school and I said 'What happened?' She said, 'Oh, I wasn't at home, I had gone for my mother's brother's son's wedding.' The mother is never at home. The father comes home tired from office – he starts shouting at the children. There's no confidence at all in that child, and then they expect a good result!

Mothers hesitate to take their children to *gham-khādi* gatherings, since it involves a great deal of '*pasa kena*' (standing and sitting) or meeting and greeting. Yet leaving them in the care of a maid arouses concern and 'sadness', in the words of one Bibi, as 'your children become insecure, clinging to you when you return home'. Both

---

[10] In other contexts, social scientists studying aspects of Western work have also described its nature as a form of 'burden' (Pahl 1989: 9), indeed making the kind of social work represented by *gham-khādi* as synonymous with 'toil' (ibid.: 11).

Pukhtun and Muslim mothers are idealised as devoted figures who bestow time and love on their offspring (*kha moryane*), yet the predominant Pukhto conception of womanhood paradoxically requires their absence from the *kor*.[11] This degree of onus on women leads some Bibiane to compare their customary conventions unfavourably with those of other ethnolinguistic groups in Pakistan. One Pukhtun Bibi said:

> Punjabian are better – they visit each other for short periods, raise their hands, pray and go; but among Pukhtuns the formality is endless.

The latitude exercised by Bibiane in taking their children to *gham-khādi* or not, or travelling with their husbands, does not extend to negotiating non-attendance or forms of reciprocation in the absence of attendance. Bibiane are, thus, 'locked' into *gham-khādi* social behaviour.

Participation and exclusion: the severing of social relations

My exposition of obligatory relationships around *gham-khādi* gives substance to a concept of ceremonial performances as 'work', in the sense that work 'implements a rule'. My account situates *gham-khādi* within the context of the social relationships which it sustains, seeking to determine what space it leaves for alternate modes of thought and action (non-participation, selective participation, the individuation of gifts and so on). Yet Bibiane are keenly aware of the high stakes of performing *gham-khādi* correctly. Omission, far from opening plural or less constrained social networks to non-participants, incurs a form of 'social death' (Bourdieu 1966: 217; see also Baal 1975: 11). As two Bibiane told me:

ASMA: If you don't attend the wedding, then you have to come later for *ombaraki*. That is a very important part, because if you don't do that then all relations are broken . . .
YASMIN: The people [concerned] get *khapa* [sad] from [i.e. angry at] the person who did not attend. People say, '[s/he] didn't come for our death or wedding!' ['*Wai na marg la raghe na khādai la raghe!*'] In death if you are absent, you have got to go for the *dua* afterwards. Because if you don't do either one of these, the *ombaraki* or the *dua*, people won't do it with you!

More specifically in funerals, those who miss the important days are not invited to the Fortieth-day commemoration, and are subtly shunned in social gatherings.

The following incident indicates the importance of attending both *gham* and *khādi*. Samina Bibi (aged about forty-eight) is from a wealthy and prestigious household from Swat. She teaches, works and lives in Islamabad with her non-Pukhtun husband (from a Nawab family of Indian origin based in Lahore). Samina

---

[11] Many mothers found the role of mothering and doing *gham-khādi* difficult to maintain. One young mother said, 'I breastfed my son for two and a half years and during that time when there was *gham-khādi* I found it very difficult: as I could not leave him at home because he was attached to me. I had to take him everywhere with me, and feed him on demand. It was a very difficult time.'

injured her back, which caused her to miss her second cousin's daughter's wedding. She told me: '*Jān* ['my life', addressed to me: it's a term of affection for younger people], I stayed back. I didn't want to go to the wedding in Swat. My [older male] cousin told me: "If you do not do *gham-khādi* no one will come to you either and you'll die a lonely woman with no one by your graveside."' Compliance is thus enforced not only through the prospect of unfortunate consequences, but more directly, through the urgings of close relatives.[12] There is nothing uncommon in someone taking it on themselves to upbraid another for their errors. Such a formula of 'commanding right and forbidding wrong' is often observed in Pukhtun contexts in interpretations of Islam, becoming an arena for conflict in Al-Huda's application of literal scripture.

Looking at non-compliance from the reverse perspective, that of snubbed Bibiane, absence from *gham-khādi* causes serious offence. When I accompanied a group of Bibiane to visit their niece, Parveen, in Islamabad on a congratulatory birth-visit (*ombaraki*) for her first-born baby girl, Parveen (married to a Mardan Khan and originally Swati) complained that her mother-in-law and sisters-in-law had failed to perform her *ombaraki*, although her baby was born after several years of marriage and was thus eagerly anticipated. An earlier property dispute had led to mutual avoidance in *gham-khādi*, even though the events were often shared. Referring to her mother-in-law, Parveen said: 'It is also *her* happiness, but she doesn't understand [*kho poyegee na*].' Looking tenderly at her crying baby girl, she added: 'She reminds me of my mother-in-law when she looks angrily at me.'

A family's prioritising of certain engagements over others may also cause relational problems. In one case, a Bibi's husband's female cousins neglected to visit her hospitalised husband a month after his operation, while they travelled to a remote village for another cousin's *dai*'s (wet-nurse's) husband's death. Shehnaz, the snubbed Bibi, cried: 'If they don't care about us, why should we care about them! Illness is the time when all relatives come together [*khpal ratol shee*].' She declared, 'I am not going to do any more *gham-khādi* with them!' These simmering resentments are rarely vented in direct confrontation (*rishtinee*), which, one Bibi told me, 'is very rude' (cf. Pitt-Rivers 1966: 40). I was present during a number of different Bibiane's *rishtinee*, where the most common response was '*munkaredal*' (to deny or reject) or evasion, especially in response to accusations of intentional wound or insult.

Disputes among Bibiane escalate from neglect of the customary '*salām*', usually accompanied by an embrace and a kiss on either cheek, to coldness and discreet avoidance, and finally to outright and widely understood aversion altogether (in a *badal*).[13] The confusion over whether a festivity is missed for genuine reasons or in retaliation, provokes much anxiety for Bibiane. As *gham-khādi* contexts are

---

[12] Analogously, Foucault in *Discipline and Punish* (1991) describes the constitution of power in the modern era as being a matter of the 'molecular' interactions of individuals insofar as they exert normative expectations (regarding custom or morality) on each other. On Foucault, see also Nola 1998.

[13] 'There is nothing worse than to pass unnoticed: thus, not to salute someone is to treat him [or her] like a thing, an animal' (Bourdieu 1991: 11).

segregated public spaces, 'the constant concern over "seeing" who sees whom, when and where' (Gilsenan 1990: 190) becomes of crucial importance. Relatedly, 'not being seen', or to avoid another's *gham-khādi* intentionally in an act of subversion, is also a characteristic feature of Pukhtun social life.

Juggling professional work, housework and the work of existence

Gham-khādi places multiple and competing demands on women's time, energy and responsibilities in their roles as mothers and wives (in their *kor-kār*: housework*)*, kinswomen (their *zeest-rozgār* or *gham-khādi*) and professional employees (their *kār-rozgār*). The tensions of the 'work of existence' for women (tug of war between professional life, home life and obligations to family/religious community) apply not just to Pukhtun or Pakistani women, but to many contemporary women's lives more generally. But the near-exclusive form of Pukhtun female adult sociality, *gham-khādi* and *tlal-ratlal* also prohibited women from any form of employment outside the *kor*. Women (and men) give moral precedence to *zeest-rozgār* or *gham-khādi*, as they define Pukhtun ethnic identity and provide a particular philosophy of life. The imperative of maintaining social bonds overrides both childcare, as we have seen, and housework in the sense of Bibiane's supervision of menial tasks. The *tlal-ratlal* requirements of spontaneous hosting often oblige Bibiane to be in two places at the same time, sitting with the guests and providing tea and food. One Bibi whose maid had gone on holiday stated, 'If I receive guests I have to sit with them – to leave them is said to be *badtameezee* [impolite].'

The requirement on Bibiane to host *gham-khādi* sits uneasily with some women's perception of their household roles and instincts. One thirty-five-year-old Bibi, resident in Islamabad and married to a Mardan Khan, argued: 'I think when a woman has a baby, then people should not even visit for the first three months. When my son was born, some people apologised for coming so late, but in my heart I said *shukkar de* [thank goodness], because receiving and entertaining guests the way we do is difficult when your hands are fully occupied.' The task of hosting, particularly in Islamabad where Bibiane's *gham-khādi* networks vastly increase and intensify, is broadly but secretly sometimes seen as an unwelcome pressure, as in the words of a Bibi:

Entertaining guests is like a tug of war – having a family, keeping a house and doing *gham-khādi* all at the same time. Nothing is relaxed or enjoyable now. You have to be obliged. You have to be there for your children's needs, for the needs of *gham-khādi* and society, for your husband's needs, your in-law's needs. So it's always needy, needy of a woman, and a woman's own needs are ignored.

It is difficult to convey an appropriately multilayered sense of how arduous a Bibi's work of directing household labour can seem to the women involved. In the local context, the maids on whom Bibiane's social reputation depends are often illiterate, untrained, unused to electrical appliances (microwaves and electric lighting) and unversed in the scrupulous differentiations of hosting practices. Bibiane's labour, although partially physical, requires constant thought and watchfulness, particularly in negotiating differences of propriety across locations and classes. Maids, in their Barthian capacity as independent 'players', may make increasing demands for gifts and privileges, and Bibiane do not feel able to 'call their bluff' and drop *zeest-rozgār* responsibilities entirely. During my entire fieldwork period, I knew of only one Bibi, Shandana, who explicitly chose not to employ maids for childcare, and looked after her six children herself, even at the cost of avoiding *gham-khādi*. Once Shandana's children were old enough for full-time education, she returned to *gham-khādi* participation, though only among a small circle of close family, cousins and friends. The additional time afforded her, enviably to some, with her limited *gham-khādi* responsibilities allows Shandana to serve in organisational contexts, such as the monthly meetings, lunches and exhibitions of the All-Pakistan Women's Association (APWA).

Some Bibiane juggle the customary obligations of *gham-khādi* with professional work (*kār-rozgār*). Khanān often avoid marriage to highly educated, professional career women because careers are held to distract from childcare and house management (see also Alavi 1991: 130). Even the *tlal-ratlal* displacement that characterises *gham-khādi* poses enormous obstacles for Bibiane wishing to take on full-time work. Bibiane often indicated that these *gham-khādi* demands proved insuperable. Zara, a fifty-five-year-old living in Islamabad, described in English that she was forced to give up teaching 'because of *gham-khādi*. When my father's brother died, I actually went to the *kille* [village] for one night only! But even one night meant I missed two days of teaching my schoolchildren.' Even this highly unconventional pared-down version of *gham-khādi* attendance left Zara feeling that she had violated proper standards of professional conduct.

Although Bibiane may wish to determine their own future goals, they find many to be incompatible with *gham-khādi*. Yasmin Bibi, from Mardan, revealed her desire to take the one-year diploma course at Al-Huda. Although she perceived it as a beneficial religious undertaking, the course would constrain her time for *gham-khādi*. Yasmin felt forced to discard her plan, stating, 'If I decide to do the diploma at Al-Huda, I can't do *gham-khādi;* and if people know that I am in the country and I don't go for someone's death, the close relatives will never forgive me!' A more dramatic illustration of the strains caused by these conflicts can be seen in the case of Arifa, the non-Pukhtun wife from Karachi, previously mentioned above, and married for eighteen years to a Mardan Khan. Arifa found her career as a United Nations development professional in Islamabad impeded by the demands of 'going and coming':

With some *gham-khādi* we had to go to villages in Mardan, like Shiva or Hoti where I did not know the people at all but with whom my in-laws did *gham-khādi*. But then this is it. There is no question of 'not' going. My husband takes time off from his work. And I've been working since the second year of my marriage. But I 'had' to take time off. And that's one of the reasons I couldn't continue working in the UN . . . I remember when my husband's aunt who was living in Mardan died in the afternoon. I was there in the middle of a Gender

Training Programme. My husband said: '[Auntie] has died and they [her entire cohort of affines] are all leaving immediately for the funeral.'

While her husband initially supported the idea of his wife's employment, the couple's flexibility was limited through the equally conscientious Pukhto training inculcated in both husband and wife:

I was thrown in a great dilemma. I was the lead trainer at the UN. So what I did was I continued with my training. My husband [and the extended family] left for the village. He left the second car and the driver for me. My programme ended at 5 o'clock pm and then I left. But that was the only time I gave priority to my professional work. Otherwise, there were a number of times when I was in the middle of a project I had to just leave 'everything'!

Arifa's non-Pukhtun work colleagues could not appreciate her required absences, nor evolve some form of flexibility allowing her to work more intermittently. She describes another occasion:

My sister-in-law's daughter's husband died in Bannu. In the morning I had to go to the office – I was working for UNICEF at that time and was waiting for a mission that was here from Philippines, but again I just 'had' to go. What did I do? I attended the meeting halfway through, and then again I went with the driver whereas the whole family left early all the way to Bannu [six hours' drive from Islamabad] for two nights. But I 'had' to go. There is no way I could say: 'I am a working or career woman, and I may come the next day.' No! You had to show your face there!

The conflicts between work schedules and *gham-khādi* responsibilities (felt also by employed husbands) have led Bibiane such as Zara and Arifa to negotiate a space, both physically and symbolically, for Pukhtun self-representations and practice within the world of work. Arifa gave up her UN career, but opened a successful private primary school in half of her Islamabad house. The school and its garden are divided from the family portion of the house (both parts of which she personally owns). A wooden partition divides the garden, with parallel driveways and gates to the house. Within the house, a swinging door from the home-kitchen connects to the adjoining school. Arifa's maid makes tea and savouries like *samose* at her own home, and brings them over to the school for the visiting mothers of schoolchildren (some of whom are also her in-laws) and other guests. Thus, presence in her professional role at school does not preclude Arifa's performance of the norms of Pukhto, such as *melmastia* (hospitality), which remain incumbent on her as a Bibi.

Rewāj and Islam: dimensions of personhood

Morality in Muslim societies is the subject of a rich body of anthropological debate.[14] However, it is often assumed that the central moral faculty, *aql* (the

---

[14] On morality and *aql*, 'the faculty of moral discrimination', see Metcalf 1984a: 10, 1984b; and Kurin 1984; Nancy Tapper translates *aql* as 'responsibility' (1991: 15, 209), the following authors

power of moral discrimination, or social sense), in different Muslim societies is derived singularly from religious authority. Anthropologists of Muslim societies point to an 'Islamic theory of personhood' (Shalinski 1986), which views humans as being endowed with two important faculties: *aql*, social reason acquired through discipline and education or *ilm*;[15] and the *nafs*, the human will and undisciplined impulses of the lower soul, which is contrasted with and controlled by the *aql*. The properly instructed person has a developed sense of *aql*, and thus seeks to act with propriety (*adab*) at all times. *Nafs* uncontrolled by *aql* creates *fitna* (disorder). Some anthropologists claim to have taken Muslim societies at their word in according a greater capacity of *aql* to men than to their female kin or counterparts (see Shalinski 1986; Torab 1996; Metcalf 1984b).

Bibiane's use of the term *aql*, however, to denote thoughtfulness, cognition and an engaged attention in relation to social procedures, suggests a greater plurality of the concept. Different senses of *aql* are deployed to refer to religious observance and social self-possession or rationality. In practice, these different uses are contradictory, though social agents manifest both. Bibiane envision their actions in ceremonies as being highly deliberate, while their self-conception is a matter of both 'Muslim' and 'Pukhtun' identifications. While the Western media often portray (in the wake of the recent rout of the Taliban) Pukhtun or Pashtun life and thought as extremist and monolithic Islam,[16] many educated young Pukhtun Bibiane consider Pukhto and Islamic practices to be in certain ways antithetical. These Bibiane experience a continual tension between the *aql* of *rewāj* (custom) or *Pukhtunwali*, and the *aql* of *mazhab* (religion) or Islam. Religion thought to encompass every aspect of Muslims' life (see Gilmartin and Lawrence 2000: 1) has been problematically construed by some Bibiane as proscribing certain *gham-khādi* rituals (as seen in Chapter 3).

The idea of *aql* is integrated into the (self-)representation of distinctively Pukhto values in a nuanced fashion. People who perform *gham-khādi* well, maintaining relations of *tlal-ratlal* (going and coming) with a wide social circle, are said to be persons who 'know' and 'understand' Pukhto (*poyegee*). In other words, they possess a degree of social *aql* that has been cultivated through experience, time (*wakht*) and age (*umar*). Elders or *masharān* of both sexes may be described as '*aqalmand banyadamān*' (persons of *aql*); they are shown great respect in *gham-khādi* events, and their participation consecrates observances as socially significant. At the other end of the age spectrum, children are widely referred to as '*kamaql*' or '*be-aql*', or persons with little or no *aql*, disqualifying them from a full role in *gham-khādi* events. While girls may attend with their mothers, they

---

as 'social reason' or 'sense': Abu-Lughod 1986: 90–1; Anderson 1985; Ewing 1988: 8; Marsden 2002: 76; Metcalf 1990: 8; Shalinski 1986: 325; Torab 1996: 236. In the context of South Asian Islam, Ewing notes: 'guidance by *aql* bring[s] one closer to God, and also higher on the social scale' (1988: 8).

[15] Knowledge of the Quran, Hadith and *Sharia*, which provide a guide for living correctly in this world (Shalinski 1986: 325).

[16] Richard Tapper argues 'there is no simple equation Taliban = Pashtun = Islam = terrorism' (2001: 13).

have no formal obligations in gifting, attending, or in offering congratulations or condolences. Between elders and children lies a wide range of persons who may or may not have cultivated different levels and degrees of *aql*. *Aql*, as developed in a person's *gham-khādi* performances, influences others' wider moral evaluation of that person's '*khawale*' (goodness), sometimes even above acts of lying or theft (see Hart 1987).

Bibiane's judgements of individual *gham-khādi* performances are supremely important in evaluations of persons' character and status, not only in morality but also in social skill. In conversation, '*kha*' (good) people, those supposedly diligent in *gham-khādi*, are contrasted with others who omitted attendance in the past. Such belittling of women's social *aql* works as a disciplining technique, however humorously it is expressed, reaffirming family relationships and household hierarchies. People falling short of prompt reciprocity in *gham-khādi* practices are referred to as *bad* (literally, bad), *na poyegee* (lacking understanding), *lewanai* (mad) or *maghroora* (proud). In contrast, '*Khogmun* people' (responsive to another's hurt) perform *gham-khādi* out of sensitivity and respect. Others often comment about these *khogmun* people. A statement I widely heard was: 'Bibi and Khan are "good" [*kha*]: they do our *tapos* [enquiry visit].' Bibi Gul, referring to her deceased paternal uncle, remembers: 'Kaka was a very good man: he did everyone's *gham-khādi* and so many people came to his funeral. His children are just like him. When my young son had a heart operation, Kaka's sons and daughters were the first to come for *tapos*.' Diligent familial attendance at ceremonies absolves young Khanān, in particular, of the accusation of headstrongness or selfishness. Those present every day at commemorations (including the Fortieth (*Salwekhtamma*) and year (*kāl*)) are said to show a greater understanding of Pukhto, and thus a greater social sense. Yet the judgement of a person's morality in their performance of *gham-khādi* creates confusion for many young Bibiane due to their purist understandings of Islamic Hadith.

Al-Huda graduates of the word-by-word Quranic exegesis and of the Fahm-al-Quran programme during Ramadan are increasingly returning to the village context, seeking to modify Pukhtun practices. Bibiane with diplomas from the Institute see themselves as emerging with a far deeper understanding of the Quran and Hadith (the basis of Islam) both in philological terms and as a living practice, than is prevalent in Pukhtun society generally. Bibiane's grasp of the meaning of the scriptures may especially be contrasted with that promulgated by the mullahs, who, in Pakistan, are typically summoned to wealthier persons' houses to teach children the Quran by rote in Arabic. Al-Huda is distinctive and novel in the Pukhtun context in that women interpret religion for a female audience. At the time of my fieldwork, much debate and interest developed around the women's Al-Huda courses and *dars* classes primarily taught by the organisation's founder, Dr Farhat Hashmi, among a wide array of Bibiane, and among other women from multiethnic backgrounds in Islamabad.

Within the context of Al-Huda lectures themselves, conventional *gham-khādi* practices are referred to critically as '*rewāj*' in Urdu, or 'customs' in English. Bibiane who attend classes necessarily become aware of the contradictions between Islam and Pukhto, allowing them vocally to express their disapproval in Frontier villages (cf. Mahmood 2001). There are two means by which such women express their dissent: in speech, 'forbidding wrong' at or after *gham-khādi* gatherings, or (more commonly) in choosing not to attend on particular days. One Bibi who had gained a diploma at Al-Huda refused to commemorate the traditional Fortieth day after a particular death. Describing her explanation to her would-be host, she stated: '*Khorai* [sister], please don't be sad, but I cannot come because I don't perform the Fortieth any more.' On different occasions, a few Bibiane absented themselves from the *Nakreeza*.

In exercising this power of religious discrimination, Dr Hashmi's students have in effect taken up a challenge to 'command right and forbid wrong' in local village contexts. As graduates, they conscientiously translate Quranic Arabic into the local languages of Urdu, English and Pukhto. Several Bibiane now give daily Quranic classes in their houses in Swat, Mardan and Islamabad, bringing together small groups of local women and children (of up to thirty to sixty persons) daily or weekly. See plate 18: Village children at a madrassa opened by a Khan in Mardan now supervised from Islamabad by Bibiane. In 2003, a group of Bibiane established a satellite institution in a Mardan *kille-kor*, instructing village-women in Pukhto. See plate 19: Women in *sazare* seen for the first time outside their homes for this kind of Islamic activity in a Mardan madrassa (school) now supervised by a Bibi who lives in Islamabad. Dr Hashmi herself has been invited to the Frontier on a number of small *khādi* occasions, once giving a talk during the Quran *khattam* (completion) ceremony of a child of the Toru Nawab family. Her courses seem continually to be gaining popularity among Bibiane: in 2000, she relocated to Karachi, and reputedly draws more than five hundred women to the Marriott Hotel hall, with many turned away. Islamic scholarly learning bestows authority on its possessor regardless of age, gender or socio-ethnic background (cf. Cook 2000: 528): a Prophetic teaching states: 'the ink of the scholar is more sacred than the blood of the martyr'. The involvement of elite and middle-class Pakistani women in Al-Huda creates a co-ordinated network of instruction spanning rural Pakistan from Swat in the north to Karachi in the south. Students at these classes may be wealthy family members of politicians, businessmen or diplomats, or poor village-women. In principle, all women gain equal merit through attendance and study.

The reforming spirit of Al-Huda-educated Bibiane is comparable to the arguments deployed by the late nineteenth-century north Indian Deoband movement that claimed women's ceremonial 'customs' for marriages and funerals were *gunah* (sinful) in the absence of a Quranic basis.[17] Maulana Ashraf Ali Thanawi (1864–1943), one leader of the Deoband movement, defines an entire female curriculum of 'proper' education in his book *Bihishti Zewar* (Heavenly Ornaments) (1905). According to the *Bihishti Zewar*, female accomplishments range from the alphabet to styles of letter writing, polite conversation, recipes, managing household funds

---

[17] On the Islamist critique of *taqlid* (blind imitation of customs and traditions) in Egypt in discourses of proper pedagogy for children and mothers, see Shakry 1998. Cf. Gilmartin and Lawrence (2000: 1).

and religious observances. In particular, book six focuses on women's activities at life-cycle events. While written for the 'wellborn' and 'grand ladies' (Metcalf 1990: 25, 110), the *Bihishti Zewar* became widely popular with the Muslim women of the subcontinent. Thanawi's text is particularly significant due to its translation into many languages, including Pukhto (ibid.: 26), encouraging women to reject, in theory at least, *gham-khādi* customs. Thanawi, ironically, describes each customary practice entailed in life-cycle events among Muslim women of the subcontinent as 'the false *shari'at* that thwarts proper order [Islamic law]' (Metcalf 1990: 3) as it entails, he contends, extravagance, indulgence and licence: 'It is evil to consider something required that is not so specified in the *shari'at*' (ibid.: 158). This is, he argues, to invent new traditions which are thus considered *bid'at*: 'reprehensible innovation that is the negative counterpart of the *sunna* towards which the *shari'at* leads' (ibid.: 31). This effort of regulation bequeathed nineteenth-century Muslim women a religious identity – as seekers of the 'jewels of heaven', and partly trained as 'ulama' or religious clerics – even as it contested the anglicisation of elite society in the imperial era (see Devji 1994).[18] Echoes of such ideas have actually been expressed by certain sections of Pukhtun society itself. For example, the ruler of Swat, Badshah Sahib, in his account of *The Story of Swat* writes:

Many an absurd custom on the occasions of marriage and death was prevalent in the State. People incurred huge expenditure, much above their means or status, and involved themselves in serious monetary difficulties. I abolished all such practices and decreed that ceremonies should in future be held modestly and inostentatiously. Women folk were restored to their rightful place in society, and were given the rights and privileges in the *Shariat* . . . In short, I spared no effort in weeding out all moral and social evils. (Wadud 1962: 115)

Whether the people of Swat celebrated *gham-khādi* modestly after Badshah Sahib came to power remains undocumented. My own research into contemporary practices indicates that *gham-khādi* remains ingrained in Pukhtun society. Yet without necessarily referencing the Deoband intervention, the Al-Huda Bibiane – some of whom are the descendants of Badshah Sahib and the Sufi saint, the Akhund of Swat – are, in a more female-centred language, contesting and negotiating 'custom' through life-cycle events.[19]

Many Frontier Bibiane living in Islamabad spoke of the transformation Al-Huda has brought to their lives and spiritual practices. One Bibi from Swat remarked:

Before Al-Huda we were doing the traditional *purdah*: for example, we would observe *purdah* from men in the village but not in Islamabad; we would remain bareheaded in front of some *na-mahram* men [marriageable men] like our brothers-in-law and not others. Now, *Mashallah*, I am trying to avoid that and be consistent. I am trying my best to do everything Islamic.

---

[18] Abu-Lughod writes, 'Thanawi will empower women with literacy but relegate them to a newly created private sphere where they can even develop some modern forms of housewifery (. . . weights and measures . . .)' (1998a: 19).

[19] One of the Akhund's descendants was Bandai Bibi, a female saint (cf. Smith 1994). Sherani observes that 'the *pir* has dominated the whole countryside since the advent of Islam'.

Visible changes show in Bibiane's dress, as well as in their enactment of *gham-khādi*. Participation in *dars* entitles Bibiane to leave their houses under religious auspices, wearing a *hijab* and *loopata* (veil). Young married and also unmarried Bibiane may leave the *kor* for religious destinations. The increasing prevalence of the *hijab* attracts both approval and criticism from other Bibiane. One convent-educated Bibi in her late thirties, who had been wearing the *hijab* for seven years after moving to Islamabad, said:

> Some people think being 'modern' is to wear sleeveless *kameezes*, have the latest hair-do, go for parties, drink *sharāb* [alcohol] and talk in English. But if someone, like me with a *hijab*, is in that party, they'll ignore me. People tell me, "Are you crazy wearing the *hijab*? You're a *Fundo* [a fundamentalist]" [she fixes her *hijab*]. Pakistan is a Muslim country, and covering your hair is the first identity of a Muslim woman, yet people here never fail to ask me why I wear a *hijab*.

Many Al-Huda graduates impose higher moral standards on themselves, although their right to Muslim authority is contested or problematic in different contexts. Young women's arrogation of Islamic prerogative as having priority over customary privileges, especially, is often vexed, leading to conflicts within families. In one instance in 2004, a sixteen-year-old daughter, who recently adopted the *hijab* and attends Al-Huda, reputedly cited Islamic prohibitions in refusing to be kissed on her forehead (as customary in some families) by her visiting 'uncle', or the male cousin of her father. Her father took offence, construing her action as a rebuff to his authority and an outrage to Pukhtun hospitality. However, in effect, the ambiguous relationship between scriptural precedent and everyday Pukhto allows most Bibiane from day to day to reconcile opposing values and plural personal inclinations and identifications.[20] Anthropologists focusing on South Asian Islam have noted this ambiguity whereby Islamic law (*Sharia*) is given 'unconditional theoretical acknowledgement' without being enforced in practice (Ewing 1988: 7; cf. Chhachhi 1994: 82).

Differences of outlook between Al-Huda and non-Al-Huda Bibiane are more usually accommodated into gossip and tacit forms of contrariety, than explored in debate or *rishtinee*. A number of Bibiane, of various ages and educational backgrounds, dismiss *hijab*-wearing relatives 'behind their backs' as 'narrow-minded hypocrites'. For them, the adoption of Islam by cousins or sisters-in-law tends to represent another strategy of rivals to win social pre-eminence or personal esteem. One Bibi said, in English, that her *hijab*-wearing cousins 'push religion down our throats'. Another, in the company of several Bibiane and Khanān, said that the women who say their prayers five times a day make a show of themselves and often do not have the best characters. Yet knowing more about Islam than their husbands, than older Pukhtun women, kin and affines, enables middle-aged and younger Bibiane to transcend 'patriarchal' and social norms by

---

[20] In the Jain context, Laidlaw describes personhood in a field of cultural multiplicity, not as 'a stable coherent self' but rather as something ' "distributed" ... This gives us the notion of a self which may be divided against itself, an assemblage of possibly conflicting "subject positions" ' (1995: 20).

referring to the higher moral order of the Quran and Hadith. As the account of the washing of a corpse in Chapter 3 showed, these Bibiane command much authority in Bibiane's Frontier village houses. Many Muslims are illiterate and cannot read the Quran (Eickelman 1992: 644); even some Western-educated Khanān (sent abroad to school at early ages) cannot read the Arabic script. Convent-educated Bibiane are literate in Urdu and thus see themselves as well placed to become the reformers and teachers of Islam (cf. Horvatich 1994: 812; and Turner 2000: 94). Moreover, women exercise power as the orchestrators of the 'women's work' of *gham-khādi*, where changes in the form of observance are binding on both sexes. In this way, women's centrality in the ceremonial continuity of Pukhtun society grants them particular leverage for defining the terms of *gham-khādi* – although always in partial and contested ways.

In this chapter, I have explored the ways in which some Bibiane are beginning to exploit uncertainties in Pukhtun definitions of work, morality, religion and *Pukhtunwali*, in order to better fit *gham-khādi* obligations to their own concerns (childcare, professional employment, personal friendships and antipathies, religious convictions). But it would be wrong to conceive of Bibiane in terms of a 'theory of resistance' refusing their *gham-khādi* obligations within a wider 'patriarchal' society. Saba Mahmood, looking at women's mosque movements in Cairo, suggests that we should 'think of agency not as a synonym for resistance to relations of domination, but as a capacity for action that historically specific relations of subordination enable and create' (2001: 203). Customary practices in *gham-khādi*, as an especially important node of Pukhto, are successively refined through slight and incremental variants. These changes may be authorised by religion, by Western-inflected modernity or by reinterpretations of tradition. Their combined effect, in any event, influences Pukhtun social relationships as these are made and displayed through life-events. Whatever the dilemmas faced by educated Bibiane, most elite Pukhtuns continue with *gham-khādi* even when questions are raised over practicality or religious warrant. Within this context, an awareness of the contradictions in the work of *gham-khādi* is growing. Young educated Bibiane, unlike many of their husbands, broadly implement the Islamic challenge 'to command right and forbid wrong'. This is an important development, as Bibiane embody religious knowledge in the context of present-day *gham-khādi*.

This chapter has sought to explore Bibianes' performances of *gham-khādi* as complex undertakings that engage the most fundamental, and fundamentally contradictory, ideas in Pukhtun experience. Through *gham-khādi*, women reinforce their social relationships through highly regulated procedures, understood as forms of work. The discourse of actors themselves reveals the term *gham-khādi* as both individual and collective, moral and potentially immoral, and voluntary and obligatory. Affines and other members of society evaluate each other's performances in terms of quality (immediacy of attendance, degree of mourning/celebration) and quantity (amount of money given, time spent at the event), while failure to participate incurs severed relationships and lost social respectability (*ezat*). Meanwhile, heightened consciousness of *gham-khādi*'s partial incompatibilities with Islam, brought to the NWFP by Al-Huda graduates, leads to the incorporation of diverse or novel elements in the ceremonies themselves. This small but influential group of Bibiane urge the reformation of practices impugning their sense of Muslim selfhood, and are met in turn by opposition from older and some middle-aged Bibiane.

The degree of paradox inherent in *gham-khādi* practices deepens its intractability in the lives of educated Bibiane. Bibiane may understand that *gham-khādi* obligations (visiting and house-*purdah*, 'tradition' and reform) are incoherent, yet this does not lessen their obligatoriness. Paradoxically, a central set of practices through which Bibiane are beginning to alter the terms of engagement with *gham-khādi* is that of textually sanctioned Islamic discipline. The prominent and productive role of educated women as instruments of Islamisation in the Frontier contests many Western and local portrayals of Bibiane as pampered 'socialites' (BBC News: Ali 2003), while associating Islam with poor young men, or the 'Taliban' (meaning students) (see Tapper 2001). Bibiane's increasing, contestatory engagement with customary *gham-khādi* is wrongly conceived within a feminist rhetoric of liberation from 'patriarchy' or 'tradition'. Plural forms of women's participation rather renew and bring complexity to ceremonies and social processes. The social continuity of Pukhtun ceremonial forms through time, and the social solidarity of Pukhtun society, are thus not necessarily damaged by Bibiane's ongoing reinterpretation of the 'work of life'.

CONCLUSION

Before returning to Cambridge from fieldwork in northern Pakistan, I visited a number of Khan households in Mardan and Swat. One of the last families I called on was Mashar Khan's, a Khan household in the small and verdant village Sher Palam in upper Swat. Mashar Khan's wife, Bibi Khana, is his second cousin. Their two sons recently married young British Pukhtun girls from Manchester in England. Their only daughter, Saira (in her early twenties), is married to her mother's *mairazane* (step) cousin's son (*de mama zwe*) in Jura, another adjoining village.

Over tea, chicken and local bread (*parathe*), I asked Bibi Khana about her daughter, Saira, who is six years younger than me, and was in my informal charge as a relative of my mother at the Murree Convent. Bibi Khana told me that Saira had recently given birth to a baby girl, so we decided to pay her a spontaneous visit, in accordance with minor *khādi*. Bibi's eldest son, Asif Khan, three years my junior and briefly back from Manchester, volunteered to drive. We veiled our heads and faces and got into the landcruiser. The barking of Mashar Khan's dogs was muffled as a *saukidar* (gatekeeper) shut the black gates behind us. Passing small huts and houses, the evening air was filled with the dust stirred by the vehicle and smoke from Jura's *tanooroona* (mud-ovens).

During this fifteen-minute journey, Bibi Khana warned that Saira's widowed mother-in-law ruled her household with an iron fist – the mother required her only son, Abdullah Khan (in his early thirties), to obtain her permission for all social or political activity or decisions in or beyond the house. Saira's husband oversees the cultivation of his substantial land and orchards (cherries, apples and peaches), which he then sells to the fruit market in Lahore. His mother would not allow her son to take Saira with him on his distant journeys to Lahore. Saira was said to be far too young and inexperienced in domestic politics to challenge her mother-in-law's authority in any major way.

On arrival, barking Alsatians, restrained by the house gatekeeper, greeted us. As the only man, Asif Khan led us through the central courtyard to the veranda and his sister's rooms. The house-dogs alerted the residents of our arrival. In semi-darkness behind heavily curtained windows, Saira sat up with her new baby to greet her mother and an old school-fellow. Bibi explained that I had come to do the *ombaraki* of her newborn daughter. Just then Saira's mother-in-law walked in and greeted us. I was introduced as my mother's daughter. Though Saira's mother-in-law was not related to my mother by blood, her husband was a distant relative of my mother's mother. Saira's mother-in-law sat us down to enquire briskly how my mother was, and when she would be returning to Swat from America (where my parents live). Then she left the room to organise the drinks.

In the privacy of the room, Asif Khan sniggered at his sister's mother-in-law, saying that he always felt nervous in her house. Bibi Khana, with her granddaughter in her arms, kept glancing at the door, anticipating the mother-in-law's return. We were served a glass of *sharbet*, which we each sipped only once, before placing it nervously to one side. At this stage, Saira's mother-in-law entered again and complained that my mother had not yet performed the *lās niwa* (condolence) after her husband's death in a car crash on the Malakand Road over four years ago. Forced into a corner, I assured her my mother would perform the *lās niwa* when she returned to Swat. Pushing further, the mother-in-law said that she had been aware of my mother coming to Pakistan two years ago (for a short period) and not visiting her. Now visibly angry at me, she got up a number of times and returned only to check whether we had left her house. On our way out, I caught a glimpse of tears in Bibi Khana's eyes at the thought that her only daughter and *masoom* (innocent) granddaughter were obliged to remain in Saira's mother-in-law's house. In the car, as Asif Khan told me not to take the mother-in-law's words to heart, Bibi Khana could only say, choked: 'I have taken my *nazbeena* [delicate] daughter with my own hands and [by marrying her into this household] slaughtered [*alal*] her like a lamb [*beeza*]' (cf. Bhattacharya 2000).

This vignette reveals the significance for Pukhtun Bibiane of the patterning of *tlal-ratlal* obligations of attendance, fulfilled at *gham* and *khādi*, and crossing over between persons, here from mother to daughter. Even though I came to perform a birth *ombaraki* visit on a *khādi* occasion, my relationship was already tenuous given Saira's mother-in-law's complaint about my mother not doing *gham* with her. My performance of this particular *khādi* was one element in a continuous sequence of previous acts of reciprocation between my own mother's mother and the Khanān of Jura, which were then expected to continue in my mother's and my own relationship with the family. The posting of my parents to the UK, followed by their migration to America, meant an inevitable lessening of *gham-khādi* contact with their extensive kin in distant Swati villages. In northern Pakistan's inherited generational scheme, however, each Pukhtun individual, rather than being conceptualised as an autonomous agent, is connected to a tightly knit web of social relationships that links near and far kin and affines. Non-performance of major *gham-khādi* even for legitimate reasons, such as migration from the country, potentially sours relations widely: in one funeral, for example, the daughters of a man with three wives publicly complained that two of their cousins (one returning from abroad) had not asked about their father (*tapos*) or performed their father's *lās niwa*, and had therefore insulted and injured them personally. In contrast, the performance of *gham-khādi* among Bibiane continually bonds families through the women's work of making relationships.

This book has sought to capture the sense in which the performance of such familial and social obligations, pivotally through attendance at *gham-khādi* ceremonies, is understood among Pukhtuns as a form of work. My phrase, 'the work of existence', brings together the 'experiential and analytical interpretations' (Gray and Mearns 1989: 31) of Bibiane's lives by presenting the wide array of organised and meaningful activities that comprise female actions at weddings and funerals. I have demonstrated how the term *gham-khādi* refers to these occasions and denotes a wider conception of life that is paradoxically sorrowful and joyful – to the extent that the conventional separation of weddings and funerals fails to capture Pukhtun ways of thinking. Using descriptive ethnography, I spoke about Bibiane while trying not to speak 'for' them (Moore 1994: 9). The book introduced *gham-khādi* for Bibiane both as a philosophy and as an explicitly female set of practices ('women's work'), demonstrating the continuity between female sociality at weddings and funerals and wider patterns of *tlal-ratlal*. I also showed the centrality of female sociality in ideas of Pukhtun identity and cultural distinctiveness.

Much of the anthropological interest in *gham-khādi* derives from its ambiguous interface between different social categories: male and female, public and private, local and transregional. While Chapter 1 sought to place *gham-khādi* within a context of Pukhtuns' self-identity, the second chapter described the segregated, multi-family *kor* as the context for these transactions. The different layouts and uses of the *kor* in the Frontier and Islamabad were shown to reflect contradictory interpretations of 'Pukhto', Islam and 'modernity'. The house's staging of *gham-khādi* enacts both familial relations, and also inter- and cross-class relationships, as women's work is understood (however ambivalently) to achieve the reproduction of a socially unifying 'traditional Pukhto'. It does this through the performance of ceremonies invoking precedent. As the site of *gham-khādi* and Bibiane's sociality, Chapter 2 attempted to capture the significance of the women's *kor*. This fuller ethnographic account of female domesticity sought to enrich conventional anthropological accounts of Pukhtun society focusing solely on the *hujra* (men's house) as defining *Pukhtunwali*.

Chapters 3 and 4, dealing with *gham* and *khādi* respectively, provided ethnographic descriptions of Bibiane's *gham-khādi* procedures hitherto undocumented in anthropology. Case studies sought to convey the variety and dynamism of funeral and wedding practices, showing how the impetus towards religious revision (or towards a more individualistic, extra-familial exercise of agency) can pose extremely painful dilemmas for Bibiane. Inherited moral and 'cultural' schemes no longer fit new ethical phenomena, nor can such schemes persist unaltered in the face of the global dispersion of Frontier Pukhtuns to other Pakistani regions and abroad, to Britain, the United States and United Arab Emirates. When members of Khan or Badshah families return as expatriates to the *kille-kor* for *gham-khādi*, they introduce new ideas to local settings. The fifth chapter laid out many of the contradictions that characteristically mark women's performance of their ceremonial obligations. Drawing from Bibiane's own speech, I portrayed *gham-khādi* to be both an individual and a collective practice; both an action 'forced' by prior convention

Conclusion 159

and one amenable to individuals' choices and sense of personal morality; and both Islamic and at variance with scriptural Islam. The increasing realisation of heterodoxy within *gham-khādi* procedures, particularly their deviance from textual Islam, inspires Al-Huda graduates to initiate highly contentious reforms. Islam does not encourage hierarchy. Yet the paradox is that both Pukhtun society and the Islamic republic of Pakistan is, in practice, hierarchical. The paradox between the egalitarian nature of Islam and the hierarchical one of Pakistan society creates an underlying tension potentially leading to an explosive situation. While this work aims to situate itself at the forefront of many strands of Frontier ethnography (of women and social elites), it nonetheless problematises its object, demonstrating how forms of *gham-khādi* practices are, indeed, one of Pukhtun society's most sensitive registers of heterogeneity in the contemporary world.

Throughout the book, I emphasised the making of social relationships as work because, as is also explicit and implicit in my examples, close relationships (rooted in agnatic rivalry) among Pukhtuns are generally very tense (Barnard 2000; Barth 1958, 1986; Grima 1998; Lindholm 1982, 1988; Cherry Lindholm 1996). Within households particularly, *gham-khādi* bears moral weight as good relations depend on attending and participation (being *kha* ('good') and 'caring' – in English (see Alvi 2001: 52)). Compliance in the dimension of personal morality overlaps with questions of wider social membership. The Bibiane's careful and reflective following of *gham-khādi* conventions regulates the practical cohesion of society (Tapper 1991: 209). The discourse of Bibiane challenges accounts of Muslim societies which claim that its men grant women inferior powers of reflection and self-scrutiny (see Metcalf 1990: 14; Shalinski 1986: 326; Tapper 1991; Torab 1996: 237, 241). Correct performance of *gham-khādi* draws on a repertoire of learnt skills, including aspects of dress, deportment, self-presentation, artful speech and social 'networking'.

There are further grounds for borrowing the local conceptualisation of the 'work of existence' as the basis for an alternate analytical category (of 'work'). A Bibi's *gham-khādi* is not merely punctual or ceremonial, but spreads out over the course of her (reflection upon her) life. Situated at the intersections of a Bibi's personhood, family and social position, eschatological belief and cultural identity, the 'processual' nature of *gham-khādi* encompasses an ongoing set of actions. As described in Chapter 4, women equip their daughter's marital trousseau while she is still a child; and the accumulation of *ezat* through diligent performance of *gham-khādi* obligations anticipates a Bibi's accession into the senior ranks of a household's most esteemed women. As they live out their social roles, Bibiane learn to be responsible for the actions of their maids. They juggle the competing priorities of childcare and professional employment with household management, visits and hosting. In a single year, there can be hundreds of *gham-khādi* calling on any individual Bibi's time and energy. The *gham-khādi* network of one woman may involve twenty-seven or so different villages, towns and cities, may represent the domiciles of servants (and their families) and kin, and may include the proliferating affinal connections she gains through marriage.

What is at stake for a Pukhtun Bibi who does not perform *gham-khādi* at all or inappropriately, is her personhood as publicly conceived – that is, her reputation or *ezat*. Due to *purdah*, a Bibi's *ezat* represents the only aspect of her personhood that circulates freely in all public contexts, and its cheapening (by her failure to perform adequately) impairs her social status. Criteria of *gham-khādi* performance are thus tied to individuals' sustained ethnic identity (Tapper 1991: 107). In this sense, behaviours presumed antithetical to *ezat* – miserliness, failure to perform or return *gham-khādi* visits, inadequate gifts, unseemly emotion and confrontation (*rishtinee*) – detract from a person's embodiment of Pukhto. On the level of collective representation, the nonconformity of wedding or funeral procedures with social expectations (as described through an internet marriage in Chapter 4) renders those procedures socially inadmissible, vexatiously 'half-done' or non-existent for close family members.

Another especially interesting dimension of female ceremonial performance is its linkage with male political power. While some Khanān were hesitant to attribute any extra-domestic influence on a woman's skill at *gham-khādi*, both women and men suggested that the standing of a Bibi's family, including her husband's political fortunes, does depend on this proficiency. In this sense, this discussion of Pukhtun *gham-khādi* illuminates an area of women's activity not fully explored by Nancy Tapper's account about Iranian women's formalised visiting (*khayr-u-sharr*). Tapper presupposes that women engage in hospitality, prestige- and position-building to the extent that they are excluded from male public life. She claims that their networks rarely overlap with male circuits of patronage and clientage. Yet I suggest that *gham-khādi* is continuous with male politicking, not parallel to it. Saba Mahmood's work on the Cairo women's mosque movement argues that an 'openness' on the part of the researcher in exploring 'nonliberal traditions' is intrinsic to a politically informed scholarly practice. The reach of the Al-Huda women's Islamic movement to Pukhtun *gham-khādi*, insofar as changes are brought about in segregated public aspects of Pukhtun social practices, has political implications for the study of women. Furthermore, what might be considered political power within a political anthropology of Pukhtun society is denoted as the possession of honour (Abu-Lughod 1986: 97) in this context. 'Power, properly developed, enhances *izzat* [*ezat*]; *izzat* legitimates power' (Mandelbaum 1993: 22).

In this sense, a theoretical question this study has engaged throughout concerns the appropriate frame for the description of *gham-khādi* practices: namely, that of social or political anthropology. The pioneer works of Pukhtun anthropology were couched in an androcentric political idiom, understanding social activities as strategies oriented towards Khans' 'maximization' (Barth 1986) of political power. I have offered another perspective, suggesting that *tlal-ratlal* visiting might be better conceptualised within a horizon of social phenomena. In satisfying the crowds of female onlookers at weddings and funerals, Bibiane establish a store of social capital partly constituted by their personal *ezat*. For Bourdieu, in his work on the Kabyle, the societal forms of 'symbolic capital' (1991: 180) (as in the effects of *gham-khādi*: its feasts, gatherings and clothes) and its forms of 'economic capital' (ibid.: 195) (Khan patrimonial wealth) are ultimately exchangeable or subject to equivalence. In these terms, the lavish expenditure among Khan families on wedding and funeral hospitality would represent the consolidation of familial inheritance through the maintenance of ultimately renumerative social relationships. While Bourdieu considers some forms of display as 'wastage' (of social energy; ibid.), people's participation in *gham-khādi* remains rational insofar as they serve their political interests. Such a rationalisation of *gham-khādi*, however, fails to deal with the intricate network of *zeest-rozgār* relationships on their own terms. It is the particular social and familial connection, no matter how distant, not the primacy of identification with a political class, that is important for Bibiane in attending *gham-khādi*. Individuals, describing their *gham-khādi* experiences, offer discriminating accounts of their 'individual selves', bound by imperatives other than those of their religion, supposed ethnic practice or *Pukhtunwali*, or class or family interest.

In respecifying a diverse body of practices of *Pukhto* (divided by gender, generation and location), this work sought to capture the dynamism of contemporary *Puktunwali*. With the move of Khan families to the city over the past thirty years, *Pukhto* is seen as having undergone a modification by almost all local people. One elder Pukhtun in his seventies, for example, thought the entire way of life had been lost. Others, a wide array of Pukhtuns, men and women, rich (*bakhtawar*) and poor (*gharib*), told me that Pukhto had 'changed'. Cable television and motorised transport have reduced the remoteness of 'tribal' areas. For many, especially mullahs, practices among the elite have become westernised, to the detriment of Khan morality. A thirty-eight-year-old married Bibi living in Islamabad, told me in English, 'Modern elements come into it.' The term 'modern' is a frequently used word in local English to indicate novelty and also westernisation. Significantly, many Bibiane understand *Pukhtunwali* in the present context as a 'female-oriented' framework, that allows *okhyar* (clever) and *chalāk* (adept) women to negotiate the governance of their husbands and households.[1] I have argued that while the relative prominence of male notions of *Pukhtunwali* (as described in conventional anthropological accounts), such as male honour (*gherat*), trust (*jabba*), revenge (*badal*), (male) honour (*nang*), assembly of male elders (*jirga*) and manliness (*saritob*), have declined among the transregional Pukhtuns I worked with, others such as *gham-khādi*, hospitality (*melmastia*) and agnatic rivalry (*tarburwali, indrorwali*) have intensified. In presenting *gham-khādi* as engaging a wide network of people, this account has sought to mediate between male (Barth 1986) and female (Grima 1998) emphases in stressing the transitive and transactional elements of participation. Men and women kin and affines, close and distant relatives, rich and poor, and paid and unpaid attenders contribute to the festivities in different ways.

[1] Women's real power here illustrates the 'double jeopardy' of men in patriarchal societies (Abu-Lughod 1986; Altorki 1986; Tapper 1991), where men are both frequently dominated, and depend for their honour on the continence of supposed subordinate female kin (Barth 1970: 122; Grima 1998: 164; cf. Giovannini 1981: 409; also cf. Mandelbaum 1993: 39).

On the theoretical level, *Pukhtunwali* may be grasped, in Laidlaw's terms, as a 'set of representations' (1995). Rather than having the character of a 'code' (as previously defined by anthropologists), whose operations are invariant and which may only be changed wholesale, it forms a repertoire of actions integrally attached to social meanings and processes, but articulated in such a way that individual practices may emerge or fall into abeyance without the whole pattern undergoing resignification. Such a theoretical frame is useful in helping us to perceive the many innovations that are beginning to be introduced into *gham-khādi* by Al-Huda graduates.

This study has explored the lives and thoughts of Muslim women in a Pukhtun context in northern Pakistan. In doing so it departs from the much discussed contemporary topic of the importance of 'political Islam' and 'terrorism' in Pakistan and has sought to bring a nuanced understanding of the nature of social, political and even economic life for women (and to some extent men) in northern Pakistan today. Hitherto, Pukhtun women's worlds and their perspectives are largely absent in the otherwise sophisticated body of anthropological literature on this large ethnolinguistic group important both in Pakistan and Afghanistan.

This work has sought to contribute to the study of Pukhtun society in its focus on the lives of 'elite' or wealthy and educated Pukhtun women. For too long the study of Pakistan's North-West Frontier Province has focused exclusively on the region's villages and so-called tribal areas. As a result, the multidimensionality of Pukhtun and Frontier lives has not been captured in much ethnographic work, and Pukhtun experiences of city life and social transformation have been largely obscured by a focus on tribal structure and the role played by religious specialists in Pukhtun society. This study has sought to address this gap in the literature, and, tangentially, in doing so, challenges the conclusions of much earlier work both on Frontier society and on the relationship between the Frontier and other provinces in Pakistan. More broadly, this study has to some extent explored the nature of social transformation in Pakistan – Pakistan society is often assumed to be simplistically divided between rural and urban spaces, Punjab and non-Punjab, and feudal and non-feudal peoples. Examining the ways in which city-based Pukhtun Bibiane work hard not only to maintain links with their 'home' villages, but also, through their domestic servants, to the 'ordinary' people who live within them, this study addresses this lacuna in the literature on contemporary Pakistan. In focusing on the complexity of spaces, this work has sought to capture Pakistan's spatial and cultural diversity through an examination of Pukhtun women's lives and in doing so challenged less complex analysis of the nature of ethnic relations in Pakistan, the form of the relationship between the Frontier and Punjab, and the nature of class and status divisions in Pakistan. Another dimension of the study has been its exploration of the nature of construction and maintenance of relationships between elite women and their maids and other female servants. The nature of the Bibi–maid relationship is reflective of the wider state of social relationships in Pakistan's politics and society. Bibiane and maids may address each other in kinship terminology, reflecting the egalitarian spirit of Islam within a clearly hierarchical social structure. Although this study focuses on Bibiane, in a sense a similar development is taking place in the Punjab where the elite are largely perceived as corrupt, and the poor, as a consequence, are becoming poorer and poorer. There is a marked rich–poor hierarchy in terms of wealth in Pakistan combined with President Musharraf's military dictatorship. The complex relationship between Bibiane and their maids is to some extent a reflection of the current state of Pakistan's politics and society. The social hierarchy within a supposedly egalitarian Islamic framework is the cause of much unease and societal tension.

'More than economics, more than philosophy, the crucial variable when considering any aspect of Pakistan is its religion, Islam' (A. S. Ahmed 1977b: 4). Any ethnography of Pukhtun peoples must distinguish between proponents of different styles of being Muslim in advancing any characterisation of social practices. While the Pukhtun Taliban are male, of poor background, and are educated through rote-learning in the *madrassa* by mullahs, Al-Huda graduates, particularly Pukhtun, are female, of relatively wealthy background, and are preponderantly English-speaking and convent-educated. Representing an alternative mode of Islamic modernity to any simplistically identified form of 'fundamentalism', Al-Huda seeks to make Pukhtun funerary procedures consonant with a scriptural reading of the Quran. In the face of critics who argue that Muslim girls leave convent-schools Christianised, Al-Huda graduates have taken issue with the prolongation of mourning beyond three days, in one case (Chapter 3) bringing the Fortieth-day anniversary forward to coincide with the weekly Friday anniversary. More frequently, however, graduates introduce modifications into their styles of attendance, risking their social reputation by the appearance of rudeness when they leave after the third day (cf. Shakry (in Egypt) 1998: 154). It should be noted, however, that these Bibiane are often as, or more, committed to the maintenance of *Pukhtunwali* as their contemporaries. In another apparent contradiction with their Islamic faith, Al-Huda graduates often continue to send their children to schools like the Catholic Murree Convent, which they regard as an institution that has conventionally taken generations of Pukhtun girls, and a place of knowledge valuable under Islamic auspices. Indeed, the religious commitment of such Bibiane has been able to transcend the hostility that typically exists between the Khan and mullah classes (see Barth 1995: 63; Caroe 1992: 426; many Khanān are said to perceive mullahs as 'narrow-minded', authoritarian and hypocritically fixated on what they proscribed – *houri*, alcohol, debauchery and homosexuality – while for the mullahs, the landed classes are perceived as 'infidels': A. S. Ahmed 1988: 191–2; Barth 1995). The two social factions are pitted against one another in the electoral process, a system largely riddled with corruption where votes are 'bought' in the context of reciprocal but asymmetrical agreements, such as in *gham-khādi*. Ironically, for the first time in the 2002 Pakistan elections, after the American rout of Afghanistan's Taliban government, Swat and Mardan returned a full slate of religious candidates, leading many politicians from influential families to doubt the veracity of pledges received in their *hujre* and *dere* (men's houses).[2]

This sense of the slippage between public personae and private selves, as voters turned out to have concealed their intentions, also pervasively characterises *gham-khādi*. Ceremonies occur in the midst of constant scrutiny, judgement and gossip (badly dressed women are referred to as '*daigāne*'). *Khalak* (people, public opinion) shapes Bibiane's every move. The necessity of presenting an irreproachable public front arouses great anxiety in many Bibiane. This anxiety produces feelings of inadequacy or exhaustion, and ructions between family members. Women repeatedly stated that *gham-khādi* left little time for, variously, childcare, relaxation, reading or courses of study. Many women professed the desire to escape the obligations of Pukhto entirely. Knowing I lived abroad, one respectable village-woman asked me in the most earnest manner to find her a position as a maid outside the country: 'just take me out of this Pukhtun society' (*bus ma de dae Pukhtano zee na oobasa*) (see also Grima 1998: 163; and Lindholm 1982: 193). For many, including Bibiane and their husbands, only emigration to *Lundun* (London, used as the term for Britain generally) or *Amreeka* (America) offers an outlet. Pukhtun Bibiane living outside Pakistan likewise praised the arrangement as having released them from what they saw as non-negotiable obligations: a Bibi whose husband works in Dubai said that her children's schooling could now proceed uninterrupted by *gham-khādi*. Future research into Pukhtun communities and elite immigrant Pukhtuns outside Pakistan is needed to broaden the present work by specifying *gham-khādi* as an international phenomenon.

However, translocation to Islamabad and the global dispersion of educated Bibiane open a space for flexibility in the 'work of existence' (Donnan and Werbner 1991: 12). Besides bringing about marriages like Firoza and Zain's, the internet makes possible new forms of sociality, adapting earlier practices. My husband and I, for example, received email invitations in Cambridge for Pukhtun weddings in the North-West Frontier Province of Pakistan. Technology also offers gradations of participation in *gham-khādi* for expatriate and other Pukhtuns not present at collective events.

In conclusion, this study has sought to establish not only the importance of ritual in sustaining individual members in society during times of crisis but in adapting to new circumstances. Modern times far from making the 'work of existence' marginal or redundant have only underlined its relevance. After the 7 July 2005 terror attacks on London's transport system, which killed more than fifty people, my relatives (one of whom I had not spoken to for more than ten years) phoned me in Cambridge to enquire about my welfare from various parts of the world including Canada and Swat. Their communication confirmed the importance of *tapos* in *gham-khādi*. Present-day *gham-khādi* has thus come to

---

[2] In one instance, Bibiane believed that they had successfully secured the votes of dependents for their father who stood for a position in national elections in exchange for wedding invitations. When their father was trounced by a mullah at the 2002 elections, however, they reputedly brandished sticks at their house gates to drive back many of the poor (*gharib*) villagers who had come to see the wedding.

include *tapos* on burning issues such as terrorist attacks. In another case, hearing a younger nephew had died, an illiterate maid working in a Khan household in England recorded a message of condolence on to a cassette player, and sent the message to be played by the deceased's wife in Swat. In the latter case, it would certainly be premature to say that many people accept such mediated forms of *gham* as adequate substitution for personal attendance. Nevertheless, some negotiation between different degrees of presence and social participation in *gham-khādi* events will develop. Otherwise, the arduousness of the 'work of life' risks alienating many Bibiane, predominantly middle-aged, to whom their own lives seem less attractive than the opportunities now opening up for their daughters and granddaughters. Possibly only through such an adjusted economy of 'modern' and 'customary' practices and allegiances can *gham-khādi* avoid being judged as what a few professional Khanān (one a medical doctor) summarily dismissed as a 'waste of time'. But such a dissociation from Pukhto as it is imagined and experienced by most Pukhtun people would, for the majority, be understood as the loss or estrangement of those speakers' fundamental identity – a concept that lies at the core of an understanding of Pukhtun selfhood. It is this sense of selfhood that provides sustenance and stability in times of change.

Appendix 1
Pukhtun putative genealogy

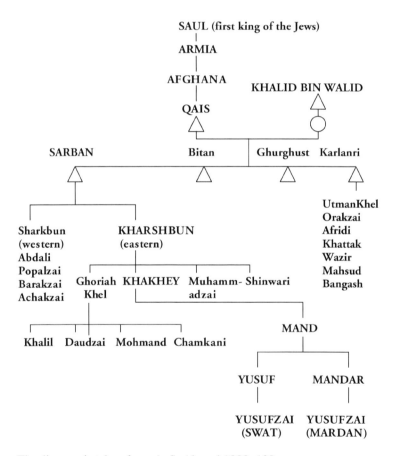

The diagram is taken from A. S. Ahmed 1980: 129.

Appendix 2
Kinship terminology: affinal and consanguinal

ENGLISH	PUKHTO
Affinal	***Skhargannai***
Husband	*Khawand*
Wife	*Khaza*
Mother-in-Law	*Khwakhe*
Daughter/s-in-Law	*Ingor/Ingiande*
Father-in-Law	*Skhar*
Husband's Sister/s	*Indror/ane*
Husband's Brother/s	*Lewar/oona*
Husband's Brother's Wife	*Yor/ane*
Husband's Brother's Wife's Offspring	*De yor bachee*
Husband's Brother's Offspring	*Lewarzay*
Brother's Wife	*Wrandar*
A Man's Wife's Sister	*Kheena*
Sister's Husband	*Ookhe*
Ego's Husband's Other Wife	*Bun*
Ego's Husband's Other Wife's Offspring	*Bunzai*
Consanguinal	***Plarganai/ De Mor-Plar Kor***
Mother	*Mor*
Father	*Plar*
Brother/s	*Ror/a*
Sister/s	*Khor/Khwende*
Son/s	*Zwe/e/Zaman*
Daughter/s	*Loor/Loonra*
Grandmother	*Neea* (Nanaji)
Grandfather	*Neeka* (Babaji)
Grandson/s	*Nwase/e*
Granddaughter	*Nwasai*
Mother's Sister	*Thror*
Mother's Brother	*Mama*
Father's Sister	*Thror*
Father's Brother	*Thre*
Father's Brother's Wife	*Thandar*
Mother's Sister's Son	*De thror zwe*
Mother's Sister's Daughter	*De thror loor*

(*cont.*)

ENGLISH	PUKHTO
Father's Sister's Son	*De thror zwe*
Father's Sister's Daughter	*De thror loor*
Ego's Brother's Son	*Wrara* (from *ror*, brother)
Ego's Brother's Daughter	*Wrera*
Ego's Sister's Son	*Khwaraye* (from *khor*)
Ego's Sister's Daughter	*Khwarza*

Appendix 3
Time

Five daily prayers (local time is measured according to prayer timings)

Number	*(Pukhto)* Prayer: *Moonz*	Arabic/Urdu
1	*Sahar*	*Fajar*
2	*Maspakheen*	*Zohar*
3	*Mazeegar*	*Asar*
4	*Makhām*	*Maghrib*
5	*Maskhutan*	*Isha*

Days of the week

Friday	*Jumma*
Saturday	*Khāli*
Sunday	*Itwar*
Monday	*Gwal*
Tuesday	*Pinzamma*
Wednesday	*Shoro*
Thursday	*Ziarat*

Months in a year

January	*Waroke Akhtar*
February	*Khāli*
March	*Loi Akhtar*
April	*Asān*
May	*Safar*
June	*Wrambai Khor*
July	*Dweyamma Khor*
August	*Thdrayemma Khor*
September	*Saloramma Khor*
October	*Zbarga*
November	*Shokadar*
December	*Roja*

Appendix 4
Maid performing *gham-khādi* on behalf of her Bibi

A young, unmarried maid relates her experience of performing a wet-nurse's (*dai*'s) brother's *lās niwa* (funerary visit) on behalf of her Bibi:

Recently, Speena Dai's brother died. Bibi [who is from the family of the Khanān of Sher Palam and is married to her father's sister's son, a Badshah from the Swat Wali's family] wanted to go for the funeral. When she went to Sher Palam [in upper Swat] her brother forbade her. So, Bibi gave me Rs.500 and sent her daughter [aged nine] and myself with the driver in her car. I went as Bibi's representative [*pa khpal ze*]. The *dai*'s house is next to Bibi's father's house in Sher Palam; Bibi wanted to go herself for Badshah's sake [*waja*] because *dai* is Bacha's wet-nurse and she has spent a lifetime with them [*ao umar a wur sara ter kare de*]. As she was restricted from going she sent me in her own place [*ao pa khpal ze a zo wa legallam*]. When I went to the house I gave the [deceased's] family Rs.500 and I said to them: 'Bibi was very sad at the news of your brother's death and she has sent me on her behalf. She wanted to come herself but her younger brother did not allow her to come, *da agha bad khwee de* [literally: he is ill-tempered, i.e. he imposes stringent *purdah*]; he did not want her to leave the house in the village, so Bibi has sent me in her own place.' So, I held my hands up in prayer [*ma warta lās waneewo*] and said, 'May God bless him' ['*Khde de oobakhe*']. I had never done *lās niwa* and did not know how to do it, but Bibi had explained every detail to me. Bibi had told me where to go, what to do and what to say. So I did and said all that she had explained to me. When we were about to leave, *dai* gave me Rs.200 to keep and some eggs for Bibi. So *dai* did *badal* (exchange/reciprocity) at that very moment. When I came back, Bibi asked me what I had told them and I related the details of the entire visit to her.

Appendix 5
Income and household expenditure

(A thirty-five-year-old Bibi with three children by her matrilateral cross-cousin)

Source of income	Husband's	Total amount of husband's income about Rs.75,000 per month. Husband gets income in lump sum not a fixed amount, once a year from inherited lands and property (shops etc.) rented in Swat. Bibi says, 'He gives me this money and I spend it on the house; he doesn't take anything . . . He gives the money to me to keep; when he needs it he asks for it.
	Her own	Bibi sold her gold wedding jewellery in Swat and her inherited land (from her father); she invested all the money in property, buying two apartments (flats), in Islamabad. The second apartment was bought jointly with some of her husband's money. She says, 'The two flats are in my name and the rent that comes from them – Rs.24,000 – collects in my bank. My husband doesn't touch it. I am going to change this money into dollars in an account abroad. The other thing I want to do is to buy land here in Swat.' She adds, 'My husband insisted on writing his lands and shops in my name.'
	Other	For 'other' source of income Bibi says, 'My mother-in-law [they live jointly] will start contributing to the [large village house] house expenditure to ease the pressure on her son.'
Expenditure on house	Food shopping and cleaning	She states, 'Chickens, cleaning items etc., whatever I need I write it on a piece of paper and in my expenditure notebook; I give it to Mama [her servant] who takes it to the shopkeeper. We have a fixed rate with particular shopkeepers who keep a monthly book and at the end of the month I compare my notes with his bills to see if they are the same and pay him the amount through our servants.' 'Apart from that every time I go to Islamabad to drop or pick up my daughters from the boarding school I do about Rs.10,000 worth food shopping; those things you can't get in Swat like foreign cornflakes, chocolates, tin foods; and the things you feel too ashamed to ask for, in a place like Swat, like toiletries such as women's personal stuff – sanitary towels, creams, and so on.'

Expenditure on children	Schools	Bibi has two daughters in the convent boarding school. For each daughter it costs her Rs.7,000 per month. This excludes expenditure on 'tuck' (food/snacks) which comes to about Rs.2,500. Holidays and trips cost Rs.10,000 in total. The bedding, hold-all, trunks and uniforms cost an initial amount of Rs.50,000 on first admission into school.
	Toys	Playstation, video games and children's video cassettes: 'My daughter has more than seventy Disney videos.' Stuffed toys and books are passed down from the eldest.
Expenditure on personal items	Clothes	Bibi spends Rs.20,000 on three-piece suits, *partoog-kameez-loopatta*, per season (six months) buying about twelve pairs of clothes for summer, and eight pairs for winter. In addition, she adds, 'and the other pairs my husband gifts to me'.
	Jewellery	'I don't like the big gold wedding jewellery . . . I sold most of mine to buy property; I prefer precious stones. When I went to Lahore I bought a diamond set.'
	Shoes etc.	'When I go abroad I buy a supply of shoes and bags so that I can wear them for *gham-khādi*.'
Expenditure on *melmastia* (hospitality)	At home	For hospitality, Bibi says, she spends about Rs.38,000 on dinners (Bibi has a reputation for being very sociable and hospitable). She adds, 'Whoever used to come to Swat we would give them dinners. But since our mills [flour] have closed down we are beginning to become more careful. We give fewer dinners. But we always serve our guests *sherbat* in summers and tea in winters.'
	Restaurants	Her statement here reveals the city–village complex: 'It is unthinkable to go to a restaurant in Swat. But in Islamabad if someone has taken us out for dinner then we are particular to return the favour. In Islamabad we go to restaurants three to four times a month and take people out, because I can't handle it in the flat: the space is too small and I want to rest, not work in Islamabad.'
Expenditure on *gham-khādi*	Deaths	She says, 'If it is a poor person's death, I do not attend because of *purdah*, but I send Rs.200 or Rs.300 to them through my husband's *dai's ingor* (wet-nurse's daughter-in-law) or I send them *ghwaro teen* (a pot of cooking oil). If the death is in my own family then I give Rs.15,000 *khairat* and attend all the days and even the Fridays [*Jumme*] after death.'
	Weddings	In a *khādi* context she states, 'It is tit for tat during *gham-khādi*. Whatever I received in the past from that person I must give the same. If it is a poor person's wedding I will send Rs.200–300 or an unstitched suit, *jora*. If it is a friend's or relative's wedding I will take an [expensive] and beautiful suit, *khkwale jora* or then give money, about Rs.1,000.'
	Births	In the context of birth, she points out, 'Whatever amount someone gave me [at the birth of her daughter] I write it down in my diary, their name and the amount and when they have a child I return the exact amount. It's an exchange, *badal*. Whatever they give me I give back.'

REFERENCES

Abu-Lughod, L. 1986. *Veiled Sentiments: Honour and Poetry in Bedouin Society*. Berkeley: University of California Press.
— 1990. The Romance of Resistance: Tracing Transformations of Power through Bedouin Women. *American Ethnologist* 17: 1, 41–55.
— 1993a. Not Falcon Crest: Culture as Politics in Egyptian Television. ASA Decennial unpublished paper, 1–24. New York University.
— 1993b. *Writing Women's Worlds: Bedouin Stories*. Berkeley: University of California Press.
— 1998a. Introduction: Feminist Longings and Postcolonial Conditions. In *Remaking Women: Feminism and Modernity in the Middle East* (ed.) L. Abu-Lughod, 3–31. Princeton: Princeton University Press.
— 1998b. The Marriage of Feminism and Islamism in Egypt: Selective Repudiation as a Dynamic of Postcolonial Cultural Politics. In *Remaking Women: Feminism and Modernity in the Middle East* (ed.) L. Abu-Lughod, 243–69. Princeton: Princeton University Press.
Ahmad, I. (ed.) 1978. *Caste and Social Stratification Among Muslims in India*. Delhi: Manohar.
Ahmad, T. 1998. *Dajjal*. London: Ta-Ha Publishers.
Ahmed, A. 1994. Change and Continuity in Pathan Tribes: A Critical Comparison of the Swat and Mohmand Pathans, unpublished Special Essay Paper, London School of Economics and Political Sciences.
— 2000. Gendering *Pukhtunwali*. *The News*, Islamabad: 16 November.
— 2004. 'The World is Established Through the Work of Existence': The Performance of Gham-Khadi Among Pukhtun Bibiane in Northern Pakistan, unpublished PhD Thesis, University of Cambridge.
— 2005. Death and Celebration among Muslim Women: A Case Study From Pakistan. *Modern Asian Studies* 39, part 4, 935–82.
Ahmed, A. S. 1975. *Mataloona: Pukhto Proverbs*. Karachi: Oxford University Press.
— 1976. *Millennium and Charisma Among Pathans: A Critical Essay in Social Anthropology*. London: Routledge and Kegan Paul.
— 1977a. *Social and Economic Change in the Tribal Areas, 1972–1976*. Karachi: Oxford University Press.
— 1977b. *Pieces of Green: The Sociology of Change in Pakistan*. Karachi: Royal Book Company.

References

1980. *Pukhtun Economy and Society: Traditional Structure and Economic Development in a Tribal Society*. London: Routledge and Kegan Paul.

1984. Religious Presence and Symbolism in Pukhtun Society. In *Islam in Tribal Societies: From the Atlas to the Indus* (eds.) A. S. Ahmed and D. M. Hart, 310–30. London: Routledge and Kegan Paul.

1987. *Toward Islamic Anthropology: Definition, Dogma and Direction*. Lahore: Vanguard.

1988. The Mullah of Waziristan: Leadership and Islam in a Pakistani District. In *Shari'at and Ambiguity in South Asian Islam* (ed.) K. P. Ewing, 180–202. Berkeley: University of California Press.

1991. Migration, Death and Martyrdom in Rural Pakistan. In *Economy and Culture in Pakistan: Migrants and Cities in a Muslim Society* (eds.) H. Donnan and P. Werbner, 247–68. London: Macmillan.

1993. *Living Islam: From Samarkand to Stornoway*. London: BBC Books.

2003. *Islam Under Siege: Living Dangerously in a Post-Honor World*. Cambridge: Polity Press.

Ahmed, L. 1992. *Women and Gender in Islam: Historical Roots of a Modern Debate*. New Haven: Yale University Press.

Ahmed, P. S., Abdul-Mueed and N. Khan, 1980–2. The Role of Maktab Scheme in the Muslim Society of Mardan District, unpublished MA Thesis, University of Peshawar.

Ahmed, Q. I. 1994. Hujra an Institution of Pukhtoon Culture. *The Frontier Post*, Peshawar: 29 September.

Al-Akili. (trans.) 1993. *Medicine of the Prophet*. Philadelphia: Pearl Publishing House.

Alavi, H. 1991. Pakistani Women in a Changing Society. In *Economy and Culture in Pakistan: Migrants and Cities in a Muslim Society* (eds.) H. Donnan and P. Werbner, 124–42. London: Macmillan.

Al-Hilali, M. T. and M. Muhsin Khan. 1996. *The Noble Quran*. Islamic University, Al-Madina Al-Munawwarah. Riyadh: Darussalam.

Ali, A. Y. (trans.) 1989. *The Holy Qur'an: Text, Translation and Commentary*. Brentwood, MD: Amana Corporation.

Ali, L. 1984–6. The Socio-Cultural Impact of TV on Swati Youth, unpublished MA Thesis, University of Peshawar.

Ali, S. 2003. Pakistan Women Socialites Embrace Islam. BBC News (Thursday, 6 November).

Al-Ja'fari, F. S. 1977. *Muslim Names*. Brentwood, MD: American Trust Publications.

Altorki, S. 1986. *Women in Saudi Arabia: Ideology and Behaviour Among the Elite*. New York: Columbia University Press.

Altorki, S. and C. El-Solh (eds.) 1999 (first published 1988). *Arab Women in the Field: Studying Your Own Society*. New York: Syracuse University Press.

Alvi, A. 2001. The Category of the Person in Rural Punjab. *Social Anthropology* 9: 1, 45–63.

Andersen, M. L. 2000. *Thinking About Women: Sociological Perspectives on Sex and Gender*. Boston: Allyn and Bacon.

Anderson, J. W. 1985. Sentimental Ambivalence and the Exegesis of 'Self' in Afghanistan. *Anthropological Quarterly* 58: 4, 203–11.

Ang, I. 1997. Dallas and Feminism. In *Media Studies: A Reader* (eds.) P. Marris and S. Thornham. Edinburgh: Edinburgh University Press.

References

Ansari, F. D. Sarah. 1992. *Sufi Saints and State Power: The Pirs of Sindh, 1843–1947*. Cambridge: Cambridge University Press.
Appadurai, A. (ed.) 1986. *The Social Life of Things: Commodities in Cultural Perspective*. Cambridge: Cambridge University Press.
Ardener, E. 1975. Belief and the Problem of Women. In *Perceiving Women* (ed.) S. Ardener. London: Malaby Press.
Ardener, S. 1981. Ground Rules and Social Maps for Women: An Introduction. In *Women and Space: Ground Rules and Social Maps* (ed.) S. Ardener, 11–34. London: Oxford University Women's Studies Committee/Croom Helm.
Arensberg, C. M. 1968. The Urban in Crosscultural Perspective. In *Urban Anthropology: Research Perspectives and Strategies* (ed.) E. M. Eddy. Southern Anthropological Society Proceedings, Athens: Distributed by University of Georgia Press.
Asad, I. S. 2003. The Institution of Wakf. *Dawn Newspaper*, 8 August.
Asad, T. 1972. Market Model, Class Structure and Consent: A Reconsideration of Swat Political Organisation. *Man* 7: 1, 74–94.
— (ed.) 1983 (first published 1973). *Anthropology and the Colonial Encounter*. London: Ithaca Press.
Ask, K. 1993. Ishq aur Mohabbat: Ideas About Love and Friendship in a Northern Pakistani Community. In *Carved Flesh Cast Selves: Gender Symbols and Social Practices* (eds.) V. Broch-Due, I. Rudie and T. Bleie, 207–23. Oxford: Berg Publishers.
Aswad, B. C. 1978. Women, Class, and Power: Examples from the Hatay, Turkey. In *Women in the Muslim World* (eds.) L. Beck and N. Keddie, 473–81. Cambridge, MA: Harvard University Press.
Baal, J. V. 1975. *Reciprocity and the Position of Women*. Assen/Amsterdam: Van Gorcum.
Baily, F. G. 1957. *Caste and the Economic Frontier*. Manchester: Manchester University Press.
Banerjee, M. 2000. *The Pathan Unarmed*. Karachi: Oxford University Press.
Barley, N. 1986 (first published 1983). *The Innocent Anthropologist*. Harmondsworth: Penguin.
Barnard, A. 2000. *History and Theory in Anthropology*. Cambridge: Cambridge University Press.
Barth, F. 1958. The Political Organization of Swat Pathans, unpublished PhD dissertation, University of Cambridge.
— 1959. Segmentary Opposition and the Theory of Games: A Study of Pathan Organization. *Journal of the Royal Anthropological Institute* 89: 1, 5–21.
— 1960. The System of Social Stratification in Swat, North Pakistan. In *Aspects of Caste in South India, Ceylon and North-West Pakistan* (ed.) E. Leach. Cambridge: Cambridge University Press.
— 1961. *Nomads of South Persia*. London: George Allen and Unwin.
— 1970 (first published 1969). Pathan Identity and its Maintenance. In *Ethnic Groups and Boundaries: The Social Organization of Culture Difference* (ed.) F. Barth, 117–34. Norway (Bergen): Universitetsforlaget.
— 1981a. *Process and Form in Social Life: Selected Essays of Fredrik Barth*. Vol. I. London: Routledge.
— 1981b. *Features of Person and Society in Swat: Collected Essays on Pathans. Selected Essays of Fredrik Barth*. Vol. II. London: Routledge.

1983. *Sohar: Culture and Society in an Omani Town*. Maryland: Johns Hopkins University Press.

1986 (first published 1959). *Political Leadership Among Swat Pathans*. London: Athlone Press.

1995 (first edition 1985). *The Last Wali of Swat: An Autobiography as Told to Fredrik Barth*. Oslo: Norwegian University Press.

Baudrillard, J. 1997. The Masses: The Implosion of the Social in the Media. In *Media Studies: A Reader* (eds.) P. Marris and S. Thornham, Edinburgh: Edinburgh University Press.

Bayly, C. A. 1980. The Small Town and Islamic Gentry in North India: The Case of Kara. In *The City in South Asia: Pre-Modern and Modern* (eds.) K. Ballhatchet and J. Harrison, 20–48. London: Curzon Press.

1998. From Rituals to Ceremony: Death Ritual and Society in Hindu North India Since 1600. In *Origins of Nationality in South Asia: Patriotism and Ethical Government in the Making of Modern India* (ed.) C. A. Bayly, 133–71. Delhi: Oxford University Press.

2001 (first published 1986). The Origins of Swadeshi (Home Industry): Cloth and Indian Society, 1700–1930. In *The Social Life of Things: Commodities in Cultural Perspective* (ed.) Arjun Appadurai, 285–321. Cambridge: Cambridge University Press.

Bayly, S. 2000. Cult Saints, Heroes, and Warrior Kings: South Asian Islam in the Making. In *Religion and Public Culture: Encounters and Identities in Modern South India* (eds.) K. E. Yandell and J. J. Paul, 193–210. Surrey: Curzon.

2001 (first published 1999). *Caste, Society and Politics in India: From the Eighteenth Century to the Modern Age*. Cambridge: Cambridge University Press.

Beattie, J. 1985 (first published 1964). *Other Cultures*. London: Routledge and Kegan Paul.

Beck, L. and N. Keddie. 1978. Introduction. In *Women in the Muslim World* (eds.) L. Beck and N. Keddie, 1–34. Cambridge, MA: Harvard University Press.

Bellew, H. W. (n.d.). *A Dictionary of the Pukkhto or Pukshto Language in which the Words are Traced to their Sources in the Indian and Persian Languages*. Peshawar: Saeed Book Bank.

1986 (reprinted). *Pushto Instructor: A Grammer of the Pukhto or Pukshto Language*. Peshawar: Saeed Book Bank.

1994 (first published 1864). *A General Report on the Yusufzai*. Lahore: Sang-e-Meel.

Berland, J. C. 1982. *No Five Fingers Are Alike: Cognitive Amplifiers in Social Context*. Cambridge, MA: Harvard University Press.

Beveridge, A. S. (trans.) 1987. *Babur-Nama: Memiors of Babur*. Lahore: Sang-e-Meel publication.

Bhattacharya, M. 2000. Iron Bangles to Iron Shackles: A Study of Women's Marriage and Subordination within Poor Households in Calcutta. *Man in India* 80: 1 and 2, 1–29.

Bloch, M. 1971. *Placing the Dead: Tombs, Ancestral Villages, and Kinship Organization in Madagascar.* New York: Academic Press.

1996 (first published 1982). Death, Women and Power. In *Death and the Regeneration of Life* (eds.) M. Bloch and J. Parry, 211–30. Cambridge: Cambridge University Press.

Bloch, M. and J. Parry. 1989 (first published 1982). Introduction: Death and the Regeneration of Life. In *Death and the Regeneration of Life* (eds.) M. Bloch and J. Parry, 1–44. Cambridge: Cambridge University Press.

1995 (first published 1989). *Money and the Morality of Exchange*. Cambridge: Cambridge University Press.

Boon, J. A. 1982. *Other Tribes, Other Scribes: Symbolic Anthropology in the Comparative Study of Cultures, Histories, Religions, and Texts*. Cambridge: Cambridge University Press.

Bourdieu, P. 1966. The Sentiment of Honour in Kabyle Society. In *Honour and Shame: The Values of Mediterranean Society* (ed.) J. G. Peristiany, 191–241. Chicago: The University of Chicago Press.

1991 (first published 1977). *Outline of a Theory of Practice*. Cambridge: Cambridge University Press.

Bowen, J. 1989. *Salat* in Indonesia: The Social Meanings of an Islamic Ritual. *Man* (NS) 24, 600–19.

Bowen, J. C. E. 1982. *Plain Tales of the Afghan Border*. London: Springwood Books.

Bowman, G. 1997. Identifying Versus Identifying with 'The Other': Reflections on the Siting of the Subject in Anthropological Discourse. In *After Writing Culture: Epistemology and Praxis in Contemporary Anthropology* (eds.) A. James, J. Hockey and A. Dawson, 34–50. London: Routledge.

Brenner, S. 1996. Reconstructing Self and Society: Javanese Muslim Women and 'The Veil'. *American Ethnologist* 23: 4, 573–691.

Brijbhushan, J. 1980. *Muslim Women in Purdah and Out of it*. Delhi: Vikas Publishing House.

Broch-Due, V. and I. Rudie. 1993. Carved Flesh/Cast Selves: An Introduction. In *Carved Flesh/Cast Selves: Gender Symbols and Social Practices* (eds.) V. Broch-Due, I. Rudie and T. Bleie. Oxford: Berg Publishers.

Bukhari, S. 1994. *Summarized Sahih Al-Bukhari*. Arabic–English (trans.) Dr Muhammad Muhsin Khan. Riyadh: Maktaba Dar-us-Sallam.

Bumiller, E. 1991. *May You Be the Mother of a Hundred Sons: A Journey Among the Women of India*. New Delhi: Penguin.

Callaway, H. 1994. Review of Hansen: African Encounters With Domesticity. *Man* 29: 205–6.

Caroe, O. 1992 (first published 1958). *The Pathans: 550 BC–AD 1957*. London: Macmillan and Company Limited.

Carsten, J. 1997. *The Heat of the Hearth: The Process of Kinship in a Malay Fishing Community*. Oxford: Oxford University Press.

Carsten, J. and S. Hugh-Jones. 1995. Introduction. In *About the House: Lévi-Strauss and Beyond* (eds.) J. Carsten and S. Hugh-Jones, 1–46. Cambridge: Cambridge University Press.

Castells, M. 1999. *The Power of Identity*. Oxford: Blackwell.

Chakravarty, S. 1976. *From Khyber to Oxus: A Study in Imperial Expansion*. New Delhi: Orient Longman Limited.

Chang, J. 1992, 1993. *Wild Swans: Three Daughters of China*. London: HarperCollins Audio Books.

Chhachhi, A. 1994. Identity Politics, Secularism and Women: A South Asian Perspective. In *Forging Identities: Gender, Communities and the State in India* (ed.) Z. Hasan, 74–95. Boulder, CO: Westview Press.

Cohn, B. S. 1989. Cloth, Clothes, and Colonialism: India in the Nineteenth Century. In *Cloth and the Human Experience* (eds.) A. B. Weiner and J. Schneider, 303–53. Wenner-Gren Foundation, Washington DC: Smithsonian Institution Press.

1996. *Colonialism and its Forms of Knowledge: The British in India*. Princeton: Princeton University Press.

Cole, D. P. 1984. Alliance and Descent in the Middle East and the Problem of Patrilateral Parallel Cousin Marriage. In *Islam in Tribal Societies: From the Atlas to the Indus* (eds.) A. S. Ahmed and D. M. Hart, 169–86. London: Routledge and Kegan Paul.

Colen, S. and R. Sanjek. 1990. Introduction: At Work in Homes 1: Orientations. In *At Work in Homes: Household Workers in World Perspective* (eds.) R. Sanjek and S. Colen, 1–13. Washington DC: American Ethnological Society Monograph Series, Number 3.

Collier, J. F. and M. Z. Rosaldo. 1981. Politics and Gender in Simple Societies. In *Sexual Meanings: The Cultural Construction of Gender and Sexuality* (eds.) S. B. Ortner and H. Whitehead, 275–329. Cambridge: Cambridge University Press.

Comaroff, J. and J. Comaroff. 1992. *Ethnography and the Historical Imagination*. Boulder, CO: Westview Press.

Cook, M. 2000. *Commanding Right and Forbidding Wrong in Islamic Thought*. Cambridge: Cambridge University Press.

Crystal, D. 1997. *The Cambridge Encyclopedia of the English Language*. Cambridge: Cambridge University Press.

Csordas, T. J. 1999. The Body's Career in Anthropology. In *Anthropological Theory Today* (ed.) H. Moore, 172–205. Malden, MA: Blackwell.

Dalrymple, W. 2002. *White Mughals: Love and Betrayal in Eighteenth Century India*. London: Harper Collins.

Daniel, V. E. 1984. *Fluid Signs: Being a Person the Tamil Way*. Berkeley: University of California Press.

Daniels, A. K. 1988. *Invisible Careers*. Chicago: University of Chicago Press.

Darish, P. 1989. Dressing for the Next Life. In *Cloth and Human Experience* (eds.) J. Schneider and A. B. Weiner, 117–40. Wenner-Gren Foundation. Washington DC: Smithsonian Institution Press.

Das, V. 1986. The Work of Mourning: Death in a Punjabi Family. In *The Cultural Transition: Human Experience and Social Transformation in the Third World and Japan* (eds.) M. I. White and S. Pollak, 179–210. Boston: Routledge and Kegan Paul.

Delaney, C. 1991. *The Seed and the Soil: Gender and Cosmology in Turkish Village Society*. Berkeley: University of California Press.

Deutsch, K. A. 1998. Muslim Women in Colonial North India Circa 1920–1947: Politics, Law and Community Identity, unpublished PhD Dissertation, University of Cambridge.

Devji, F. F. 1994. Gender and the Politics of Space: The Movement for Women's Reform, 1857–1900. In *Forging Identities: Gender, Communities and the State in India* (ed.) Z. Hasan, 22–37. Boulder, CO: Westview Press.

Donnan, H. 1987. Issues in Pakistani Ethnography. *Anthropology Today* 3: 4, 21–2.
  1988. *Marriage Among Muslims: Preferences and Choice in Northern Pakistan*. Delhi: Hindustan Publication Corporation.

Donnan, H. and P. Werbner. 1991. Introduction. In *Economy and Culture in Pakistan: Migrants and Cities in a Muslim Society* (eds.) H. Donnan and P. Werbner, 1–34. London: Macmillan.

Donner, W. W. 1992. Lineages and Land Disputes on a Polynesian Outlier. *Man* 27: 2, 319–39.

Drucker-Brown, S. 1982. Joking at Death: The Mamprusi Grandparent–Grandchild Joking Relationship. *Man* (NS) 17, 714–27.

Dube, L. 1969. *Matriliny and Islam: Religion and Society in Laccadives*. Delhi: National Publishing House.
Dumont, L. 1980. *Homo Hierarchicus: The Caste System and Its Implications*. Chicago: University of Chicago Press.
Dunbar, R. 1997. *Grooming, Gossip and the Evolution of Language*. London: Faber and Faber.
Dupree, L. 1977. On Two Views of the Swat Pushtun. *Current Anthropology* 18: 3, 514–18.
  1978. Pushtun. In *Muslim Peoples: A World Ethnographic Survey* (ed.) Richard V. Weekes, 323–9. Connecticut: Greenwood Press.
  1984. Tribal Warfare in Afghanistan and Pakistan: A Reflection of the Segmentary Lineage System. In *Islam in Tribal Societies: From the Atlas to the Indus* (eds.) A. S. Ahmed and D. M. Hart, 266–86. London: Routledge and Kegan Paul.
Easwaran, E. 1999. *Nonviolent Soldier of Islam: Badshah Khan, a Man to Match His Mountains*. California: Nilgiri Press.
Eddy, E. M. (ed.) 1968. Urban Anthropology: An Introductory Note. In *Urban Anthropology: Research Perspectives and Strategies*. Southern Anthropological Society Proceedings, Number 2. Athens: Distributed by University of Georgia Press.
Edwards, D. B. 1996. *Heroes of the Age: Moral Fault Lines on the Afghan Frontier*. Berkeley: University of California Press.
  1998. Learning from the Swat Pathans: Political Leadership in Afghanistan, 1978–97. *American Ethnologist* 25: 4, 712–28.
Eickelman, D. F. 1992. Mass Higher Education and the Religious Imagination in Contemporary Arab Societies. *American Ethnologist* 19: 4, 643–55.
Eliot, T. S. 1963 (first published 1941). *A Choice of Kipling's Verse*. London: Faber and Faber.
Ellen, R. F. 1992. *Ethnographic Research: A Guide to General Conduct*. London: Academic Press.
Elliot, J. G. 1968. *The Frontier 1839–1947*. London: Cassell and Company.
Elphinstone, M. 1815. *An Account of the Kingdom of Caubul, and its Dependencies in Persia, Tartary, and India*. London: Longman.
Enevoldsen, J. 1993. *The Nightingale of Peshawar: Selections From Rahman Baba*. Peshawar: InterLit Foundation.
Epstein, A. L. (ed.) 1967. *The Craft of Social Anthropology*. London: Tavistock Publications.
Esposito, J. L. 1998. Women in Islam and Muslim Societies. In *Islam, Gender and Social Change* (eds.) Y. Y. Haddad and J. L. Esposito, viii–xxviii. New York: Oxford University Press.
Ewing, K. P. (ed.) 1988. *Shari'at and Ambiguity in South Asian Islam*. Berkeley: University of California Press.
Farhat-ul-Ain. 1980–2. Effect of Television on Children, unpublished MA Thesis, University of Peshawar.
Fazila-Yacoobali, V. 1999. A Rite of Passage: The Partition of History and the Dawn of Pakistan. *Interventions: International Journal of Postcolonial Studies*. 1: 2, 183–200.
Fazlur-Rehman. 1999. The Religio Political Movement of Faqir of Ippi. Islamabad: National Institute of Pakistan Studies, unpublished PhD Dissertation, Quaid-i-Azam University, Islamabad.
Ferdows, A. K. 1985. The Status and Rights of Women in *Ithna 'Ashari* Shi'i Islam. In *Women and the Family in Iran* (ed.) A. Fathi, 13–36. Leiden, Netherlands: E. J. Brill.

Fischer, M. D. 1991. Marriage and Power: Tradition and Transition in an Urban Punjabi Community. In *Economy and Culture in Pakistan: Migrants and Cities in a Muslim Society* (eds.) H. Donnan and P. Werbner, 97–123. London: Macmillan.

Fiske, J. 1997. The Codes of Television. In *Media Studies: A Reader* (eds.) P. Marris and S. Thornham. Edinburgh: Edinburgh University Press.

Forbes, G. 1999. *Women in Modern India*. Cambridge: Cambridge University Press.

Foucault, M. 1991. *Discipline and Punish: The Birth of the Prison*. Harmondsworth: Penguin.

Franks, S. 1999. *Having None of It: Women, Men and the Future of Work*. London: Granta Books.

Frazer, J. 1993 (first published 1922). *The Golden Bough*. Ware, Hertfordshire: Wordsworth.

Freeman, S. T. 1970. *Neighbors: The Social Contract in a Castilian Hamlet*. Chicago: Chicago University Press.

Freitag, S. B. 1988. Ambiguous Public Arenas and Coherent Personal Practice: Kanpur Muslims 1913–1931. In *Shari'at and Ambiguity in South Asian Islam* (eds.) K. P. Ewing, 143–63. Berkeley: University of California Press.

Gellner, D. N. 1994. Priests, Healers, Mediums and Witches: The Context of Possession in the Kathmandu Valley, Nepal. *Man* 29: 1, 27–48.

Gellner, E. 1969. *Saints of the Atlas*. London: Weidenfeld & Nicolson.

1993 (first published 1982). *Muslim Society*. Cambridge: Cambridge University Press.

Gibb, H. A. R. and J. H. Kramers (eds.) 1974. *Shorter Encyclopaedia of Islam*. Netherlands: Leiden.

Giddens, A. 1978. *Durkheim*. London: Fontana.

Gilbert, M. 1994. Vengeance as Illusion and Reality: The Case of the Battered wife. *Man* 29: 4, 853–873.

Gilmartin, D. 1984. Shrines, Succession, and Sources of Moral Authority. In *Moral Conduct and Authority: The Place of Adab in South Asian Islam* (ed.) B. D. Metcalf, 221–40. Berkeley: University of California Press.

Gilmartin, D. and B. B. Lawrence (eds.) 2000. *Beyond Turk and Hindu: Rethinking Religious Identities in Islamicate South Asia*. Gainesville: University Press of Florida.

Gilsenan, M. 1990. *Recognizing Islam: Religion and Society in the Modern Middle East*. London: I. B. Tauris.

1996. *Lords of the Lebanese Marches: Violence and Narrative in an Arab Society*. London: I. B. Tauris.

2000. Signs of Truth: Enchantment, Modernity and the Dreams of Peasant Women. *Journal of the Royal Anthropological Institute* (NS) 6: 4, 597–615.

Giovannini, M. J. 1981. Woman: A Dominant Symbol within the Cultural System of a Sicilian Town. *Man* 16: 3, 408–26.

Glasse, C. 1991. *The Concise Encyclopaedia of Islam*. London: Stacey International.

Goffman, E. 1968. *Asylums*. Harmondsworth: Penguin.

Goodwin, B. 1969. *Life Among the Pathans*. London: RAI-Museum of Mankind Library.

Goody, J. 1962. *Death Property and the Ancestors: A Study of the Mortuary Customs of the LoDagaa of West Africa*. London: Tavistock.

Gray, J. N. and D. J. Mearns (eds.) 1989. *Society from the Inside Out: Anthropological Perspectives on the South Asian Household*. New Delhi: Sage Publications.

Greenleaf, R. K. 1977. *Servant Leadership: A Journey into the Nature of Legitimate Power and Greatness*. New York: Paulist Press.

Grima, B. 1998. *The Performance of Emotion Among Paxtun Women: 'The Misfortunes Which Have Befallen Me'*. Karachi: Oxford University Press.

Grint, K. 1991. *The Sociology of Work*. Cambridge: Polity Press.

— 1994. Review of Herbert Applebaum's *The Concept of Work: Ancient, Medieval, and Modern*. *Man* 29, 193–4.

Gul, S. 1995–7. Working Girl Child, Their Problems and Prospects, unpublished MA Thesis, University of Peshawar.

Habermas, J. 2002. *The Structural Transformation of the Public Sphere: An Inquiry into a Category of Bourgeois Society*. Cambridge: Polity Press.

Haddad, Y. Y. and J. L. Esposito (eds.) 1998. *Islam, Gender and Social Change*. New York: Oxford University Press.

Hagen, J. M. 1999. The Good Behind the Gift: Morality and Exchange Among the Maneo of Eastern Indonesia. *Man* 5: 3, 361–74.

Hall, S. 1997. Encoding/Decoding. In *Media Studies: A Reader* (eds.) P. Marris and S. Thornham. Edinburgh: Edinburgh University Press.

Hanifi, J. M. 1976. Preindustrial Kabul: Its Structure and Function in Transformational Processes in Afghanistan. In *The Mutual Interaction of People and Their Built Environment: A Cross-Cultural Perspective* (ed.) A. Rapoport, 441–51. The Hague: Mouton.

Hansen, K. T. 1994. Review of *Maids in the USA*. *Man* 29, 216–17.

Harrison, S. 1992. Ritual as Intellectual Property. *Man* 27: 2, 225–43.

Hart, D. M. 1987. *Banditry in Islam: Case Studies From Morocco, Algeria and the Pakistan North West Frontier*. Outwell, Wisbech, Cambridgeshire: Middle East and North African Studies Press.

Hasan, A. G. 1996. *The Rights and Duties of Women in Islam*. Riyadh: Darussalam.

Hertz. R. 1960. *Death and the Right Hand*. London: Routledge and Kegan Paul.

Hegland, M. E. 1998. Flagellation and Fundamentalism: (Trans)forming Meaning, Identity, and Gender through Pakistani Women's Rituals of Mourning. *American Ethnologist* 25: 2, 240–66.

Heston, W. L. and Mumtaz Nasir (n.d.) *The Bazar of the Storytellers*. Islamabad: Lok Virsa.

Hill, B. 1996. *Servants: English Domestics in the Eighteenth Century*. New York: Oxford University Press.

Hirschkind, C. 2001. Civic Virtue and Religious Reason: An Islamic Counterpart. *Cultural Anthropology* 16: 1.

Hobson, D. 1997. Housewives and the Mass Media. In *Media Studies: A Reader* (eds.) P. Marris and S. Thornham. Edinburgh: Edinburgh University Press.

Hochschild, A. R. 1997. *The Time Bind: When Home Becomes Work and Work Becomes Home*. New York: Metropolitan Books.

Hoch-Smith, J. and A. Spring (eds.) 1978. *Women in Ritual and Symbolic Roles*. New York: Plenum Press.

Holland, P. 1997. When a Woman Reads the News. In *Media Studies: A Reader* (ed.) P. Marris and S. Thornham. Edinburgh: Edinburgh University Press.

Hoodfar, H. 1991. Return to the Veil: Personal Strategy and Public Participation in Egypt. In *Working Women: International Perspectives on Labour and Gender Ideology* (eds.) N. Redclift and M. T. Sinclair, 104–24. London: Routledge.

Horvatich, P. 1994. Ways of Knowing Islam. *American Ethnologist* 21: 4, 811–26.
Hoti, A. K. (n.d.) *History of the Hoti Family*. Compiled during the time of Lt Col Nawab Sir Mohammad Akbar Khan of Hoti: Mardan.
   1942. *Pathan a Mis-nomer for an 'Afghan'*. Peshawar: The London Book Company (India).
Howell, E. 1979. *Mizh: A Monograph on Government Relations with the Mahsud Tribe*. Karachi: Oxford University Press.
Humphrey, C. 1992. Women and Ideology in Hierarchical Societies in East Asia. In *Persons and Power of Women in Diverse Cultures* (ed.) S. Ardener, 173–92. New York: Berg.
   1999. Shamans in the City. *Anthropology Today* 15: 3, 3–10.
Humphrey, C. and J. Laidlaw. 1994. *The Archetypal Actions of Ritual: A Theory of Ritual Illustrated by the Jain Rite of Worship*. Oxford: Clarendon Press.
Humphrey, C. and P. Vitebsky. 1997. *Sacred Architecture*. London: Duncan Baird.
Huntington, R. and P. Metcalf. 1980. *Celebrations of Death: The Anthropology of Mortuary Rituals*. Cambridge: Cambridge University Press.
Hussain, A. 1979–81. Attitude of People Towards Female Education in Village Turlandi Tehsil Swabi, unpublished MA Thesis, University of Peshawar.
Ikramullah, S. S. 1992. *Ceremonies, Customs and Colour Behind the Veil*. Karachi: Oxford University Press.
   1998. *From Purdah to Parliament*. Karachi: Oxford University Press.
Iqbal, S. 1997. Inner Structures and Dynamics of Intra Female Conflicts in Domestic and Public Domain and its Implications for Women's Status, unpublished MA Thesis, Quaid-i-Azam University, Islamabad.
Jacobson, D. 1982. Purdah and the Hindu Family in Central India. In *Separate Worlds: Studies of Purdah in South Asia* (eds.) H. Papanek and G. Minault, 81–109. Delhi: Chanakya Publications.
Jahoda, M. 1982. *Employment and Unemployment: A Socio-Psychological Analysis*. Cambridge: Cambridge University Press.
Jalal, A. 1985. *The Sole Spokesman: Jinnah, the Muslim League and the Demand for Pakistan*. Cambridge: Cambridge University Press.
James, A. H. J. and A. Dawson. 1997. Introduction: The Road from Santa Fe. In *After Writing Culture: Epistemology and Praxis in Contemporary Anthropology* (eds.) A. Hockey, J. James and A. Dawson, 1–15. London: Routledge.
Jansson, E. 1988. *India, Pakistan or Pukhtunistan*. Uppsala: Acta Universitatis Upsaliensis.
Jeffery, P. 1979. *Frogs in a Well: Indian Women in Purdah*. London: Zed Press.
Joshi, R. 1985. *The Afghan Nobility and the Mughals (1526–1707)*. New Delhi: Vikas.
Kabbani, R. 1986. Innocents Abroad? Some European Travellers and their Orient, unpublished PhD Dissertation, University of Cambridge.
Keiser, L. 1991. *Friend by Day, Enemy by Night: Organized Vengeance in a Kohistani Community*. Orlando: Holt, Rinehart and Winston.
Kelly, M. P. F. 1986. *Women's Work: Development and the Division of Labor by Gender*. Massachusetts: Bergin and Garvey.
Ibn Khaldun. 1986 (first print 1958). *The Muqaddimah: An Introduction to History* (trans. from the Arabic by Franz Rosenthal), 3 vols. London: Routledge and Kegan Paul.
   1989. *The Muqaddimah: An Introduction to History* (abridged by N. J. Dawood; trans. from the Arabic by Franz Rosenthal). Princeton: Princeton University Press.
Khan, A. M. 1994. *Da Pukhtunkhwa Ghag* (in Pukhto). Sadar Pukhtunkhwa Quomi Party. Lahore: Millat.

Khan, Ali. 2003. Representing Children: Power, Policy and the Discourse on Child Labour in the Football Manufacturing Industry of Sialkot, unpublished PhD Dissertation, University of Cambridge.
Khan, B. 1992–4. Status of Women in Pukhtoons (Problems and Prospects): A Case Study of Saidu Sharif, Swat, unpublished MA Thesis, University of Peshawar.
Khan, B. 1999. Frontier Taliban. *Newsline Journal*, Pakistan: February.
Khan, G. 1990 (first published 1947). *The Pathans*. Islamabad: Pushto Adabi Society.
Khan, M. S. 1979–81. Thesis on the Impact of Afghan Refugees on Our Society, unpublished MA Thesis, University of Peshawar.
Khan, M. T. 2000. Pukhto and the Pukhtunwali. *The News*, Islamabad: 1 November.
Khan, M. W. 1998. *Women in Islamic Shari'ah*. New Delhi: Al-Risala Books.
Khan, S. A. 1996. *Anthropology as Science: The Problem of Indigenization in Pakistan*. Lahore: Sang-e-Meel Publications.
Khan, S. M. 1997. *Pukhtuno Ka Tarekhe Safar* (in Urdu). Karachi: Zaki Sons.
Khan, S. M. 2000. *The Begums of Bhopal: A Dynasty of Women Rulers in Raj India*. London: I. B. Tauris.
Khedairi, B. 2003. An Etiquette of Condolences. *The Guardian Newspaper* (UK) Monday 30 June.
Khoury, P. S. and J. Kostiner (ed.) 1990. *Tribes and State Formation in the Middle East*. Berkeley: University of California Press.
King, L. W. 1984. *The Orakzai, Country and Clan*. Lahore: Vanguard Books.
Kipling, R. 1987 (first published 1901). *Kim*. Oxford: Oxford University Press.
Kolenda, P. 1989. The Joint Family Household in Rural Rajasthan: Ecological, Cultural and Demographic Conditions for its Occurrence. In *Society From the Inside Out: Anthropological Perspectives on the South Asian Household* (eds.) J. N. Gray and D. J. Mearns, 55–106. New Delhi: Sage.
2000. Memories of Brahman Agraharam in Travancore. In *Religion and Public Culture: Encounters and Identities in Modern South India* (eds.) K. E. Yandell and J. J. Paul, 162–89. Surrey: Curzon.
Kondos, V. 1989. Subjection and the Domicile: Some Problematic Issues Relating to High Caste Nepalese Women. In *Society From the Inside Out: Anthropological Perspectives on the South Asian Household*. (eds.) J. N. Gray and D. J. Mearns, 162–91. New Delhi: Sage.
Kuhn, A. 1997. The Power of the Image. In *Media Studies: A Reader* (eds.) P. Marris and S. Thornham. Edinburgh: Edinburgh University Press.
Kurin, R. 1984. Morality, Personhood, and the Exemplary Life: Popular Conceptions of Muslims in Paradise. In *Moral Conduct and Authority: The Place of Adab in South Asian Islam* (ed.) B. D. Metcalf, 196–220. Berkeley: University of California Press.
Kurti, L. 1999. Cameras and other Gadgets: Reflections on Fieldwork Experiences in Socialist and Post-Socialist Hungarian Communities. *Social Anthropology* 7: 2, 169–85.
La Fontaine, J. 1992. The Persons of Women. In *Persons and Power of Women in Diverse Cultures* (ed.) Shirley Ardener, 89–104. New York: Berg.
Laidlaw, J. 1995. *Riches and Renunciation: Religion, Economy, and Society among the Jains*. Oxford: Oxford University Press.
2000. A Free Gift Makes No Friends. *Journal of the Royal Anthropological Institute* 6: 4, 617–34.
Lamb, C. 2002. *The Sewing Circles of Herat: A Memoir of Afghanistan*. London: HarperCollins.

Le Wita, B. 1994. *French Bourgeois Culture* (trans. from the French by J. A. Underwood). Cambridge: Cambridge University Press.

Lees, W. N. 1871. *Indian Musalmans: Being Three Letters*. London: Williams and Norgate.

Leonardo, M. D. 1991. Introduction: Gender, Culture, and Political Economy: Feminist Anthropology in Historical Perspective. In *Gender at the Crossroads of Knowledge: Feminist Anthropology in the Postmodern Era* (ed.) Micaela di Leonardo, 1–48. Berkeley: University of California Press.

Lévi-Strauss, C. 1963. Do Dual Organizations Exist? In *Structural Anthropology*, 132–63. New York: Basic Books.

Lewenhak, S. 1980. *Women and Work*. London: Macmillan.

  1992. *The Revaluation of Women's Work*. London: Earthscan Publications.

Lewis, R. 1996. *Gendering Orientalism: Race, Femininity and Representation*. London: Routledge.

Lindholm, Charles. 1981. History and the Heroic Pakhtun. *Man* 16: 3, 463–7.

  1982. *Generosity and Jealousy: The Swat Pukhtun of Northern Pakistan*. New York: Columbia University Press.

  1988. The Social Structure of Emotional Constraint: The Court of Louis XIV and the Pukhtun of Northern Pakistan. *Ethos* 16: 3, 227–46.

  1995. Quandaries of Command in Egalitarian Societies: Examples from Swat and Morocco. In *Comparing Muslim Societies: Knowledge and State in a World Civilization* (ed.) J. R. I. Cole, 63–87. Ann Arbor, MI: University of Michigan Press.

  1996. *Frontier Perspectives: Essays in Comparative Anthropology*. Karachi: Oxford University Press.

Lindholm, Cherry. 1996. The Swat Pukhtun Family as a Political Training Ground. In *Frontier Perspectives: Essays in Contemporary Anthropology*, Charles Lindholm, 17–27. Karachi: Oxford University Press.

Loizos, P. 1981. *The Heart Grown Bitter*. Cambridge: Cambridge University Press.

Lupton, D. 1996. *Food, the Body and the Self*. London: Sage.

Lutz, C. 1986. Emotion, Thought, and Estrangement: Emotion as a Cultural Category. *Cultural Anthropology* 1: 3, 287–309.

Macaulay, T., Lord. 1935. *Selected Speeches by Lord Macaulay with his Minute on Indian Education*. Oxford: Oxford University Press.

Macfarlane, A. 1981. Death and the Demographic Transition: A Note on English Evidence on Death 1500–750. In *Mortality and Immortality: the Anthropology and Archaeology of Death* (eds.) S. C. Humphreys and Helen King, 249–59. London: Academic Press.

Macfarlane, A. and I. Macfarlane. 2003. *Green Gold: The Empire of Tea*. London: Ebury Press.

Mackintosh, M. M. 1979. Domestic Labour and the Household. In *Fit Work for Women* (ed.) S. Burman, 173–91. London: Croom Helm.

McLuhan, M. 1997. The Medium is the Message. In *Media Studies: A Reader* (eds.) P. Marris and S. Thornham. Edinburgh: Edinburgh University Press.

Madan, T. N. 2002. *Family and Kinship: A Study of the Pandits of Rural Kashmir*. New Delhi: Oxford University Press.

Mahmood, S. 2001. Feminist Theory, Embodiment, and the Docile Agent: Some Reflections on the Egyptian Islamic Revival. *Cultural Anthropology* 16: 2, 202–36.

  2003. Ethical Formation and Politics of Individual Autonomy in Contemporary Egypt. *Social Research* 70: 3 (Fall).

Malik, H. A. 1991. *The Sharia Rules for Marriage.* Pennsylvania: Institute for Research and Islamic Education.

Malinowski, B. 1982 (first published 1948). *Magic, Science and Religion and other Essays.* London: Souvenir Press.

Mandelbaum, D. G. 1993. *Women's Seclusion and Men's Honor: Sex Roles in North India, Bangladesh and Pakistan.* Tucson and London: The University of Arizona Press.

Mannan, M. 1994–6. Religio-Cultural Importance of Purdah: A Descriptive Study of Village "Toormang" District Dir, unpublished MA Thesis, University of Peshawar.

Marsden, M. 2002. Islamization and Globalization in Chitral, Northern Pakistan, unpublished PhD Dissertation, University of Cambridge.

Matri, S. 2003. The Opiate of the Elite. *Newsline,* Pakistan: December, 35–7.

Matthews, D. (trans.) 1996. *Umrao Jan Ada* (original in Urdu by Mirza Muhammad Hadi Rusva). Lahore: Sang-e-Meel.

Mauss, M. 1990 (first published 1954). *The Gift: The Form and Reason for Exchange in Archaic Societies.* London: Routledge.

Maza, S. C. 1983. *Servants and Maids in Eighteenth Century France: The Uses of Loyalty.* New Jersey: Princeton University Press.

Mead, M. 1950. *Male and Female: A Study of the Sexes in a Changing World.* London: Victor Gollancz.

Merk, W. R. H. 1984. *The Mohmands.* Lahore: Vanguard Books.

Mernissi, F. 1985. *Beyond the Veil: Male–Female Dynamics in Modern Muslim Society.* London: Al Saqi Books.

  1988. *Doing Daily Battles: Interviews with Moroccan Women.* London: The Women's Press.

Metcalf, B. D. 1984a. Introduction. In *Moral Conduct and Authority: The Place of Adab in South Asian Islam* (ed.) B. D. Metcalf, 1–20. Berkeley: University of California Press.

  1984b. Islamic Reform and Islamic Women: Maulana Thanawi's *Jewelry of Paradise.* In *Moral Conduct and Authority: The Place of Adab in South Asian Islam* (ed.) B. D. Metcalf, 184–95. Berkeley: University of California Press.

  1990. *Perfecting Women.* Berkeley: University of California.

Metcalf, P. 1982. *A Borneo Journey into Death: Berawan Eschatology from Its Rituals.* Philadelphia: University of Pennsylvania Press.

Metcalf, T. R. 1979. *Lands, Landlords, and the British Raj: Northern India in the Nineteenth Century.* Berkeley: University of California Press.

Mir-Hosseini, Z. 2000 (first published 1999). *Islam and Gender: The Religious Debate in Contemporary Iran.* London: I. B. Tauris.

Modleski, T. 1997. The Search for Tomorrow in Today's Soap Operas. In *Media Studies: A Reader* (eds.) P. Marris and S. Thornham. Edinburgh: Edinburgh University Press.

Mody Spencer, P. 2000. Love Marriage in Delhi, unpublished PhD Dissertation, University of Cambridge.

Mohmand, J. S. 1966. Social Organization of Musa Khel Mohmand, unpublished MA Thesis, Punjab University, Pakistan.

Moore, H. L. 1994. *A Passion for Difference.* Cambridge: Polity Press.

  1997 (first published 1988). *Feminism and Anthropology.* Oxford: Polity Press in association with Blackwell.

  1999. *Anthropological Theory Today.* Malden: Blackwell Publishers.

Moore, J. D. 1997. *Visions of Culture: An Introduction to Anthropological Theories and Theorists*. Walnut Creek, CA: AltaMira Press.

Morgan, Lewis H. 1965. *Houses and House-Life of the American Aborigines*. Chicago: University of Chicago Press.

Morris, L. 1990. *The Workings of the Household*. Cambridge: Polity Press.

Morris, R. C. 1995. All Made Up: Performance Theory and the New Anthropology of Sex and Gender. *Annual Review of Anthropology* 24, 567–92.

Muhammad, F. and M. A. Jan. 1992–4. Impact of Mass Media Communication (TV) on Changing Behaviour of Teenagers (A Case Study of Town Committee Area Charsadda), unpublished MA Thesis, University of Peshawar.

Mumtaz, K. and F. Shaheed. 1987. *Women of Pakistan*. London: Zed Books.

Munn, N. D. 1990. Constructing Regional Worlds in Experience: Kula Exchange, Witchcraft and Gawan Local Events. *Man* 25: 1, 1–17.

Nadelson, L. 1981. Pigs, Women, and the Men's House in Amazonia: An Analysis of Six Mundurucu Myths. In *Sexual Meanings: The Cultural Construction of Gender and Sexuality* (eds.) S. B. Ortner and H. Whitehead, 240–72. Cambridge: Cambridge University Press.

Nadvi, M. S. A, M. A-S. Nadvi and A. S. S. Nadvi. 1999. *Biographies of the Women Companions of the Holy Prophet*. Karachi: Darul-Ishaat.

Najmabadi, A. 1998. Crafting an Educated Housewife in Iran. In *Remaking Women: Feminism and Modernity in the Middle East* (ed.) L. Abu-Lughod, 91–125. Princeton: Princeton University Press.

Namihira, E. 1987. Pollution in the Folk Belief System. *Current Anthropology* 28: 4, S65–S74. Supplement: An Anthropological Profile of Japan. August–October.

Naveed-i-Rahat. 1990. *Male Outmigration and Matri-Weighted Households: A Case Study of a Punjabi Village in Pakistan*. New Delhi: Hindustan Publishing Corporation.

Nelson, C. 1974. Public and Private Politics: Women in the Middle Eastern World. *American Ethnologist* 1: 3, 551–63.

The News International. 2000a. Protection of Kids from Harmful Mass Media Programmes Urged. Islamabad: 31 July.

2000b. Islamic Activists Torch TV Sets in Mardan. Islamabad: 31 October.

2001. Pakistan's Population Reaches 140.5m. Islamabad: 17 June.

Nizami, R. 2001. Islamabad: 15 minutes away from Pakistan. *Dawn*, Karachi: 3 July.

Nola, R. 1998. *Foucault*. London: Frank Cass.

Novarra, V. 1980. *Women's Work, Men's Work: The Ambivalence of Equality*. London: Marion Boyars.

Okely, J. 1996. *Own or Other Culture*. London: Routledge.

Ong, A. 1996. Cultural Citizenship as Subject-Making: Immigrants Negotiate Racial and Cultural Boundaries in the United States. *Current Anthropology* 37: 5, 737–51.

Oppong, C. 1994. Introduction. In *Gender, Work and Population in Sub-Saharan Africa* (eds.) A. Adepoju and C. Oppong, 1–16. London: James Currey.

Otterbein, K. F. 1977 (first published 1972). *Comparative Cultural Analysis*. New York: Holt, Rinehart and Winston.

Pahl, R. E. (ed.) 1989. *On Work: Historical, Comparative and Theoretical Approaches*. Oxford: Basil Blackwell.

Paine, R. 1982. The Stamp of Swat: A Brief Ethnography of Some of the Writings of Fredrik Barth. *Man* 17: 2, 328–39.

Papanek, H. 1982. Purdah: Separate Worlds and Symbolic Shelter. In *Separate Worlds: Studies of Purdah in South Asia* (eds.) H. Papanek and G. Minault, 5–53. Delhi: Chanakya Publications.

Parfitt, T. 2002. *The Lost Tribes of Israel: The History of a Myth*. London: Phoenix.

Parry, J. P. 1972. Caste and Kinship in Kangra, unpublished PhD Dissertation, University of Cambridge.

1989. Sacrificial Death and the Necrophagous Ascetic. In *Death and the Regeneration of Life* (eds.) M. Bloch and J. Parry, 74–107. Cambridge: Cambridge University Press.

Pashto Dictionary. 1982. Peshawar: Saeed Book Bank.

Pastner, C. Mc C. 1978. The Status of Women and Property on a Baluchistan Oasis in Pakistan. In *Women in the Muslim World* (eds.) L. Beck and N. Keddie, 434–50. Cambridge, MA: Harvard University Press.

Pitt-Rivers, J. 1966. Honour and Social Status. In *Honour and Shame: The Values of Mediterranean Society* (ed.) J. G. Peristiany, 19–77. Chicago: University of Chicago Press.

Povinelli, E. A. 1993. *Labor's Lot*. Chicago: University of Chicago Press.

Price, G. P. 2000. Acting in Public versus Forming a Public: Conflict Processing and Political Mobilization in Nineteenth Century South India. In *Religion and Public Culture: Encounters and Identities in Modern South India* (eds.) K. E. Yandell and J. J. Paul, 27–55. Surrey: Curzon.

Rabinow, P. (ed.) 1986. *The Foucault Reader*. Harmondsworth: Penguin.

Rahman, T. 1997. The Urdu–English Controversy in Pakistan. *Modern Asian Studies* 31: 1, 177–207.

Raj, D. S. 1997. Shifting Culture in the Global Terrain: Cultural Identity Constructions Amongst British Punjabi Hindus, unpublished PhD Dissertation, University of Cambridge.

Rapoport, A. (ed.) 1976. *The Mutual Interaction of People and Their Built Environment: A Cross-Cultural Perspective*. The Hague: Mouton.

Raverty, H. G. 1982. *A Dictionary of Pukhto, Pushto or Languages of the Afghans*. Peshawar: Saeed Book Bank.

Reagan, B. B. and M. Blaxall. 1976. Introduction: Occupational Segregation in International Women's Year. In *Women and the Workplace: The Implications of Occupational Segregation* (eds.) M. Blaxall and B. Reagan, 1–5. Chicago: University of Chicago Press.

Rehman Baba. (n.d.) *Deewan-e Rehman Baba* (in Pukhto). Muhalla Jangi, Peshawar: Zeb Art Publishers.

Reiter, R. R. 1975. Men and Women in the South of France: Public and Private Domain. In *Towards an Anthropology of Women* (ed.) R. R. Reiter, 252–82. New York: Monthly Review Press.

Reynell, J. 1985. Honour, Nurture and Festivity: Aspects of Female Religiosity amongst Jain Women in Jaipur, unpublished PhD Dissertation, University of Cambridge.

Richards, D. S. 1990. *The Savage Frontier: A History of the Anglo-Afghan Wars*. London: Macmillan.

Rifaqat, Z. 1998. Gender Mobility Among Pathan Women, unpublished MA Thesis, Quaid-i-Azam University, Islamabad.

Robina B. 1994–6. The Problems of Maids in Haripur City, unpublished MA Thesis, University of Peshawar.

Roded, R. (ed.) 1999. *Women in Islam and the Middle East*. London: I. B. Tauris.

Safdar, S. 1997. *Kinship and Marriage in Pukhtoon Society*. Lahore: Pak Book Empire.
Saiyid, D. H. 1997. Sir Sayed, Hali and Nazir Ahmed on the New Role of Women. *The Nation* (8 June), Pakistan: 8–9.
Sandborg, K. 1993. Malay Dress Symbolism. In *Carved Flesh Cast Selves: Gender Symbols and Social Practices* (eds.) V. Broch-Due, I. Rudie and T. Bleie, 195–206. Oxford: Berg Publishers.
Sayyed, M. 1994–6. Psycho-Social Implications of Women Having no Male Child: Study of Village Bickotgung Mardan, unpublished MA Thesis, University of Peshawar.
Scheper-Hughes, N. 1992. *Death Without Weeping: The Violence of Everyday Life in Brazil*. Berkeley: University of California Press.
Schneider, J. and A. B. Weiner (eds.) 1989. *Cloth and Human Experience*. Wenner-Gren Foundation. Washington DC: Smithsonian Institution Press.
Schwartz, N. B. 1977. A Pragmatic Past: Folk History, Environmental Change, and Society in a Peten, Guatemala Town. *American Ethnologist* 4: 2, 339–58.
Seaman, G. 1981. The Sexual Politics of Karmic Retribution. *The Anthropology of Taiwanese Society* (eds.) E. M. Ahern and H. Gates, 381–96. Stanford, CA: Stanford University Press.
Sehrai, N. 1994–6. The Attitude of Pukhtuns Toward Female Education (A Study of Village Baghicha Dheri District Mardan), unpublished MA Thesis, University of Peshawar.
Sexton, L. D. 1984. Pigs, Pearlshells, and 'Women's Work': Collective Responses to Change in Highland Papua New Guinea. In *Rethinking Women's Roles* (eds.) D. O'Brien and S. W. Tiffany, 120–52. Berkeley: University of California Press.
Shabnam, D. 1994–6. Contribution of Rural Women in Agriculture: Their Problems [and] Prospects (A Case Study of Village Jowar District Bunair), unpublished MA Thesis, University of Peshawar.
Shah, S. I. 1993. *Socio-Economic Development in the Tribal Areas: A Case Study of Mohmand Agency (1975–85)*. Islamabad: National Institute of Pakistan Studies, Quaid-i-Azam University.
Shah, S. W. A. 1999. *Ethnicity, Islam and Nationalism: Muslim Politics in the North West Frontier Province 1937–47*. Karachi: Oxford University Press.
Shah, S. Y. 1980–2. Labour Export and Honour in Pukhtoons (A Case Study of Village Toru), unpublished MA Thesis, University of Peshawar.
Shakry, O. 1998. Schooled Mothers and Structured Play: Child Rearing in Turn-of-the Century Egypt. In *Remaking Women: Feminism and Modernity in the Middle East* (ed.) L. Abu-Lughod, 126–70. Princeton: Princeton University Press.
Shalinski, A. C. 1986. Reason, Desire, and Sexuality: The Meaning of Gender in Northern Afghanistan. *Ethos* 14: 4, 323–43.
Sharma, U. M. 1980. Purdah and Public Space. In *Women in Contemporary India and South Asia* (ed.) A. de Souza, 213–39. New Delhi: Manohar.
Shaukat Ali, Z. 1997. *The Empowerment of Women in Islam*. Mumbai: Vakils, Feffer and Simons.
Shaw, A. 1997. Women, the Household and Family Ties: Pakistani Migrants in Britain. In *Family and Gender in Pakistan: Domestic Organization in a Muslim Society* (eds.) H. Donnan and F. Selier, 132–55. New Delhi: Hindustan Publishing Corporation.
— 2000. *Kinship and Continuity: Pakistani Families in Britain*. London: Routledge.

2001. Kinship, Cultural Preference and Immigration: Consanguineous Marriage Among British Pakistanis. *Man* 7: 2, 315–34.

Sherani, S. R. 1991. *Ulema* and *Pir* in the Politics of Pakistan. In *Economy and Culture in Pakistan: Migrants and Cities in a Muslim Society* (eds.) H. Donnan and P. Werbner, 216–46. London: Macmillan.

Sherif, B. 1999. Gender Contradictions in Families: Official v. Practical Representations among Upper Middle-class Muslims. *Anthropology Today* 15: 4, 9–13.

Sheriff, S. 1996. *Women's Rights in Islam.* London: Ta-Ha Publishers.

Shinwari, S. A. 2000. One Hundred Years of Pashto Language and Literature. *The Frontier Post*, Peshawar: 13 February.

Shore, C. 2002. Introduction: Towards an Anthropology of Elites. In *Elite Cultures: Anthropological Perspectives* (ed.) C. Shore, 1–21. London: Routledge.

Shostak, M. 1982. *Nisa: The Life and Words of a Kung Woman.* London: Penguin.

Silver, B. 1984. The *Adab* of Musicians. In *Moral Conduct and Authority: The Place of Adab in South Asian Islam* (ed.) B. D. Metcalf, 315–29. Berkeley: University of California Press.

Singer, A. 1982. *Guardians of the North-West Frontier: The Pathans.* Amsterdam: Time Life Books.

Singh, K. 1992. *Women Entrepreneurs.* New Delhi: Ashish Publishing House.

Sinha, M. 1995. *Colonial Masculinity: The 'Manly Englishman' and the 'Effeminate Bengali' in the Late Nineteenth Century.* Manchester: Manchester University Press.

Slocum, S. 1975. Woman the Gatherer: Male Bias in Anthropology. In *Towards an Anthropology of Women* (ed.) R. R. Reiter, 36–50. New York: Monthly Review Press.

Smith, M. 1994. *Rabi'a: The Life and Work of Rabi'a and Other Women Mystics in Islam.* Oxford: One World Publications.

Spain, J. W. 1962. *People of the Khyber.* New York: Frederick A. Praeger.

—— 1963. *The Pathan Borderland.* The Hague: Mouton.

—— 1995. *Pathans of the Latter Day.* Karachi: Oxford University Press.

Spender, D. 1980. *Manmade Language.* London: Routledge and Kegan Paul.

Sterling, P. 1965. *A Turkish Village.* London: Weidenfeld and Nicolson.

Strathern, M. 1972. *Women in Between: Female Roles in a Male World: Mount Hagen, New Guinea.* London: Seminar Press.

—— 1981a. Self-interest and the Social Good: Some Implications of Hagen Gender Imagery. In *Sexual Meanings: The Cultural Construction of Gender and Sexuality* (eds.) S. B. Ortner and H. Whitehead, 166–91. Cambridge: Cambridge University Press.

—— 1981b. *Kinship at the Core: An Anthropology of Elmdon a Village in North-West Essex in the Nineteen Sixties.* Cambridge: Cambridge University Press.

—— 1984. Domesticity and the Denigration of Women. In *Rethinking Women's Roles* (eds.) D. O'Brien and S. W. Tiffany, 13–31. Berkeley: University of California Press.

—— 1990 (first published 1988). *The Gender of the Gift: Problems with Women and Problems with Society in Melanesia.* Berkeley: University of California Press.

Sung, L-S. 1981. Property and Family Division. In *The Anthropology of Taiwanese Society* (eds.) E. M. Ahern and H. Gates, 361–78. Stanford, CA: Stanford University Press.

Tahir, M. N. 1980. *Tappa ao Zwand* (in Pukhto). Peshawar: Pukhto Academy.

Tair, M. N. and T. C. Edwards. 1982. *Rohi Mataluna* (Pashto Proverbs). (A collection of Pashto proverbs with translations into English.) Peshawar: Pashto Academy, University of Peshawar.

Tamanoi, M. A. 1991. Songs as Weapons: Culture and History of *Komori* (Nursemaids) in Modern Japan. *Journal of Asian Studies* 50: 4, 793–817.

Tapper, N. 1978. The Women's Subsociety Among the Shahsevan Nomads of Iran. In *Women in the Muslim World* (eds.) L. Beck and N. Keddie, 374–98. Cambridge, MA: Harvard University Press.

1981. Direct Exchange and Brideprice: Alternative Forms in a Complex Marriage System. *Man* 16: 3, 387–407.

1991. *Bartered Brides: Politics, Gender and Marriage in an Afghan Tribal Society*. Cambridge: Cambridge University Press.

Tapper, R. 1984. Holier Than Thou: Islam in Three Tribal Societies. In *Islam in Tribal Societies: From the Atlas to the Indus* (eds.) A. S. Ahmed and D. M. Hart, 244–65. London: Routledge and Kegan Paul.

2001. Anthropology and (the) Crisis. *Anthropology Today* 17: 6, 13–16.

Tapper, R. and N. Tapper. 1986. 'Eat This, It'll Do You a Power of Good': Food and Commensality among Durrani Pashtuns. *American Ethnologist* 13: 1, 62–79.

Tarlo, E. 1996. *Clothing Matters: Dress and Identity in India*. London: Hurst and Company.

Tellis-Nayak, V. 1983. Power and Solidarity: Clientage in Domestic Service. *Current Anthropology* 24: 1, 67–74.

Thackston, W. M. (ed.) 1999. *The Jahangirnama: Memoirs of Jahangir, Emperor of India*. New York: Oxford University Press.

Thomas, N. 1992. The Inversion of Tradition. *American Ethnologist* 19: 2, 213–32.

Tiffany, S. W. 1984. Introduction: Feminist Perceptions in Anthropology. In *Rethinking Women's Roles* (eds.) D. O'Brien and S. W. Tiffany, 1–11. Berkeley: University of California Press.

Titus, P. 1998. Honor the Baloch, Buy the Pushtun: Stereotypes, Social Organization and History in Western Pakistan. *Modern Asian Studies* 32, 657–87.

Todorov, T. 1984. *The Conquest of America: The Question of the Other*. New York: Harper and Row.

Tonkiss, F. and A. Passey (eds.) 2000. *Trust and Civil Society*. Basingstoke: Macmillan.

Torab, A. 1996. Piety as Gendered Agency: A Study of Jalaseh Ritual Discourse in an Urban Neighbourhood in Iran. *Journal of the Royal Anthropological Institute* 2: 2, 235–52.

Toynbee, A. J. 1961. *Between Oxus and Jumna*. Oxford: Oxford University Press.

Turner, C. 2000. *The Muslim World*. Gloucestershire: Sutton Publishing Limited.

Van Gennep, A. 1977. *The Rites of Passage*. London: Routledge and Kegan Paul.

Veblen, T. 1953. *The Theory of the Leisure Class*. New York: Mentor Book.

Venkatesan, S. 2001. Crafting Discourse: Mat Weaving in Pattamadai, South India, unpublished PhD Dissertation, University of Cambridge.

Vogel, D. W. 2000. Liturgical Theology: A Conceptual Geography. In *Primary Sources of Liturgical Theology* (ed.) D. W. Vogel, 3–14. Minnesota: The Liturgical Press.

Wadud, M. A. 1962. *The Story of Swat* (trans.) Ashruf Altaf Husain (told to Muhammad Asif Khan). Peshawar: Ferozsons.

Wali Swat, Shahzada Muhammad Abdul Haq. 1953. *Tarruf Peshkash* (in Urdu). Mingora, Swat State: Asmat Industries.

Wallace, C. 1987. *For Richer, For Poorer: Growing Up In and Out of Work*. London: Tavistock Publications.

Wallman, S. 1979. Introduction: A Social Anthropology of Work? In *Social Anthropology of Work* (ed.) S. Wallman, 1–24. London: Academic Press.

Walter, J. H. (ed.) 1967. *Romeo and Juliet*. Oxford: Heinemann Educational Books.

Ward, H. 1997. Worth its Weight: Gold, Women and Value in North West India, unpublished PhD Dissertation, University of Cambridge.

Warrier, M. 2000. The Appeal of a Modern Godperson in Contemporary India: The Case of Mata Amritanandamayi and Her Mission, unpublished PhD Dissertation, University of Cambridge.

Wasti, S. A. T. and M. Z. Osmani (eds.) (n.d.) *Islamabad*. Islamabad: Capital Development Authority (CDA).

Waterson, R. 1990. *The Living House: An Anthropology of Architecture in South-East Asia*. Oxford: Oxford University Press.

Watson, H. 1992. *Women in the City of the Dead*. London: Hurst and Company.

Weber, M. 1968. *The Protestant Ethic and the Spirit of Capitalism* (trans.) Talcott Parsons. London: Allen and Unwin.

Weiss, A. M. 1991. Introduction: Industrial Development and Social Change. In *Culture, Class, and Development in Pakistan: The Emergence of an Industrial Bourgeoisie in Punjab*, 1–18. Boulder, CO: Westview Press.

1998. The Slow yet Steady Path to Women's Empowerment in Pakistan. In *Islam, Gender and Social Change* (eds.) Y. Y. Haddad and J. L. Esposito, 124–43. New York: Oxford University Press.

Werbner, P. 1986. The Virgin and the Clown Ritual Elaboration in Pakistani Migrants' Weddings. *Man* 21: 2, 227–50.

1992. Processes of Community Formation (in Commentaries). *American Anthropologist* 94: 4, 926.

2001. The Limits of Cultural Hybridity: Ritual Monsters, Poetic Licence and Contested Postcolonial Purifications. *Journal of the Royal Anthropological Institute* 7: 1, 133–52.

Wikan, U. 1982. *Behind the Veil in Arabia: Women in Oman*. Baltimore, MD: The Johns Hopkins University Press.

Yasmeen, D. 1995–7. The Role of Karakoram Handicraft Development Program in Enhancing the Status of Women (A Study of Hyderabad Village in Central Hunza), unpublished MA Thesis, University of Peshawar.

Yin, A. C-C. 1981. Voluntary Associations and Rural–Urban Migration. In *The Anthropology of Taiwanese Society* (eds.) E. M. Ahern and H. Gates, 319–37. Stanford, CA: Stanford University Press.

York, S. 1997. Beyond the Household: An Exploration of Private and Public Spheres in the Yasin Valley. In *Family and Gender in Pakistan: Domestic Organization in a Muslim Society* (eds.) H. Donnan and F. Selier, 208–33. New Delhi: Hindustan Publishing Corporation.

Youssef, N. H. 1978. The Status and Fertility Patterns of Muslim Women. In *Women in the Muslim World* (eds.) L. Beck and N. Keddie, 69–99. Cambridge, MA: Harvard University Press.

Yusuf, A. A. (trans.) 1989. *The Holy Qur'an*. Brentwood, MD: Amana Corporation.

Yusufzai, R. 2000. Frontier Loses its Last Witty Ex-Civil Servant. *The News*, Islamabad: 9 October.

2001. Islami Jirga Sets TV and VCRs on Fire in Mardan. *The News*, Islamabad: 19 February.

INDEX

NB: page numbers in bold refer to plates and tables

Abbottabad 47, 53, 54
Abdul Gaffur 21
Abu-Lughod, L. 35, 44, 137, 160
   dual lives and 49, 78
   mourning and 82, 89, 90, 97
   weddings and 119, 124, 125
affinal terminology **167**
Afghan Nobility and the Mughals (1526–1707) (Joshi) 31
Afghan ruling family 22
Afghana 31
Afghanistan 1, 5, 19–21, 25, 31
agency 4, 11, 71, 78, 101–6
Ahmad, I. 31
Ahmed, A. S. 3, 10, 91, 163
   dual lives and 13, 50, 51, 67, 77
   gham-khādi and 15, 21, 32, 36, 134, 139
   weddings and 11, 108, 125
Ahmed, L. 50
Ahmed, Q. I. 50
Akbar Khan, Patriarch Nawab 6
Akhtar (Eid) 47, 81, 89, 101, 102, 103
Akhund of Swat 6, 21, 22, 152
Al-Huda International Institute of Islamic Education for Women 12, 159, 160, 162, 163
   dual lives and 48, **73**
   gham-khādi and 15–16, 29, 39, 145, 147
   personhood 150–3, 155
   mourning and 79, 88, 92–3, 95, 99
      agency 101, 103, 104, 105
      seniority 99, 100
   weddings and 110, 111, 123
Alavi, H. 4, 26, 147
Alexander the Great 5, 21, 23
Ali, S. 27, 29, 155
All Pakistan Women's Association (APWA) 26, 70, 147
alliances 111
Altorki, S. 43, 44, 49, 116, 125, 134
Alvi, A. 125, 126, 159

American Pakistanis 25
Anderson, J. W. 4
anglicisation 33
Ansari, F. D. S. 123
Appadurai, A. 76
aql 114, 130, 148, 149–50
Arabia 31
Arabic 150, 151, 154
Ardener, S. 50, 60
Arensberg, C. M. 66
'arranged' marriages 125
Asad, T. 10, 22
Ask, K. 125
Aswad, B. C. 35, 54
attending 7
Australia 28

Baal, J. V. 141, 144
Baba, Rehman 91
Babar, Mughal Emperor 21
Babylon 31
Bacha, Adnan 74, 75
Bacha, Amirzeb 35
Bacha, Asfandiar 74
Bacha, Aurangzeb 23, 35
Badshah Sahib (Wali of Swat) 5, 21, 22, 152
Badshahyan (definition) 6
Baluchis 25, 26, 33
Banerjee, M. 15, 32
'Bangla' 52
Barnard, A. 159
Barth, F. 10, 11, 13
   dual lives and 50, 53, 54, 67, 77
   gham-khādi and 15, 20, 22, 29, 30, 34, 36
      work 134, 139, 147, 159, 160, 161, 163
   land and 6, 10
   mourning and 89, 94
   Pukhtunwali and 3
   weddings and 111, 123, 130
bathing 86, 96, 100
Bayly, C. A. 104

Index 193

Beck, L. 125
Bellew, H. W. 9
Berland, J. C. 125
Beveridge, A. S. 21
Bhattacharya, M. 157
Bibiane (people) 29–40
  agency 101–6
  definition 6
  dress 39–40
  education 32–4
  forging bonds 54–6
  genealogy and history 31, 32
  generations 40
  inter-household tensions 35–7
  khidmatgarān (helpers) 6, 37–8
  marriage 34–5
  wealth and income 38–9
  weddings 117–21
  see also dual lives
Bihishti Zewar (Thanawi) 151, 152
birth (*ombaraki*) 8, 128–31, 139, 156, 157
  celebration (*Salwekhtee*) 129
Bitan 10, 31
Bloch, M. 80, 85
bonds, forging 54–6
Bourdieu, P. 160, 161
  dual lives and 48, 53, 54
  gham-khādi and 15, 43, 144
  weddings and 110, 113, 127, 130
Bowen, J. C. E. 91
Brahminical Hindu rajahs 23
Brenner, S. 100, 105
brides, finding 110–12
British colonial rule 5, 6, 21, 23, 31–2
Buddhist emperors 23
Buddhist Gandhara civilisation 21
Bukhari, S. 72
Burn Hall (school) 32
Bush, President G. W. 1

Cairo 17, 71, 111, 154, 160
Canada 28
Capital Development Authority (CDA) 25
Caroe, O. 15, 163
Carsten, J. 9
  dual lives and 47, 50, 53, 59, 61
  visiting 53, 54, 55
Castells, M. 15
castings-out 60
Chak Shehzad 141
Chhachhi, A. 153
childcare 143–4
children 61–2, 75, 135, 164
  weddings and 109, 115, 125
Chitral 22, 57
choice 110–12
Christians 23, 25, 33, 70
circumcisions (*sunnat*) 8

clothing matters 97–9
  see also dress
cohabitation 60
Cole, D. P. 31
Colen, S. 12
collective and individual work 133–6
Comaroff, J. 10, 133
conflicts 57–60, 125, 148
confrontation 57–60, 145
consanguinal terminology 167
Convent of Jesus and Mary (school) 32, 43, 143, 156, 163
convents 12, 32–4, 105, 163
Cook, M. 13, 71, 72, 100, 123, 151
Crystal, D. 32

daigāne see wet-nurses (*daigāne*)
'Dalbar' (house) 51–3
dancing 117–18, 121–5, 127, 129
  group 116
  preparations 110, 116, 117
Daniel, V. E. 7, 51
Darish, P. 85
Das, V. 80, 89, 90, 91, 104, 113
dawa 28
days of week 169
de wada wraz 118–20
death and dismay *see* mourning
decorum 7, 89–93
deference 35–7
Delaney, C. 34, 35, 43, 44
  dual lives and 49, 52, 54, 63
  weddings and 116, 119, 122, 130
Deutsch, K. A. 13
Devji, F. F. 78, 152
Dir 22
disputes 110, 145
domestic helpers 6, 37–8
Donnan, H. 10, 25, 164
  dual lives and 47, 49, 71, 75, 77
Donner, W. W. 38
double-rootedness 75–8
dowry 110, 114, 120
dress 39–40, 109, 110, 143, 153
  mourning 82, 84, 86, 89, 97–9
  wedding 114, 118
  see also jewellery
Drucker-Brown, S. 92
dual lives 13, 47
  Al-Huda 70–5
  double-rootedness 75–8
  house from inside-out 48–51
  household relationships 56–66
  houses from inside-out 48–51
  Islamabad 66–70
  kille-kor (village house) layout 51–4
  visiting etiquette 54–6
Dube, L. 87

Index

Dunbar, R. 63
Dupree, L. 11, 16
Durkheim (Giddens) 90

Easwaran, E. 15
Eddy, E. M. 40
education 32–4
   see also Al-Huda International Institute of Islamic Education for Women; converts
Edwards, D. B. 54, 77
Edwards, T. C. 81, 92, 97, 109
Egypt 71, 100, 163
Egyptian *du'at* 28
Egyptian women's mosque movement 17
Eickelman, D. F. 32, 154
Eid (Islamic festival) 47, 81, 89, 101, 102, 103
El-Solh, C. 43, 44
Elizabeth II, Queen 23
Elphinstone, M. 32
England 165
English 27, 28, 32–4, 151, 163
   -medium schools 40, 66
enquiry visit (*tapos*) 82–3, 128, 150
entertainment 121–5
ethnic endogamy 110
etiquette, visiting 54–6
Evans-Pritchard, Sir E. E. 10
Ewing, K. P. 105, 153
existence 8, 146–8
'existence, work of' 2, 8–9, 146, 158, 159, 165
expenditure
   household 171
   wedding **115**
expression in *gham* 89–93
ezat 104, 134, 159, 160
   weddings and 110, 111, 112, 117, 125, 127, 130

Fahm-al-Quran programme 150
Faisal Mosque 73
Faisalabad 39
'family' 3
Farsi 33
Fatima Jinnah Park 70
Fazlur-Rehman, M. 21
female agency 11, 101–6
fieldsites 21–9
   Islamabad 25–9
   plains of Mardan 23–4
   valley of Swat 21–3
fieldwork 43–6
first cousins 50
Fischer, M. D. 125
flats, city
food 109, 110, 117, 120
   distribution
   hierarchy **94**
   hospitality and 93–7

Forbes, G. 32
forging bonds 54–6
Fortieth day 18, 81, 88, 94, 129, 144, 163
   agency and 101, 103
   birth and 129
   personhood and 150, 151
Frazer, J. 36
Freeman, S. T. 116
Freitag, S. B. 123
Fridays 81, 94, 104, 163
Frontier villages 25
'fundamentalism' 163

games 119
Gandhara kingdom 23
Gellner, E. 87, 105
genealogy and history 31–32, 166
General Army Headquarters 25, 65
generational differences 40
gham see mourning
gham-khādi 3, **8**, 15–17, **73**
   Bibiane (people) 29–40
   definition 2–3, 132–3
   fieldsites 21–29, 43–6
   maids performing 170
   networks **42**, 40–3
   Pukhtunwali and 15–18
   socio-political 73–5
   village organisation 21
   see also work of *gham-khādi*
Ghani Khan 20, 125
Al-Ghazzali, Imam 72
Ghurghust 10, 31
Giddens, A. 90
gifts 57, 64, 142
   see also money
Gilmartin, D. 149
Gilsenan, M. 63, 77, 95, 146
Goffman, E. 59
Goody, J. 93
Gray, J. N. 12, 48, 54, 158
Grima, B. 2, 3, 4, 11, 13, 54
   gham-khādi and 15, 16, 17, 43, 139, 141
   mourning and 81, 91, 93, 95, 96
   sequence of *gham* 82, 85, 86
   Pukhtun society and 159, 161, 164
   weddings and 108, 119
Grint, K. 9
Guides Cavalry 23

Habermas, J. 13
Hadith 72, 100, 104, 120
   gham-khādi 27, 29, 150, 154
Hagen, J. M. 41
haj pilgrimage 8
Harrison, S. 102
Hart, D. M. 150

Hashmi, Dr Farhat 27, 150, 151
  dual lives and 70, 71
Hayatabad market 69
Hegland, M. E. 105
helpers (*khidmatgarān*) 6, 37–8
Hertz, R. 80
Heston, W. L. 35
hijab 110, 153
Hindukush Mountains 21
Hindus 18, 21, 23, 72, 80
Hirschkind, C. 13, 28
historical roots 31, 32, 110
'holding' the bride 119
holy groups 19
Hoodfar, H. 50, 100
Horvatich, P. 154
hospitality (*melmastia*) 54, 79, 93–7, 142, 148
  wedding 117, 119, 127, 129
hosting 7, 20, 54, 146
Hoti, A. K. 3
Hoti family 30, 33
Hoti (Mardan) 5, 43
Hoti, Nawab of 24, 31
Hotis 24
household
  expenditure 171
  labour 146–7, 148
  Moroccan 59
  relationships 56–66
    beyond the village 64–6
  rented
  tensions 35–7
houses from inside-out 48–51
  purdah and 49–51
  see also dual lives
Hugh-Jones, S. 50, 53, 61
hujra 53, 84, 85–7, 101, 133
Humphrey, C. 9, 50, 76
Huntington, R. 88, 90, 99
Hussain, A. 33

Ibn Khaldūn 18, 49
Ibrahim, Prophet 31
identity 7, 9, 15–18, 43
Ikramullah, S. S. 24, 115
income 38–9
  household expenditure and 171
India 65
Indian Deoband movement 151, 152
individual work 133–6
International Foreign Women's Association (IFWA) 26, 70
internet 125–8, 164
invitations and preparations 113–17
Iqbal, S. 54, 57, 60
Iranians 25, 160
Islam 148–55

Islamabad 5, 13, 18, 43, 102
  dual lives and 66–70, 75–8, 85
  as fieldsite 21, 23, 25–9
Islamabad International Airport 25
Islamic law (*Sharia*) 28, 100, 152, 153
Islamic revival movement 27

Jahanzeb College 23, 52
Jamila, Begum 35
jewellery 98, 140
  wedding 114, 117, 118
jhanj (convoy of in-laws) 120
Jiddah 116
Jinnah, Mohammad Ali 1
Joshi, R. 31
7 July 2005, 1, 164
Jura 22, 157

Kabul valley 19
kameezoona 82
Karachi 1, 27, 29, 39, 41
Karlanri 31
Kashmiris 25
Keddie, N. 125
Keiser, L. 16, 57
Kennedy, President J. F. 23
khādi, celebrating *see* weddings
Khalid bin Walid 31
Khan, Ajab 75
Khan, Ali 12
Khan, Nawab Colonel Amir 31
Khan, President Ayub 23, 25, 35, 84
Khan, Aziz 74, 75, 76
Khan, B. 29
Khan, Liaqat 39
Khan, M. S. 25
Khan, S. M. 3
Khan, Deputy Inspector General Salim 74
Khan status 6
Khanān 3, 6, 10, 22, 23
Khans 10
khattam 89, 92, 101, 103
khidmatgarān (helpers) 6, 37–8
kille-kor (village house) layout 51–4
kinship 7, 11, 40–1, 57
  obligations 93–7
  terminology 167
  weddings and 110, 121, 124, 127
Kohistan 22
Kolenda, P. 32, 135
Kondos, V. 9, 13, 47, 48, 58
kor 133
  mourning and 90, 101, 102
  sequence of *gham* 84, 86–7, 89
Kurti, L. 119

La Fontaine, J. 44
Lahore 39, 41

Index

Laidlaw, J. 9, 162
land 110
landlords 54, 67
  see also Khanān
Lawrence, B. B. 149
Lawrence College 32
Lees, W. N. 32
Lévi-Strauss, C. 48
Lewenhak, S. 9
Lindholm, Charles 2, 3, 11, 159, 164
  dual lives and 49, 50, 55, 57, 59, 67, 75, 77
  gham-khādi and 15, 30, 32, 34, 36, 43, 134
  mourning and 79, 81, 82, 91, 96
  weddings and 108, 123
Lindholm, Cherry 159
Lodhi, Bahlol 31
Loizos, P. 45
London 1, 164
love 125–8
Lupton, D. 54, 87
Lutz, C. 81

Macaulay, T. 32
Macfarlane, A. 58, 96
Macfarlane, I. 58, 96
Mackintosh, M. M. 9
Mahmood, S. 17, 18, 71, 79, 151, 154, 160
Mahmud of Ghazni 21
Mahsood 5
maids 6, 162
  birth and 129
  dual lives and 52, 68
    relationships 57, 59, 60, 62–3, 65
  gham-khādi and 17, 36, 37–8
  work 137, 139–40, 143, 146–7, 148
  mourning and 81, 84, 86, 87, 101, 102, 103
  weddings and 111, 117, 118, 119
    preparations 113, 114, 115–16
Malakand 22, 23
male servants 37, 53, 65, 68, 101
  helpers 6, 37–8
Malinowski, B. 80
Mandelbaum, D. G. 40, 57, 160
Mardan 5–6, 7, 23–4, 33
  views of
Margalla Hills 25, 26
marriage 34–5, 50
  see also weddings
Marriott Hotel
  Islamabad 26
  Karachi 151
Marsden, M. 51, 57, 100, 123
Marxist anthropologists 10
Matri, S. 27
Mauss, M. 137
Mearns, D. J. 12, 48, 54, 158
melmastia see hospitality
'Men's Paxto [Pukhto]' 16

Mernissi, F. 39, 110, 125
  dual lives and 50, 57, 59, 61, 65, 73
Metcalf, B. D. 29, 92, 149, 152, 159
Metcalf, P. 85, 88, 89, 90, 99, 139
Mir-Hosseini, Z. 44
Mody Spencer 125
money **139**
  birth and 128, 129
  weddings and 110, 114, 116, 136
    Bibiane's 117, 118, 119
    dancing 124
months of year 169
Moore, H. L. 13, 16, 158
morality 136–42
Morocco 59, 110
Morris, L. 9
mourning 79
  Bibiane's agency 101–6
  clothing matters 97–9
  decorum and expression in *gham* 89–93
  food and hospitality 93–7
  sequence of *gham* 81–9
  transcending seniority 99–101
Mughal empire 31
Mumtaz, K. 26, 29
Munn, N. D. 69
Murree 26, 47
Murree Convent *see* Convent of Jesus and Mary
Musharraf, President Pervez 163
Muslim Brotherhood 28

Nadelson, L. 54
Najmabadi, A. 62, 78
Nakreeza 113, 116, 117–18, 129, 151
  Al-Huda and 72
  dancing and 121, 123, 124
nakreeza (henna) 117–18
naming and hair-shaving ceremonies (*haqiqa*) 8
Naseem Bibi 23
Nasim, Begum 35
Nasir, M. 35
National Assembly 12, 75
Naveed-i-Rahat, Dr 54, 86
Nawab Khanān 23
Nawabs 3, 6, 39
Nelson, C. 11, 16, 49, 78
networks, *gham-khādi* 40–3
New York 1–7
nikah 118
Nizami, R. 25
North-West Frontier Province (NWFP), map of
Novarra, V. 9

obligations 93–7, 142–4
Okely, J. 33
ombaraki (birth) 8, 128–31, 139, 156, 157
Otterbein, K. F. 53, 62

Pakistan 18
Pakistan Country Statistics 38
Papanek, H. 13, 86, 95, 125, 133
  dual lives and 50, 54, 65
Papua New Guinea 13
Parry, J. P. 80
Passey, A. 116
personhood 148–55
Peshawar 69, 93, 143
  gham-khādi and 19, 21, 23, 33, 41, 44
Pindi (Rawalpindi) 25, 26, 65, 66
Pitt-Rivers, J. 62, 145
politics 43, 97, 135
  arena for 11, 12, 110
  power and 11, 160, 162
Povinelli, E. A. 9
power-struggles 103
prayers, five daily 169
preference 110–12, 142–4
preparations and invitations 113–17
Presentation (school) 32
procedure 7, 109
professional work 146–8
Prophet Muhammad (SAW) 19, 27, 31, 72, 92
Provincial Assemblies 12
public spheres 12–13
  private areas and 48
Pukhto-speaking regions 33
Pukhtun 3, **17**
  putative genealogy 166
Pukhtuns 5, 12, 16, 25
Pukhtunwali 3, 5, 6, 9, 13
  dual lives and 50, 54, 76, 161–2
  gham-khādi and 15–18, 19, 36, 45
  work 134, 149, 154, 158, 163
  mourning and 79, 86, 93, 99, 103, 105
  weddings and 108, 120, 125, 126, 127, 129, 131
Punjab 65
Punjab Regiment 23
Punjabis 70, 111
  gham-khādi and 25, 26, 29, 30, 33, 34, 35
purdah 4, 5, 13, 155, 160
  dual lives and 48, 49–51, 64, 65, 67–8, 72–3, 76
  gham-khādi and 16, 21, 24, 36, 37, 44
  mourning and 79, 82, 83, 86, 90, 102
  weddings and 113, 117, 119, 121, 124, 130

qabar
Qadiani sect 35
Qais bin Rashid 10, 31
Quetta 41
Quran 60, 72, 100, 120, 163
  gham-khādi and 27–9, 35
  work 150, 151, 154

Quranic Arabic 33
Quranic *khattam* 89, 92, 101, 103

Radcliffe-Brown, A. R. 10
Rahman, T. 32
Ramadan 27, 33, 70, 89, 150
Raverty, H. G. 8, 9, 17, 49
Rawal Dam 26
reciprocity and morality 136–42
relocation 85
resentments 145
respect names 36–7
respectability 124
revenge 141
rewāj and Islam 148–55
Rifaqat, Z. 50
rites de passage 4, 33, 71, 76, 110
ritual 7
rivalry, female 135
Roded, R. 11
Roman Catholic nuns 32–4

Sadozai 22, 33
Safdar, S. 34
Safi Mohmand 22
Saidu Baba 21, 22, 74
Saidu Sharif 23
Saidu (Swat) 5, 21, 43
St Dennies (school) 32
Salwekhtamma see Fortieth day
Salwekhtee (birth celebration) 129
Sangota Convent school 23, 32
Sanjek, R. 12
Sarban 10, 31
Sargodha 27
Saul, King 31
Sayyed, M. 35
sazare (veiling) 117, 118, 129, 130, 156
  mourning and 79, 82, 88, 90, 99, 102
segmentation 31
Sehrai, N. 33
seniority, transcending 99–101
11 September 2001 1, 25
servants 6, 62, 106
  helpers 6, 37–8
  male 37, 53, 65, 68, 101
  see also maids
Shah, S. Y. 25
Shaheed, F. 26, 29
Shaikh Malli 19
Shakry, O. 100, 163
Shalinski, A. C. 4, 49, 149, 159
shame (*sharam*) 49, 122, 130, 132–9
Sharia (Islamic law) 28, 100, 152, 153
Sharma, U. M. 13, 18, 33, 50, 65
Shaukat Ali 34, 130
Shaw, A. 18, 34, 54, 94, 133, 134
  weddings and 110, 125

Index

Sher Palam 22, 65
Sherani, S. R. 21
Sherif, B. 40
Sheriff, S. 111
Shia sect 33, 35, 111
Shinwari, S. A. 3
Shore, C. 4
Sindhis 25, 26, 33, 35
Singer, A. 3, 50, 51, 56, 95, 125
singing 118, 121, 122, 127, 129
social agent 109
social diacritica 39–40
social relations, severing of 144–6
socio-political *gham-khādi* 73–5
space of agency 4, 78
Spain, J. W. 3, 31, 49
Spender, D. 63
status 6, 110
Steul, W. 15
Strathern, M. 4, 9, 12, 13
    dual lives and 56, 78, 97
    gham-khādi and 41
    weddings and 114, 121
Sufi 10, 21
Sung, I-S. 38
Sunni 111
Swat 5–6, 7, 21–3
    views of
Swat-Kohistan 22
Al-Tabari, Jafari 72

Tair, M. N. 81, 92, 97, 109
Taliban 1, 2, 29, 65, 163
    students 155
tapos (enquiry visit) 82–83, 128, 150
Tapper, N. 11, 34, 159, 160
    dual lives and 56, 78
    mourning and 80, 105
    weddings and 111, 118, 122, 125, 128
Tapper, R. 45, 80, 105, 155
Tarlo, E. 97, 114
Tellis-Nayak, V. 62
tenants 67
tensions, household 35–7, 56–66
Thanawi, Maulana Ashraf Ali 151, 152
Thomas, N. 15
Tiffany, S. W. 13, 18
time
Titus, P. 67
Todorov, T. 32
Tonkiss, F. 116
Torab, A. 4, 149, 159
Toru family 30, 33, 151
Toru, Nawab of 24
Torus 24

Toynbee, A. J. 22
'translocality' 69, 77
Turner, C. 154

United Arab Emirates (UAE) 23, 28, 110, 158
United Kingdom (UK) 23, 27, 45, 158
United Nations (UN) 147, 148
United States of America (USA) 1, 23, 27, 28, 158
Urdu 70, 71, 105, 121
    gham-khādi and 27, 29, 32, 33, 151, 154

Van Gennep, A. 129
veiling *see sazare* (veiling)
Venkatesan, S. 34
villages 51–4, 64–6
violence 125
visiting 41–3, 69–70, 142, 143
    etiquette 54–6
    tapos (enquiry visit) 82–3, 128, 150
Vitebsky, P. 50
Vogel, D. W. 80

wada see weddings
Wadud, Abdul 22
Wadud, M. A. 152
'Walayat Seb' 52
Wali Ahad of Swat 25
Wali of Swat 3, 6, 10, 51, 74
    family 10, 23, 30, 52, 74
    first wife 52
    gham-khādi and 22, 23, 35
    mourning and 84, 98
Walima 117, 120, 121
Wallace, C. 9
Walter, J. H. 35
Ward, H. 140
Washington DC 1
Waterson, R. 12, 48
Watson, H. 44, 111
Wazir 5
wealth 38–9, 110
weddings (*wada*) 7, 8, 107–15
    Bibiane's 117–21
    birth (*ombaraki*) 128–31
    dances 121–25
    expenditure **115**
    finding brides 110–12
    internet love 125–8
    invitations and preparations 113–17
Weiss, A. M. 13, 30
Werbner, P. 10, 15, 25, 120, 134, 164
    dual lives and 47, 49, 71, 75, 77
wet-nurses (*daigāne*) 6, 109, 115, 129, 139
    dual lives and 60, 61, 63–4, 75
    gham-khādi and 17, 37, 38, 44
Wikan, U. 54

witchcraft 60
'Women's Paxto' 16
work of *gham-khādi* 132–9
   collective and individual 133–6
   juggling work 146–8
   money and **139**
   obligation and preference 142–4
   participation and exclusion 144–6
   personhood 148–55
   reciprocity and morality 136–42
   see also gham-khādi

Yasin valley 13
Yin, A. C-C. 40
York, S. 13, 35, 49, 56, 57
Youssef, N. H. 44
Yusuf, A. A. 72
Yusuf (descendant of Qais) 31
Yusufzai, R. 83
Yusufzai tribe 3, 5, 10, 77
   gham-khādi and 16, 22, 23, 31

Zubair, Dr Idrees 27

University of Cambridge
Oriental Publications published for the
Faculty of Oriental Studies

1. *Averroes' commentary on Plato's Republic*, edited and translated by E. I. J. Rosenthal
2. *FitzGerald's "Salaman and Absal"*, edited by A. J. Arberry
3. *Ihara Saikaku: the Japanese family storehouse*, translated and edited by G. W. Sargent
4. *The Avestan Hymn to Mithra*, edited and translated by Ilya Gershevitch
5. *The Fuṣūl al-Madanī of al-Fārābī*, edited by D. M. Dunlop (out of print)
6. *Dun Karn, poet of Malta*, texts chosen and translated by A. J. Arberry; introduction, notes and glossary by P. Grech
7. *The political writings of Ogyū Sorai*, by J. R. McEwan
8. *Financial administration under the T'ang dynasty*, by D. C. Twitchett
9. *Neolithic cattle-keepers of south India: a study of the Deccan Ashmounds*, by F. R. Allchin
10. *The Japanese enlightenment: a study of the writings of Fukuzawa Yukichi*, by Carmen Blacker
11. *Records of Han administration*. Vol. I *Historical assessment*, by M. Loewe
12. *Records of Han administration*. Vol. II *Documents*, by M. Loewe
13. *The language of Indrajit of Orchā: a study of early Braj Bhāṣā prose*, by R. S. McGregor
14. *Japan's first general election, 1890*, by R. H. P. Mason
15. *A collection of tales from Uji: a study and translation of "Uji Shūi Monogatari,"* by D. E. Mills
16. *Studia semitica*. Vol. I *Jewish themes*, by E. I. J. Rosenthal
17. *Studia semitica*. Vol. II *Islamic themes*, by E. I. J. Rosenthal
18. *A Nestorian collection of Christological texts*. Vol. I *Syriac text*, by Luise Abramowski and Alan E. Goodman
19. *A Nestorian collection of Christological texts*. Vol. II *Introduction, translation, indexes*, by Luise Abramowski and Alan E. Goodman
20. *The Syriac version of the Pseudo-Nonnos mythological scholia*, by Sebastian Brock
21. *Water rights and irrigation practices in Lajih*, by A. M. A. Maktari
22. *The commentary of Rabbi David Kimhi on Psalms cxx–cl*, edited and translated by Joshua Baker and Ernest W. Nicholson
23. *Jalāl al-dīn al-Suyūtī*. Vol. I *Biography and background*, by E. M. Sartain
24. *Jalāl al-dīn al-Suyūtī*. Vol. II *Al-Tahadduth bini'mat allāh*, Arabic text, by E. M. Sartain
25. *Origen and the Jews: studies in Jewish–Christian relations in third-century Palestine*, by N. R. M. de Lange
26. *The Vīsaladevarāsa: a restoration of the text*, by John D. Smith
27. *Shabbethai Sofer and his prayer-book*, by Stefan C. Reif

28. *Mori Ōgai and the modernization of Japanese culture*, by Richard John Bowring
29. *The rebel lands: an investigation into the origins of early Mesopotamian mythology*, by J. V. Kinnier Wilson
30. *Saladin: the politics of the holy war*, by Malcolm C. Lyons and David Jackson
31. *Khotanese Buddhist texts* (revised edition), edited by H. W. Bailey
32. *Interpreting the Hebrew Bible: essays in honour of E. I. J. Rosenthal*, edited by J. A. Emerton and Stefan C. Reif
33. *The traditional interpretation of the Apocalypse of St John in the Ethiopian orthodox church*, by Roger W. Cowley
34. *South Asian archaeology 1981: proceedings of the sixth international conference of South Asian archaeologists in western Europe*, edited by Bridget Allchin (with assistance from Raymond Allchin and Miriam Sidell)
35. *God's conflict with the dragon and the sea. Echoes of a Canaanite myth in the Old Testament*, by John Day
36. *Land and sovereignty in India. Agrarian society and politics under the eighteenth-century Maratha Svarājya*, by André Wink
37. *God's caliph: religious authority in the first centuries of Islam*, by Patricia Crone and Martin Hinds
38. *Ethiopian Biblical interpretation: a study in exegetical tradition and hermeneutics*, by Roger W. Cowley
39. *Monk and mason on the Tigris frontier: the early history of Ṭur 'Abdin*, by Andrew Palmer
40. *Early Japanese books in Cambridge University Library: a catalogue of the Aston, Satow and Von Siebold collections*, by Nozumu Hayashi and Peter Kornicki
41. *Molech: a god of human sacrifice in the Old Testament*, by John Day
42. *Arabian studies*, edited by R. B. Serjeant and R. L. Bidwewll
43. *Naukar, Rajput and Sepoy: the ethnohistory of the military labour market in Hindustan, 1450–1850*, by Dirk H. A. Kolff
44. *The epic of Pabūjī: a study, transcription and translation*, by John D. Smith
45. *Anti-Christian polemic in Early Islam: Abū 'Īsā al-Warrāq's "Against the Trinity"*, by David Thomas
46. *Devotional literature in South Asia: current research, 1985–8. Papers of the fourth conference on devotional literature in New indo-Aryan languages*,
47. *Genizah research after ninety years: the case of Judaeo-Arabic. Papers read at the third congress of the Society for Judaeo-Arabic Studies*, edited by Joshua Blau and Stefan C. Reif
48. *Divination, mythology and monarchy in Han China*, by Michael Loewe
49. *The Arabian epic: heroic and oral storytelling*, volumes I–III, by M. C. Lyons
50. *Religion in Japan: arrows to heaven and earth*, edited by P. F. Kornicki and I. J. McMullen
51. *Kingship and political practice in colonial India*, by Pamela G. Price

52. *Hebrew manuscripts at Cambridge University Library: a description and introduction*, by Stefan C. Reif
53. *Selected letters of Rabindranath Tagore*, edited by Krishna Dutta and Andrew Robinson
54. *State and court ritual in China*, edited by Joseph P. McDermott
55. *Indian semantic analysis: the* nirvacana *tradition*, by Eivind Kahrs
56. *The Syraic version of the Old Testament: an introduction*, by M. P. Weitzman
57. *The cult of Asharah in ancient Israel and Judah: evidence for a Hebrew goddess*, by Judith M. Hadley
58. *The transformation of nomadic society in the Arab East*, edited by Martha Mundy and Basim Musallam
59. *Early Muslim polemic against Christianity: Abū 'Īsā al-Warrāq's "Against the Incarnation"*, edited and translated by David Thomas
60. *Seeking Bāuls of Bengal*, by Jeanne Openshaw
61. *State and locality in Mughal India: Power Relations in Western India, c. 1572–1730*, by Farhat Hasan
62. *Love in South Asia: A Cultural History*, edited by Francesca Orsini
63. *Sorrow and Joy among Muslim Women: The Pukhtuns of Northern Pakistan*, by Amineh Ahmed Hoti